# Systematic Lexicography

JURI APRESJAN

*translated by Kevin Windle*

OXFORD
UNIVERSITY PRESS

# OXFORD
UNIVERSITY PRESS

Great Clarendon Street, Oxford OX2 6DP
Oxford University Press is a department of the University of Oxford.
It furthers the University's objective of excellence in research, scholarship,
and education by publishing worldwide in

Oxford New York

Athens Auckland Bangkok Bogotá Buenos Aires Calcutta
Cape Town Chennai Dar es Salaam Delhi Florence Hong Kong Istanbul
Karachi Kuala Lumpur Madrid Melbourne Mexico City Mumbai
Nairobi Paris São Paulo Singapore Taipei Tokyo Toronto Warsaw

with associated companies in Berlin Ibadan

Published in the United States
by Oxford University Press Inc., New York

First published 2000

British Library Cataloguing in Publication Data
Data available

Library of Congress Cataloging in Publication Data

Data applied for

ISBN 0–19–823780–4

10 9 8 7 6 5 4 3 2 1

Typeset in Minion
by Peter Kahrel, Lancaster
Printed in Great Britain
on acid-free paper by
Biddles Ltd., Guildford and King's Lynn

# Acknowledgements

Chapter 1, 'English Synonyms and a Dictionary of Synonyms', was first published as 'Angliiskie sinonimy i sinonimicheskii slovar'', an afterword to J. Apresjan *et al.*, *Anglo-russkii sinonimicheskii slovar'* (Moscow, 1979).

Chapter 2, 'Types of Information in a Dictionary of Synonyms', was first published as 'Tipy informatsii dlia slovaria sinonimov', the fourth section of an article written as an introduction to the collective monograph *A New Explanatory Dictionary of Russian Synonyms. A Prospectus* [*Novyi ob"iasnitel'nyi slovar' sinonimov russkogo iazyka. Prospekt*] (Moscow, 1995) and entitled 'A New Synonym Dictionary: The Concept and Types of Information' [*Novyi slovar' sinonimov: kontseptsiia, tipy informatsii*]. This work was supported by a grant from the Russian Foundation for the Humanities.

Chapter 3, 'The Picture of Man as Reconstructed from Linguistic Data: An Attempt at a Systematic Description', was first published as 'Obraz cheloveka po dannym iazyka: Popytka sistemnogo opisaniia' in *Voprosy iazykoznaniia*, No. 1 (1995). It was made possible by an award to the author from the Alexander von Humboldt Foundation and an invitation from Professor P. Hellwig to visit the University of Heidelberg. The author wishes to thank his colleagues from the Humboldt Foundation and Professor Hellwig for providing ideal working conditions. It is his pleasant duty to also thank V. J. Apresjan, M. Ia. Glovinskaia, L. L. Iomdin, L. N. Iordanskaja, and I. A. Mel'čuk, who read the manuscript and made valuable critical comments.

Chapter 4, 'The Synonymy of Mental Predicates: *schitat'* [to consider] and its Synonyms', was first published as 'Sinonimiia mental'nykh predikatov: Gruppa *schitat'*' in the collection *Logicheskii analiz iazyka. Mental'nye deistviia* (Moscow, 1993).

Chapter 5, 'The Problem of Factivity: *znat'* [to know] and its Synonyms', was first published as 'Problema faktivnosti: *znat'* i ego sinonimy' in *Voprosy iazykoznaniia*, No. 4 (1995). It was supported by the Russian Foundation for the Humanities and the Soros Foundation's 'Cultural Initiative' and dedicated to Anna Wierzbicka.

This series was discussed at a working meeting of the Theoretical Semantics Section at the Russian Language Institute of the Russian Academy of Sciences. The author expresses his sincere gratitude to all participants in the seminar—O. Iu. Boguslavskaia, M. Ia. Glovinskaia, T. Krylova, I. V. Levontina, and E. V. Uryson—for their critical observations. The author is also grateful to the participants in N. D. Arutiunova's seminar at which this work was presented, for their interesting questions and comments.

Chapter 6, '*Khotet'* [to want] and its Synonyms: Notes about Words', was first published as '*Khotet'* i ego sinonimy: Zametki o slovakh' in *Filologicheskii sbornik* (*k 100-letiiu so dnia rozhdeniia V. V. Vinogradova*) (Moscow, 1995). The research was made possible by an award to the author from the Alexander von Humboldt Foundation and an invitation to the University of Heidelberg, where Professor P. Hellwig and his colleagues provided ideal working conditions. This article was completed with financial support from the Russian Foundation for the Humanities.

Chapter 7, 'Metaphor in the Semantic Representation of Emotions', by V. J. Apresjan and J. D. Apresjan, first appeared as 'Metafora v semanticheskom predstavlenii emotsii' in *Voprosy iazykoznaniia*, No. 3 (1993).

Chapter 8, 'On the Language of Explications and Semantic Primitives', was first published as 'O iazyke tolkovanii i semanticheskikh primitivakh' in *Izvestiia RAN, Seriia literatury i iazyka*, No. 4 (1994). It was made possible by an award to the author from the Alexander von Humboldt Foundation and an invitation to Professor Hellwig's department at the University of Heidelberg. The author is grateful to the Humboldt Foundation and to Professor Hellwig for the ideal living and working conditions provided for him by his German colleagues.

Chapter 9, 'Lexicographic Portraits (A Case Study of the Verb *Byt'* [to be])', was first published as 'Leksikograficheskie portrety (Na primere glagola *byt'*)' in *Nauchno-tekhnicheskaia informatsiia*, Series 2, No. 3 (1992). The text was read by L. L. Iomdin, I. A. Mel'čuk, and E. V. Paducheva, to whom the author expresses his gratitude for valuable critical comments.

Chapter 10, 'A Lexicographic Portrait of the Verb *vyiti* [to emerge, come out]', was first published as 'Leksikograficheskii portret glagola *vyiti*' in the collection *Voprosy kibernetiki. Iazyk logiki i logika iazyka* (Moscow, 1990).

# Contents

# Translator's Note

This translation is based on the Russian text published in J. D. Apresjan, *Izbran-nye trudy, t. II, Integral'noe opisanie iazyka i sistemnaia leksikografiia* (Moscow, 1995). Since it was made in close collaboration with the author, who introduced numerous revisions and approved some deletions, the English version may be said to represent an updated version and does not fully correspond to the original. In many places the Russian examples have been shortened and some of the more complex examples, particularly those from poetic sources, have been omitted. For different reasons, adjustments have been made to some of the English examples in Part I.

In preparing this translation I have tried to bear in mind two distinct groups of potential readers whose interests will inevitably differ. On the one hand, there are the academic linguists who are conversant with the field of semantics and may have a grasp of Russian grammar but little vocabulary. For these the Cyrillic script may present difficulties, hence the need for transliteration and for brief, manageable examples. On the other hand, advanced students of Russian will find much that is valuable in the author's detailed treatment of Russian synonyms. No doubt these readers, if they choose to read this translation rather than the original, would prefer to read the Russian examples in Cyrillic. I hope, however, that this latter group will understand the needs of readers with less knowledge of Russian, and will not be deterred by the amount of transliterated Russian.

The transliteration system followed is that applied by the Library of Congress. Exception is made for certain individuals who have become well known under other forms of their names. These include Juri Apresjan himself (and therefore his daughter Valentina Apresjan), Lidija Iordanskaja, Igor Mel'čuk, I. M. Boguslavsky, Roman Jakobson, V. A. Uspensky, and A. K. Zholkovsky. In order to avoid confusion by allowing the same names to appear in two different forms, the transliteration used in these names in the text has been retained in the references. Where the author quotes non-Russian sources in which other systems of transliteration are used, those systems are adhered to only in the quoted material.

## Symbols Used in the Text

An asterisk preceding a collocation or sentence indicates that it is incorrect. A superscript question mark preceding a phrase indicates that the given usage is dubious.

## Note on Terminology

Readers should note that the author's terminology does not always coincide with more traditional grammatical usage in Russian and English. In particular, the class of Russian verbs familiar to students of Russian as 'verbs of motion' [*glagoly dvizheniia*] (*idti, khodit'; ekhat', ezdit'*, etc., and their prefixed derivatives) are now referred to by some specialists, including Juri Apresjan, as 'verbs of locomotion' [*glagoly peremeshcheniia*], while the term 'verbs of motion' denotes verbs expressing movements other than locomotion. The author has introduced his own English term 'non-proper' to describe senses which are not primary or intrinsic to a given word. It serves as a translation of the Russian *nesobstvennyi* and is used here as an antonym of *proper* ('sobstvennyi') in the sense 'proper to'.

*Translator's Acknowledgements*

For their generous help throughout this project the translator is deeply indebted to two friends and colleagues at the Australian National University, Anna Wierzbicka and Margaret Travers. The former was able to give most valuable advice on numerous problems of translation in the field of semantics and lexicography. The latter devoted much time to checking and preparing the typescript, vetting the English phrasing by reference to the Russian original, and helping to compile the indices. Without their help the task of making this translation would have been much more difficult than it was.

Juri Apresjan himself has been deeply involved in all stages of the translation project. His guidance has been invaluable, and I am grateful for his readiness to deal with my many queries, both by e-mail to Canberra and in person during my visits to Moscow.

K.W.

# Publisher's Note

Oxford University Press is extremely grateful both to Kevin Windle for providing such an excellent translation in such a relatively short time, and to the author for having provided an English introduction to the work at its request.

# Abbreviations[1]

| | |
|---|---|
| A | adjective |
| acc | accusative |
| ANAL | analogue |
| ANT | antonym |
| comp | comparative |
| Conj | conjunction |
| CONV | conversive |
| D | adverb or adverbial phrase |
| dat | dative |
| fem | feminine |
| fut | future |
| gen | genitive |
| imper | imperative |
| imperf | imperfective |
| impers | impersonal |
| inf | infinitive |
| inst | instrumental |
| intrans | intransitive |
| masc | masculine |
| N | noun |
| neut | neuter |
| nom | nominative |
| num | numeral |
| P | preposition |
| $P_1$ | preposition denoting the starting point |
| $P_2$ | preposition denoting the point of arrival |
| $P_3$ | locative preposition |
| pass | passive |
| pf | perfective |
| pl | plural |
| prep | prepositional |
| propos | proposition |
| Rel | interrogative word introducing a relative clause |
| S | whole clause |
| sg | singular |
| SYN | synonym |
| trans | transitive |
| V | verb |

[1] These apply particularly to the dictionary entries for the verbs *byt'* and *vyiti* in Chapters 9 and 10.

# Introduction

This book is a collection of articles, yet there is a unity to it. Throughout the book I am concerned with two main issues—linguistic theory and lexicography. Until quite recently there has been a gap between the two. Moreover, in some quarters lexicography was looked down upon as a purely practical enterprise unworthy of scholarly interest. The present author is convinced, however, that sound lexicography can only be based on sound linguistic theory and that recent theoretical developments are of paramount importance for the practical skills of compiling a dictionary. The goal of this book is to show how a lexicographer can avail himself of the findings of theoreticians and how his own work can serve the aims of linguistic theory.

There are four trends in modern linguistic theory that are of immediate relevance to systematic lexicography:

1. The search for the 'naïve' (language) picture of the world, or the pattern of conceptualizations underlying lexical and grammatical meanings of the given language.

2. The breakthrough into linguistic macrocosm as manifested in the shift from the study of separate words to the study of large lexicographic types.

3. The breakthrough into linguistic microcosm as manifested in the shift to 'lexicographic portrayal', that is, meticulous studies of separate word senses in all of their linguistically relevant aspects.

4. The convergence of grammatical and lexicological studies, which resulted in what may be called a unified, or integrated theory of linguistic description.

It is precisely these trends and their impact on lexicography that are the subject-matter of the present book, so I shall briefly outline each of the four topics. To help the reader who may have difficulty with the Russian material in the bulk of the book I shall use mostly English examples in this introduction.

## 1. The 'Naïve', or Language Picture of the World

One of the most fascinating manifestations of a specific 'world-view' are the so-called obligatory meanings, i.e. meanings which a certain language *forces* its speakers to express whether they are important for the essence of their messages or not. After F. Boas and R. Jakobson it has become customary to contrast grammatical and lexical meanings as obligatory and non-obligatory. Grammatical meanings, for example, number in English substantives, are claimed to be obligatory in the sense that they must be expressed every time the speaker uses the respective part of speech. For example, in the phrase *The telephone is a useful invention* the noun *telephone* is used in the singular, although quantity is absolutely immaterial for the essence of the speaker's thought. What is actually spoken of is not the number of concrete objects but a certain technical way of conveying messages. By contrast, lexical meanings were presumed to be optional in the sense that they are expressed only when there is actual communicative need for them.

In recent decades research has shown that the opposition of grammatical and lexical meanings is not so sharp. Some elements of lexical meanings have also been demonstrated to be obligatorily and quite systematically expressed.

For instance, Russian forces its speakers, whenever they talk of locomotion, to specify the manner of locomotion (walking, flying, crawling, and so on), although it may be irrelevant to their thought. In particular, the idea of 'a certain living being having left at the point of observation a certain place' is expressed in good Russian by the phrases *Sobaka vyshla iz konury* 'The dog walked out of its kennel', *Ptitsa vyletela iz gnezda* 'The bird flew out of its nest', *Zmeia vypolzla iz nory* 'The snake crawled out of its hole', *Ryba vyplyla iz grota* 'The fish swam out of the grotto'. On purely logical grounds the verb *pokinut'* 'to leave' seems to come closer to the required meaning, yet the phrases ?*Sobaka pokinula konuru* 'The dog left its kennel', ?*Ptitsa pokinula gnezdo* 'The bird left its nest', ?*Zmeia pokinula noru* 'The snake left its hole', ?*Ryba pokinula grot* 'The fish left the grotto' are at least doubtful. They sound unmotivatedly elevated with regard to the required meaning or else express an entirely different idea of 'leaving a certain place *for good*'.

In this respect Russian is opposed to French, where the idea at issue is uniformly expressed by the same verb *sortir*: *Le chien est sorti de sa niche, Le serpent est sorti de son trou*, etc. Only when it is necessary to emphasize the way of leaving a certain place does French allow it to be specified by adding an adverbial phrase like *en marchant, à la nage*, etc. English seems to be intermediate between Russian and French. The required idea can be quite idiomatically rendered by the verbs *to walk, to fly, to crawl, to swim*, specifying the ways of locomotion in precisely the same way as Russian does (see the English glosses above). On the other hand, one can freely resort to the indiscriminate verb *to leave*, which comes closer to the French way of thinking: *The dog left its kennel, The bird left its nest, The snake left its hole, The fish left the grotto*.

The same predilection of Russian for specifying the *way* things are done can be further substantiated by the vocabulary of spatial position. Russian forces its speakers, when talking about the spatial orientation of certain physical bodies with regard to some other bodies, to specify the way they are positioned (e.g. whether they stand, lie, or hang). Cf. *U okna stoial Ivan* 'John stood at the window', *Na stene viseli kartiny* 'Some pictures hung on the wall', *V uglu lezhali knigi* 'Some books lay in the corner'. What the speaker actually *means* to communicate may be limited to the idea of 'to be placed, to be located somewhere'. This idea is prototypically rendered in Russian by the verb *nakhodit'sia*. Yet the phrases *U okna nakhodilsia Ivan, Na stene nakhodilis' kartiny, V uglu nakhodilis' knigi* would be odd or at least non-idiomatic.

French is again opposed to Russian because in similar circumstances it does not express any difference between the ways objects are positioned in space. It uses the neutral verb *se trouver* or the equally neutral construction *il y a*, unless it is necessary, for some reason or other, to specify their spatial positions. English again stands halfway between Russian and French, admitting both forms of expression.

The *language picture of the world*, including language-specific meanings, is thus the first keynote of this book.

## 2 Lexicographic Types

A lexicographic type is a group of lexemes with a shared property or properties, not necessarily semantic, which are sensitive to the same linguistic rules and which should therefore be uniformly described in the dictionary. I shall exemplify this concept with the classes of factive and putative predicates. Both of them will be narrowed down to the subclasses of verbs denoting mental *states* (not processes or actions).

Following Z. Vendler, the label 'factive' in this book is assigned to the verbs *to know* ⟨*to understand, to guess, to remember . . .*⟩ (*that P*) and similar predicates which govern propositions denoting facts. All of them are decomposable into semantic structures with the sense 'to know' at their root and presuppose the truth of the subordinate clause. This means that irrespective of whether the knowledge of P is asserted or denied, P always remains true. Such sentences as *He knew that he was under police surveillance* and *He didn't know that he was under police surveillance* are alike in asserting that he was under police surveillance.

The label 'putative' in this book is assigned to the verbs *to think* ⟨*to believe, to consider, to find, to hold, to doubt . . .*⟩ *that P* and similar predicates which denote opinions. Opinions, unlike knowledge, are not necessarily true. In other words, it cannot be deduced either from the sentence *He thought that he was under police surveillance*, or from the sentence *He didn't think that he was under police surveillance* whether he was in fact under surveillance or not.

Both lexicographic types share the common feature of all statives, namely, a specific relation to the idea of duration. It manifests itself above all in the fact that *to know* ⟨*to understand, to guess, to remember*⟩ (*that P*) and *to think* ⟨*to believe, to consider, to find, to hold, to doubt . . .*⟩ *that P* cannot occur in the progressive tenses (in the senses under consideration). Indeed, the phrases *\*When I entered he was knowing* ⟨*understanding, guessing*⟩ *that the meeting had been cancelled* or *\*When I entered he was believing* ⟨*considering, doubting*⟩ *that the meeting had been cancelled* are highly ungrammatical.

On other points factive and putative statives differ from one another. All of their formal differences are quite systematic and semantically well motivated, so that two consistently organized classes emerge. To make them accessible to certain rules of grammar and other sufficiently general linguistic rules we have to posit two distinct lexicographic types which should be uniformly described throughout the dictionary. I shall exemplify these types mostly with material from the descriptions of the verbs *to know* and *to think*.

A characteristic syntactic feature of factives noted by Z. Vendler is the ability to govern an indirect question introduced by the *wh*-words such as *what, who, which, where, when,* and so on: *He knew what was in store for him ⟨why his father kept silent, where to look for the mistake⟩.* Putatives do not govern indirect questions; in particular, they cannot replace factives in the above sentences.

The next syntactic peculiarity of *to know* and other prototypical factives is rooted in the fact that knowledge has a source, but not a reason. Therefore factives can govern nominal groups denoting sources of information and cannot subordinate adverbial modifiers of cause. Compare the well-formed *How do you know it?, I know it from the newspapers* and the ungrammatical *\*Why do you know it?*

By contrast, opinions have a reason, but never a source. Therefore putative verbs can subordinate adverbial modifiers of cause but not those denoting a source of information. Compare the well-formed *Why do you think so?* and the ungrammatical *\*I think so from the newspapers.*

The last syntactic difference between factives and putatives is motivated by the semantics of the latter. Prototypical putative verbs denote all sorts of opinions, that is, evaluative judgements. Therefore most of them can in some way or other govern assessment constructions with the second complement denoting the essence of evaluation: *to think ⟨to consider, to find⟩ somebody young, to regard ⟨to look upon⟩ this marriage as a mistake*, etc. For putatives the second complement is obligatory. Phrases like *\*I think him, \*I consider him* (in the sense at issue) are ungrammatical.

At first sight factives like *to know* (in a slightly different meaning) and *to remember* are also able to form this construction: *I knew ⟨remember⟩ her young.* However, the similarity is purely superficial. The second complement in this case does not fill in any semantic valency of the verb but fulfils the function of a co-predicative dependent. Syntactically it is optional, and its semantic relation to the verb is entirely different from that of the putative verbs. *I remember her young* means 'I remember her at a *time* when she was young'. This reference to time is totally alien to putatives.

There is at least one more formal feature which distinguishes factives and putatives—their prosodic and communicative properties. Curiously enough these have been almost totally neglected in theoretical studies, not to speak of dictionaries.

Factive words convey information about the real state of things. Therefore they can bear a strong phrasal accent (the so-called main phrasal stress) and serve as the rheme of the utterance, as in the phrase *I ↓knew she would marry him, I ↓remember how it all ended.* There is a rational motivation for it—it is pragmatically and psychologically reasonable to call the addressee's attention to the undoubtedly true information by phonically accentuating it.

Putative words express somebody's opinion about something which may be either true or false. Therefore they are never marked off by the main phrasal stress and are usually located in the thematic part of the utterance. The only type of phrasal stress they can bear is the so-called logical, or contrastive stress marking the contrastive rheme of the utterance, as in the sentence *Do you ↑↑believe you are under police surveillance, or do you ↓↓know it?*

These distinctions are so strong that they occur even within a single word if it happens to have a factive and a putative sense. Note the difference in the interpretation of the verb *to understand* in such sentences as *I ↓understand he is in trouble* (He is in trouble) and *I understand he is in ↓trouble* (I am doubtful about whether he is in trouble or not and am asking for information rather than asserting anything).

These differences carry over to all sorts of factives and putatives, in particular, to factive and putative adjectives and adverbs. For instance, a written sentence like *His son is a real gangster* is homographic and conceals two different propositions. The first is *His son is a ↓real gangster* (robs people and engages in all sorts of criminal activities, i. e. 'belongs to the class Y and has all its essential properties', factive). The second is *His son is a real ↓gangster* (naughty, disorderly, misbehaving, i.e. 'resembles an object of class Y but lacks its crucial property', putative).

To sum up, *lexicographic types* and the need to describe them in uniform fashion in a consistent dictionary is the second keynote of this book.

## 3. Lexicographic Portraits

To follow up the example considered in the preceding section, it should be noted that not all of the factives and not all of the putatives can be expected to display the prototypical properties of those two lexicographic types.

For instance, the factive verb *to understand* which, as noted above, may ultimately be reduced to the idea of 'to know', has no valency of an outward source of information. Understanding is a process too deep-seated in the mind of the subject himself and involving too much of his own activity. This accounts for the ungrammaticality or the dubiousness of sentences like *\*Where do you understand it from?*, *ʾI understand it from the newspapers.*

Various putative stative verbs display varying degrees of incompatibility with the idea of duration mentioned above. For instance, the verb *to think (that P)*, which is a close synonym of *to believe* and *to consider*, can be used in the progressive tenses, especially when it is conjoined with a genuinely actional verb: *As I lay thinking that my book was quite close to completion, I heard the phone ring.* Neither *to believe*, nor *to consider* can replace *to think* in such contexts.

The explanation is to be sought in the semantic structure of *to think* as a whole. The second basic sense of *to think* is purely actional: *I was thinking about tomorrow's session when the phone rang.* Now, closely related senses of a single word are apt to 'grow' into one another and impart to the neighbouring senses at least some of their properties. In such cases deviation from the prototype becomes highly probable.

This adds a new dimension to the facts discussed so far. It appears that in lexical description one should give equal attention to the shared properties of lexemes (the problem of lexicographic types, or *unification*) and to what distinguishes them (the problem of lexicographic portraits, or *individuation*).

A lexicographic portrait is an exhaustive account of all the linguistically relevant properties of a lexeme, with particular emphasis on the semantic motivation of its formal properties. A certain property is considered to be linguistically relevant if there is a rule of grammar or some other sufficiently general rule (semantic rules included) that accesses this property. Once the given lexeme is viewed against the whole set of linguistic rules, an entirely novel point of observation is created. It highlights new facets of lexemes and helps to uncover a number of their lexicographically relevant and semantically motivated properties that have never been recorded in dictionaries.

Consider the word *alone* in the following two uses: (1) *The house stands on the hillside all alone, He likes living alone*; (2) *Smith alone knows what happened, You alone can help me*. *Alone 1* is assigned the following definition in current dictionaries: 'by oneself, without the company or help of others'. *Alone 2* is defined as follows: 'and no other, no one else, the only one'.

It should be noted that *alone 1* and *alone 2* have different scopes. This is borne out by (*a*) the semantic contrast between *He lives there alone 1* and *He alone 2 lives there*; (*b*) the fact that *He lives alone 1* is grammatical while *?He alone 2 lives* is odd; (*c*) the fact that *He alone 2 knows the truth* is grammatical, while *?He knows alone 1 the truth* is not. Yet the dictionary definitions cited above fail to bring out this difference in the scopes. I propose the following more explicit definitions: *X does P alone 1* = 'X does P; one could expect that someone else would do P simultaneously or together with X; no one else does P simultaneously or together with X'; *X alone 2 does P* = 'X does P; there is no one else that does P'.

These definitions account for the following more formal properties of *alone 1* and *alone 2* which should be recorded in a dictionary of lexicographic portraits.

Syntactically *alone 1* is an adverbial modifier, that is, a verbal dependent (*Don't go there alone*), whereas *alone 2* is a noun attribute (cf. *Smith alone, you alone*).

Communicatively *alone 1* has no permanent value. It may mark off the verbal group as the theme (topic) of the utterance, as in *Living alone 1* [theme] *is a nuisance ⟨a pleasure⟩*. On the other hand, it may serve as the rheme (comment), as in *The house stands on the hillside all alone 1* [rheme]. Unlike it, *alone 2* always marks off the nominal group to which it refers as the rheme of the utterance; cf. *Smith* [rheme] *alone 2 knows what happened*.

The above distinctions are mirrored in the prosodic properties of the two lexemes. *Alone 1* can bear the main phrasal stress, as in *The house stands on the hillside all ↓alone 1*, or it may be left phrasally unstressed, as in *He ↓likes living alone 1*. On the other hand *alone 2* always bears the main phrasal stress, cf. *Smith ↓alone 2 knows what happened, You ↓alone 2 can help me.*

Exhaustive *lexicographic portraits* are thus the third keynote of this book.

### 4. The Unified, or Integrated Theory of Linguistic Description

Every complete linguistic description is ultimately made up of a grammar and a dictionary. It is reasonable to expect that these two documents should be mutually adjusted, i.e. co-ordinated with regard to the types of information included and the formal devices used to record them.

Unfortunately, until quite recently these natural principles had not been clearly formulated, much less adhered to. Originally dictionaries and grammars were produced by different people. The result was basically discordant grammars and dictionaries that did not give a coherent picture of the language as a whole. Let me quote one of the most intriguing examples of such a discrepancy.

English grammar has always recognized (cardinal) numerals as a discrete part of speech, distinct from nouns and adjectives. Indeed, their morphological, derivational, syntactic, and semantic properties are very different from those of nouns and adjectives. (*a*) In such prototypical uses as *five books, twenty-five, room five, to divide ⟨to multiply⟩ five by five*, and some others they can have no number marking—the basic morphological category of genuine nouns. (*b*) Derivationally they are set off from nouns and adjectives by such patterns as 'X + *teen*', 'X + *ty*', 'X + *th*', 'X + *fold*', as in *fifteen, fifty, fifth, fivefold*. (*c*) Syntactically they require that the nouns they combine with have the plural form, as in *five books*. They can also form the multiplicative construction *five by five* featuring a unique meaning of the preposition *by*. Prototypical nouns and adjectives have none of these properties. (*d*) In co-occurring with one another they form a specific concatenated syntactic construction with an additive meaning: *twenty-five* = '20 + 5'. Semantically this construction is entirely different from the typically substantive or adjectival constructions conjoining two nouns or adjectives, like *cannonball, computer system, dark blue, English–Russian* and so on.

Within a scientific description of English, classing numerals as nouns or adjectives in the dictionary is bound to play havoc with the grammatical rules geared to genuine nouns and adjectives. However, there is virtually no comprehensive dictionary of British, American, Australian, or any other variety of English that has the grammatical label 'num'. In many of the most authoritative dictionaries numerals are labelled either as nouns or as adjectives. Most inconsistently many of them include an entry for *numeral*, with the definition 'a word ⟨a name⟩ denoting ⟨expressing⟩ a number', and some of them even quote *cardinal numerals* as an example.

As can be seen from this account, traditional grammars and dictionaries at this point are glaringly incompatible. Insistence on the need for *integrated* linguistic descriptions, with a perfectly co-ordinated dictionary and grammar, thus becomes the last major keynote of the present book.

### 5. Conclusion

In his very apt dictum the great founder of modern English lexicography Samuel Johnson called dictionary-makers 'harmless drudges', and it is precisely the art of such drudges (in its theoretical aspects) that this book is devoted to. A harmless art is hardly a thing which is likely to catch the public attention. In our times risks, dangers, and upheavals hold far greater attraction. And yet the author hopes that the book he offers will not be altogether lost upon the English public. The English are famous for their love of dictionaries. According to recent statistical data, up to 90 per cent of English families have at least one dictionary in the household. If that percentage holds true for students of languages, this book has a chance of finding its readership.

# Part I
# PROBLEMS OF SYNONYMY

# 1

# English Synonyms and a Dictionary of Synonyms

As its title shows, this chapter has a dual purpose: first, it is intended to provide a theoretical introduction into that field of contemporary semantics which deals with lexical synonyms and to explain the meaning of the theoretical concepts used in the dictionary; second, it is intended to provide a lexicographical introduction to the dictionary, showing what information about synonyms may be found in it and in what form. The connection between these two topics is clear: a theory of lexical synonyms should (ideally) define the practical principles of their lexicographical description. This dictates the structure of the introductory chapter: theoretical matters are not relegated to a separate section but form the background to a presentation of the design of the dictionary and the structure and composition of a standard entry; these matters are explored to the extent required to clarify the lexicographical principles of processing the material and of subsequent use of the dictionary.

The theory of lexical semantics in general and of lexical synonyms in particular, which forms the basis of work on the dictionary, has been published in fairly full form and with all necessary references (J. Apresjan 1974). For this reason no bibliographical survey is given here, no other viewpoints are examined, the underlying arguments are not set forth. Instead the essentials of the chosen position are set out in fairly dogmatic fashion. Nor do we venture into the field of the history of English dictionaries of synonyms; a brief but extremely valuable article on this subject may be found in *Webster's New Dictionary of Synonyms* (Webster 1968). As far as possible, complex specialist terminology has been avoided and presentation shaped to be accessible to the non-linguist.

## 1. The Design of the Dictionary

The present dictionary is experimental. It aims not to provide a comprehensive account of all synonyms in the English language, but to demonstrate, on the basis of a small but fairly representative body of material, certain new principles in the description of series of synonyms. These principles derive from the practical and theoretical positions adopted.

First, this dictionary is designed above all to foster an active command of

English vocabulary (of that vocabulary which is included in the dictionary). On the other hand, unlike ordinary dictionaries of synonyms, it is conceived as a bilingual dictionary: it describes English synonyms in Russian. Finally, our last and perhaps most important aim was to compile a dictionary which would meet modern theoretical and lexicographical requirements, in line with modern scholarship and practice. More detailed consideration is given below to the complex of problems which need to be resolved if the aim of compiling a modern bilingual production dictionary of synonyms is to be achieved.

## 1.1. A PRODUCTION DICTIONARY

An active command of the vocabulary of a language, be it a speaker's native language or a foreign language, manifests itself above all in the semantic precision of his speech, that is, in his skill in selecting from the lexis and grammar of that language precisely those items which exactly express his thoughts. It is clear what a vital role is played here by a command of lexical synonyms.

Let us suppose that the speaker wishes to express the idea that somebody has met with an accident. If he chooses the second of two inexact synonyms *victim* and *prey*, and says, *he has fallen prey to an accident* he will commit a semantic error: *prey* presupposes an agent applying initiative and performing an *intentional* act of *violence*, for example: *he carefully marked down his prey before dealing the blow*. There will be no such error if we use the word *victim*, as this word, as distinct from *prey*, does not contain in its meaning any reference to whether intentional violence was applied or whether there was an accidental, though fateful, coincidence: *they could not identify the victim nor the man who had killed him; the victims of an earthquake/shipwreck*.

To take another example: should there be a need to express the idea of an unexpected attack on an encampment or fortress, from the pair of inexact synonyms *to surprise* and *to ambush* the first should be selected: *to surprise* [not *to ambush*] *the enemy camp/fortress*. If, on the other hand, we are speaking of an unexpected attack, especially from a concealed position, on a motorcyclist travelling along a road, we should say, *to ambush* [not *to surprise*] *a motorcyclist*. *Surprise* presupposes an immobile object while the subject is usually mobile (the attacker approaches his victim). *Ambush* presupposes a mobile object and a subject which is usually immobile (the victim approaches the attacker).

Semantic correctness may be absolute or relative. The sentence *he has fallen prey to an accident* is *absolutely* incorrect, that is, it is incorrect however it is used. An example of *relative* incorrectness is the sentence *he stopped to talk to his neighbour*: it is incorrect with regard to the meaning *he stopped talking . . .* but correct with regard to the meaning *he stopped in order to talk . . .*

It is clear that if a dictionary of synonyms is to help the user towards accurate expression it should contain a full, non-redundant, and absolutely explicit description of their semantic similarities and distinctions. A description is full if it mentions all substantive characteristics of the lexemes at issue; it is non-redundant if no superfluous characteristics are ascribed to any lexeme; lastly, it is explicit if nothing is left unsaid and every characteristic is clearly stated in a manner which can and should be understood literally, with no recourse to the reader's deductive powers.

The second distinguishing feature of a good command of a language is idiomatic usage, in the broad sense of the word, i.e. the ability to observe lexical and syntactic co-occurrence constraints.

Each of the adjectives *healthy, healthful, wholesome, salubrious*, and *salutary* has the sense 'fostering the improvement or maintenance of health'. Thus, if we say *a salubrious diet, salubrious food*, or *a salubrious way of life* we are making no semantic error: in principle the synonym selected is capable of expressing the required idea and we may be assured that we will be correctly understood. Nevertheless none of the above collocations is fully correct (the best choices will be: *a healthy diet, wholesome food, a healthy way of life*). Each of them violates a co-occurrence constraint, which, though not binding, is observed in pedantic and literary discourse, and requires that *salubrious*, unlike all its synonyms, be used chiefly with the nouns *air* and *climate*.

Nor is there any error of sense in the sentence *\*he sprang the fence*, yet this cannot be said in English. Unlike the synonymous verbs *to jump/leap*, which in this sense may either govern a direct object denoting the obstacle to be surmounted or be followed by a preposition (*to jump/leap a stream* or *to jump/leap over a stream*), the verb *to spring* must be accompanied by the preposition *over*: *he sprang over the fence*.

It is clear, then, that in order to ensure idiomatic use of language a dictionary of synonyms must contain a full, explicit and non-redundant description of the similarities and distinctions between them in their co-occurrence constraints—both lexico-semantic, and syntactic.

The third important indicator of language competence is flexibility, more precisely, a speaker's ability to paraphrase, i.e. his skill in expressing an idea in a wide variety of ways while leaving the content unchanged. If the speaker possesses just one means of expressing each idea he has most likely simply memorized it while actually having a very poor knowledge of the language; conversely, the better he knows the lexis and grammar of a language, the greater the ease with which he paraphrases his utterances when the need arises.

At the basis of this ability to paraphrase lies a knowledge of the synonym system of the language in the broad sense of the word, a knowledge of its synonymic resources. These are far from being limited to synonyms (note the following pairs of synonymous sentences which do not contain any lexical synonyms proper: *he writes short stories = he is a writer of short stories; he sold me a book for two dollars = I bought a book from him for two dollars; he is never present when needed most = he is always absent when needed most; linguistics is his hobby = linguistic science is his hobby = the science of language is his hobby*). It is natural,

however, to expect a dictionary of synonyms to answer the question of the connection between lexical synonyms and the paraphrasing system of a language.

With reference to lexical synonyms the question of their place in a language's
paraphrasing system comes down to the question of which synonyms can replace
one another in which contextual circumstances. Clearly this property is characteristic above all of semantically exact synonyms, when their lexical, semantic,
and syntactic co-occurrence constraints coincide at least partially. On the other
hand some inexact synonyms may also replace one another. For this it is essential, first of all, that their semantic distinctions be neutralizable, and secondly
that their co-occurrence characteristics be similar. The concepts of exact synonymy and neutralization are considered in detail below, so two illustrations will
suffice here.

An example of semantically exact synonyms with coincident co-occurrence
constraints is the pair of verbs *to gather* and *to collect* in the sense shown in the
sentence *dust gathered/collected in all the corners.* An example showing (partially)
neutralizable semantic distinctions is the pair *to menace* and *to threaten.* The
former denotes a promise to cause harm: *to menace smb. with ostracism/new
miseries.* The latter usually denotes a promise to cause harm if some demand is
not complied with: *'If you interfere with my sister, I shall call an officer,'* he
*threatened.* This distinction between *menace* and *threaten* is neutralized at least
in part when the subject lacks the ability to formulate demands, for example, if
the subject is a dog: *the dog menaced/threatened them with bared fangs.*

Another kind of synonym variation is motivated by a stylistic need to vary the
means of expressing the same idea within a small fragment of text. For this kind
of interchange it is immaterial whether the items at issue are semantically exact
synonyms or inexact synonyms with neutralizable semantic distinctions. If there
is a difference between the synonyms it can be disregarded since in the given
text they are used not to express shades of meaning, but purely to observe the
aforementioned stylistic rule.

The converse of a speaker's ability to paraphrase is his selective ability—the
fourth and last important element of the phenomenon known as 'good command of a language'. This ability manifests itself in the capacity to select from
a large number of theoretically possible ways of expressing a certain idea the one
which most closely corresponds to the social, cultural, and other features of the
speech situation and most fully expresses the personality of the participants.

If a language possesses a number of stylistically varied synonyms, irrespective
of whether these are semantically exact, it is by no means immaterial which of
them is used in a given speech situation.

It is important, for example, to know that in the series of synonyms *situation,
place, position, post, office,* the former has characteristics of genre. It is favoured
in newspaper advertisements: *situation wanted; situations vacant/available.* Without this knowledge a *stylistic* error can easily occur: *?place wanted, ?places vacant.*

Clearly, in a dictionary of synonyms aimed at fostering an active command of a language—that is, in a production dictionary—meticulous descriptions must be given of stylistic similarities and distinctions between synonyms—those of genre, function, geography, etc.

Thus consideration of the principle of active command of a language leads us to the conclusion that a dictionary of synonyms should describe synonyms from the standpoints of meaning, their lexical and semantic co-occurrence constraints, grammatical constructions, and stylistic features. In each of these cases all their similarities and differences must be described in such a way that for each synonym in a given series the types of contexts specific to it are listed and for any pair of synonyms the types of context in which they are mutually interchangeable are given (if, of course, they are in principle interchangeable). Finally, it is essential that the description be as full, non-redundant, and explicit as possible, i.e. constructed in such a way that on its basis the student may learn the correct use of synonyms in a broad range of situations.

## 1.2. A BILINGUAL DICTIONARY

For Russian compilers and users a bilingual dictionary of English synonyms is preferable in certain respects to a monolingual dictionary: it is easier to prepare and to understand. On the other hand, however, there are serious dangers: for the compiler, the temptation to provide translations rather than explicit definitions, and for the user the temptation to transfer the properties of a Russian word to an English word with similar meaning. Both these temptations derive from the same delusion, or perhaps the same type of linguistic inertia which sees units which are merely similar as identical. As has already been noted more than once, cases of full correspondence between lexical units in different languages are fairly uncommon, except for technical terms and similar words. More typical are cases of partial correspondence, sometimes very substantial, but still less than full coincidence.

Russian *rubit'* corresponds only approximately to English *to chop*: good equivalents with this verb exist for the phrases *rubit' drova, rubit' kapustu* [to chop wood, to chop (up) cabbage], but the phrases *rubit' kanaty* [to cut away the rigging] and *rubit' derev'ia* [to fell/chop down trees] cannot be translated by this verb.

The case of the verb *kolot'* [to split], which when closely examined turns out to be a very inexact synonym for *rubit'*, is even more complex. For meat and cabbage (assuming, of course, that these are in their natural state) the verb *rubit'* may be applied, but *kolot'* must be ruled out; *rubit'* may be used of *poleno* [log] if it is cut either lengthways or across the grain, while *kolot'* is only lengthways; nuts, chalk, ice, and similar objects may, generally speaking, be broken by the actions of both *kolot'* and *rubit'*; however, if we seek to achieve the desired result by throwing them against something hard or striking them against a hard surface, or crushing them in various ways by hand we can only use the verb *kolot'*. Here, in a first approximation, is the complex of ideas expressed by the verb *kolot'*: 'the process of division of a hard object with a rigid structure by a blow or by exerting pressure (not necessarily by the use of any special tool!), in such a way that the object suddenly breaks up completely into pieces or parts'. This cluster of ideas is so complex as to make it most unlikely for another language, with a different history and literary tradition, to have developed the means to express exactly the same combination in a single word. It is no surprise, therefore, that for the Russian collocations using one and the same verb the corresponding English collocations use very different verbs: *kolot' drova—to split/chop wood* (as for *rubit' drova*), *kolot' led—to break ice* (as for *lomat' led*), *kolot' orekhi—to crack nuts*. It is clear that in each of these cases only part of the complex of ideas which forms the content of *kolot'* is conveyed.

The same is true of English. Let us take, for example, the word *thrill* as shown in the sentence *What a thrill it was to go down the rapids in a tiny boat!* In this sense *thrill* combines within itself the ideas of an almost physical palpitation, of a piquant and exciting experience, of novelty and splendid sensations, when everything within one seems to sing. A Russian translation such as *ostrye oshchushcheniia* [piquant sensations], which does not convey even half of these ideas, would seem a disappointing failure were it not for the fact that in our comprehension of texts we are accustomed to rely on our experience, knowledge of reality, and our imagination. When we are told of shooting dangerous rapids in a small fragile boat, we need no more than a hint (*ostrye oshchushcheniia*) to allow us to reconstruct, with the aid of extralinguistic means, a fuller picture of the inner state described here.

The noun *abandon* is very English and has no equivalent in Russian. Dictionary translations—*neprinuzhdennost'* [unconstrainedness], *razviaznost'* [free-and-easy behaviour], *nesderzhannost'* [lack of restraint]—do not bring out its essence. It is apparent that there is no single over-arching translation possible in this case; more successful correspondences, new in each case, may be found only for entire collocations or even situations: *to sing with abandon—pet' s chuvstvom* [to sing with feeling], *to act with abandon—deistvovat', pozabyv obo vsem* [to act, forgetting about everything] (*v poryve, impul'sivno ili zhertvenno* [on an impulse, selflessly]), *he spoke with complete abandon—on govoril, ne sderzhivaias'* [he spoke without restraint] (*ego slovno prorvalo* [≈ as if carried away]).

This lexical 'incommensurability' is typical above all of words with fairly complex meanings: the greater the number of different ideas encapsulated in one dictionary sense, the greater the likelihood that the combination of ideas will be unique. Conversely, the simpler the meaning, the fewer basic ideas contained in it, the greater the likelihood that it will be expressed in one word in many, perhaps all the languages of the world. Sometimes, however, even relatively simple senses display similar incommensurability. Let us consider, for example, the following simple idea: 'P existed at moment $T_1$ and P did not exist at moment $T_2$ and $T_2$ is later than $T_1$.' This is an approximate description of the meaning of verbs such as *prekratit'sia* [to cease] and *to stop*. The above formula is not comprehensive, however; *stop* differs in that it implies the *sudden* cessation of a process (cf. *to cease*, which usually implies gradual cessation). In other words, paradoxical though it may seem, *prekratit'sia* and *to stop* are not fully exact translations of each other.

Since in many cases there is no exact correspondence even within individual pairs (*rubit'*—*to chop*, *thrill*—*ostroe oshchushchenie*), the same must apply to whole synonym series to an even greater extent.

The lack of correspondence between series of synonyms is at the same time quantitative and qualitative: first, in two roughly matching series the number of elements almost always differs; secondly, the synonyms within the series differ or resemble one another in different semantic, selectional, syntactical, and stylistic dimensions.

The English series consisting of three elements, *help, aid, assist*, is matched by a Russian series of two elements, *pomogat', podsobliat'*. *Help* and *pomogat'* correspond to each other fairly closely: they denote assistance in productive work, be it physical or mental (*pomogat' komu-l. rubit' drova*—*to help smb. to chop wood*), or in actions focused on the recipient—supplying, movement, etc. (*pomogat' komu-l. den'gami/sovetom*—*to help smb. with money/advice*; *pomogat' komu-l. pereiti ulitsu/sest' v mashinu*—*to help smb. across the road/into a car*). Here, however, the semantic and stylistic correspondence ends (the attentive reader may have noticed that the syntactic correspondences ended even earlier).

Russian *podsobliat'*, perhaps because of its slightly substandard nature, usually denotes purely physical help in some technically simple, uncomplicated labour process. The English synonyms of the verb *to help*—the words *aid* and *assist*—on the other hand, make it possible to foreground quite different aspects. *Aid* is preferred when speaking of organizational matters (*to aid in the funeral preparations*), or when it is necessary to emphasize the abundance of power and resources possessed by the subject, and the recipient's lack of these: *to aid the underdeveloped countries*; *to aid a government with subsidies*. *Assist*, on the other hand, presupposes the subordinate position of the subject, who performs some secondary task, perhaps following the directions of the recipient of the help (this semantic peculiarity of *assist* is clearly manifested in Russian *assistent* and *assistirovat'*).

Let us briefly consider one more series of synonyms from English and Russian. In the series *choose, select, opt, elect*—*vybirat', izbirat', otbirat', podbirat'*, only *choose* and *vybirat'*, which have the most general meaning of singling out one or a number of objects from a collection, are a direct match. *Select* indicates a range of possibilities from which a choice is made; *opt* usually indicates the presence of a single alternative (either one thing or the other); *elect*—the seriousness of the choice. In Russian the synonyms are differentiated by other features. *Izbirat'* indicates not only the seriousness of the choice but also its finality (possibly also the difficulty of the decision); *otbirat'* denotes choice of several objects with a common property designed to suit a certain purpose, while *podbirat'* denotes the choice of an object corresponding to another object or to a certain purpose.

The picture of these varied and nuanced distinctions between synonyms within one language and semantically close words in two different languages would be obscured and in some cases distorted beyond recognition if translation were the main method of explicating distinctions in a bilingual dictionary of synonyms.

It may seem at first sight as if translation could nevertheless remain the basic medium for the description of synonyms if it were utilized in some more interesting way—following the practice of standard bilingual dictionaries, for example, in which almost every common word (excluding technical terms) in each of its senses is given not one translation equivalent but a number of quasi-equivalents, each of which describes only one aspect of the word in question. In that case, however, the task of forming a correct idea of the original word is placed squarely upon the user: he himself must extract it by comparing the quasi-equivalents and guessing whether only their shared component corresponds to the original word or whether their specific features also correspond. It is clear that in a bilingual dictionary of synonyms, where the main aim is not translation but the explication of all the similarities and distinctions between synonyms, this method is out of the question.

But then the only remaining possibility is to describe the semantic, collocational, selectional, and stylistic similarities and distinctions between synonyms not via translation into the native language but via a special lexicographical language in which all the substantive properties of synonyms may be described as fully and explicitly as possible, and without redundancy. Translation may serve as a secondary means of description.

Thus our consideration of the problems of the bilingual dictionary leads, on the one hand, to the same conclusions as our consideration of the principle of the production dictionary. On the other, since translation cannot serve as the main means of explication, the question of a special descriptive language arises. As we shall see, there is a need not for one such special language, but several.

## 1.3. A MODERN DICTIONARY

A dictionary of English synonyms should comply with contemporary lexicographical and theoretical requirements.

The lexicographical requirements which it should meet are set by the level attained in the best Russian and foreign dictionaries of synonyms.

The most scholarly Russian synonym dictionary is the two-volume *Slovar' sinonimov russkogo iazyka* edited by A. P. Evgen'eva (Leningrad, Nauka, 1970, vol. i; 1971, vol. ii). For one thing it bridges the traditional gap which manifests itself between dictionaries of synonyms and explanatory dictionaries in the non-correspondence of the items of description. Explanatory dictionaries handle separate senses of words while most synonym dictionaries handle whole words in all of their senses. In *Slovar' sinonimov russkogo iazyka*, in most cases the items described correspond to the senses given in an explanatory dictionary. Secondly, in spite of very brief (from our standpoint, quite inadequate) notes on the series of synonyms, it contains a wealth of illustrative material, not interspersed with commentary but in a special zone of the dictionary entry. Both these principles seem to us sensible.

The best non-Russian dictionary of synonyms, to our way of thinking, is *Webster's New Dictionary of Synonyms*, of which a new edition, substantially amended and revised, appeared in 1968. It is unsurpassed in the wealth of observations, and contains an interesting attempt at a theoretical interpretation: similarities and differences between synonyms are described on the basis of their implications, applications, and connotations. For this reason, in compiling our dictionary of English synonyms we have given most careful consideration to the data in Webster's dictionary.

In view of the role *Webster's New Dictionary of Synonyms* has played in this work as a lexicographical source, a few words need to be said about its deficiencies as well as its virtues. It should be borne in mind that Webster reflects the level of linguistic science of the early 1950s and in particular the limited notions of synonymy then prevailing. The essence of these may be summarized as follows:

(*a*) Synonymy is regarded as a rather incomplete correspondence of senses, permitting substantial semantic distinctions between 'synonyms', for example *door, gate, portal, postern, doorway*. It would seem impossible to construct a general and sufficiently rigorous definition of synonymy which would subsume the listed words as synonyms without at the same time entailing solutions, with regard to some other facts, that would be utterly unacceptable to the author of the definition.

(*b*) A synonymic relationship is often established between whole polysemous words rather than between individual senses of words. Thus, in the series *mend, repair, patch, rebuild* the first synonym is represented by three senses: (1) *to mend* as in *to mend one's dress*; (2) *to correct, improve*, as in *to mend your manners/ways*; (3) *to heal*, as in *the wound mended slowly*. *Repair* is also included in the series in three senses: (1) *to repair*, as in *to repair a car*; (2) *to make good*, as in *to repair the lack of early education*; (3) *to restore*, as in *peace can be repaired*. *Patch* is represented by four senses: (1) *to patch*, as in *to patch overalls*; (2) *to save from collapse*, as in *to patch up one's marriage*; (3) *to put together*, as in *to patch a car together from pieces from a junkyard*; (4) *to produce an incomplete picture of something on the basis of fragmentary information*; *his life must be patched together from scattered references*. Finally, *rebuild* is represented by two senses: (1) *to restore, rebuild*, as in *to rebuild a house*; (2) *to remake, reassemble*, as in *to rebuild a typewriter*. As can be seen, in certain senses (e.g. the third sense of *mend*, the second sense of *repair*, the fourth sense of *patch*, and either sense of *rebuild*) these words are not synonymous; but even if some words are synonymous in several senses at once, the types of semantic, stylistic, combinatorial, and syntactic differentiation within the series are by no means always the same.

Theoretically, therefore, each series should be accorded a separate description (see below, § 2.1).

(*c*) In cases where a synonymic relationship is established not between words but between senses of words, account is usually taken of two types of meaning—direct and primary meanings (the senses most often used). This means that a vast stratum of lexical synonyms—words which are synonymous in their derived, figurative, or lexically constrained senses—is almost completely left out of account. Thus the following series do not appear: *give, lend, render,* as in *to give/ lend/render assistance; foot, bottom; head, top* as in *foot/bottom (head/top) of the stairs; back, ago* as in *a few years back/ago; get, bring, make* as in *I couldn't get him to help me; she couldn't quite bring herself to do it; good, clever* as in *to be good/clever at arithmetic.* The series for the word *courage* does not contain the word *heart* although it has a synonymous sense: *Rawdon had not the heart for that manœuvre* (Thackeray); the series *perform, fulfil,* etc. does not contain the verb *to do* which in this sense differs from *perform* and *fulfil* mainly stylistically. More examples could easily be cited.

(*d*) Semantic distinctions between synonyms are regarded as their central characteristic and are described in some detail. Collocational and stylistic distinctions, particularly those of bookish or archaic register, are often ignored, i.e. bookish and archaic words are treated as neutral, while syntactic and some grammatical distinctions are not mentioned at all. There is no attempt to trace interesting stylistic, syntactic, and collocational features of synonyms to their semantic sources. (This question is considered in more detail in § 2.1, 2.2, 2.4, 2.6, and 2.7.) Cases of semantically exact synonyms and inexact synonyms whose semantic distinctions are neutralizable in certain conditions are either not described at all or not fully described.

(*e*) There is an imbalance in treatment of vocabulary of high and low styles. Specifically, bookish and even archaic vocabulary is accorded a marked preference over colloquial and substandard. This is evidently the reason for the absence of such series as *child,* coll. *kid; head,* coll. *chump; lie,* coll. *tale;* in the series *nerve, effrontery, gall* etc. the colloquial synonyms *face, brass, sauce* are not given; in the series *courage, mettle* the colloquial *spunk* does not appear.

(*f*) The notion of a metalinguistic vocabulary with which to define synonyms is lacking, and as a result the definitions of separate items do not meet the requirements of fullness, non-redundancy, and explicitness.

While taking Webster's work as our model, we clearly could not follow it blindly in everything. A detailed account will be found below (§ 2.1) of our departures from Webster. Here it will suffice to say that they are all motivated by a general desire to compile a dictionary of synonyms incorporating the theoretical findings of the 1970s.

The theoretical demands which our dictionary should meet are defined by the state of contemporary linguistic semantics. In those studies which guide our work (above all, I. A. Mel'čuk's writings), semantics is seen as one of the components of a formal model of language. The 'formal model of language' is the term applied to a logical automaton which imitates command of a language in the sense defined above (see § 1.1). In the final analysis this automaton should be able to establish formally the correspondence between a given meaning and all the correct texts which express that meaning, on the one hand, and between a given text and all the meanings it expresses, on the other. Since a logical automaton is able to work only with absolutely precise and comprehensive instructions, it will establish correctly the correspondence between senses and texts only if it is programmed with a full, sufficient, and explicit description of all linguistic objects and rules. But this is precisely the kind of description which is needed, quite independently, by a bilingual production dictionary of synonyms. In other words the principles of a modern, bilingual production dictionary demand of the lexicographer the implementation of exactly the same set of conditions, not of several different sets.

A slant towards modern computer linguistics also brings another benefit. The task of establishing correspondences between meanings and texts is posed in theoretical semantics as one of translation from an artificial semantic language to a natural language (which corresponds to speaking, or the synthesis of texts) and from natural language into a semantic language (which corresponds to understanding, or the analysis of texts).

The advantages of a special semantic language with which to record the initial information to be subsequently translated into natural language are obvious: a semantic language is universal, that is, it is free of everything that makes up the specifics of expression in natural languages. Every meaning which in any natural language is expressed implicitly, for example, within a large combination of senses of the kind considered above or by means of a grammatical construction or with the aid of word order and the like, should be expressed explicitly—by a single word of the semantic language. It follows that the lexical correspondences between semantic and natural language are not word-for-word matches. They are more complex: as a rule a single word of natural language with a complex meaning will be matched by a whole collocation or phrase in the semantic language.

It is clear how important this semantic language is to the compiler of a dictionary of synonyms: it is the tool which ideally suits the aim of providing an explicit description of all the semantic properties of synonyms.

In contemporary theoretical semantics, special formal languages are being developed not only to describe the meanings of words, but also their lexico-semantic and syntactic co-occurrence constraints. In semantics they are essential, as without them it is impossible to resolve the problem of automatic synthesis of correct, idiomatic texts; but once they have been created it is expedient to utilize them for other applied tasks in which similar problems arise, in particular for the compilation of a dictionary of synonyms.

As is clear from the foregoing remarks, at the present stage of development of linguistics and its applications—for the first time in the history of linguistic study—the opportunity has arisen for a fruitful synthesis of lexicography and semantics, which until very recently developed separately. In order to make clear how we envisage the synthesis of lexicography and theoretical semantics in a dictionary of synonyms and how *The English–Russian Dictionary of Synonyms* differs from its predecessors, we shall consider the structure and composition of its entries.

## 2. The Structure and Composition of Entries

Each dictionary entry contains a detailed analysis of a single series of synonyms. By 'series of synonyms' we mean a group of words belonging to the same part of speech and having the same semantic description or descriptions with much in common (a semantic description is made up of an explication, a list of semantic associations, information concerning logical emphasis, and other kinds of information; explications, semantic associations, and logical emphasis are considered below under § 2.2). Only words of the first type (those whose semantic descriptions coincide fully) are synonyms in the strict sense; those of the second type (whose semantic descriptions coincide partially) should be termed quasi-synonyms. However, following the tradition of dictionaries of synonyms, we shall preserve the term 'synonym' for words of the second type and call those of the first type 'exact synonyms'.

Our dictionary sets forth approximately 400 of the most widely used synonym series in English. In terms of scope, this is only a small part of the material contained in Webster's dictionary of synonyms. For various reasons, most of them technical, many of Webster's series have been left out, and we have not added any new series not given by Webster. Generally speaking, as we have said, in view of the experimental nature of this dictionary we do not attempt to cover all the vocabulary of English but rather to describe fully each synonym series given.

A standard entry comprises the following zones: (1) headword, (2) explication, (3) translation, (4) meaning, (5) notes, (6) syntax, (7) co-occurrence constraints, (8) illustrations. We shall consider each of these in detail.

### 2.1. HEADWORDS

The opening line of a dictionary entry comprises the synonym series itself, that is, the ordered list of synonyms to be considered. In most cases it coincides formally with the corresponding one in Webster's synonym dictionary. Departures from Webster are as follows:

(*a*) sometimes synonyms unaccountably missing in Webster are added to the series; for example in the series *solitude, seclusion, isolation* the word *loneliness*, which is semantically very close to *solitude*, is added;

(*b*) sometimes certain words are omitted from a series when they are semantically fairly remote from its basic meaning. Thus, from the series *remember, recollect, recall* the verb *remind* (cause somebody to remember) is excluded. From the series *recede, retreat* etc. the verb *retract*, having a transitive and causative meaning, is dropped. In the series *slide, glide, glissade, slip* etc. the verbs *coast* and *toboggan* are removed;

(*c*) where two series are close they may be combined if this produces a more consistent treatment of the material in the dictionary as a whole. For example, differences in the amount of movement, when the nature of that movement coincides, are usually treated by Webster within a single entry, producing series such as the following: *swing, sway, undulate, fluctuate, oscillate, vibrate; shake, quake, shiver*, and many others. This justifies the amalgamation of the two series *jump, leap, spring, bound, vault* and *skip, hop*;

(*d*) any series which brings together several different meanings of synonyms in Webster is broken down into a number of new series such that in each new series all the synonyms are represented by just one meaning, and such that all synonyms in the series have this meaning. Here there are three possible situations.

The first and most important of these is usually, though not always, linked with so-called regular (recurrent) polysemy. One type of regular polysemy which is broadly represented in the dictionary deserves special mention. It concerns adjectives denoting the intellectual, emotional, moral, and physical characteristics and states of human beings. These adjectives systematically manifest a combination of senses of the following two types: (1) 'having a certain property/being in a certain state', and (2) 'expressing this property/state', 'manifesting this property /state'; e.g. *intelligent/stupid man—intelligent/stupid look/answer, merry/sad boy —merry/sad eyes/smiles, agile/awkward animals—agile/awkward movements, honest /sly person—honest/sly question*. The first type of meaning is expressed in combination with nouns denoting humans, animals, or the organ which is the bearer of the given features, e.g. *intelligent mind, sad soul, deft hands, upright character*; the second type in combination with nouns denoting speech acts, facial expression, gestures or actions.

If all synonyms of the group in question display this kind of regular polysemy, the group is divided into a number of subgroups under the same heading but with different sense numbers. The series *intelligent, clever, bright, smart*, etc. is divided in this way, as is *angry, wrathful, indignant, mad*, etc. and many others.

It goes without saying that exactly the same procedure is followed with other series when all members of a series possess the same combination of meanings, irrespective of whether they display this or another type of regular polysemy or not. Webster's single series *threaten, menace* is divided in our dictionary into two meaning series: (1) 'to promise to cause smb. harm': *to threaten/menace smb. with destruction (to kill smb)*; (2) 'to be imminent, to constitute danger' (cf. *grozit'*—threaten): *death/the earthquake was threatening/menacing*.

The second situation differs from the first in that not all members of one of

Webster's series, but only some of them, have the same combination of meanings. A series of this type is broken down into completely independent series—each with its own headword. Thus Webster's series *summon, call, convene, convoke, muster* is divided into the following three series: (1) *convene, convoke, call, summon, muster* (bring together parliament, a sessional meeting, etc.), (2) *summon, call, muster* (gather, mobilize inner resources, courage, strength, mental powers, energy), (3) *summon, call* (tell somebody to come).

In the third and last case one word or a number of words from a Webster series are represented in the appropriate entry not only by the meaning in which they are synonymous with all the other words, but also by certain other meanings which fall outside the series. These meanings are treated in the zone headed Notes (see § 2.5 below).

In connection with point (*d*) it should be emphasized that the principle of differentiation of senses upheld here makes it possible to demonstrate a complex and delicate network of semantic intersections among individual words and whole word groups.

(*e*) In those cases in which a Webster series has been in any way reorganized, the 'dominant' of the series—the introductory headword—may also be changed. It is clear, for example, that the verb *to summon*, which introduces the series with the meaning 'tell somebody to come', cannot head the series with the meaning 'convoke': this meaning, which is peripheral to *summon*, is central to the verb *convene*, which should be placed at the head of the series in this case.

(*f*) The order of synonyms within a series (and the order in which they are described within the entry) may differ from that adopted in Webster. This may occur when it leads to a clearer description of the semantic structure of the series, that is, the identification of semantic groups and subgroups in it. Thus the series *slide, slip, glide, skid, glissade, slither* is reordered as *slide, glide, glissade, slip, skid, slither* in order to emphasize the closer semantic links between *glide* and *glissade* (a graceful, flowing sliding movement, usually deliberate) and *slip* and *skid* (a sliding movement resulting from loss of balance or stability, unintentional and often connected with danger).

(*g*) The headword series contains, besides a list of synonyms, a description of their stylistic properties. This is effected by means of the stylistic labels customarily used in lexicography. This form of description of stylistic properties is far more economical than the lengthy notes given in the explicatory part of the entry in Webster (and other synonym dictionaries).

It is essential to note that although the stylistic properties of synonyms, on the one hand, and their semantic, combinatorial, and syntactic properties, on the other, are logically independent of each other, in many cases there is a quite palpable connection between them. To be more precise, certain semantic, combinatorial, and syntactic properties of synonyms are motivated by their stylistic properties.

In the synonym series *face, countenance, visage* only the first word, being stylistically neutral, can denote the front of an animal's head as well as that of a human head, and therefore combine with the names of animals: *the monkey's face*; *the face of Katy* [a pig, J.A.] *was a tiger's face* (Steinbeck). The bookish terms *countenance* and *visage* inevitably bear connotations of beauty or grandeur and cannot denote the face of an animal. They are therefore used exclusively of humans (a similar example is examined in § 2.2).

In the series *effrontery, nerve, cheek, gall,* the last three synonyms, by virtue of their colloquial nature, are syntactically far less free than *effrontery*. There are few constructions in which all four may be used: *to have the effrontery/nerve/cheek/gall to do smth.*; *smb.'s effrontery/nerve/cheek/gall maddened him*; *the effrontery/nerve/cheek/gall of smb.* (*was maddening*). *Cheek* and less frequently *nerve* are also used in the construction *it's* (*awful*) *cheek my coming so late*, and as the object of the verb *to give*: *Nothing but genuine inspiration could give a woman such cheek* (Shaw). But in constructions such as *the effrontery of looking into her soul, a kind of haughty effrontery, the cool effrontery of a Yankee, cheek, nerve* and *gall* are not normally used.

In those cases where we have been able to trace such links they are described in the appropriate zone of the entry ('Meaning', 'Syntax', or 'Co-occurrence constraints').

Up till now we have been dealing solely with those departures from Webster which concern the head series of an entry. Of course the differences between the English-Russian synonym dictionary and Webster do not end here—if they did there would be no need to compile a new dictionary. The most substantive and fundamental differences relate to the explication of the meaning of a synonym series, the description of the semantic, combinatorial, and syntactic features of synonyms, the specification of conditions in which they are interchangeable, and like matters.

## 2.2. EXPLICATION

In connection with the problem of explications we shall consider briefly the concept of the object of the explication, that is the meaning of a word or synonym series (the thing explicated) and, in more detail, the concept of the means of explication, that is, the metalanguage in which the explication is formulated.

Generally speaking the meaning of a word comprises two components:

(1) the naïve concept of the thing, situation, property, state, process, etc. denoted by the word; compare the naïve concept of water as a transparent colourless liquid used for drinking and other purposes and the scientific description of water as a chemical substance comprising two atoms of hydrogen and one of oxygen. The naïve concept of a situation (the participants, their characteristics, and the relations between them) may include details of the role played by the narrator or observer. For the adjectives *distant, far, far-off, faraway* the position of the observer has no relevance. The synonym *remote* indicates that a

certain object A is distant from point B and that B is perceived by the speaker as the position of the observer or a central point from which distances are measured: *I went abroad to a remote place where I thought I wasn't likely to meet anyone who knew me.* Certain meanings (and, consequently, certain explications) have two distinct components—presuppositions and assertions. Presuppositions are those elements of an explication which are not affected by negation. In the word *bachelor* (= unmarried man of marriageable age) the element 'man' is a presupposition for *bachelor*, while 'unmarried' is its assertion, i.e. the semantic component affected by negation. If we say *Peter is not a bachelor* we are in no sense denying that Peter is a man, merely that he has never been married. Presuppositions became a subject of linguistic study only in the 1960s and the material accumulated is as yet insufficient for their full lexicographical treatment. For this reason in the English-Russian synonym dictionary presuppositions are hardly ever described separately from the other components of meaning.

(2) an evaluation of the thing, situation, etc. as good or bad, plausible or implausible, desirable or undesirable, etc. from the point of view of the interlocutors, that is, the speaker or listener. Evaluative components are especially typical of the meanings of delimiting, contrastive, and emphatic particles (such as *dazhe* [even], *uzh* [certainly, indeed], *tol'ko* [only, just], *ved'* [after all]), concessive and contrastive conjunctions (such as *khotia* [although], *no* [but], *odnako* [however]) and certain semantic classes of modal words and adverbs (such as *sovsem* [completely], *vsego* [in all, only], *otniud'* [by no means]). These form the so-called modal framework of the explication.

Although, as stated, these evaluative components are typical above all of the meanings of particles, some conjunctions, and adverbs, they are by no means the exclusive property of these word categories. Consider, for example, the phraseme *take care* and the verb *bother* in the sense 'take the trouble (to do something)'. *Take care* may be used quite freely in the most varied sentence types, especially in affirmative sentences: *the criminal took care to rub off his finger-prints. Bother,* however, is severely restricted in this meaning: it is used predominantly in negative, interrogative, modal, and hypothetical sentences, such as, *the criminal didn't bother to rub off his finger-prints; do you think he will bother to rub off his finger-prints?; he would scarcely bother to rub off his finger-prints.* We cannot say *\*the criminal bothered to rub off his finger-prints.* The distinction in syntactic behaviour between *take care* and *bother* is due to the fact that *bother* contains an evaluative component which is not present in *take care.* This evaluative component can be described naturally by means of the following modal framework: *bother (to do P)* = 'the speaker considers it unlikely that the subject will make an effort to do P' (see also § 2.6).

The naïve concept and evaluation (if the latter is relevant, which for many words is far from being the case) conclude the subject of the explication proper. The description of the naïve concept forms the core of the explication and the description of the evaluation its modal framework. However, a complete *seman-*

*tic description* of a word, which is of primary importance in a dictionary of synonyms, is broader than its meaning, and includes, in addition, information about its presuppositions, the semantic associations, or connotations, that it evokes, its logical stress, and a number of other matters of less concern here.

Semantic associations reflect the cultural concepts and traditions related to a word, the history of its use in literature, its etymology, the predominant applications of the given referent in a given society, and many other extralinguistic factors. The word *prey* may serve as an example: it suggests ideas of cruelty and evil, which may be traced to its etymology. The synonym *victim* lacks these associations.

The third concept—logical stress, emphasizing or highlighting one component of meaning—may be illustrated by the synonyms *grateful* and *thankful* (such as a person who believes or knows that he is the recipient of good and feels obliged to repay it by verbal acknowledgement or a reciprocal good deed). *Grateful* is preferred when there is a need to stress the significance of the service rendered, and *thankful* when it is necessary to express the intensity of the feeling experienced by the subject: *you've helped me, and I'm grateful to you; I'm thankful that his life was spared in the accident.*

The semantic components which form part of the meaning of a word and can therefore be recorded in its explication may be permanent features present in any example of its usage, or non-permanent, possible, but not obligatory. In the series *stern, severe, austere, ascetic*, the first denotes a characteristic which manifests itself in making harsh demands upon others, while the last implies harsh demands made upon oneself. These are permanent components of the meanings of *stern* and *ascetic*. Unlike these, *severe* usually implies severity with regard to others, but may sometimes denote self-directed severity as well: *a severe teacher; he was as severe with himself as with others.* When alone in predicative usage, *severe* is typically understood in the first sense: *he is a severe one. Austere*, on the other hand, more commonly denotes ascetic severity, that is, self-directed severity, but may also denote severity directed towards others: *an austere character; an austere father*. For *severe* and *austere*, then, the components 'with regard to others' and 'with regard to oneself' are possible, but not obligatory. For this reason they are accompanied in the explications by components such as 'usually', 'sometimes', 'often', and 'may'. (Strictly speaking, these components are not elements of meaning, but meta-statements about the typical conditions of use of the corresponding words.)

A component of meaning must be distinguished from its co-occurrence features. The fact that *salubrious* occurs mostly with the words *climate* and *air* (see § 1.1) in no way permits us to include these words in its explication. This feature is purely a co-occurrence characteristic of *salubrious*, and not a component of its meaning.

We move on to the second topic—a semantic language, which, as we attempted to demonstrate in § 1.2, is needed to describe the semantic similarities and distinctions between synonyms. Bearing in mind that in an area as traditional as lexicography reforms are more useful than revolution, we have developed a compromise medium of description for a dictionary of synonyms, a simplified form of standard Russian, consisting of a limited number of relatively simple words and structures.

Before describing this standardized language, we shall demonstrate some of its features as clearly as possible by contrasting some explications in that language with the respective explications from Webster.

*Grateful, thankful* (see above), Webster: 'feeling or expressing one's gratitude'.

*Attachment, affection, love*: 'a feeling experienced towards an object which is pleasant to the subject and causes a wish to have contact with the object or do good to it'. Webster: 'a feeling which animates a person who is genuinely fond of somebody or something'.

*Hatred, detestation, abhorrence, abomination, loathing*: 'feeling experienced towards an object which is unpleasant to the subject and causes a wish to have no contact with the object or to do harm to it'. Webster: 'extreme aversion, especially as coupled with enmity or malice'.

*Enemy, foe*: 'one who is in conflict with someone and seeks to destroy him or do him harm'. Webster: 'person or body of persons that is hostile or that manifests hostility to another'.

*Misfortune, adversity, mischance, mishap*: 'an event having negative or damaging influence on a person's normal activities'. Webster: 'bad luck or adverse fortune' or 'an instance of adverse fortune'.

*Accident, casualty, mishap*: 'an accidental event having negative or damaging influence on a person's normal activities or functioning'. Webster: 'chance or a chance event bringing injury or loss'.

*Jump, leap, spring, bound, skip, hop*: (*a*) 'by a sudden muscular effort to move oneself spatially, losing contact with any support', or (*b*) 'to move by this means'. Webster: 'suddenly move in space by or as if by muscular effort'.

*Beat, pound, pummel, thrash, buffet, baste, belabour*: 'to repeatedly bring a compact object into forceful contact with the body of a living being in order to cause physical pain to that being'. Webster: 'to strike repeatedly'.

Even a cursory comparison of these explications makes the following features obvious: (*a*) our explications are long, Webster's brief; (*b*) our explications are sometimes stylistically clumsy, while Webster's are almost always stylistically impeccable; (*c*) owing to their unusual form, a certain effort is required to understand our definitions, while Webster's can be grasped easily; (*d*) our explications are constructed on the basis of relatively simple meanings, Webster's on the basis of fairly complex meanings; (*e*) our explications contain artificial words such as (*kauzirovat'*—'to cause') while Webster's do not; (*f*) our definitions contain numerous words which recur in various definitions (*good, harm, to do, to cause, feeling, subject, object, pleasant, not, contact, negative, normal*, etc.), while in Webster's there is hardly any repetition of words.

These differences are not accidental but are due to certain general principles of the description of meanings. The most important of these are the following:

(*a*) A complex meaning should be explicated by means of simpler meanings (see above examples). Although the explications produced may be clumsy and inelegant, they permit a natural resolution of the main problems of a dictionary of synonyms: first, they make it easy to express the semantic similarities and distinctions between synonyms in a given series, for example the fact that *hatred* implies 'a wish to cause harm to a person', while *detestation* is 'a wish to have no contact with him' (see also the analysis of the pair *grateful—thankful*, above); secondly, they bring out the semantic similarities and distinctions between different but related synonym series (e.g. between *attachment, affection, love* and *hatred, detestation, abhorrence, abomination, loathing*; between *misfortune, adversity, mischance, mishap* and *accident, casualty, mishap*).

Webster's explications are ill-suited to these purposes since a single complex meaning (*love* [noun], *hate, enemy, disaster*) is defined by means of another which is no less complex (*love* [verb], *loathing, hostile, misfortune*). Consequently a tautologous circle occurs in the explications, or in the worst cases a lack of precision. If *grateful* and *thankful* are different, as emerges from Webster's further description, they can hardly both mean *gratitude*; *thankful* should signify *thankfulness*. *Hatred* is clearly not a variety of *aversion*; these are two different feelings, related though they may be. The same may be said of *misfortune* and *bad luck*, *attachment* and *fondness*.

The principle of gradual reduction of complex meanings to simpler ones presupposes that certain meanings must be accepted as primary or indefinable meanings, such as *khotet'* [to want], for example, which cannot be explicated via simpler meanings since simpler meanings do not exist. In such cases the explication of a series coincides verbally with one of its translation equivalents: *desire, wish, want* has the translations *khotet', zhelat'*.

(*b*) Explications should be complete and non-redundant. Clearly, if the explications are incomplete, they will not demonstrate all the semantic similarities and distinctions between synonyms; if there is redundancy, the synonyms will acquire non-existent similarities and distinctions. Because of this, in certain situations artificial words are needed. One of these, the verb *kauzirovat'* [to cause], deserves special mention.

*To cause P* means, by definition, 'to act in such a way that a situation P directly occurs or begins'. In this sense the word *kauzirovat'* is used in the explication of many causative verbs, e.g., *to open* = 'to cause to become open', *to kill* = 'to cause to die', etc. The question arises: is it not possible in these and similar explications to replace this artificial Russian verb with some word from natural language? This issue has been widely discussed in the theoretical literature in connection with a proposal to explicate causative verbs such as *open, kill, break, grow, burn*, etc. with the aid of the English verb *cause*. At first sight it appears that English *to cause* has the required meaning: *to open* (*the door*) = 'to cause (the door) to open', *to kill* (*a bird*) = 'to cause (a bird) to die', *to break* (*the window*) = 'to cause (the window) to break', *to burn* (*the toast*) = 'to cause (the toast) to burn', etc. It was noted, however, that collocations containing the verb *to cause* did not have quite the same meaning as the corresponding causative verbs. It is possible to say, *he caused the door to open by tickling Sally who was pressed against it*, but not *\*he opened the door by tickling Sally who was pressed against it*: in the latter case the door was opened by Sally, not by him. By the same token, *John's negligence caused the toast to burn* is not the same as *\*John's negligence burned the toast*, and so on. The point is that *to open the door, to burn the toast*, and similar collocations express the idea of direct causation, which is alien to the English verb *to cause*. This means that the explication *to open* (*the door*) = 'to cause (the door) to open' and others like it are semantically incomplete. The same clearly applies to the closest Russian equivalent of the verb 'to cause'—*vyzyvat'*: *ubit' privratnika* [to kill the door-keeper] and *vyzvat' smert' privratnika* [to cause the death of the door-keeper] are plainly different in meaning; hence *ubit'* is not equal to *vyzvat' smert'*.

However, if we try to define verbs of the type *open, kill, grow, break* (or their Russian equivalents) by means of other causative verbs, such as *budit'* (*mysli, liubopytstvo*) [to awaken (thoughts, curiosity)], *vnushat'* (*uvazhenie, chuvstvo zhalosti*) [to inspire (respect, a feeling of pity)], *vozbuzhdat'* (*liubopytstvo, interes*) [to awaken (curiosity, interest)], *zastavliat'* (*rabotat', otstupat'*) [to compel (to work, to retreat)], *porozhdat'* (*neuverennost', nedovol'stvo soboi*) [to engender (uncertainty, dissatisfaction with oneself)], *privodit'* (*k putanitse, k raspadeniiu*) [to lead (to confusion, disintegration)], *prinosit'* (*neschast'e, stradaniia*) [to bring (misfortune, suffering)], *prichiniat'* (*bol', vred*) [to cause (pain, harm)], *chinit'* (*prepiatstviia*) [to create (obstacles)] we shall produce semantic redundancy in the explications, that is, the result will be an excess of superfluous semantic components: it is clear that each of the verbs listed here differs from *kauzirovat'* in some particular semantic feature which is peculiar to it alone.

Thus in the explication of verbs of the type *to open, to break, to burn*, and others of similar nature, there is a need for a sense which cannot be expressed by any actually existing Russian verb. We have no choice but to introduce the artificial verb *kauzirovat'* to express this sense concisely.

(*c*) Each Russian word appearing in the explication should be used in one sense only, and each semantic component in the explication should be expressed by one word only; in other words, the words and senses of the standardized language should ideally form a one-to-one semantic match (there should be no synonyms and no homonyms). Observance of this requirement makes possible an explicit description of all the similarities and differences between complex meanings; meanings are the same if their explications coincide literally, that is, contain the very same words in the same configurations; they are different if the explications diverge even slightly (see the above explications).

As is clear from the above, the requirements formulated here are no caprice or modish whim. They are dictated by the central issues themselves. If they are not observed the explications become so unclear that at times they become riddles which can lead even the best-intentioned of readers into a blind alley. Let us take an example which is typical of synonym dictionaries.

Webster's dictionary presents the following two synonym series as different: *desire, wish, want, crave, covet,* with the explication 'to have a longing for something', and *long, yearn, hanker, pine, hunger, thirst* with the explication 'to have a strong and urgent desire for something'. Of *crave* it is separately stated that this verb 'implies strongly the force of physical or mental appetite', and of *covet* that it 'implies a strong, eager desire'. This description generates a great many questions without supplying answers to any of them. First of all, is there a difference between *desire* and *longing* or do they mean exactly the same thing? If we are to believe the second definition, there is a difference: *longing* is a 'strong and urgent desire'; but then how can *desire* and its closest synonyms *wish* and *want* mean simply longing, as suggested by the first definition? If we are to believe the first definition, why does the dictionary supply two synonym series in place of one? If we are to believe the second, why are *crave* and *covet* placed in the first series rather than the second? Is there a semantic distinction between 'strong and urgent desire' (*long, yearn, hanker,* etc.) and 'strong and eager desire' (*covet*), or is this distinction purely verbal and what is meant in both cases is the same 'strong and urgent desire'? Are we supposed to understand differently (and if so, in what ways) the definitions 'means a strong and urgent desire' and 'implies strongly the force of physical or mental appetite', or is this a stylistic refinement on the part of the compilers, who shun hackneyed phrases? One can go on asking such questions (inevitably occurring to any attentive user of synonym dictionaries) by the dozen.

These remarks are not intended to detract from the worth of Webster's dictionary, particularly because we have deliberately selected one of the weakest descriptions from material which is objectively very difficult. Yet we should like to state most categorically that in difficult cases (and these cases are the majority) there is only one alternative to descriptions of the type we have just considered—precisely those awkward, cumbersome, unidiomatic explications expressed in a standardized form of language.

It needs to be said that the idea of a standardized language is not alien to traditional lexicography, though it has not been previously formulated clearly and has never been consistently implemented. A moment's reflection will tell us that the language of explication in an ordinary monolingual dictionary is different from the language being explicated, if only in being much poorer. Russian has approximately ten words (including substandard and slang) with the meaning 'eyes': *glaza, ochi, zenki, burkaly, gliadelki, migalki, bel'ma, shary,* etc. But only one of these—*glaza*—is selected for the explicatory part and appears in the definitions not only of all the other synonyms in the series, but also of such words as *belki* [whites], *brovi* [eyebrows], *veki* [eyelids], *vylupit'* [to goggle], *glaznitsa* [socket], *glaznoi* [ocular], *glaukoma* [glaucoma], *gliadet'* [to look], *dal'tonizm* [colour blindness], *zakatyvat'* [to roll (the eyes)], *zrachok* [pupil], *zrenie* [eyesight], *karii* [brown (of eyes)], *okulist* [oculist], *ochki* [spectacles], *podglaz'e* [bag under the eye], *puchit'* [to goggle], *pialit'* [to stare], *raduzhnaia obolochka* [iris], *smotret'* [to look], *tarashchit'* [to goggle], *trakhoma* [trachoma], etc. Nobody would think of using *ochi* in an explication of *dal'tonizm* [colour blindness], for example, or the substandard *zenki* in an explication of *ochki* [spectacles].

It would be wrong to think that in this example the choice of explicatory vocabulary is dictated by considerations which are fundamentally different from those in the example with causative verbs, that in one case stylistic considerations apply (the most neutral word is chosen) while in the other they are semantic. In fact in both cases the choice is motivated by semantics, although the lexicographer may not always realize this. As stated elsewhere, *ochi* are large and beautiful eyes; *burkaly*, *bel'ma*, and *shary* are large and unattractive eyes, while *migalki*, *gliadelki*, and *zenki* are small eyes which are unattractive or which produce an unpleasant impression. We may add that all these synonyms for *glaza*, outwardly purely stylistic, differ from this word in that they denote predominantly human eyes; *glaza* is normally the only word used to denote the organs of vision of animals, fish, and insects, as well as humans. *Glaza* is therefore the most general word, semantically speaking, in the synonym series under consideration. If we were to choose any other synonym for use in the explications we would commit errors not only of style, but of semantics too. Although *karii* [brown] is used to describe the colour of human eyes and *podglaz'ia* [bags under the eyes] are also usually a feature of human beings, the verbs *gliadet'*, *smotret'* [to look] as well as *puchit'*, *pialit'*, and *tarashchit'* [to goggle] can apply not only to humans. Therefore the nouns *ochi* and *zenki* are unsuited to the explication of these words on semantic grounds.

As is clear from this example, even in traditional lexicography the choice of words used in explications is not arbitrary, but subject to certain principles. It is the consistent application of these principles that leads to the concept of explication and standardized language set forth above.

## 2.3. TRANSLATION

The Russian translation provided immediately following the explication has two purposes: to make it easier for the reader to grasp the explication, and to compare, in so far as this is possible in a bilingual dictionary, corresponding fragments of the synonym systems of English and Russian.

In the translation zone a series of Russian synonyms is usually given, systematically ordered so that the transition from the first to the last element of the Russian series matches, at least approximately, the transition from first to last in the English series, for example *want*, *wish*, *desire*, *crave*, *covet*—*khotet'*, *zhelat'*, *zhazhdat'*; *care, concern, solicitude, anxiety, worry—ozabochennost', opaseniia, bespokoistvo, trevoga*; *throw, cast, fling, hurl, pitch, toss, sling—brosat', kidat', shvyriat', metat'.*

In selecting translations we have attempted to ensure a transition from the English text to the Russian in varied lexical and syntactic conditions of the use of synonyms: *frigid climate—kholodnyi klimat, frigid wind—ledeniashchii veter*; *chilly weather—promozglaia pogoda, chilly wind—pronizyvaiushchii veter*; *proficient /expert player—iskusnyi igrok, proficient/expert in the art of self-defence—v sovershenstve vladeiushchii iskusstvom samozashchity.*

If any of the English synonyms have fairly close Russian equivalents, these are given against each word in the next zone of the entry: *attachment—priviazannost', affection—teploe chuvstvo, love—liubov', cold—kholodnyi, cool—prokhladnyi, frosty—moroznyi.*

However, in most cases opportunities to use such single-word translations are severely restricted by the non-correspondence of the lexical systems of the two languages, with which we dealt in § 1.2. Many English synonym series have only a single exact Russian translation (*sharp, keen—ostryi*; *victim, prey—zhertva*) and some have none at all. Such is the series *brawl, broil,* coll. *row,* coll. *rumpus,* substandard *scrap(e)* whose sense is only approximately conveyed by *ssora, skandal, perebranka, draka,* because an important semantic component of a number of the English synonyms, absent in the Russian translations (except, perhaps, for *skandal*), is the fact that the conflict is acted out in a public place. The translations should therefore be regarded as an auxiliary and purely heuristic means of description, while the zones headed Explication and Meaning are the primary means.

This zone is not the only one in which Russian translations appear. They occur in three more zones—Meaning, Notes, and Co-occurrence, in which not only single words are translated, but also locutions and quotations from English literature. In these zones the translation of individual words is done in accordance with the principles set forth above. As for the locutions and quotations, in translating these we have adhered to tactics of two different types.

In the translation of anonymous utterances we have attempted to give the closest possible equivalent to the English item, sometimes even at the risk of being excessively literal: *the invaders looted and robbed throughout the entire country—zakhvatchiki maroderstvovali i grabili po vsei strane; a group of officials who looted the treasury—gruppa dolzhnostnykh lits, rastaskivavshikh kaznu.*

In the translations of quotations from literature we have attempted not only to convey the meaning, but also to preserve the style and expressiveness of the original, even at the price of departing considerably from its syntax and lexis.

## 2.4. MEANING

In this zone of the entry—the most important of all—a description is first given of the semantic similarities and differences between the members of the given synonym series. The description is arranged on the basis of the semantic features by which the synonyms in a given series are distinguished.

By semantic features we mean the generic names of the meanings which form part of the explications. If, for example, one of the synonyms denotes slow loco-motion with no particular direction and usually undertaken for pleasure (*roam* ≈ *brodit'*), and another denotes energetic locomotion with constant changes of direction, sometimes—particularly in its older sense—in search of booty, food, etc. (*rove* ≈ *ryskat'*), while a third denotes languid, aimless locomotion with frequent changes of direction (*meander*), we can say that the synonyms are dis-tinguished by the semantic features of speed of locomotion (slow, energetic, languid), its pattern (the idea of non-linear motion in *rove*, and twisting and turning in *meander*), and aim (pleasure, booty, or absence of aim).

When the number of such features exceeds two, they are listed explicitly, with numbers, at the beginning of the zone, immediately preceding a detailed descrip-tion of the series.

Generally speaking, if there is a full, non-redundant, and unequivocal explica-tion of each synonym, any supplementary description becomes theoretically superfluous: all the essential information about semantic similarities and differ-ences between synonyms may be deduced automatically—by comparing one explication with another and establishing which parts coincide and which differ. However, even if this theoretical motivation is lacking, the description retains its practical value since it greatly facilitates the task of the reader. This is all the more so since in the description we are in no way obliged to pursue a point-by-point comparison of explications. Semantic distinctions between synonyms may be formulated in terms of situations in which one may be used but not another (if a man is drowning he shouts *help!*, not *\*aid!* or *\*assist!*), or in terms of the logical inferences flowing from one synonym but not another (if, for example, an object is described as being *firm* it follows that it is difficult to bend, while if it is described as *hard* this means that it cannot be penetrated easily). In many cases information of these two kinds provides invaluable assistance in mastering all the nicer points of word-use.

For the reasons listed above, the description of semantic distinctions between synonyms is arranged in the form of a fairly free commentary, embracing all the essential elements of the explications and the semantic description as a whole.

Granted this free form, the commentary is made to conform to a set pattern, that is, to provide answers, if these exist, to a list of questions which is the same for all synonym series. The questions are as follows:

(1) What are the kinds of similarities and differences in the complete semantic descriptions of synonyms? In accordance with § 2.2, the following types of differ-ences are considered: (*a*) denotative or purely semantic, (*b*) evaluative, (*c*) asso-ciative or connotational, (*d*) differences in emphasis or logical stress.

(2) What are the possible types of semantic identity? Two types are consid-

ered: (*a*) exact synonymy, (*b*) the neutralization of semantic distinctions between synonyms.

(3) What is the semantic structure of a given synonym series? Two types of structure are considered: (*a*) intersected, (*b*) hierarchical.

In describing synonym series we illustrate and substantiate the similarities and differences between synonyms by means of utterances and short, mostly anonymous quotations from original literature and dictionaries. Alongside correct utterances (the majority), incorrect phrases and collocations are sometimes adduced, that is, that 'negative linguistic material' (L. V. Shcherba) which was considered by many classics of linguistics to play a key role in mastering a language.

## 2.4.1. Differences in the Complete Semantic Descriptions of Synonyms

### 2.4.1.1. *Purely Semantic Distinctions*

These differences are the most interesting and at the same time the most complex and varied, as they usually hold not only for a given synonym series but for a whole semantic class of words. For the verbs of locomotion, for example, differences of purpose are typical. Words denoting human emotional and intellectual properties and states are frequently distinguished by the features of cause and the way in which these properties and states are manifested. Physical actions are distinguished by types of objects and instruments, and actions giving rise to situations by the nature of their results.

It is obvious that an exhaustive set of all semantic differences can be presented only in a large, scholarly dictionary. Nevertheless we shall attempt to point out the most common types of features on the basis of which semantic differences between synonyms arise.

In order to summarize these features rationally, we should note that the semantically inexact synonyms mostly concern actions, situations, events, processes, states, and properties (unlike stylistic synonyms, which mostly apply to objects). Actions, situations, events, etc. may be distinguished by their participants (subject, object, addressee, instrument, means) and by their own characteristics (cause, effect, purpose, motivation, place, starting-point, point of arrival, time, method of performance, nature, degree, form of manifestation, etc.). It is precisely the kinds of participant and the generalized features of the actions, situations, or states which in many cases provide the distinguishing features of synonyms. As we shall see, the same notions are significant in the description of the syntactic and co-occurrence features of synonyms.

The subject of the action, property, or state. In the series *escape, avoid, evade, elude*, the first verb indicates that success depends on the subject's skill or good luck (*he managed to escape punishment, he escaped death by a mere chance*); *avoid* points to the subject's foresight, his ability to take precautions (*to avoid an accident/responsibility*); *evade* suggests that the subject avoids an undesirable situation by means of a ploy, thanks to his cunning or resourcefulness (*to evade one's pursuers/duties/military service/the question*); *elude* indicates that the subject has the ability to hide suddenly, to be 'uncatchable' (*to elude the enemy/creditors*).

*Temerity, audacity, hardihood* stress different aspects of the nature and psychological characteristics of the subject. *Temerity* is the result of having little regard for danger, of overestimating one's own powers or underestimating the complexity of a situation (*such temerity in attack can be expected only of young and inexperienced leaders*); *audacity* is the result of flouting *convention*, and readiness to challenge public taste (*to show audacity in speech/dress*); finally, *hardihood* flows from steadiness of character, readiness to go forward heedless of everything, spurning danger or convention to achieve one's purpose (*it took hardihood in Copernicus to deny the current conception of the universe*).

Object, content. The idea of the object is of importance in describing synonym series which denote physical actions of various kinds. The action denoted by the verb *throw* is compatible with any physical body as its object; as for *cast* and especially *toss*, the object is something light, while in the case of *hurl*, on the other hand, it is something heavy: *to cast a fishing rod; he cast his cigarette ash on the carpet; to toss a penny to a beggar; tossing pebbles on her palm; he tossed an envelope into the fire; to hurl a spear at the bear* (*wood into the fire*).

The idea of content, which is close to that of the object, is relevant in describing synonym series which denote intellectual activity, ability, emotion, and wishes. Consider, for example, the words *imagination, fancy, fantasy. Imagination* denotes the ability to conjure up any mental images, regardless of whether there is anything to correspond with them in the real world or whether they are entirely divorced from reality: *he had enough imagination to see the possible consequences; she has a powerful imagination and systematically thinks the worst of everyone* (cf. *u tebia razygralos' voobrazhenie—your imagination is running away with you*). *Fancy* and *fantasy* denote the ability to conjure up images only remotely resembling real objects or having nothing at all in common with them: *the power of fancy/fantasy, a flight of fancy/fantasy. Fantasy* additionally suggests the *whimsical* or *unnatural nature* of the images conjured up (*his fantasy has created an unreal world*), while *fancy* suggests that there is less depth to the images.

The content of *desire* is usually some situation which is actually *achievable* (*he received the position he desired, people desire political reforms*), while *wish* and *crave* often denote unachievable wishes: *I wish I were a Gipsy; to crave for fresh fruit in the Antarctic winter*.

Addressee. In the series *swing, wave, flourish*, the second of the three, unlike the other synonyms, presupposes a semantically optional addressee, a person whose attention the subject seeks to attract by hand movements, to whom he seeks to impart information or to urge to act: *to wave to the man to go on*.

In the series *commend, recommend, applaud, compliment*, the first two mean 'to comment approvingly on someone or something, trying to draw the attention of others to the virtues of the object'. This is as much as to say that the addressee of the message and the object of praise are two distinct participants in the situation. Cf. *I did not fail to commend these things to her as they deserved; he is an expert watchmaker and greatly recommended.* In the case of *applaud* and *compliment* the addressee of the message is the same as the object of praise: *we applaud your decision; to compliment a lady on her appearance.* A partially similar distinction may be found in Russian between *khvalit'* [to praise] and *odobriat'* [to approve, endorse]: in the first instance an external addressee is possible (*on khvalil mne moego syna* [he praised my son to me], but not in the second. It is interesting that with the antonym *rugat'* [to curse] the expression of an addressee is more difficult.

Instrument, operative part. In the series *beat, pummel, thrash, buffet,* the first verb denotes beating with some *extremity* (hand, tail) or some *object, pummel* with the hand or fist, *thrash* with some object which serves as an *instrument of punishment, buffet* with the *palm.*

In the series *defend, protect, shield, guard, safeguard,* the first three verbs permit the use of some special objects—instruments or tools of defence: *to defend oneself with a stick, the fortress is protected by walls, to shield one's eyes with one's hand.* In the actions denoted by the last two verbs, on the other hand, there is no reference to special instruments of defence: *to guard a fortress, to safeguard children who play in the street.*

Cause, effect. In the series *lean, spare, gaunt,* the first denotes simply the absence of fat and rotundity, regardless of cause: *lean, good-looking young men; he had an excessively long and lean brown face. Spare* denotes thinness usually as a result of abstinence or moderation in eating habits, and often implies approval (cf. *sukhoshchavyi, podzharyi*): *he was slight and spare.* Lastly *gaunt* signifies thinness resulting from exhausting work, permanently inadequate diet, or other privations: *a gaunt old man; his gaunt, weather-beaten features pinched with cold and fatigue.*

*Try, torment, torture* may indicate either an external or an internal cause of suffering: *the great heat of the sun tries his body; rheumatism tries me a good deal; the horses are tormented/tortured by flies; headaches/suspicions tormented him.* Unlike these, the synonym *rack* always indicates that the cause, the source of the suffering is within the subject: *his body was racked with pain; to be racked with doubts/jealousy.*

The idea of effect is closely linked to that of cause. *Intimidate* and *cow* differ particularly in the nature of the resulting state of the object. *Intimidate* describes a broad range of the object's states resulting from the act of intimidation, ranging from inability to act to unwillingness to act: *to intimidate workers by the threat of discharge; her deficiencies in this subject intimidated her. Cow* indicates not only the loss of ability or will to act, but also the complete subordination of the object to the will of another: *the population was thoroughly cowed.*

Purpose. *Examine* and *inspect* are synonymous in the sense 'to consider something in detail with the aim of understanding or evaluating it'. *Examine* may equally denote considering something out of idle curiosity (*he examined the passers-by, then with the same lack of intensity he examined his fingers*), and inspection with serious intent (*he raised his eyes to examine her face very carefully; the jury examined the cups closely*). Unlike this, *inspect* always denotes a fairly close consideration, usually with the aim of checking, monitoring, or exposing defects: *to inspect each car* (*the pearl under magnification; the fire-prevention system of the plant*); *to inspect every length of cloth for defects*.

*Sharp* denotes both useful sharpness (*sharp knife/blade/needle*) and sharpness serving no purpose at all (*the sharp edge of a table; sharp elbow; sharp icicles*). Unlike this, *keen* is appropriate only in those cases where sharpness required for some definite purpose is meant: *the keen edge of a knife, a keen razor*, but not *\*the keen edge of a mountain*.

Motivation. Meanings of cause and purpose form part of the more complex meaning of motivation, which is relevant for the series *swing, wave, flourish, brandish*, for example. These synonyms make reference to different states motivating the movement. In *swing* motivation plays no particular part: *to swing a scythe in mowing; to swing the pump-handle/hammock; to swing one's arms to circulate the blood; to swings one's arms/one's stick in walking*. *Wave* in most cases denotes a deliberate movement motivated by a need to express one's inner state (joy, agitation, impatience), a desire to *attract attention*, a need to convey information (a signal, a request, an order, etc.): *to wave flags; the excited men waved and shouted to them; he waved his hand in return; to wave to the man to go on; to wave smb. aside/away*. *Flourish* means 'to make energetic waving movements with something, defiantly, triumphantly or with bravado': *he flourished the certificate in Andrew's face* (Cronin); *the deer flourished his first antler and was very proud of it*. *Brandish*, on the other hand, implies a threat as motivation: *to brandish a sword/club/stick/revolver; they began to shout and brandish their fists* (Winsor).

Place. *Pain, ache, twinge* are synonymous in denoting physical pain. *Pain* is preferred in reference to an unpleasant sensation in the external tissues of the organism, whether localized in a small area or covering a larger surface: *she felt a sharp pain in her back/knee/chest; he felt pain when the needle touched his skin*. *Ache* signifies a pain localized in the internal organs or spread throughout the body: *a dull ache in one's bones; the racking ache seemed continually an element of her being; muscular aches*. In the case of *twinge*, the pain is localized, but the locus cannot be definitely pinpointed: *a twinge of gout/rheumatism*. Finally *stitch* usually means a pain localized in one definite part of the body, in the side, in the intercostal tissue: *a stitch in the side*.

Time. *Associate, pal*, and *comrade* presuppose the existence of social and emotional bonds between people over a significant period of time. They cannot signify short-term contacts which are easily established and broken off (in games, in train journeys, etc.) *Companion* may serve this purpose. *Crony* signifies a long-standing friendship, begun in childhood or youth and enduring—perhaps with interruptions—into mature years: *his cronies at Harrow*.

Manner, nature. In the series *ponder, meditate, muse*, etc., *ponder* denotes an attempt to take account of all factors or aspects of something, to make sense of it from various points of view (cf. *vzvesit'*): *to ponder the situation (the mystery, the problem of how she could help him); the government should ponder well whether the prize would be worth the cost*. *Meditate* presupposes not a comprehensive consideration of the object of thought, but thought focused on isolated details with the aim of completely understanding them: *to meditate on the nature of happiness (on holy things, on the hypocrisy and spiritual stagnation of the High Church party)*. A typical situation for *muse* is absorption, feeling removed from one's immediate surroundings, with elements of day-dreaming or contemplation in the process of thought, even to the extent of losing the ability to act: *to muse on the happy events of one's childhood; where Elizabeth hesitated, mused, suffered, Fanny acted; up till then he had been musing but now he woke up with a start*.

*Pain*, from the series considered above in the meaning 'physical pain', in no way specifies the nature of that pain as subjectively perceived: *she felt a sharp/ dull pain*. *Ache* generally denotes a dull pain, *pang* a sudden, sharp, momentary pain (*I feel a sharp pang if I touch an aching tooth*; cf. *streliaiushchaia bol'* [shooting pain]), while *throe* denotes forms of severe, spasmodic pain accompanied by cramps, convulsions, and twitches: *the throes and gripings of the belly*.

Degree. *Expert* signifies a higher degree of skill than *skilful*. Analagous distinctions emerge in the series *surprise, astonish, amaze*, and *cool, cold, frosty, icy*.

Distinctions of degree are the ones most often mentioned in the specialist and instructional literature. Few authors, however, make mention of the much more interesting fact that differences of degree are usually motivated, that is, they are the result of deeper, qualitative distinctions of sense. In the series *summon, call, muster* in the lexically constrained sense 'by an effort of will to bring one's inner resources (mental powers, strength, courage) to a state in which they can be used' (cf. Russian *prizvat', napriach', sobrat', mobilizovat'*), *muster* implies a greater effort of will than *summon* and *call*. The latter two mean that the subject possesses the necessary reserves of a particular property and that, in order to put this property to use, it is sufficient for the subject to transfer it by an effort of will from its passive state to an active, operational one: *she resolved to summon (up) her courage to refuse him; you'd better call (up) your pluck and resolution before starting the conversation*. Unlike this, *muster (up)* means that the subject does not have sufficient reserves of the required property in a state of readiness for use (perhaps because he has already expended some), and in order to put it to use it is not enough merely to transfer it from the passive to active state, but first to build up reserves; for these two operations, naturally, a greater effort of will is required than in the case of *summon* or *call*: *it seemed as though she could not muster enough strength to move again; they could see the effort with which she mustered up her self-command*.

Properties (states) versus their external manifestations. In the pair *loving, affectionate*, the first differs from the second by indicating the depth of feeling and by the absence of any indication of a need to demonstrate it: *let us continue to be a loving and united family.* Affectionate denotes not necessarily deep, but always tender feelings, expressed through caresses and in other outward forms, which may sometimes be perceived as excessively demonstrative: *she was gay and sweet and affectionate*; *an affectionate brother/child*; *you are much too affectionate to me.*

In the series *afraid, aghast,* the first is neutral with regard to outward manifestation of the subject's inner state, while the second denotes a feeling of horror directly evoked by an impending danger, accompanied by surprise and finding expression in loss of the ability to speak or act, etc. (see examples below).

Permanent property versus temporary state. *Afraid* may denote a permanent feature (*to be afraid of the dark/snakes*) or a temporary state experienced at a given moment (*he was afraid to fall; don't be afraid*), while *aghast* refers only to a temporary state: *the door opened and a big dog ran in; the girl stood aghast.*

In the pair *honest, upright,* the former signifies both a property (*he is an honest man*) and a temporary condition (*be honest about it*), while the latter has only the first sense (*he was an upright man,* but not *\*be upright about it*).

Active versus passive mode. In the series *crass, dull, dense,* etc., the first denotes a lack of capacity for active intellectual processes, forming one's own opinions or independent analysis of complex or nuanced phenomena: *crass minds whose reflexive scales could only weigh things in a lump* (Webster). *Dull* and *dense* are used of 'those to whom it is difficult to explain things; those who have difficulty in grasping the thoughts of others', that is, they describe a lack of mental ability in passive intellectual processes: *a dull pupil; it is difficult to explain even elementary arithmetic to a dull child; a particularly dense group of students.*

Similar distinctions appear in the opposite series *quick-witted, smart, bright.* The first two describe active intellectual ability—the ability to size up a situation or make the best decision: *he was quick-witted/smart enough to see the danger and change the subject.* Although *bright* could also be used here, it occurs typically in contexts having to do with passive intellectual ability—the ability to assimilate knowledge provided by another: *a bright boy/pupil/student.*

Static versus dynamic mode. *Awkward* and *clumsy* differ in meaning as follows: *awkward* signifies only an absence of co-ordination in movement, although there may be nothing wrong with the subject's physical shape and build: *he is an awkward dancer, awkward in gait/gestures/manners, some animals are awkward on land but able to move easily in the water.* The property denoted by *clumsy* is displayed not only in motion but also at rest: it is the *absence of proportion* in parts of the body, manifesting itself in poorly co-ordinated movements: *he was rather heavy and clumsy; clumsy in shape and build.*

Mind versus emotion. *Passionate* stresses an emotional quality in a person's nature and is fully appropriate in describing one in whom passion predominates over reason: *a passionate nature; he was hot-blooded and passionate.* Unlike this, *ardent* primarily describes a person's intellectual characteristics, his deep *interest* in some form of activity or intention to do something useful: *an ardent stamp-collector/theatre-goer/globe-trotter; an ardent follower of an idea/advocate of a principle.*

Physical versus spiritual aspects. *Thoughtful* is generally used of a person who is attentive to the physical needs of others and is prepared to cater to their *material* convenience and protect them from the need to expend physical effort: *the thoughtful girl undertook the house-cleaning for her sick aunt*; *'Leaving me to gather the sticks . . . Not very thoughtful of you'* (Cronin). *Considerate* is usually used of one who attends to the emotional well-being of others, spares their *feelings*, protects them from suffering and embarrassment: *he was too considerate to let her see his distress at her sickly look*; *to be considerate to smb. in his grief.*

Intentional versus unintentional action. In the series *gather, collect, assemble* (transitive), *gather* does not express intention: *he soon gathered a crowd around himself* may be said both in a situation where it was intended to gather a crowd and in one when this was not intended, for example, by unusual behaviour. *Collect* always implies that the subject has a definite intention (*to collect the flock/ pupils/group for a lecture*), while *assemble* implies, in addition, that the subject and the object share the same aims, or that these are similar and usually of a social or political nature (*to assemble the committee/government*).

*Stop* and *cease* may mean either intentional or unintentional cessation: *to stop/ cease stroking the dog, to cease trembling.* The synonyms *quit, discontinue, desist* can mean only deliberate cessation: *to quit laughing/talking; to discontinue a subscription/payment/systematic training; to desist from one's occupation; to desist from one's intention to write to a friend.*

The action signified by the verb *remember* may occur with or without an effort of will: *he remembers every detail of that occurrence; he suddenly remembered an appointment; I can't remember his name; I tried to remember his name but gave it up.* The action signified by the synonym *recollect* is always accompanied by an effort of will: *recollect where you were on the night of June 17.*

In establishing certain semantic distinctions between the members of a synonym series, we do not in any sense wish to suggest that these distinctions surface in all instances of use. In actual speech, as a rule, a speaker is concerned with only part (the most important part, it is true) of the complex of ideas which a given word expresses. It is this feature of word-use which lies at the basis of the stylistic rule of compulsory variation of synonyms within a limited context, of which we spoke in § 1.1.

It is clear, for example, that in this extract from Bernard Shaw's *Caesar and Cleopatra*, 'Caesar: *Are you trembling?* Cleopatra (*shivering with dread*): No, I— I . . . No', the distinctions between *tremble* (rapid shivering provoked by strong emotion, physical weakness or cold) and *shiver* (rapid shivering of short duration provoked by cold or fear and affecting the whole body) do not emerge in any way. A weakening, sometimes total lifting of peripheral components of meaning also occurs in conditions in which semantic distinctions are neutralized (neutralization is examined in detail below, in § 2.4.2.2). Nevertheless it is essential to draw the fullest possible picture of the semantic composition of each element in a synonym series because situations when only one member will serve the purpose are very common. In this regard cases of specifying or contrasting usage of synonyms, when they are used as homogeneous members of coordinative or parallel constructions and when the distinctions between them are given special emphasis, are particularly useful: *He never had an ache or pain, ate his food with gusto and ruled his brothers with a rod of iron* (T. Dreiser, *The Financier*); 'Malone: *My father died of starvation in Ireland, in the black 47. Maybe you've heard of it.* Violet: *The Famine?* Malone (*with smouldering passion*): *No, the starvation. When a country is full of food, and exporting it, there can be no famine*' (W. Collins, *The Moonstone*).

### 2.4.1.2. *Evaluative Distinctions*

While examining the evaluative component of meaning in § 2.2 we noted that a situation denoted by a word or the participants in that situation may theoretically be appraised by the speaker or his listeners from a wide variety of points of view. However, in the nomenclature of semantic features which distinguish various synonyms, two kinds of appraisal actually figure: the speaker's positive or negative opinion of the object of his utterance.

*Vehement* differs from its synonym *intense* in that it implies a greater degree of intensity and usually presupposes a negative evaluation of the phenomenon described by the speaker: *intense heat* corresponds to Russian *sil'naia zhara*; *vehement heat* to *nevynosimaia* [*unbearable*] *zhara*. Similarly, *intense cold—vehement cold*; *intense pain—vehement pain*, *intense red—vehement red—*(approximately 'red which hurts the eye'). This, incidentally, explains the fact that only *intense* combines with the names of properties which a given society usually regards favourably: *the letter was of intense significance*, but not *\*the letter was of vehement significance*, because the latter sentence features that type of logical contradiction which is avoided in language.[1]

*Stir, flurry, fuss, ado* mean disorderly or hurried activity and sometimes the excited human state which causes it (cf. Russian *sumatokha, sueta, perepolokh*). The last two synonyms differ from the first two above all by their implication of the speaker's disapproval of excessive activity expended on trifles.

*Sharp* and *keen* have a figurative sense 'acting powerfully upon the organs of perception' (cf. Russian *ostryi, rezkii, pronzitel'nyi*—of smell, taste, sound, light,

---

[1] This does not of course mean that any utterance which is logically contradictory is linguistically incorrect. The sentence *kholostiaki byvaiut zhenaty* [bachelors may sometimes be married men], for example, fully corresponds to Russian norms, although *kholostiak* denotes an unmarried man (remember *zhivoi trup* [living corpse], *kruglyi kvadrat* [round square], and other established oxymorons, leaving aside the oxymorons of poetic language such as *prostoe i slozhnoe schast'e* [simple and complex happiness], *zhestokoe dobroe vremia* [cruel kind time], *veselye grustnye pesni* [happy sad songs], *korotkaia dolgaia zhizn'* [short long life]). Language does not avoid all logical contradictions, but only those which occur in the evaluative component of meaning (more precisely: linguistic errors are generated by contradictions between the modal frame and the assertive parts of meaning).

wind, cold, etc.). In most cases *sharp* is neutral with regard to evaluation: collocations with nouns denoting auditory irritants, in which it conveys a negative appraisal by the speaker, tend to be exceptional: *a sharp voice/whisper/cry/yelp; a sharp flash of lightning; a sharp wind. Keen* has the sense of a positive assessment, attributing to the object described or to some phenomenon the quality of piquancy, spiciness, and the ability to refresh: *the keen savour of the roast beef; the wind came keen with a tang of frost.*

### 2.4.1.3. *Differing Semantic Associations*

*Jump, leap, spring, bound, skip, hop* display the following characteristics: *jump* has the most general meaning. *Leap* describes a long, light, flowing, and rapid jump, like that of an antelope: *to leap into the saddle; the chamois was leaping from crag to crag; I love to watch a dancer leap. Spring* and to a lesser extent *bound* denote a powerful springy jump, pushing off sharply from the departure point. In addition *bound* usually implies a series of leaps associated with the leaps of a predatory animal. Cf. *to spring across the stream; the cat sprang upon the bird; to spring onto a moving train; she sprang to her feet and bounded across the intervening space like a tiger. Skip* and *hop*, signifying little jumps, are not associated with any idea of strength and are therefore not used to describe an attack, for example. *Skip* implies speed, lightness, and grace in jumps often made on alternating feet: *to skip along the road; to skip out of the way; to skip upstairs two at a time. Hop* means 'to make one or a series of short jumps, perhaps clumsily, on one foot, on both feet together, or with alternating feet'; it is associated with the movements of frogs, grasshoppers, and certain birds: *the kids chalked out a hopscotch game and began to hop around its squares; the sparrows hopped nearer; how far can you hop on your right leg?; he hopped on one leg and then the other to shake the water out of his ears.*

*Tickle* and *regale* in their figurative senses of giving pleasure are distinguished by the semantic associations which lie in their literal, and non-synonymous, senses. The verb *tickle* in its literal sense has associations of agreeable nervous excitement and jollity, while *regale* is associated with gastronomic enjoyment: *the joke will really tickle you; to regale smb. with one's own story; when in humour, he would regale her with the choicer gossip of the town.*

*Naked*, unlike *bare*, usually means the absence of clothing on the human body or at least on those parts which, according to established codes of behaviour, should be covered. For this reason, ethical, social, and aesthetic associations are possible: an affront to public taste (*naked woman*), poverty, material hardship (*naked children playing on the heaps of rubbish*), naturalness, beauty (*a charming naked baby; a perfectly shaped naked body*).

In the series *imagination, fancy, fantasy*, the first, as we have said, means the ability to conjure up any mental images, regardless of whether there is anything to correspond with them in the real world or whether they are entirely divorced from reality, while the other two denote the ability to conjure up images which have little or nothing to do with reality. On this basis there naturally arise differences between the semantic associations of *imagination,* on the one hand, and *fancy, fantasy* on the other. When used in the first situation (when there is some correspondence between the image and the object), *imagination* is associated with creativity and suggests the ability to imagine as part of a broader scholarly, aesthetic, logical, and emotional perception of the world: *a job that requires imagination; poets, artists and inventors need imagination; it's only through imagination that men become aware of what the world might be* (Russell); *he is a man of no imagination.* A different set of semantic associations is characteristic of *fancy* and *fantasy.* It includes dreaminess, illusoriness, and falsity. It is curious that the Russian word *fantaziia,* the closest equivalent of *fancy* and *fantasy,* unlike these two, may easily be associated with the idea of creativity.

### 2.4.1.4. *Differing Logical Emphasis*

*Stoop* and *condescend* mean 'to do something incompatible with one's social position or moral principles' (cf. Russian *ne gnushat'sia, ne brezgat'*). *Stoop* emphasizes a departure from moral norms (the second element of its meaning), while *condescend* means forgetting one's high social standing (the first element of its meaning): *to stoop to stealing/cheating/meanness/begging/lies; to condescend to trickery; he said he would never condescend to their society.*

*Hard* and *difficult* mean 'requiring great efforts due to the complexity of the task or the pressure of obstacles'. *Hard* gives emphasis to the idea of the need to expend much effort: *we have a hard lesson to learn; chopping wood is a hard job.* *Difficult* places more emphasis on complexities and obstacles in the way of accomplishing a given task: *she came across a difficult passage in translation; he is a difficult writer; it was a difficult problem for a pupil of the fourth class; designing a sputnik is a difficult task.*

*Sparing* and *frugal* mean 'limiting one's living expenses', 'thrifty', 'economical'. *Sparing* stresses the idea of limiting one's expenses: *he is sparing enough and never runs into debt.* In the case of *frugal* the emphasis is on the small amount spent on essentials, hence the idea of *thrift* in food and clothing, sometimes even of material hardship: *with fifteen shillings a week and a family he had to be frugal* (this may also be understood as meaning that he denied himself much).

*Guard* and *safeguard* mean not a current defensive action but constant readiness to defend something against a potential threat. The meaning of *guard* (like Russian *stoiat' na strazhe, okhraniat'*) stresses the element of readiness to repel an attack and the related element of vigilance in expecting danger: *the entrances are well guarded; the president is always guarded by secret service men.* *Safeguard* stresses the element of potential threat, sometimes no more than a theoretical threat, hence the readiness for defence is seen more as prophylactic, as forestalling danger: *to safeguard our health; to safeguard one's country from a surprise attack; to safeguard children who play in the street.*

Logically naïve concepts, evaluation, semantic associations, and emphasis are independent of one another. In practice, however, the nature of the last three components is in many cases motivated by the content of the corresponding naïve concept.

## 2.4.2. Types of Semantic Identity

As noted earlier, our dictionary describes two types of semantic identity: exact synonymy and the neutralization of semantic distinctions between synonyms. We shall consider these in more detail.

### 2.4.2.1. *Exact Synonyms*

The concept of exact synonyms was set forth at the very beginning of Section 2: these are lexemes whose semantic descriptions fully coincide. In other words, they feature the same naïve concepts, evaluation, semantic associations, and logical emphasis. At the same time they may differ in their stylistic properties (as long as this entails no semantic differences—see § 2.1 and 2.2), as well as in their lexico-semantic co-occurrence and syntactic features.

The possibility of semantic identity, in the sense indicated here, is seen by many as problematic, especially in the presence of distinctions in the areas of lexico-semantic and syntactic co-occurrence. However, there is really nothing surprising about it, as a word's co-occurrence features are determined not only by its meaning but also by many other factors, including some which are purely a matter of chance or tradition. This statement is so trivial as to hardly require any factual evidence, but perhaps one example will be useful. The synonyms *sharp, keen, acute*, applied to the organs of perception, fully coincide in meaning but differ in certain co-occurrence preferences. They all occur with nouns naming the five basic senses and their organs; but *sharp* is most often used of sight and hearing (*sharp eyes/sight/hearing*), *keen* of sight and smell (*keen eyes, a keen sense of smell*), and *acute* almost exclusively of hearing; collocations such as *acute eyesight, acute sense of smell* are extremely uncommon.

Although in theory any word may have an exact synonym, exact synonymy is by no means equally characteristic of all layers of language. For a number of reasons which we shall not discuss in detail here, it occurs most often in the area of figurative meanings (see below), loan-words (cf. native English *calling* versus the borrowed *vocation*: *to make one's choice of a calling/vocation; to mistake one's calling/vocation*), archaisms (*healthy* and the obsolescent *healthful* in the sense 'good for the improvement or maintenance of physical health': *healthy/ healthful diet/exercise*), expressive vocabulary (*damn, bit, snap*, etc. in expressions such as *I don't care a damn/bit/snap about it*), and certain types of derived forms and compounds (*far-off, faraway* as in *far-off/faraway hills/sounds*).

The number of exact synonyms is particularly high among words which are synonymous in their figurative and collocation-bound senses.

In most cases the rise of such senses is connected with the development of metaphor, and in its most typical form this process consists of the loss of one or more semantic components from the literal meaning. In their literal sense, *anger, wrath, rage,* and *fury* differ in at least three features: (1) intensity (*wrath* is stronger than *anger,* and *rage* and *fury* are stronger than *wrath*); (2) the properties of the subject experiencing the emotion (a feeling of righteousness in the case of *wrath*; irritability and ill temper in the case of *rage* and *fury*); (3) the nature of the manifestation of the emotion (*anger* is neutral in this regard; *wrath* implies punishment as its natural result; while *rage* and *fury* manifest themselves in loss of self-control and destructive urges). The figurative senses shown in the phrases *the anger of the sea, the wrath of the elements, the fury/rage of the storm* are formed by the loss of the second and third semantic components. In this synonym series, then, expression is given only to the distinctions in intensity; this is to say that in their figurative senses *anger, wrath, rage,* and *fury* differ to a far lesser degree than in their literal senses, and *rage* and *fury* do not differ at all.

More examples of this type may be adduced. *Hunger* and *thirst* are the same in the sense 'to want something desperately', since what is preserved of their literal and non-synonymous meanings is only the idea of 'strong desire', perceived as a physical need for something: *to hunger/to thirst for knowledge/ information*; *to hunger for friends*; *to thirst for peace*; *to hunger/to thirst for power/ wealth/revenge.*

*Summon* (*up*) and *call* (*up*) are the same in the sense of 'bringing one's abilities into an active state': *to summon up one's energy/courage/wits/self-command*; *to call up all one's pluck/wits/resolution/dignity.*

### 2.4.2.2. *Neutralization of Semantic Distinctions between Synonyms*

A characteristic feature of many lexical meanings which comprise several semantic components is the fact that these components are not fully materialized in all contexts: certain contexts preclude the materialization of certain of the components. If two inexact synonyms which differ in sense 'A' occur in a context in which the presence of this sense is for some reason ruled out, the semantic distinction between them is neutralized in this context and they acquire the capacity to replace each other without affecting the content of the utterance.

Generally, this is the only case of true neutralization. Here semantic identity, and hence the theoretical possibility of replacing one synonym by another, arises as a result of semantic change occurring within one of the synonyms, that is, within one word.

Let us now consider another situation. Two inexact synonyms $C_1$ and $C_2$ differ in sense 'A', which is expressed by one of them (let us say $C_1$) and not by the other. Let us now imagine that each of the synonyms is syntactically linked with a word $C_3$ in a meaning which includes precisely this sense 'A'. Then in the collocation $C_1C_3$ sense 'A' will be expressed twice and in the collocation $C_2C_3$ once. In most cases the repetition of senses produces a pleonasm, and thus the collocations $C_1C_3$ and $C_2C_3$ in full may be synonymous, although the inexact synonyms $C_1$ and $C_2$ themselves will preserve the distinction deriving from sense 'A'. We shall consider some examples.

*Stay* differs from *remain* chiefly on grounds of purpose: *stay* more often implies a definite intent or purpose, while *remain* more often presupposes the absence of these: *to stay to dinner/supper; we remained there much longer than we expected*. *Remain*, for its part, is more likely than *stay* to indicate the continuing presence of the subject after others have departed: *few remained in the building after the alarm was given; he remained behind*. If the meaning of purpose, intent, or wish is expressed separately in the sentence (for example, by an infinitive or a verb of the class *decide, intend, wish, try*, etc.) and if there are no indications of the actions of others, the semantic distinctions between *stay* and *remain* are neutralized and the two verbs become mutually interchangeable: *he stayed to learn the doctor's verdict; he remained on the platform to wave farewell to his friends; we decided/intended to stay/to remain in the hotel till the end of the month; I had to stay/to remain at home till I felt better*.

*Remember, recollect*, and *recall* are distinguished by three features: (1) the presence or the restoration of information (*remember* signifies either the presence of information or the restoration of it, while *recollect* and *recall* denote only its restoration; thus, for example, in the context *no one remembers the exact number of casualties, recollect* and *recall* are not possible or have a different meaning); (2) effort of will in the process of recalling (vital for *recollect* and *recall*, but not for *remember*); (3) degree of effort (the action in *recall* requires an effort, *recollecting* requires more effort, while for *remember* it is immaterial). In contexts in which these synonyms are syntactically subordinated to words denoting an intention, an attempt or some other act of will, the semantic distinctions based on the first two features are neutralized: *try to remember/to recollect/to recall his exact words; try to remember/to recollect/to recall where you were on the night of June 17*.

Thus in the series *stay, remain* and *remember, recollect, recall* the semantic coincidence (or lesser degree of semantic difference), and hence interchangeability, comes about as a result of semantic changes not within a single word but within a collocation. Such cases are distinct from neutralization in the strict sense and should be termed quasi-neutralization.

We pass on to another pair of concepts which describe the phenomenon of neutralization. In comparing the series *stay, remain*, and *remember, recollect, recall* we note that in the former a situation is possible where it makes no difference to the content which of the pair is used: the distinction between the synonyms is fully neutralized. In the latter we cannot identify such a situation: *remember, recollect*, and *recall*, in any instance of use, show distinctions based on the degree of effort expended. Here, therefore, we can speak only of partial neutralization of semantic distinctions. Let us consider another example of partial neutralization, the verbs *support*, in its figurative sense, and *uphold*. *To support the principle/demand/decision* may be said regardless of whether the principle (demand, decision) has broad support and a good chance of being adopted or has so little support as to be at risk. *To uphold the principle/demand/decision*, on the other hand, is appropriate only when that principle (demand, decision) has little support and its chances are debatable, so that supporting it takes courage. If the object of *uphold* is a fact which by its nature cannot be revoked or cancelled out, *support* and *uphold* become closer in meaning: *he could not support/ uphold their behaviour*. However, even in cases such as these only a partial neutralization occurs because *uphold* always signifies firmer support.

We shall therefore speak of partial neutralization if synonyms are distinguished by senses 'A' and 'B', and if in a given context distinction 'A' alone is lifted, while distinction 'B' remains.

All in all we have four types of neutralization of semantic distinctions between synonyms: complete neutralization, partial neutralization, complete quasi-neutralization, and partial quasi-neutralization. For reasons of space, we shall concentrate below almost exclusively on the first type, bearing in mind that the concepts proposed are equally applicable to the other three.

The crucial issue of the linguistic theory of neutralization is the issue of the conditions in which it occurs. Without making any claim to factual or even logical completeness, we shall describe below four types of factors especially characteristic of neutralization: stylistic, syntactic, combinatorial, and semantic.

One stylistic factor which is more propitious than others for neutralization is well known—the use of synonyms in colloquial speech, which exerts a surprisingly strong levelling influence on various nuances of meaning and usage. *Odd, queer*, and *quaint* all mean 'departing from accepted notions of the normal or natural', with the following distinctions: *odd* is used as an evaluation of a person, object, or fact which is difficult to explain or even puzzling: *an odd fellow, an odd laugh; the old man and the boy have formed an odd friendship; the odd thing was that he was happy through all that hard year*. *Queer* signifies that some object or fact is not only puzzling but occasions suspicion of something bad: *a queer character, a queer bird, queer aches in his body; it's queer that he's made a lot of money lately—he is not very clever at business*. *Quaint*, on the other hand, describes an attractive quality which evokes positive feelings, especially if applied to something very old or old-fashioned: *a quaint old castle; there are many quaint nooks and corners in this town; she was a quaint, kind old woman; the quaintest and simplest and trustingest race* (Twain). In colloquial speech these distinctions may be neutralized to the point at which the synonyms are fully interchangeable: *it was an odd/queer/quaint way to look at things; he had an odd/queer/quaint habit of using phrases of hers*.

In the pair *hard, difficult*, the semantic distinction described above is also neutralized in colloquial speech: *it's a hard/difficult problem/book/language*.

Another stylistic property of speech, its heightened emotional pitch, exerts almost as much levelling influence on the semantic distinctions between synonyms. The synonyms *stupid* and *dull* (of a person's feelings or behaviour, the product of his mental activity, his face, appearance, etc.) differ in that the first is semantically broader than the second. *Dull* usually signifies those manifestations of slow wit (minimal reaction or slow thought processes) which are typical of passive mental activity: *dull persistence/apathy, dull face/look.* Both words are used in emotional speech for impressionistic evaluations which should not be understood literally and which in such cases partially neutralize the distinctions mentioned above.

Of more direct linguistic interest is neutralization in conditions which may be formulated in terms of the purely linguistic features of the context—syntactic, lexical, or semantic.

*Want*, as distinct from *wish*, implies that the subject has the determination, the will to act and is prepared to apply some effort to achieve the desired end: *the young Forsyte meant having what she wanted* (Galsworthy); *they wanted only truth, justice.* These elements of the meaning of *want* are expressed especially clearly in constructions with nouns or pronouns as their direct object (see above examples). Neither this meaning, nor this construction is usual for *wish*, which only points to the desirability of a situation, whether the subject personally intends to make efforts to achieve it or hopes that it will come about without his interference (cf. Russian *khochetsia*): *he wished to be alone; eagerly I wished for tomorrow.* Moreover, *wish* may signify a completely abstract desire, essentially *unfulfillable*, when it governs a subordinate clause with a predicate in the subjunctive: *I wish I were a Gipsy; I wish the week were over.* In the latter case, *wish* stands in sharp contrast to *want* not only semantically, but also syntactically: *want* cannot govern a subordinate clause with a predicate in the subjunctive. In some other constructions, especially those with a complex infinitive predicate (*accusativus cum infinitivo*), the meanings of *want* and *wish* may be reduced to the sense of 'wish proper' (with no indication of determination or of abstract desire respectively), so these two synonyms become practically interchangeable (although minor stylistic distinctions remain): *She was ambitious for me. She wanted me to rise in the world* (Anderson); *I want you to come for the afternoon next Sunday; do you wish me to see him about it?; Now, with this visit in prospect he wished her to accompany him* (Cronin).

*Grateful* and *thankful* are distinguished mainly by their logical emphasis: *grateful* emphasizes the significance of a service rendered to the subject, *thankful* the force of the emotion experienced (see examples in § 2.2). Some syntactic distinctions between them are connected with this difference in emphasis: *grateful* usually requires mention of the subject of the service (*grateful to smb.*) or of the service itself (*grateful for smth.*). *Thankful* requires neither. Since attention is concentrated on a feeling, which may be, for example, satisfaction due to the fact that something has turned out more or less successfully, the notion of the service and its subject is shifted into the background: *I am thankful that he is no worse/ that there were no casualties* (this is a form of government which is totally untypical of *grateful*). Theoretically, however, *thankful* may be used in the constructions *to be thankful for smth., to be thankful to smb.,* and *to be thankful to smb. for smth.* In these syntactic contexts the distinctions in logical emphasis between the two are neutralized and they become mutually interchangeable: *I'm grateful/*

*thankful to you* (*for your help*); *I'm grateful/thankful for all you have done for me.*

We pass on to cases in which the conditions of neutralization can be formulated in terms of co-occurrence features. *Apt* and *liable*, of a person or thing who/which is likely to be involved in or undergo something, differ in the following respects: in the case of *apt*, the possible event is seen as resulting from the inner properties of the main participant denoted by the subject of the given sentence: *idle children are apt to get into mischief; he is apt to lose his head under stress; china cups are apt to break; dry wood is apt to catch fire.* In the case of *liable* the likelihood of the event occurring is connected with the structure of the situation as a whole, along with the circumstances which have taken shape before that moment: *he is liable to be punished/killed; he is liable to encounter difficulties.* Thus, if the main participant in a situation (the subject) is a creature or object, *apt* and *liable* may have contrasting senses: *this car is apt to skid* (it is a characteristic of this car)—*cars are liable to skid on wet roads* (it is characteristic of any car on a wet road). These distinctions are neutralized in the context of a subject which is not a creature or object but a fact or situation: *snow is apt/liable to fall in these parts as early as September; difficulties are apt/liable to occur.*

Finally we shall consider an example of neutralization in specific semantic conditions. *Doubtful* and *dubious* are synonymous when applied to a person who has doubts about the veracity or reality of something (like Russian *somnevaiushchiisia, kolebliushchiisia*). *Doubtful* is usually used to describe somebody who does not know for sure whether a statement is true or whether a specific situation is real, but is inclined, on the basis of the information he has, to believe that these are not so: *he was doubtful about the outcome of this project/of the prospects of the rebellion; he was more than ever doubtful whether the battery would last him home* (Greene). *Dubious* is close to *doubtful* in implying that the subject questions the truth of a statement or the reality of a situation, but differs from it in suggesting a different source of doubt: in the case of *dubious* the doubts are based less on information in the subject's possession than on his own mistrust or anxiety: *I'm dubious about his stories of early success; I'm dubious of his honesty.* If what is at issue are the statements, characteristics, or actions of the doubter himself then these semantic distinctions are neutralized, because the subject cannot be suspicious or mistrustful of himself: *I'm doubtful/dubious about what I ought to do.* As a result a fine distinction appears in sentences such as *John was doubtful/dubious about his ability to cope with the situation*: if the noun *John* and the possessive pronoun *his* are not coreferential (denote different people) the semantic distinction noted above between *doubtful* and *dubious* is preserved; if *John* and *his* are coreferential (if they refer to the same person), this distinction is neutralized.

### 2.4.3. The Structure of Synonym Series

Two basic types of relation between synonyms within a series are possible: (*a*) the semantic closeness (as measured, for example, by the number of matching and non-matching components in the explications) of any pair of synonyms in a given series is roughly the same, that is, each is equally close to all the others; and (*b*) the semantic closeness is greater for some pairs of synonyms than for others, so that groups and subgroups of synonyms may be identified within a series according to the degree of closeness. We shall speak of a synonym series with an intersected structure in the first case and a hierarchical structure in the second.

The distinction between these two types of structure matters less from a theoretical point of view than from a practical one, as it makes it possible to facilitate the exposition and assimilation of information regarding synonym series. Each type of structure is assigned its own type of description.

The description of the semantics of a synonym series contains, basically speaking, two kinds of elements: the synonyms themselves (the object of the description) and their semantic features (the instrument of description). In the case of an intersected structure it is more convenient to register a synonym and describe it against all features, then pass on to the next synonym and repeat the operation, and so on; in the case of a hierarchical structure it is more convenient to register a *feature* and show how it divides a series into groups and the groups into subgroups, then pass on to the next feature and so on. However, neither type of description is immutably applied to a particular type of structure.

### 2.4.3.1. *Intersected Structure*

*Calculate, compute, reckon, estimate* differ by the following features: (1) the nature of the action; (2) the nature of the original data; (3) the nature of the final results. *Calculate* may mean the most varied kind of reckoning, from mathematically complex operations to simple arithmetic, and actions in which the original data are obtained by theoretical or hypothetical means, extrapolated from other factors but not given in advance, while the result is expressed in fully exact terms: *to calculate the velocity of light/speed of a rocket/cost of furnishing a house/purchasing power*. *Compute* and *reckon* do not differ from *calculate* with regard to the precision of the result obtained, but denote operations based on definite original data, known in advance: *to compute/reckon the number of women in American colleges*. It is natural, for example, to *compute* the amount of material needed for a building, all of whose parameters (area, height, purpose, etc.) are known; it is natural to *calculate* the position of a flock of migratory birds if the calculations are based on hypothetical factors such as starting-point, direction, average speed and total flying time, average wind speeds, etc. On the other hand, *compute* differs from *reckon* but resembles *calculate* in denoting the most varied calculations, regardless of their complexity, while *reckon* implies a relatively simple process, often performed mentally: *to reckon (up) the bill/number of people present*. *Estimate* differs from all three in being neutral with regard to the first two features but always implying an approximate result.

*Discuss, argue, debate, dispute* differ by the following features: (1) the type of argumentation (biased, attempting to prove that only one party is right; broad, considering all factors which may confirm or deny the standpoint set forth); (2) the topic of discussion (ordinary or political issues); (3) the character of the discussion itself (organized, disorganized, calm, heated). On the first point, *argue*, *dispute*, and to a lesser extent *debate* stand in opposition to *discuss*, which denotes an objective and unbiased debate of an issue, considering all arguments for and against a person's standpoint. According to the second feature, *discuss* and *argue* which are neutral with regard to topic, stand in opposition to *debate*, which usually describes the discussion of political matters, and to *dispute* which usually denotes more ordinary matters. Finally, on the last point, *debate* and *dispute* can be contrasted, each in its own way, with the other two: *debate* means *organized* discussion (for example, with a set order of speeches), while the other three are neutral in this regard; *dispute* suggests a relatively heated discussion, while the other three say nothing about this.

### 2.4.3.2. *Hierarchical Structure*

*Sullen, morose, sulky, surly, glum, gloomy* differ by the following features: (1) the permanence or transience of the property or state; (2) its causes (the psychological make-up of the individual); (3) its outward manifestations. With regard to the first feature, *sullen* and *morose* differ from the other members of the series in that they may denote both permanent characteristics and transient states: *he was a sullen/morose man; suddenly he grew sullen/morose.* All the other synonyms primarily denote states. *Sullen* and *morose* differ in that *sullen* implies as a cause an inability to communicate, the absence of the vitality required for communication with others, while *morose* points rather to an unwillingness to communicate owing to the individual's ill nature—arrogance, spleen or ill will: *Sheridan was generally very dull in society and sat sullen and silent* (Webster); *one must be very cold-blooded and morose not to like this book.* *Sulky* and *surly* differ from *glum* and *gloomy* in that their direct cause is dissatisfaction or irritation with someone or something, whereas the state described by *glum* and *gloomy* is a result of a bad mood, or depression brought on by unpleasant experiences. In the group *sulky, surly* the first differs from the second in the outward symptoms of the state. *Sulky* suggests a tendency to take offence and show one's feelings in a sour expression, while *surly* suggests a tendency to get angry and show one's feelings in words or deeds: *he turned sulky and did not answer the question; the surly maid shut the door in my face.* In the group *glum, gloomy* the first differs from the second in degree (cf. *pasmurnyi—mrachnyi*); *glum* implies being (mildly) downcast, in low spirits, while *gloomy* implies deep unhappiness: *you sit there as glum as the mutes at a funeral; he was gloomy all these days because he didn't see a gleam of hope.*

*Sly, cunning, crafty, artful, tricky, foxy, wily* signify one who goes about achieving his aims by deceit (cf. Russian *khitryi, kovarnyi, lukavyi, lovkii*). *Sly* and *cunning* imply insincere behaviour, hypocrisy, an ability to act with caution and conceal one's true intentions. Both usually presuppose an aim *near at hand*, which can be achieved without great foresight. They may therefore be used of people of modest ability: *it was not intelligence, but a low kind of cunning/slyness*. *Crafty* and *artful*, on the other hand, usually imply a highly developed *mind* and an ability to make comprehensive plans and achieve *more distant, complex, and serious* aims by skilled manœuvring. *Foxy* and *wily* occupy an intermediate position between these two groups. They are close to the first in implying hypocrisy and guile, and close to the second in implying cleverness and foresight. *Tricky* stands on its own, describing a mendacious, resourceful, and unreliable person: *fear a tricky opponent more than a crafty one* (Webster). In the pair *sly, cunning*, the first implies that the behavioural symptoms are not so much a result of conscious calculation as an extension of personal characteristics, a manifestation of innate duplicity or perfidy: *she was extremely sly and could always get the better of her partners*. *Cunning*, on the other hand, implies calculation rather than an innate tendency to duplicity: *he was very cunning in dealing with his customers*. In the pair *crafty, artful*, the second implies cleverer and defter manipulation, with resourcefulness, etc. being demonstrated: *crafty man of affairs/ money-changer*; *being artful she cajoled him with honey-mouthed flattery*. In the pair *foxy, wily* the former implies a degree of experience of life, knowledge of human nature, and ability to exploit weaknesses, especially susceptibility to flattery; *foxy* is therefore usually used to describe older people: *he is a foxy old man*. *Wily* differs from *foxy* in almost the same way as *sly* differs from *cunning*, implying not so much calculating exploitation of others for one's own ends as craftiness as a personal characteristic: *a wily fox! We never knew what a rascal he was*.

The series *polite, civil, courteous, courtly, gallant, chivalrous* may be divided into three groups. *Polite* and, to a lesser extent, *civil* describe a person who observes the rules governing intercourse with others to at least a minimal degree. *Polite* usually describes a person who is well brought up, attentive, and tactful: *she was always polite to the servants*; *he was too polite to ask such questions*. *Civil* signifies a minimal degree of good manners, beyond which a person will risk seeming rude: *he forced his son to be civil to the stranger*; *the servant was sullen, but civil*. *Courteous* and *courtly* imply not only the maintenance of prescribed rules of behaviour, but also that the subject does this with a sense of his own dignity. Moreover *courteous* emphasizes a friendly manner, readiness to help or perform favours: *the young man was quite courteous and helpful*; *he was so charming and courteous to the old lady*. *Courtly* denotes a refinement of aristocratic manners reaching the point of standing on ceremony and visible in all forms of behaviour: *a courtly and stately old gentleman*. *Gallant* and *chivalrous* mainly describe men who show kindness or attention to a woman. Here *gallant* denotes politeness and courtesy shown above all in elegant manners and outward polish: *trying to be gallant, he bowed*. *Chivalrous* suggests the inner nobility of the subject, a selfless readiness to help others: *he was kind and chivalrous to women of all ages; he felt strangely chivalrous and paternal towards her.*

## 2.5. NOTES

This zone lists, with explication, translation, examples, and illustrations, those meanings of the words making up the series which are close to the meaning under consideration. From the aforementioned series *desire, wish, want*, etc., the verb *desire* may serve as an example: in the obsolete construction *to desire smb. to do smth.* it means 'to express a wish' (*he desired me to stay in a peremptory tone*), and in this case has no single-word synonyms. In the series *love, affection, attachment*, the first, unlike the other two, has the special meaning 'love for a person of the opposite sex': *love at first sight; to fall in (out of) love.*

In such cases the Notes function essentially as fragments of an explanatory dictionary.

Notes fulfil one more function. Sometimes they contain a synonym series presented in reduced form. This happens whenever some of the synonyms treated in the basic series have a closely related but rare meaning poorly represented in the texts.

In the series *angry, indignant, wrathful, irate, furious, acrimonious, mad*, the words *angry, wrathful* and *furious* appear under 'Notes'. They all have a figurative sense, applied to the elements, and differ from one another mainly in their degree of intensity: *an angry/wrathful sea; a furious storm.*

Sometimes there is more than one meaning of this type. For example, in the series *support, uphold, back (up), champion*, the verbs *support* and *back (up)* are synonymous in two senses at once which are close to the basic meaning of the series: (1) 'to adduce evidence in support of smth.' (*he could not find any arguments to support/back his story*), (2) 'to be evidence in support of smth.' (*this information supports the suspicion; the bills will not be discounted unless they are backed by responsible names.*)

In these and similar cases the Notes basically fulfil the function of a dictionary of synonyms, though on a limited scale.

## 2.6. SYNTAX

We shall term 'syntactic' any distinctions which may be described with the aid of grammatical features, be they syntactic or morphological. They manifest themselves within words, collocations, and sentences. The most interesting and widespread is the second type of distinction, which is analysed in detail below; however, for the sake of completeness the first and third types must be mentioned, however briefly.

Syntactic distinctions within a word occur, for example, when that word tends to be used in a single grammatical form, whereas the other synonyms may freely be used in any form of the respective grammatical paradigm. The fixed use of one member of a series of verbs in its past participle form is one such widespread instance.

Of greater interest are syntactic distinctions which appear within the limits of a *sentence*. We shall note two typical patterns: sentences with the expletive *it*, and negative, interrogative, and various modal sentences.

In the series *try, torment, torture, afflict, rack*, the first three are used in sentences with the expletive *it* introducing an infinitive construction, while the last two cannot be used in this way: *it tried/tormented/tortured him to think that*, but not *\*it afflicted/racked him to think that*. The adjectives *hard, difficult* on the one hand, and *arduous* on the other, are distinguished in the same way: *it was hard/difficult to climb up the steep slope*, but not *\*it was arduous to climb up the steep slope*.

*Condescend* and *deign* differ in that *deign* is fixed in modal, interrogative, and negative sentences and in outwardly affirmative sentences containing words implying negation (usually adverbs such as *hardly* or *scarcely*): *to deign no reply; I do/will not deign to reply to such impertinence; will you deign to answer my question?; he hardly/scarcely deigned a comment*. *Condescend* is used freely in all types of sentence: *he condescended to his younger brother; he condescended to the suggestion; he condescended to accept the message; to condescend no answer; will you condescend to answer my question?*, etc. Exactly the same distinction may be seen between *abstain*, on the one hand, and *resist, withstand* in a similar sense on the other: *he abstained from drinking; I can't resist a cigarette; I could hardly resist a cigarette; the curiosity that I could hardly withstand; human nature could not withstand those bewildering temptations; will you be able to resist/withstand such a temptation?*

There are even tighter constraints upon the use of *budge*, compared to *stir*: *budge*, a typical 'negative polarity item', is used almost exclusively in negative sentences or modal sentences with implied negation: *he did not budge; he could hardly budge*.

It may be presumed that these syntactic constraints are motivated by profound semantic causes. *Stir* and *budge, condescend* and *deign, abstain* and *withstand* are evidently not exact synonyms. One fine semantic distinction lies in the fact that in each pair the second member has in its explication a modal frame which establishes the speaker's attitude to the given situation. For the verb *budge*, for example, the explication may look like this: *budge* = 'to make a slight movement; the speaker thinks that certain elements in the situation make it extremely unlikely that the subject will be willing or able to move'. The phrase *\*he budged* is incorrect because it creates a tension between the assertive and the modal components of meaning, and such a situation is avoided in language.

We move on to syntactic distinctions manifested within the limits of a collocation. These fall into two classes: (1) distinctions linked with the ability to be subordinate elements in a collocation, and (2) those linked with the ability to be the main element in it.

The first class of distinction, as may readily be foreseen, is characteristic of noun and adjective series.

With regard to nouns, this means the ability to be governed by a preposition or verb. In the series *pleasure, joy, delight*, all three may be governed by the preposition *with* (*with pleasure/joy/delight*), but only *delight* may be governed by the preposition *in*: *to jump in delight*, whereas *\*to jump in pleasure/joy* are impossible. *Rest* and *ease*, unlike the synonym *comfort*, may follow the preposition *at*: *my mind is at rest/ease* (*about it*), whereas *\*my mind is at comfort* (*about it*) is impossible.

With regard to adjectives, it means the ability to be used attributively (with a noun) or predicatively (with a linking verb). In the series *affectionate, devoted, fond, doting*, etc., the first three are used in both an attributive and predicative function, while *doting* is only attributive: *an affectionate/devoted/fond/doting mother*, but only *she is affectionate; she is devoted to me; she is fond of him*. In this respect the series at issue contrasts with the series *watchful, vigilant, alert, awake*; in the latter the first three synonyms are used both attributively and predicatively, while the last one is fixed not in attributive but in predicative use: *to be watchful/vigilant of/against danger/the enemy; to be alert/awake for/to a new adventure*, but only *a watchful/vigilant/alert sentinel*. *\*An awake sentinel* is not possible.

The second class of distinction, the most widely represented in a dictionary of synonyms, is characteristic of verbs and other word classes which are capable of syntactically governing others. They may be syntactically motivated or unmotivated.

Consider the series *bare, naked, nude*. As will be remembered, *bare* denotes an absence of clothing on a part of the body, *naked* on the whole body or those parts which should, according to accepted convention, be covered, while *nude* implies the absence of all clothing. Therefore *bare* and *naked* may govern the form *to smth.*, indicating the limit of the exposed area, while *nude* cannot: *bare/naked to the waist*, but not *\*nude to the waist*.

The verb *to wave*, unlike its synonyms *swing* and *flourish*, as previously stated, denotes a movement of the arms intended to attract the attention of another person or pass on information to him (usually a request or an order). Accordingly, *wave* is freely used in the constructions *to wave to smb.* (meaning the addressee of the signal), and *to wave* (*to*) *smb. to do smth., to wave smb. to smth.* (for example *to silence*), *to wave smb. away/on/aside* (with the meaning of the content of a request or order). *Swing* and *flourish*, which do not express the idea of the addressee, are unable, naturally, to govern such forms.

In both the cases indicated above the syntactic distinctions are semantically conditioned, motivated by the meanings of the respective words (cf. also the analysis of the pair *stir—budge*, earlier in this section). However, a syntactic feature can by no means always be explained by reference to its meaning. It is not clear, for example, why *leap* can govern both a preposition and a direct object (*to leap over a fence; to leap a fence*), while the synonym *spring* can only be used with a preposition (*to spring over a fence*); why *attain* may have either a direct or a prepositional object (*to attain success/glory; to attain to power/ to prosperity*), while the synonym *gain* may have only a direct object (*to gain success/glory*). In these instances, syntactic distinctions do not appear to be semantically motivated.

The types of government, irrespective of whether they are semantically motivated or not, are described from three different but mutually complementary viewpoints: semantic, syntactic, and morphological. In the example given above with the verb *to wave*, the forms *smb., to smb.* semantically denote the *addressee* (other possible roles of the governed forms are subject, object, content, instrument, means, place, end point, starting-point, time, cause, result, purpose, etc., that is, the same roles which appear as distinguishing features in the semantic description of synonym series); syntactically they function as a direct object (*smb.*) or a prepositional object (*to smb.*); and lastly, morphologically they are represented by a noun (or pronoun), or a preposition with a noun (or pronoun).

Any difference in semantic roles, syntactic function, or morphological expression and any combination of such differences will be listed as a difference in syntactic government.

As governed forms we shall class not only nominal groups preceded or not preceded by prepositions, but also infinitives, phrases, and gerunds. Some examples follow.

The verbs *discuss, argue, debate, dispute* govern forms denoting the object (the topic of discussion) and forms denoting the second subject (the other participant in the conversation). With all four verbs the former may be a direct object: *to discuss/argue/debate/dispute a point*. With the verbs *argue* and *debate* a complement introduced by the prepositions (*up*)*on, about, over* and the semantically more independent *round* is also possible: *to argue/debate on art; to argue/debate about/over religion; to argue/debate round the topic*. With the verb *dispute* the same semantic role may be represented by the prepositional objects *about smth.* and *over smth.*, but not *on smth.*: *to dispute about/over religion*. With *discuss* and *debate* it may be in the form of a subordinate clause: *to discuss/debate how to do it*.

*Beg, entreat, beseech, implore, supplicate, adjure, conjure* govern forms denoting the addressee of the request and the content of the request. In all cases the addressee may be expressed by a direct object. The content of the request is then expressed by an infinitive, a subordinate clause, or direct speech: *to beg/entreat/ beseech (etc.) smb. to listen (that he should grant permission)*; '*Help me,*' he *begged/ entreated/beseeched*. With all these synonyms except *adjure* and *conjure* the content of the request may be expressed by the prepositional complement *for smth.*: *to beg/entreat/beseech* (but not *\*to adjure/conjure*) *smb. for a loan*.

With all of them the content of the request may also be expressed by a direct object. In this case *beg* and *entreat*, unlike all the others, may have the prepositional complement *of smb.* to denote the addressee of the request: *to beg/entreat/ beseech/implore smb.'s help/protection*, but only *to beg/entreat leave of smb.*

*Commend, applaud, compliment* govern prepositional objects denoting the object of the praise. The first two verbs are followed by the form *for smth.*, while the last is followed by *on smth.*: *to commend/applaud smb. for his performance;*

*to compliment smb. on his presence of mind. Commend* and *applaud*, unlike *compliment*, may be followed by a direct object denoting the object of the praise: *to commend/applaud smb.'s presence of mind*, but not *\*to compliment smb.'s presence of mind*.

*Companion, comrade, pal* are often used with the prepositional government *to smb.*, to indicate the subject of the friendship, which is untypical of *crony* and *buddy* and impossible with *associate*: *he was a good companion/comrade/pal to me.*

*Hard* and *difficult*, unlike *arduous*, may govern an infinitive denoting the substance of the difficulty: *the lesson was hard/difficult to learn*, but not *\*the lesson was arduous to learn.*

*Appear* and *emerge* occur with the prepositional object *from smth.* denoting a starting-point: *to appear from nowhere; he emerged from the side door of the house.* In addition, *appear* may have the prepositional object to indicate the place where something appears, which is untypical of *emerge*: *to appear in the doorway/ on the threshold; the city appeared beyond it.*

In many cases distinctions in the syntactic properties of synonyms have corresponding co-occurrence distinctions.

A well known example of this correspondence is the word *love*, which governs two different prepositional objects to indicate the object of the emotion: *for smb.* (most usual with nouns denoting living beings, *love for one's wife*), and *of smth.* (more common with nouns denoting things, actions and so on, *love of adventure*). The word *attachment*, however, which is synonymous with *love*, is linked to the name of any object (be it human or non-human) by the preposition *to*: *attachment to one's daughter/one's home.*

The adjectives *attentive, considerate, thoughtful* are linked by prepositions with the object of attention or consideration, with *attentive* always taking the preposition *to*, and *thoughtful* taking the preposition *of*, whether the object is a human being or a state: *attentive to a friend/to smb.'s needs; thoughtful of other people/of his son's well-being.* As for the synonym *considerate*, it usually governs the form *to smb.* if the object is human and *of smth.* if the object is a state: *considerate to old people; considerate of the comfort of old people.*

*Discuss, argue, debate, dispute*, as noted above, govern their objects both directly and with the aid of prepositions. In the case of prepositional government the object may be a noun of any semantic class. However, if the object is direct, the choice of nouns for the verbs *argue, debate*, and *dispute* is semantically restricted. In particular, only *discuss* may combine with a noun denoting a person in the function of a direct object: *to discuss the people who attended the funeral; we are discussing you, not mankind in the abstract.*

## 2.7. CO-OCCURRENCE CONSTRAINTS

A full lexicographic description of a word should include an account of its co-occurrence constraints—lexical, semantic, and referential.

Lexical co-occurrence constraints are recorded in the form of a list of specific words which may be syntactically linked with the word in question. The adjectives *doubtful* and *dubious* as predicatives do not combine with all copula verbs, but only with a limited number, principally *to feel, to look, to seem, to sound*; not, for example, with *to turn out*: *even after they had been assured that there was no danger, they looked/felt/seemed/sounded doubtful/dubious*, whereas *\*he turned out doubtful/dubious about it* is incorrect. For *doubtful* and *dubious* it is therefore necessary to provide a list of copula verbs for which these two synonyms may serve as predicatives.

On the other hand, a semantic co-occurrence constraint is recorded by indicating a particular semantic property which any word syntactically linked with the given word must display. In the series *escape, flee, fly, abscond, decamp*, the first three have broader co-occurrence than the last two. The subject of *escape, flee*, and *fly* may be either a human or an animal: *his best two dogs escaped from the camp*; *the dog fled into the forest*, whereas only *humans* may be the subject of *abscond* and *decamp*.

Referential co-occurrence constraints are a more complex matter. An example is the series *reach, achieve, gain, attain*. The following collocations with nouns denoting the aim or result of an action are typical of these synonyms: *to reach/ achieve, gain/attain one's aim/the object of one's desires/success/fame/glory*; *to reach an understanding/agreement*; *to achieve a reputation for being rude*; *to achieve the realization of a dream*; *to gain/attain the attention of the clerk/the confidence of the mountain people*. It is curious that in the last examples with the verbs *gain* and *attain* these cannot be replaced by *reach* or *achieve*: the collocations *\*to reach/ achieve the attention of the clerk/the confidence of the mountain people* are incorrect (not simply different in meaning). If we consider more closely the nouns *attention* and *confidence*, which may function as the direct object of *gain* and *attain* but not *reach* or *achieve*, we find the following interesting feature in the corresponding sentences: the subject of the state denoted by the nouns *attention* or *confidence* is different from the subject of the action denoted by the verbs *gain* and *attain*: the clerk's attention is attracted not by the clerk himself, but a second person, and the confidence of the mountain people is gained by somebody other than the mountain people. However, the verbs *gain* and *attain* may combine with nouns denoting states (properties, situations) whose subjects *coincide* with the subjects of the corresponding actions: in the case of *to gain/attain one's aim/success/glory*, the subject of the aim, the success, and the glory is the same person as the subject of the gaining or attaining. We can now formulate a referential co-occurrence constraint for the verbs *reach* and *achieve*: they cannot be combined with the names of states if the subject of the state is different from the subject of the actions they denote.

A similar distinction is seen in the pair of synonyms *condescend, deign*: the former may combine with the names of actions or properties whose subject *coincides* with the subject of *condescend* (*he condescended to smile*) and with the name of a property or state whose subject *does not coincide* with that of *conde-scend* (*to condescend to smb.'s folly*). *Deign,* on the other hand, combines only with the names of one's own actions and properties: *he didn't deign to smile,* but not *\*he didn't deign to their folly.*

Co-occurrence distinctions between synonyms, like syntactic distinctions, may be *motivated* or *unmotivated.*

Let us take, for example, the synonyms *surprise, amaze, astound.* They differ particularly in the degree of feeling. All three may combine with adverbial modi-fiers of measure, but *surprise* combines with any such modifier (*he was a little/ not a little/very much surprised; he was surprised beyond all measure*), while *amaze* and *astound* combine only with those which signify a great or extreme degree of the respective property, condition, or state: *he was amazed/astounded to such a degree that he could hardly talk.* Collocations such as *?he was a tiny bit amazed/ a little astounded* are at least unusual, if not anomalous. The nature of this con-straint is clear: *amaze* and *astound* alone and unaided express the idea of a great degree, and this idea can be intensified only by a meaning such as 'extreme' or 'extraordinary'.

*Concern* and *solicitude* differ from *care* in that the first two denote a state of *emotion,* while *care* has the sense of a state of activity. This semantic distinction accounts for the co-occurrence distinctions between the synonyms, above all the fact that the first two combine with qualifiers defining the degree of emotion (*deep or profound concern/solicitude*) and with verbs signifying the presence or the manifestation of an emotion: *to feel concern/solicitude; to express profound concern; to manifest/show solicitude.*

In both the cases considered above the co-occurrence distinctions naturally flow from distinctions of meaning. However, even co-occurrence distinctions may not be semantically motivated. It is difficult, if not impossible, to explain by ref-erence to semantic factors the differing co-occurrence of such adjectives as *cold* and *cool* in the sense of feeling cold. Both may combine with the name of an animate being or all of its body as the subject of the state: *I sat in the armchair feeling sick and cold; I'm perfectly cool, but open the window if you like.* In this sense, however, only *cold* may co-occur with the names of parts of the body when these are the subject of the state: *his fingers/toes felt cold* but not *his fingers/toes felt cool.* The latter sentence is either incorrect (in the sense 'his toes felt cold') or has a different meaning (objectively cold; 'his toes were cool to the touch').

In what follows no specific mention will be made of the semantic motivation or non-motivation of co-occurrence distinctions, although in the dictionary this information is fairly systematically provided.

In setting forth the co-occurrence features of synonyms, use is made of the role nomenclature which was developed to describe their semantic and syntactic similarities and differences (subject, object, content, addressee, instrument, means, purpose, cause, etc.). The applicability of this nomenclature in descriptions of the co-occurrence similarities and differences between synonyms demonstrates that it is a convenient and universal means of recording information which is relevant in theoretical research as well as in mastering the synonym system of a language.

Here we shall consider some examples of co-occurrence distinctions between synonyms. These examples cannot claim to be representative, still less to constitute a comprehensive list: types of co-occurrence distinctions are extraordinarily varied and only the dictionary can give exhaustive treatment.

*Achieve* and *gain* co-occur with a noun denoting a person as the subject of the action. The subject of *achieve*, but not *gain*, may be not only humans, but also their *words*, *deeds*, or *qualities* which help them achieve their aims: *his words achieved their aim/object*, whereas *\*his words gained their aim* is incorrect. A similar distinction arises between the Russian verbs *dostich'* and *dobit'sia* [to reach, attain]: *ego slova dostigli tseli* [his words achieved their aim], but not *\*ego slova dobilis' tseli*.

In the sense of 'arriving', *reach*, *gain*, and *attain* co-occur with a noun denoting a person as the subject of the action and one denoting a place as the goal of the action: *they couldn't reach/gain/attain the opposite shore*. *Reach* combines more often than the other two with a noun denoting a moving object as its subject: *the boat reached the shore*; *the train reaches Oxford at six*.

*Gather* differs from its synonyms *assemble* and *congregate* in that it co-occurs (in a stylistically neutral text) with animate and inanimate nouns in the function of the grammatical subject; cf. in particular: *the clouds are gathering, it will rain*. *Assemble* and *congregate* do not take inanimate subjects.

*Ponder*, *meditate*, and *ruminate* combine with nouns denoting situations, properties, and the products of thought as the objects (topics) of consideration: *to ponder/meditate/ upon the course of action*; *to ruminate over the past*; *to ponder/ meditate/ruminate the point*. The verbs *ponder* and *meditate* co-occur with nouns signifying people as the object of consideration, which is not typical of *ruminate*: *to ponder on modern young men*; *he meditated on all those people and the things they represented in his life*.

*Depress*, *oppress*, and *weigh down* occur with nouns signifying feelings, actions, properties, and so forth as the cause of the state of oppression: *a feeling of isolation depressed/oppressed her*; *she was oppressed by fear*; *she was oppressed/weighed down by the heat*. In addition, *depress* and *oppress* occur with the names of specific things and animate beings in the same function, which would be unlikely with *weigh down (upon)*: *the dim room depressed/oppressed her*; *she depressed me*.

## 2.8. ILLUSTRATIONS

Illustrations drawn from literature, fairly numerous in most dictionary entries, play a dual role: first, they form a substantial part of the material upon which our description of a synonym series is constructed; second, they demonstrate how the features of these synonyms are manifested in various styles and genres of literature and speech.

It should be noted that the illustrations include numerous instances of individual usage of synonyms by writers and that this usage is characterized by departures from established co-occurrence norms, by unexpected metaphorical reinterpretation of a word, and so on. Such material, while of great value as evidence of the great wealth of possibilities of use of living language and as an indicator of the direction of potential change, should not, however, be considered when describing the semantic, syntactic, or co-occurrence norms of synonym use as set forth in the analytical part of the dictionary. The reader should not, therefore, be deterred by those very few cases of divergence between the material used in the semantic, syntactic, and co-occurrence zones and that given in the illustration zone.

Over half the illustrations are taken from literary works of the nineteenth and early twentieth centuries. The choice was determined mainly by the availability of material during the earlier stages of research. We are aware that it is desirable to use more modern material in a dictionary of synonyms, and hope that in future we shall be able to remedy this defect.

# 2

# Types of Information in a Dictionary of Synonyms

Below we present the types of lexicographical information contained in the *New Explanatory Dictionary of Russian Synonyms* [*Novyi ob"iasnitel'nyi slovar' russkogo iazyka*], in the form of a brief survey of the zonal structure of its entries.[1]

## 1. The Heading

The heading is made up of the synonym series itself, that is, of a group of lexemes with a substantial common part. In addition to synonyms of the usual kind—lexemes of the same part of speech derived from different roots—this dictionary treats the following as synonyms:

(*a*) different parts of speech, as long as these can fulfil identical syntactic functions; particles and adverbs (*Pushkin vladychestvoval tol'ko/edinstvenno siloiu svoego talanta* [Pushkin held sway only/solely by the force of his talent]); particles and adjectives (*Tol'ko/odin Vasia promolchal* [Only Vasia/Vasia alone said nothing]); adverbs and prepositions (*Sestra priekhala chut' ran'she menia/neposredstvenno peredo mnoi* [My sister arrived just/immediately before me]); adverbs and adjectives (*Emu nado/nuzhno podlechit'sia* [He must have some treatment]); verbs and adverbs or adjectives combined with copulas (*Emu sledovalo/nado bylo/bylo neobkhodimo otdokhnut'* [He needed to have a rest]; *On napominaet/pokhozh na ottsa svoei neprimirimost'iu* [He resembles his father in his uncompromising nature]; *Mne etogo khvatit/budet dostatochno* [That will be enough for me]); verbs and conjunctions (*Stoilo emu voiti, kak vse vstavali—Kak tol'ko on vkhodil, vse vstavali* [As soon as he came in everybody stood up]); adjectives and verbs in participial forms (*izmozhdennyi, izmuchennyi* [exhausted]).

(*b*) synonyms derived from the same stems, such as, *belet'* and *belet'sia* [to appear white (in the dark)], *svetit'* and *svetit'sia* [to shine (of stars)], etc.; *gret' —razogrevat', podogrevat'* [to warm up (food)]; *gret'—sogrevat'* [to warm (one's hands)], *obogrevat'* [to heat (a room)]. Of particular interest in this respect is the regular and characteristically Russian type of lexical synonym produced by back-

---

[1] Besides his own materials, the author has made use of some material from the series *boiat'sia* written by V. Apresjan and three entries compiled jointly with M. Glovinskaia: *zhalovat'sia—setovat'*, *roptat'*, etc.; *obeshchat'—obiazyvat'sia, sulit'*, etc.; *rugat'—branit'*, etc.

formation from a prefixed form: *probit'* (*probivat'*) *zoriu*/*trevogu* and *bit' zoriu*/ *trevogu* [to sound reveille/the alarm]; *razbit'* (*razbivat'*) *steklo* and *bit' steklo* [to smash glass]; *razbit'* (*razbivat'*) *vraga* and *bit' vraga* [to rout the enemy]; *sbit'* (*sbivat'*) *maslo* and *bit' maslo* [to whip cream/butter]; *vybrosit'* (*vykinut'*) *chto-libo v korzinu* and *brosit'* (*kinut'*) *chto-libo v korzinu* [to throw smth. into the bin].

(*c*) certain types of lexical and syntactic synonyms, in particular verbs as opposed to fixed negated verb forms, finite verbs governing prepositions as opposed to sentential adverbs, and a number of others. For example *nedostavat'* and *ne khvatat'* [to be insufficient]; *zhit'* [to live] as in *Nadezhda zhivet v serdtse* [Hope lives on in one's heart] and *ne ugasat'* [not to fade]; *Ia schitaiu, (chto on polovinu faktov utail)* [I think (he has concealed half of the facts)] and *Po-moemu (on polovinu faktov utail)* [In my opinion (he has concealed half of the facts)]; *Byvaet, chto on opazdyvaet* [It happens that he arrives late] and *Inogda on opazdyvaet* [He sometimes arrives late].

Fully regular series of lexical and syntactic synonyms are also formed by verbs which might be termed 'impersonal semi-conversives', such as *Ia dumaiu—Mne dumaetsia* [I think], *Ia schitaiu—Mne predstavliaetsia* [I think], *Ia khochu—Mne khochetsia* [I want], etc. However, in the present version of the dictionary pairs of the type *khotet'* and *khotet'sia* are treated in different synonym series.

## 1.1. THE DOMINANT

Each series begins with a dominant, that is, a lexeme which has the most general meaning in the given series, has the broadest application and co-occurrence, and is most neutral from the point of view of style, pragmatics, communicative values, grammar, and prosody, etc. For example *vyzyvat'* (*krizis, nenavist'*) [to cause (a crisis, hatred)]—*vesti k, porozhdat', rozhdat', budit', probuzhdat'*; *delit'* [to divide]—*razdeliat', raschleniat', razbivat', drobit'*; *zameret'* [to freeze into immobility]—*zastyt', otsepenet', okamenet', ostolbenet'*; *zashchishchat'* [to defend]— *ograzhdat', otstaivat', stoiat' za, zastupat'sia za, vstupat'sia za*; *risovat'* [to sketch] —*zarisovyvat', pisat', malevat'*; *zhalovat'sia* [to complain]—*setovat', roptat', nyt', skulit', khnykat'*; and so forth.

In many cases the meaning of the dominant is fully present in the meaning of all other members of the series, as for example in *brosat'* [to throw]—*kidat', shvyriat', metat'*. However, even in the simplest of series with a semantic primitive at the head, the dominants may differ from the other synonyms by positive semantic components which the other synonyms lack. This applies in even larger measure to synonym series which have a more complex structure of meaning.

This is a natural consequence of the fact that the dominants are almost always foreground lexemes, the words most extensively used in a language and the most deeply rooted in the whole verbal culture reflected in that language. They retain semantic traces of the varied situations in which they alone may be used and in which they suggest specific senses and connotations.

Let us consider, for example, the series *zhdat'* [to wait]—*ozhidat', dozhidat'sia, podzhidat', vyzhidat', perezhidat', podozhdat', prozhdat'*. The semantic specifics of all these words except for *zhdat'* are almost apparent: *ozhidat'* indicates the subject's inner readiness to meet some person or event; *dozhidat'sia*—patient waiting in a definite place; *podzhidat'* suggests that the subject has some special, often hostile intent towards the object of the waiting; *vyzhidat'* denotes waiting for a favourable moment in which to perform some planned action; *perezhidat'* indicates waiting for the end of some process or phenomenon as a precondition for the resumption of some activity of one's own; *podozhdat'* suggests a brief period of waiting in a definite place (except for usage of the type *Ia mogu i podozhdat'*); *prozhdat'* means that the waiting was long and futile.

In this context *zhdat'* may appear as a general and universal synonym, able to take the place of any other word in the series. Closer analysis, however, reveals that it has a number of semantic properties which distinguish it from the other members of the series. Here it is sufficient to mention one of these. In a number of cases *zhdat'* has the additional sense 'to wish that something would happen', as in this example: *Vechera futuristov sobirali neveroiatnoe kolichestvo publiki . . . Mnogie prikhodili radi skandala, no shirokaia studencheskaia publika zhdala novogo iskusstva, khotela novogo slova—prichem—i eto interesno—prozoi malo interesovalis'* [The Futurists' gatherings attracted a huge audience. Many came to enjoy a riotous scene, but most of the students in the audience expected [*zhdala*] new art and wanted to hear a new word. Curiously, however, they had little interest in prose.] (R. Jakobson). A context containing adverbs of degree is typical of this added semantic element: *ochen'* [very], *strashno* [terribly], *bol'no* [badly, very] and the emphatic particles *kak, tak* and *tak i*, as in *On ochen' vas zhdal* [He was so impatient to see you]; *Ne bol'no-to on tebia zhdet* [He hasn't been too keen to see you]; *On videl uzhe i ponimal nastroenie etikh gospod, tak i zhdavshikh teper' sluchaia pristat' k nemu* [He could already see and understand the mood of those gentlemen who were now so eager to beset him] (M. Volkonskii); *On tak zhdal, chto na nego obratiat vnimanie* [He so much wanted to be noticed]; *Ona [Dasha] podniala k nemu litso s zazhmurennymi mokrymi resnitsami: 'Ivan Il'ich, milyi, kak ia zhdala vas'* [She (Dasha) raised her face and lowered moist eyelashes to him: 'My dear Ivan Il'ich, how I longed to see you'] (A. N. Tolstoi).

The other synonyms in this series cannot co-occur with these emphatic particles, and hence cannot undergo this semantic modification.


## 1.2. STYLISTIC LABELS AND GRAMMATICAL NOTES

Every lexeme in a synonym series, when necessary, is assigned a stylistic label. The system that is applied is basically a traditional one, although in some instances it appeared to be necessary to expand it.

In order better to show the essence of our few innovations, we should recall the basis of the traditional system. The principal stylistic categories considered are the following: (*a*) literary style (*vysok.* [high style], *knizhn.* [bookish], *ofits.* [official], *poet.*, etc.); (*b*) spoken styles (*razg.* [colloquial], *prost.* [substandard], etc.); (*c*) sub-literary (*grub.* [vulgar], *zharg.* [slang], *bran.* [abusive], etc.); (*d*) the speaker's attitude to his topic or the addressee, his tone of voice, etc. (*lask.* [affectionate], *neodobr.* [disapproving], *iron.*, *prezr.* [contemptuous], *prenebr.* [deprecating], *unich.* [disparaging], etc.); (*e*) social areas or particular domains of activity (*spets.* [specialized], *polit.* [political], *isk.* [art], *ek.* [economics], *mat.* [mathematics], *khim.* [chemistry], *sport*, etc.); (*f*) temporal (*ustar.* [obsolete], *arkh.* [archaic], *ist.* [historical], *star.* [old], *nov.* [new], etc.); (*g*) spatial (*obl.* [regional], *dial.*, *fr.* [French], etc.).

Our innovations are the following: alongside the labels *knizhn.*, *vysok.*, and *poet.* we have introduced *neobikhodn.* [formal] and *narrat.* [narrative].

The label 'neobikhodn.' [formal] indicates the level between bookish and neutral in the literary language. An example is *setovat'* [to lament, complain] set against the bookish *roptat'* and the neutral *zhalovat'sia*; also *upovat'* [to hope] set against the neutral *nadeiat'sia* [to hope]; *zabluzhdat'sia* [to err] and *obmany-vat'sia* set against the neutral *oshibat'sia*; *pleniat'* [to captivate] and the neutral *privlekat'*.

The label 'narrat.' describes the phenomenon noted independently by V. J. Apresjan and O. Iu. Boguslavskaia and represented in the synonym series *tech'* [to flow], *lit'sia*, *lit'*, *struit'sia*, *idti*, *katit'sia*, *bezhat'*, etc. (an example by V. J. Apresjan) and *golyi*, *nagoi*, *obnazhennyi*, etc. [bare—of woods or fields] (series by O. Iu. Boguslavskaia) and the like. Some members of these series have their own characteristic stylistic behaviour. Let us consider sentences such as *Krov' bezhala iz rany* [Blood flowed from the wound], *Slezy struilis' iz glaz* [Tears streamed from (my/your/his, etc.) eyes], *Ia shel mimo obnazhennykh polei* [I walked past bare fields], *Lesa stoiali obnazhennye* [The forests stood bare], etc. In ordinary speech these utterances are highly improbable (they would be replaced by *Iz rany shla krov'* [Blood came from the wound], *Ona plakala* [She was crying], *Polia byli golye* [The fields were bare], etc. Their very tone marks them as belonging to the style of literary narrative, to an artistic description of facts. In reality almost all such expressions bear the hallmarks of the literary stock phrase, which differs from the harmless linguistic cliché in being artificially elevated without motivation. Thus the label 'narrat.' serves two purposes: first, like any other label, it places the lexeme in a specific stylistic class; second, it serves as a warning against use in everyday speech.

The next scale of register—official, colloquial, substandard, etc.—was divided into two separate scales. In the first, the lexemes are arranged according to a greater or lesser degree of pedantry or casualness of speech. It seemed necessary to introduce the label 'razg. snizh.' [low colloquial], in addition to 'official' and 'colloquial'. It marks the stage beyond the merely colloquial casual, which an educated speaker may employ without risk to his linguistic reputation. Compare the low colloquial synonyms *skulit'* and *khnykat'* [to whine] with the colloquial synonym *plakat'sia* and the neutral *zhalovat'sia*.

The basis for distinguishing two scales here is the label 'prost.' [substandard]. It can easily be seen that in accepted lexicographical practice it reflects not so much casualness in speech, below the level termed 'colloquial', as the speaker's level of education and general culture. An indicator of this level is the use of the familiar *ty* and the boorish *ty* address form (to use A. A. Kholodovich's terminology) in situations where an educated speaker uses the polite *vy*. The label 'prost.' [substandard] is in reality applied to those lexemes which an educated speaker cannot use without compromising his linguistic reputation. We propose to introduce another label on the same scale, 'obikhodn.' [informal], to mark words which stand halfway between neutral and substandard vocabulary. It may be applied to such forms as *dozhidat'sia* (compared with the neutral *zhdat'* [to wait]) and *vidat'* (compared with the neutral *videt'* [to see]).

Some innovations have a direct or indirect relation to a time-scale.

Words whose sphere of usage in the modern language has been substantially reduced in comparison with an earlier period are marked 'ukhodiashch.' [obsolescent]. As an example of this concept we may cite the observations of O. Iu. Boguslavskaia from her entry for *pustoi—porozhnii* [empty]. It would be incorrect to describe the adjective *porozhnii* as archaic or obsolete in collocations such as *porozhnii stakan* [empty glass] or *porozhnii sostav* [unladen train]. In the modern language, however, it is used in a small number of lexically restricted contexts, whereas in the nineteenth century its combinatorial potential was much greater; e.g. *porozhnii stul* [empty chair] (F. M. Dostoevskii), *porozhniaia troika* [empty troika] (A. S. Pushkin).

A number of linguistic manifestations of obsolescence may be noted: (*a*) the loss of a semantic rule determining word choice and its replacement by a lexical rule. Compare the correct collocations *porozhnii sostav/vagon* [empty train/ carriage] with the dubious ?*porozhnii poezd* [empty train]; *porozhnii kholodil'nik* [empty refrigerator], *porozhnii iashchik* [empty box/crate] are permissible, while ??*porozhnii shkaf/garderob* [empty cupboard/wardrobe] and ??*porozhnii chemodan/ portfel'* [empty suitcase/briefcase] are questionable. The only general class of nouns with which the adjective *porozhnii* may combine more or less freely is the names of vessels and containers for liquids. Even within this class, however, *porozhnii stakan, porozhniaia butyl'/bochka/tsisterna, porozhnee vedro* sound perceptibly more natural than ?*porozhnii kofeinik/chainik*; (*b*) ease of co-occurrence may be greater with the names of older realia: ?*porozhnii komod* [empty chest of drawers] is preferable to \**porozhnii servant* [empty sideboard], ?*porozhnii meshok* [empty sack] to \**porozhnii riukzak* [empty rucksack]; (*c*) the stylistically autonomous status of collocations which are used as more or less set expressions; compare the substandard *porozhnii stakan* [empty glass] and the stylistically neutral *porozhnii sostav* [unladen train]; (*d*) the larger potential for non-standard usage by individual writers than with neutral lexemes; e.g. the following from

Solzhenitsyn's *GULAG Archipelago*: *Kak-to vstretilsia nam dolgii porozhnii oboz* [We once encountered a long, empty train of carts]; *Da kogda zhe Butyrki stoiali porozhnie* [When did Butyrka Prison ever stand empty?]; *On, serzhant, khotel, chtoby ia, ofitser, nes ego chemodan . . . a riadom s porozhnimi rukami shli by shest' riadovykh?* [He, the sergeant, wanted me, an officer, to carry his suitcase . . . while six private soldiers walked empty-handed beside us].

The next label related to the time axis is 'stil.' [stylized]. It is applied to obsolete lexemes which may be used in the modern language when a stylized effect is required. For example, the verb *zret'* [to see, look] is freely used in poetry: *Ty videl vse moria, ves' dal'nii krai. | I v ad ty zrel—v sebe, a posle v iavi* [You have seen all the seas and all the furthest land. | You have looked into hell, within yourself and in reality] (I. Brodskii).

The last innovation in the field of stylistic labels is also connected with the time-scale, or more precisely with the projection of this scale onto the dichotomy of 'linguistic system and usage'. In traditional nomenclature this dichotomy is represented by the label 'redk.' [rare]. It is applied to lexemes which exist in the system but are rarely encountered in actual usage. Generally speaking, two factors may account for rarity in use: either the word is in the process of dying out or, on the contrary, it is entering the language, as the linguistic system has a place for it. We propose reaffirming the use of 'rare' for the former situation and introducing the label 'potent.' [potential] for the latter.

Besides stylistic labels for synonyms, grammatical notes may also appear. For verbs, in particular, the other member of an aspectual pair is indicated: *pritvoriat'sia* (sov. [pf.] *pritvorit'sia*), *prikidyvat'sia* (sov. *prikinut'sia*), *simulirovat'* (sov. *simulirovat'*).

### 1.3. SEMANTIC GROUPS WITHIN A SERIES, AND THE EXPLICATION

Synonyms within a series are arranged in such a way as to show by the spatial distance between them the degree of semantic similarity. It is clear without any analysis, for example, that in the series *prikazyvat', velet', komandovat', rasporiazhat'sia* [to give orders] the verbs *prikazyvat'* and *velet'* form one group while *komandovat'* and *rasporiazhat'sia* form another. Similarly, the series headed *nadeiat'sia* [to hope] divides into the group *nadeiat'sia* and *upovat'* on the one hand, and *rasschityvat'* and *polagat'sia* [to rely on] on the other. The series (*byt'*) *pokhozh* [to be similar] divides into *pokhozh* and *pokhodit'* on the one hand and *napominat'* [to remind] and *smakhivat'* on the other. *Privlekat'* [to attract] divides into *privlekat', vlech',* and *uvlekat'* on the one hand and *manit'* [to tempt, beckon], *tianut',* and *pritiagivat'* on the other. It is clear that the more elements a series contains, the more grounds there are for subdivisions. The series *privyknut'* 2 [to get used to] has the following four groups: *privyknut'* 2, *svyknut'sia, priterpet'sia; prisposobit'sia, adaptirovat'sia, akklimatizirovat'sia; prinorovit'sia, priladit'sia, priteret'sia, primenit'sia; vzhit'sia, szhit'sia, prizhit'sia, osvoit'sia.*

At the end of a series an explication is provided of the common component of the meanings of the lexemes within it. We shall indicate two principles which determine the structure of this part of the dictionary entry.

(1) The explications of series are arranged so as to reflect, by the choice of meaning components, the semantic links between series which are close to one another, that is, so that their semantic similarities and differences should be immediately apparent. Let us consider from this angle the series *privyknut′* 1, *priuchit′sia, vtianut′sia, priokhotit′sia, pristrastit′sia, povadit′sia* and the foregoing series *privyknut′* 2, *svyknut′sia, priterpet′sia, prisposobit′sia*, etc. The first may be represented by the examples *On privyk/priuchilsia rano vstavat′/delat′ po utram zariadku* [He got used to getting up early/to doing morning exercises], and the second by the examples *On privyk/priterpelsia k postoiannomu shumu stankov/k novoi obstanovke* [He got used to the constant noise of the machinery/to the new situation].

The distinction between the two senses of the verb *privyknut′* (one's own actions becoming habitual versus adjustment to some external factor) is made in all Russian explanatory and synonym dictionaries. However, it remains unclear from the usual explications how these two lexemes (and therefore the synonym series which they introduce) resemble each other and how they differ. Take, for example, the following explications: *privyknut′* 1 = 'priobresti privychku (delat′ chto-l., postupat′ kakim-l. obrazom' *i t.p.*) [to acquire a habit (of doing smth., behaving in a certain way, etc.)]; *privyknut′* 2 = 'osvoit′sia, svyknut′sia s chem-l'. [to adjust, adapt to smth.] (*Malyi akademicheskii slovar′* [The Shorter Academy Dictionary]); *privykat′* 1 = 'usvaivat′, priobretat′ privychku k chemu-l.; priuchat′sia chto-l. delat′, kak-l. postupat′' [to acquire a habit; to get used to doing smth., to acting in a certain way], *privykat′* 2 = 'osvaivat′sia, svykat′sia s kem, chem-l.' [to adjust, adapt to smb., smth.] (*Bol′shoi akademicheskii slovar′* [The Great Academy Dictionary]).

By using the metalanguage and the principles of explication of meanings set forth in Chapter 8 in this volume, it is possible to resolve this difficulty in a natural way. *Privyknut′* 1='after repeating a certain action or being in a certain state many times in the course of several periods of observation, to change as a result of this in such a way that doing this or being in this state becomes the subject's norm of behaviour or existence'. *Privyknut′* 2 = 'after spending some time in unusual conditions, to change as a result of this in such a way that these conditions become the norm or cease to be perceived as unusual'.

We leave it to the reader to verify that all the semantic similarities and differences between these two synonym series are recorded in these explications in the most direct manner.

(2) If a series is headed by a lexeme which cannot be semantically broken down in the given language (*khotet′* [to want]—*zhelat′, zhazhdat′, mechtat′*), in place of an explication the standard note is provided: 'the dominant of the series is a semantic primitive'.

## 2. The Zone of Meaning

In this zone attention is focused on identifying and explicating all similarities and distinctions in content (that is, semantic, referential, pragmatic, communicative, and extralinguistic) between synonyms and on formulating the conditions in which these distinctions are wholly or to some extent neutralized, so that full or partial interchange becomes possible. Prosodic features (that is, specific aspects of phrasal stress and intonation) are usually also described here as these are very closely linked to the communicative properties of the synonyms, especially their thematic and rhematic properties.

### 2.1. SYNOPSIS

The meaning zone begins with a synopsis or short guide to the dictionary entry. It lists the semantic, pragmatic and other content features which provide the basic oppositions within a given synonym series. Each feature is illustrated by several synonyms which exhibit the greatest differences with regard to that feature. Two examples follow.

The series *pytat'sia—probovat', starat'sia, silit'sia* [to attempt]. The synonyms are distinguished by the following semantic features: (1) the scale and nature of the action the subject wishes to perform (*silit'sia* may be applied to a concrete action, usually not particularly complicated, in the process of its unfolding, *pytat'sia* to any action; *starat'sia* may be applied to both controllable and uncontrollable actions, *probovat'* only to controllable actions); (2) the amount of effort and the objective need for it (*probovat'* implies the least effort, *silit'sia* the most; moreover the latter implies that the effort is essential because the action is objectively difficult to perform); (3) the possibility or impossibility of isolating a single application of effort (in the case of *probovat'*, individual attempts may be isolated, but not in the case of *starat'sia*); (4) the possibility of performing an action and the probability of achieving a result (in the case of *silit'sia* it is often impossible to perform the action itself, and therefore the desired result is hardly ever achieved, while in the case of *starat'sia* the action is more frequently performed and the desired result achieved); (5) the cause of possible failure (in the case of *pytat'sia* this may lie in an incorrect choice of means, while in the case of *silit'sia* the subject lacks the resources); (6) the subject's readiness to try alternative ways of achieving the result if the first attempt should fail (*pytat'sia* and *probovat'* admit other courses of action, while *starat'sia* and *silit'sia* do not); (7) the motivation for the action and the subject's attitude to it (in the case of *pytat'sia* the subject always wishes to perform a planned action, while in the case of *probovat'* he may wish to establish whether it can be performed at all or whether the result will be pleasing, etc.); (8) the presence of an external observer (more apparent in *silit'sia* than in *probovat'*).

The series *nadeiat'sia* [to hope; to depend on]—*upovat'* [to hope; to place one's trust in], *rasschityvat'* [to count on], *polagat'sia* [to rely]. The synonyms are distinguished by the following semantic features: (1) does the subject's inner state presuppose emotion? (It does in the case of *nadeiat'sia* and *upovat'*, but not in the case of *rasschityvat'* or *polagat'sia*); (2) what underlies the state of mind—an opinion (*nadeiat'sia*), a belief (*upovat'*), reasoning (*rasschityvat'*), or trust and previous experience (*polagat'sia*)? (3) what is the nature and scale of the force with which the subject's hopes are linked? (*Upovat'* can only apply to some higher power external to the subject, or to other people whose potential to act is much greater than the subject's); (4) what is the intensity of the expectation? (It is greater in the case of *upovat'* than in those of *nadeiat'sia* and *rasschityvat'*); (5) how sure is the subject that the desired event will come to pass and how far is it removed in time from the moment of observation? (*Polagat'sia* implies greater certainty than any other synonym in the series, and the event is expected to occur in the fairly near future); (6) what is the subject's current situation? (It may be any situation in the case of *nadeiat'sia*, but an unfavourable or grave one in the case of *upovat'*); (7) what other mental states accompany the given state? (With *nadeiat'sia* there is a measure of general optimism.)

## 2.2. SIMILARITIES AND DISTINCTIONS IN CONTENT BETWEEN SYNONYMS

The synopsis is immediately followed by the main body of the entry, describing the various groups, subgroups, and individual members of the series isolated on the basis of some feature or combination of features.

The description is arranged in a standardized but not especially rigid pattern. The standardization relates to the composition, the way in which the material is presented, and the ways in which synonyms are grouped within the series, not to the language of description. In this zone, unlike the explication zone, the language of description is free in the sense that there are no constraints on the means of expression (beyond a number of limitations on special linguistic terminology, which is employed in closely prescribed limits and must be explained in the theoretical introduction to the Dictionary). Here any form of paraphrase may be used, even metaphors if these are a short cut to understanding.[2] The

---

[2] Of course, not all metaphors are valuable, only those which may be described as 'illuminating'. Boris Pasternak brilliantly said of these, 'Metaphors are the natural consequence of the finite nature of human life and the infinite nature of man's plans. Given this disparity, man is forced to look at things with the acuity of an eagle and express himself in instant and immediately intelligible illuminations. This is what poetry is. Metaphors are the shorthand of a great personality, the stenography of his spirit' (Pasternak 1982: 394). Naturally we make no claim to anything said by Pasternak, except one thing: we have indeed tried to resort to metaphor only when it really does shorten the path to communicating essential knowledge. It is useful to emphasize this once again because cryptographic metaphors are ever more widely used to explicate meanings. These do not clarify complex meanings, but encipher simple ones. See the following metaphors from Baranov *et al.* (1993): *s trudom* [with difficulty] ≈ *beg s prepiatstviiami* [obstacle race]; *v samom dele* [really] ≈ *ot zabluzhdeniia k istine* [from error towards truth]; *na samom dele* [indeed] ≈ *pravda zhizni* [the truth of life]; *v obshchem* [in general] ≈ *iskusstvo otbrosit' lishnee* [the art of casting aside the superfluous]; *v tselom* [on the whole] ≈ *bol'shoe viditsia na rasstoianii* [the big picture can be seen at a distance]; *v printsipe* [theoretically] ≈ *poiski ideala* [the quest for the ideal], etc.

description should satisfy only one requirement—clarity in setting forth all similarities and differences in content between the synonyms.

This may appear to ignore a more natural way of compiling a dictionary of synonyms. Why is it not sufficient simply to write out their explications one after another to demonstrate all their similarities and differences? In view of such doubts it is desirable to cite a number of considerations which support the method of description chosen here.

First: if we do no more than give explications, the task of forming an accurate picture of the synonyms is handed back to the reader. He himself must perform all the comparative work, using a semi-finished product, which is all that the explications of the words can provide.

Second: some of the similarities and differences between synonyms, for example, in their pragmatic and referential aspects, their connotations and other cultural associations, would still be omitted because many such properties are usually described outside the explication proper.

Third, and most important: the combination of purely semantic description, that is, of explication in a relatively formalized semantic metalanguage, with more loosely constructed lexicographic portraits of words is justified ontologically.

Explication is only one form of paraphrase of the linguistic unit, though it is the one accorded the highest status. It performs the following four functions: (a) it explains the meaning of the given linguistic unit; (b) it indicates its place in the semantic system of the language; (c) it represents a semantic rule applicable in the movement from a deep syntactic representation of the utterance to its semantic representation and vice versa; (d) it serves as a basis for the rules of semantic interaction between the given unit and other units within the utterance.

Only an explication can perform functions (b), (c), and (d) and thus serve the needs of linguistic theory. However, the main function—the metalinguistic function of explaining the meaning of the given unit—may be performed by other paraphrases, as long as they really do progress from the unknown to the known. The same ends may be served by other means of conveying linguistic knowledge. For example, in some cases simply pointing to the realia represented by the lexemes will suffice. In actual everyday practice speakers employ these methods when it is necessary to communicate to the interlocutor what a word means. In this way they perform their metalinguistic activity.

This, in essence, exhausts the broad range of descriptive methods applied in describing the content of the linguistic units in this zone of the entry.[3]

---

[3] A combination of the two approaches is valuable not only in a synonym dictionary. It should be an obligatory principle in any description of the semantics of natural languages which claims to be exhaustive. Only then will a definitive conclusion be reached in the prolonged debate over whether circularity is permissible in describing meanings: it is not permissible in explications, but there is nothing to prevent recourse to it in freer explanations of meaning. Explications model a scientific linguistic knowledge of language, while freer paraphrase, like any other means of explaining meaning, models the metalinguistic practice of speakers.

We move on to a more detailed discussion of the information stored in the meaning zone proper. The greater part of it is devoted to possible distinctions between synonyms.

Distinctions in the assertive components of meaning are regarded as having greatest importance. In the series *risovat'*, *zarisovyvat'*, *pisat'*, *malevat'* [to draw, to paint] one of the differences relates to the fact that *zarisovyvat'* always implies an outward object, while *risovat'*, *pisat'*, and *malevat'* may be performed without it.

Although on the whole assertive elements of lexical meanings are clearer and less subtle layers of sense than modal frames, frames of observation, and various kinds of evaluative and motivational components, in some cases they too are less obvious and are very difficult to capture. Such situations are our special concern since the existing explanatory and synonym dictionaries are least articulate on these subjects.

Let us explain what we mean. When processing large corpora one fairly quickly forms an idea of large and small lexicographical types and of what kind of semantic elements need to be sought in a given synonym series. For example, in verbal series most semantic features which distinguish the verbs have to do with their actant structure: the distinctions usually bear on the properties of their subjects, objects, addressees, instruments, means, ends, place, time, and so forth. In noun series denoting natural objects we should first seek distinctions in features of form, colour, size, internal structure, application, and so forth. In noun series denoting artefacts, distinctions in the function and purpose of the objects are added to the above. In series of verbs and nouns denoting emotions, we should expect distinctions bearing on the stimulus evoking the emotion, the intellectual evaluation of the stimulus by the subject, the nature, intensity, and depth of the emotion, the desires it engenders, its outward manifestations, and so forth. These are the typical distinctions.

On occasion, however, one has to deal with less typical distinctions, for example distinctions in temporal parameters in nouns, adjectives, and adverbs not derived from verbs, or distinctions of property in verbs. In order to clarify this matter, we shall make use of the concept of proper and non-proper meaning, generalizing it for lexical meanings.[4]

Usually the proper meaning of a given grammeme is the one which coincides with its name. Thus the proper meaning of the grammeme PROSH [past] is an event which occurred in the past, that is, prior to the moment of speech, and the meaning of a future event represented in phrases based on past tense forms such as *Do svidaniia, ia poshel/poekhal/pobezhal* [Goodbye, I'm leaving] is non-proper.

Extending these concepts and this terminology to lexical meanings, we shall

---

[4] 'Proper' (Russ. 'sobstvennoe') in this context has the sense of 'prototypical, principal, inherent' in the given lexical unit, while 'non-proper' (Russ. 'nesobstvennoe') means 'transferred', 'shifted', inherent in a different lexical unit.

say that those senses which are typical (more precisely, prototypical) of the lexical meanings of a given part of speech are proper to it and non-proper to other parts of speech. In particular, temporal components as inalienable attributes of an action will be proper to a verb and non-proper to a noun, while the meaning of property will be proper to an adjective and non-proper to a verb.

It may be stated that, other things being equal, non-proper components in the lexical meanings of various parts of speech are harder to identify than proper ones, that they are harder to master practically, and that they are of greatest theoretical interest.

The adverb *zaprosto* [with ease] differs from its synonym *legko* in that it shifts the designated action into the future with reference to the moment of observation and into the realm of possibility rather than actual performance. Compare the sentences *On zaprosto vse ob"iasnit/perevedet/nachertit* [he will explain/ translate/outline everything easily] with the dubious and less natural *?on zaprosto vse ob"iasnil/perevel/nachertil* [he explained/translated/outlined everything easily]. It is clear that these constraints do not apply to *legko*.

A similar shift into the future with reference to the moment of observation (which itself may be located in the past or the present) is implied in the meaning of the word *pogibel'* [doom]. Like its more colloquial and substandard synonyms *kryshka, khana, kaiuk*, etc., it never denotes a *fait accompli*, only a forthcoming event, foretold or foreseeable, as in the classic example from Pushkin: *Tak vot gde tailas' pogibel' moia! Mne smertiiu kost' ugrozhala!* [So that was where my doom lay hidden! The bones held the threat of my death!]. Cf. also *Nam teper' kryshka/khana/kaiuk* [It's all up with us now]. The analogues of *pogibel'*, the nouns *smert', gibel', konchina*, etc. [death], on the other hand, may denote a *fait accompli*.

The adjective *blizkii* [near], in its temporal sense, differs from its synonym *nedalekii* in referring exclusively to the future, for example *blizkoe budushchee* [near future], *blizkii ot"ezd* [forthcoming departure], *blizkaia vesna* [approaching spring]. *Nedalekii*, on the other hand, may apply to both the future and the past, for example *v etot uzhe nedalekii den'* [on that day which is now not far off] and *v etot eshche nedalekii den'* [on that still recent day]. In the case of *nedalekii*, of course, location in the future or past is clarified by the words *etot* [this], *uzhe* [already] and *tot* [that], *eshche* [still] respectively but is not determined by these. In this connection we may note that the same neutrality, that is, the ability to apply to both the future and the past, also distinguishes *dalekii* [distant] from its antonym *blizkii*. However, in the context of the word *dalekii* the particles *uzhe* and *eshche* engender diametrically opposed effects: compare *den' eshche dalek* [daylight is still far off] and *noch' uzhe daleka* [night is already far behind us].

If such elusive elements of meaning are found even in the assertive part of the explications, similar covert semantic components should be expected in the more finely organized layers of sense. These include modal frames and frames of ob-

servation, evaluation, presupposition, motivation, and so forth. They are especially typical of the lexical groups which are dealt with under the name of minor
lexicographic types in Chapter 10. We shall consider a few examples.

In the synonym series *vyiti* [to turn out, to happen to be]—*poluchit'sia*,
*vypast'*, *vydat'sia* the first two imply human agency in the occurrence of an object or situation: *Roman vyshel/poluchilsia neplokhoi* [the novel turned out quite
well]. The latter two refer to situations arising by chance: *Den' vypal trudnyi* [it
turned out to be a hard day], *Leto vydalos' zharkoe* [the summer turned out to
be hot]. These are of particular interest. Both describe a situation in which one
of a number of equally probable outcomes happens to occur. *Vypast'*, however,
makes it possible to see the outcome as favourable to somebody's activities, as
a hindrance to them, or affecting human beings in some other way. *Vydat'sia*
brings out a quite different aspect, the fact that the outcome differs from other
equally probable outcomes in some of its particulars. This is why it would not
be usual to say *"Leto vydalos' obyknovennoe* [the summer turned out to be ordi-
nary]; cf. the correct *Leto vydalos' neobyknovennoe* [the summer turned out to
be extraordinary]. On the other hand, this outcome is considered much more
objectively, that is, not in connection with the activities of any particular person
but as a fact of nature granted equally to all.

*Vit'sia* and *viliat'* are synonymous in the sense which may be formulated as
follows: 'to extend across a locality, with many bends' (of roads, paths, streams,
and similar elongated objects). The usual dictionary definitions of these meanings
create no grounds for discerning semantic distinctions between sentences such
as *Doroga v'etsia mezhdu kholmami* and *Doroga viliaet mezhdu kholmami* [the
road meanders through the hills]. And yet there are differences, and these consist
in (*a*) differing appraisals of what is essentially the same reality; and (*b*) the
stance of the observer. In the former case there is a positive aesthetic appraisal
of the object (the landscape is picturesque) and the observer is detached or seem-
ingly detached from the scene. In the latter there is a negative utilitarian appraisal (the road is presented as ill-suited to passage on foot or by transport) and
the observer is a user of the road: he is the one travelling along it.

*Shutia* and *igraiuchi*, which are synonymous in the meaning 'with ease; with
no visible effort', differ from each other in their modal frame. In the former case
(*Paren' shutia podnial tiazhelennyi meshok* [the lad picked up a very heavy sack
with ease]) the speaker does not voice any presupposition with regard to the
thoughts or feelings of the subject of the action. In the latter (*Paren' igraiuchi
podnial tiazhelennyi meshok* [the lad playfully picked up a very heavy sack]), a
view is expressed: the speaker believes that the subject realizes how easily he can
perform a difficult action and that he derives pleasure from this. We may also
note the pictorial vividity with which the subject is portrayed here.

*Zhdat'* [to wait] differs from some other members of its synonym series in the
referential status of the noun group which serves as its direct object. *Podzhidat'*
usually has a definite person as its object, while *zhdat'* may apply to any individ-

ual of the generic class denoted by the respective noun: *Ona vsiu zhizn' zhdala zhenikha* [she waited all her life for a suitor].

Another type of fine distinction described in our dictionary is that between the connotations or associations of synonyms. Cf. pairs of the type *lakei* [lackey] (connotations of subservience, servility, and self-abasement) and *sluga* (connotations of loyalty); *osel* [donkey] (connotations of stupidity and stubbornness) and *ishak* [donkey] (connotations of uncomplaining diligence); *pis'mena* [letters of the alphabet] (connotations of something elevated, important and mysterious) and *bukvy* (no connotations).

We shall restrict ourselves to the above examples. Only the dictionary itself can give an idea of the nature and type of the subtle and barely perceptible distinctions between some of the synonyms to which particular attention is drawn in it.

### 2.3. PROSODY AND THE COMMUNICATIVE PROPERTIES OF SYNONYMS

In a number of other works (e.g. Chapter 9 in this volume), consideration has been given to certain cases of lexicalized prosody and communicative properties. It was noted, in particular, that the factive verbs *ponimat'* [understand], *znat'* [know], and *videt'* [see, in the sense of 'understand'] may, in neutral affirmative sentences, bear the main phrasal stress, regardless of their position in the sentence, and therefore belong to the rhematic part of the utterance. Thus they differ from the prototypical putative verbs *schitat'* [believe], *polagat'* [suppose], and *nakhodit'* [find, think], which in comparable conditions (not at the end of a sentence; not in modal or concessive contexts) cannot bear the main stress and belong to the theme of the utterance.

Let us examine some further instructive examples of instances of lexicalized prosody and communicative properties which have a more direct bearing on a dictionary of synonyms.

The principal semantic distinction between the synonyms *khotet'* [want] and *zhelat'* lies in the fact that *khotet'* denotes an active wish, presupposing the will to implement it: *plokh tot soldat, kotoryi ne khochet stat' generalom* [It's a poor soldier who doesn't want to be a general]; *Khochu byt' vladychitsei morskoiu!* [I want to be queen of the seas!]; *Ia khochu, chtoby mne seichas zhe, siiu sekundu, vernuli moego liubovnika, mastera—skazala Margarita, i litso ee iskazila sudoroga* ['I want to have my lover, the Master, returned to me immediately, this very second,' said Margarita, and a spasm distorted her face] (M. Bulgakov); *A on eshche bilsia. On nastoichivo borolsia so smert'iu, ni za chto ne khotel poddat'sia ei, tak neozhidanno i grubo navalivsheisia na nego* [But he went on resisting. He struggled doggedly with death, not wanting at any price to succumb to death, which had so unexpectedly and crudely struck at him] (I. Bunin). *Zhelat'*, on the other hand, especially in the imperfective, signifies only a wish, with no suggestion of active will: *Im [Rudinu, Karavaevu] on protivopolagaet liudei, umeiushchikh ne tol'ko zhelat', no i khotet'* [Against these people (Rudin and Karavaev) he sets those who are able not only to wish but to want] (A. F. Koni); *U kazhdogo, u kazhdogo v dushe bylo to, chto zastavliaet cheloveka zhit' i zhelat' sladkogo obmana zhizni!* [Each one of them had in his heart the thing that compels a man to live and wish for the sweet illusion of life!] (I. Bunin); *Ot vsei dushi zhelaiu, chtoby oni [prazdniki] skoree konchilis'* [With all my heart I wish they (the holidays) would end as soon as possible] (M. Bulgakov); *Doktor trevozhilsia za etu zhizn' i zhelal ei tselosti i sokhrannosti* [The doctor felt concern for this life and wished it to remain intact] (B. Pasternak).

For the reason set out above, the meaning of wishing in *khotet'* is closely bound up with the meaning of intent. Contexts may be cited which favour the expression of a wish or that of intent. Precisely these contexts are of particular interest from the standpoint of prosody and the communicative properties of lexemes.

In the expression of a wish proper, the verb *khotet'* is typically part of the rheme and, in accordance with the general rules of communicative organization of an utterance, bears the main phrasal or emphatic stress: ↑*Khotite vypit' chto-nibud'?* [Would you like something to drink?]; *Ia ↓↓khochu poekhat' v Moskvu* [I want to go to Moscow]; *Bol'she ia ne ↓khochu lgat'. Ia ne ↓khochu, chtoby u nego navsegda ostalos' v pamiati, chto ia ubezhala ot nego noch'iu* [I don't want to tell lies any more. I don't want him to remember forever that I ran away from him at night] (M. Bulgakov).

In the expression of intent (not only in the case of *khotet'*) the thematic position without phrasal stress is typical. Among the lexical and semantic conditions favouring the expression of intent with the verb *khotet'* are: (*a*) a context including verbs of physical action in the perfective: *Ia khochu po doroge zaekhat' v institut* [I want to call in at the institute on the way]; *Lara khotela ubit' cheloveka, po Pashinym poniatiiam, bezrazlichnogo ei* [Lara wanted to kill a man to whom, as far as Pasha could see, she was indifferent] (B. Pasternak); (*b*) a context including the particles *uzhe* and *bylo*, indicating a decision not to undertake an action when it was on the point of being performed: *On khotel bylo ⟨uzhe khotel⟩ vykliuchit' ratsiiu, no peredumal* [He was about to turn off the walkie-talkie, but changed his mind]; (*c*) a context including temporal words and expressions such as *teper', kak raz, tol'ko chto, pered etim, posle etogo, potom* in syntactic constructions expressing the idea of events in succession: *Ia tol'ko chto khotel soobshchit' vam, chto sobranie otmeniaetsia* [I was about to tell you the meeting is cancelled]; *Ia kak raz khotela poprosit' tebia ob"iasnit' mne kvadratnye uravneniia* [I was about to ask you to explain quadratic equations to me](B. Pasternak); *Koe-kakie materialy ia uzhe sobral i teper' khochu poekhat' v Moskvu* [I have already collected some materials and now want to go to Moscow]; *Ia khochu porabotat' v arkhivakh, pobyvat' na mestakh sobytii i pogovorit' s ikh uchastnikami* [I want to do some work in the archives, visit the scene and talk to the participants]; *Khoteli pet'—i ne smogli, | Khoteli vstat'—dugoi poshli* [They

wanted to sing but couldn't, | they wanted to get up, and were bent double]
(O. Mandel'shtam). It can easily be seen that in all the above contexts *khotet'*
has the sense of intent and lacks phrasal stress.

We shall take one further example, the synonyms *privyknut'* and *povadit'sia*
[to get used to].

Let us compare the sentences *Ia privyk vstavat'* ↓ *rano* [I have grown used to
getting up early] (with the usual phrasal stress on the last word) and *Ia* ↓ *privyk
vstavat' rano* [I have grown used to getting up early] (with the main phrasal
stress on *privyk*). The first sentence has the status of a simple statement of a
habit, containing no suggestion of forthcoming difficulties or any interpretation
of the fact of early rising in the past. The second sentence, with its rhematic
*privyknut'*, has more extensive illocutionary potential. It may be used to refer to
past experience of early rising as a guarantee that in a forthcoming situation this
will not be difficult (it has the function of reassurance). On the other hand it
may be used to explain why the speaker appears so fresh at such an early hour.

The synonymous verb *povadit'sia* in neutral conditions cannot bear the main
phrasal stress and therefore cannot occupy the position of rheme. A characteristic syntactic property of this verb also correlates well with this: like most thematic verbs, in particular all existential verbs, it may precede the grammatical
subject of the sentence: *Povadilsia medved' na paseku* [The bear got into the
habit of visiting the apiary] (for more detail on this see § 4.3).

It is curious that for the antonym of *privyknut'*, *otvyknut'* [to grow unused
to], the main phrasal stress is the norm: *Ia* ↓ *otvyk vstavat' rano*. Utterances such
as these, unlike those of the type *Ia* ↓ *privyk vstavat' rano*, are communicatively
neutral. It is reasonable to suppose that this redistribution of the role of
prosodic highlighting with antonyms is based on some general rule (most likely
it is related to negation in the meaning of the antonym).

## 2.4. PRAGMATIC AND EXTRALINGUISTIC CONDITIONS

Let us consider the lexeme *viset'* [to hang (intrans.)], which may be explicated
as follows: 'to be placed on a vertical surface X, being attached to X and lying
along it without any support from below'. It can be seen in sentences of the type
*V prikhozhei ran'she viselo zerkalo* [a mirror used to hang in the hall]; *Na stene
visit kartina/kover/karta/nebol'shoi posudnyi shkafchik* [a picture/rug/map/small
dresser hangs on the wall]; *Na grudi u nego viseli ordena i medali* [he had orders
and medals pinned to his chest].

Of particular interest to us are the uses of this lexeme when it signifies the
result of an object A being attached to the surface of another object B by means
of an adhesive applied to the whole surface of object A. This situation is usually
described by a passive form of the verb *nakleit'* [to stick, glue], but may also be
described by the verb *viset'*, which in this case is synonymous with the form *byt'
nakleen(nym)* [to be glued]: *Na stenu nakleen list bumagi* [a sheet of paper has

been stuck on the wall], *Na stene visit list bumagi* [a sheet of paper is hanging on the wall]. The second verb is selected when the object attached is seen as bearing information and the first verb in all other cases.

The rule formulated here is not semantic. The point is that the way an object is used in a specific situation may not coincide with its prototypical function. In order to use the verb *viset'* correctly it is not enough to know its dictionary definition and the dictionary definition of the noun denoting the attached object. It is essential to possess some extralinguistic information about the purpose that object serves in the given situation.

Thus Mendeleev's periodic table or a poster, even if attached to a wall by glue spread all over their surfaces but used in the accepted manner, *visit* [hangs] on that wall. On the other hand a clean sheet of Whatman paper of exactly the same size and fixed to the wall in exactly the same way but for some unknown purpose is better described as *nakleen* [stuck] to it.

If, however, we know that in the given situation the poster or the periodic table is being used as wallpaper, we will say that they are *nakleeny* [stuck] to the wall. On the other hand, if a clean sheet of paper has been stuck to a wall so that notes can be written on it we can say that it *visit* [hangs] there.

## 2.5. NEUTRALIZATION

Although neutralization of distinctions between synonyms, with the subsequent possibility of mutual replacement, is not considered an essential property, instances of this type are most carefully taken into account in the synonym dictionary. Particular attention is devoted to the formulation of contextual and situational neutralization conditions.

The difference between *zhalovat'sia* [to complain] and its closest synonym *setovat'* consists in the fact that the former usually presupposes some specific deviation from the norm in the life of the subject and that this deviation may be eliminated. The subject of the verb *zhalovat'sia* communicates to someone that he is usually in a better position than at present. By stating this he wishes to draw other people's attention to his plight, usually with the hope that it will evoke sympathy or encourage them to help him. Less often it is used to give vent to his feelings. For example: *Kak-to raz prosnulsia on, i bylo emu sovsem khudo. Pozhalovalsia:—Kolotit vsego. Ia dal emu rubl'* [Once he woke up feeling absolutely dreadful. He complained that he was shaking all over with fever. I gave him a rouble] (S. Dovlatov); *Romashev leg na spinu i nachal stonat' i zhalovat'sia na sil'nye boli* [Romashov lay down on his back and started groaning and complaining of severe pains] (V. Kaverin); *[Sasha Semenov] zhalovalsia na monotonnost' svoego sushchestvovaniia—obychno sil'no vypiv i govoria ob etom pochti plachushchim golosom* [(Sasha Semenov) complained of the tedium of his life—usually after a bout of drinking and speaking of it in an almost tearful voice] (G. Gazdanov); *[Inzhener] zhalovalsia, chto ona [zhena] vtravila ego v eto delo, ona zhe i otreklas' ot nego srazu posle aresta* [(The engineer) complained that she (his wife) had involved him in the affair and renounced him immediately after his arrest] (Iu. Daniel').

The closest synonym to *zhalovat'sia* is *setovat'*, whose meaning, however, is considerably more restricted. It is most commonly used of a state of affairs which hampers the subject's normal activity or causes him unhappiness. Moreover it may usually be supposed that there is no reason to expect any improvement in the situation: *on (po)setoval na to, chto zloe nachalo v cheloveke chereschur sil'no* [He lamented the fact that evil in man is too powerful]; cf. the incorrect *\*on (po)zhalovalsia na to, chto zloe nachalo v cheloveke chereschur sil'no.* Compare also the following: *Sestra setovala na bisernost' moego pocherka* [My sister complained about my tiny handwriting] (most likely, without any hope that my writing might improve); *V kazhdom pis'me sestra zhalovalas', chto ei trudno razbirat' moi pocherk* [in every letter my sister complained how difficult it was to read my writing] (most likely expecting me to write more clearly). The motivation of the utterance is less an expectation of real help than the hope of understanding. Compare: *Aleksandr Viktorovich setuet na to, chto militsiia nynche dorogo beret* [Aleksandr Viktorovich laments the fact that the police now take a lot of money in bribes] (*Stolitsa*, No. 29, 1992); *My neredko setuem, chto nashi lidery nedostatchno tsivilizovanno vedut sebia na mezhdunarodnoi arene* [we often lament the fact that our leaders behave in an insufficiently civilized manner in the international arena] (*Izvestiia*, 19 Nov. 1992).

Given the impossibility of remaking the world, the feelings most commonly associated with *setovanie* [lamenting] are grief and regret. The verb may therefore be applied to one's own unsuccessful actions. Here *setovat'* approaches the verb *sokrushat'sia* [to grieve], e.g. *Eks-chempion osobenno setoval na svoi grubeishii promakh v 11-i vstreche* [the ex-champion particularly regretted his most egregious blunder in the eleventh meeting] (A. Suetin). The synonym *zhalovat'sia* cannot be used in these contexts.

In some cases the synonyms *setovat'* and *zhalovat'sia* come quite close in meaning, although the distinction is not fully lost. In particular, they draw close in modal constructions signifying the futility of complaints and in contexts dealing with an abnormal state of health: *Chego popustu zhalovat'sia/setovat'?* [what's the good of pointless complaining?]; *On po vremenam derzhalsia za serdtse, byl bleden, zhalovalsia/setoval na donimaiushchuiu ego bolezn'* [from time to time he clutched at his heart, looked pale and complained of the illness that was wearing him down].

In concluding this section we shall consider the conditions in which the distinctions between *dozhidat'sia* and *zhdat'* [to wait for] are neutralized. In this pair *dozhidat'sia* has greater semantic specificity. It signifies patient, purposeful, and possibly protracted expectation of some event in a particular place, usually producing a desired result: *Nakonets my dozhdalis' ob"ektivnogo obsuzhdeniia ekologicheskikh problem* [at last we have achieved an objective discussion of ecological problems]; *Odinnadtsat'! I rovno chas, kak ia dozhidaius' vashego probuzh-deniia* [Eleven o'clock! That makes exactly one hour that I've been waiting for you to wake up] (M. Bulgakov); *A Sergei Lemeshev, samyi znamenityi tenor Rossii, radovalsia kak rebenok, chto khot' na zakate svoei kar'ery dozhdalsia vozmozhnosti, uspel zapisat'sia v svoei liubimoi partii Lenskogo* [and Sergei Lemeshev, Russia's most famous tenor, was as delighted as a child that, though in the twilight of his career, he had lived to have the opportunity to be recorded in his favourite role, as Lenskii] (G. Vishnevskaia).

Most of these features are neutralized in the imperfective in contexts describing a single act of waiting for a specific event which is to happen in a specific place when neither the process of waiting nor the event itself are specified. In such cases *dozhidat'sia* is at its closest to the dominant of the series and, leaving aside stylistic considerations, these two synonyms become mutually interchangeable: *V kholle prositeli dozhidalis'/zhdali nachala priema* [in the hall the petitioners were waiting for consulting hours to begin].

## 2.6. NOTES

The meaning zone concludes with an optional subzone of notes, in which attention is given to the following three topics: (*a*) synonyms not included for whatever reason in the given series (in most cases a lexeme is liable to be excluded because it is peripheral, obsolete, outside normal usage, and so forth); (*b*) other meanings of the words discussed, close to the one under consideration in the given series; (*c*) other words with meanings similar to the one considered in the given series. Some examples follow.

The series *dumat'—schitat', polagat', nakhodit', rassmatrivat',* etc. [to think, consider] has the following notes.

NOTE 1: In the nineteenth century and early twentieth century the verbs *pochitat', myslit',* and *mnit'* had senses synonymous with *schitat'* [to think, consider]: *Te, kotorye pochitaiut sebia zdeshnimi aristokratami, primknulis' k nei* [those who saw themselves as the local aristocracy adhered to her] (M. Lermontov); *Otkryt' im [antroposofam] glaza na Rossiiu pochital on [Belyi] svoeiu missiei, a sebia—poslom ot Rossii k antroposofii* [he (Belyi) regarded it as his mission to open their (the anthroposophers') eyes to Russia, and he regarded himself as Russia's emissary to anthroposophy] (V. Khodasevich); *Sam zhe Bunin chudovishchem sebia ne mnil* [Bunin himself did not see himself as a monster] (Z. Shakhovskaia); *Ne to, chto mnite vy, priroda, | Ne slepok, ne bezdushnyi lik* [Nature is not what you suppose it to be; it is no dummy and no soulless effigy] (F. I. Tiutchev).

In modern substandard speech and slang the lexeme *derzhat'* [to hold] occurs in evaluative use as a synonym for *schitat',* mostly in collocations of the type *derzhat' kogo-l. za duraka/za polnogo idiota* [to take smb. for a fool/a complete idiot]; e.g. *Ia v tochnosti ponimaiu, za kogo ikh i nas derzhat. Ne za podrostkov*

*—za idiotov. Za DEBILOV. Kotorye v kuple-prodazhe eshche chto-to sekut, no v vysokikh materiiakh—nichego* [I understand perfectly what they take us and them for. Not for juveniles. For idiots. For cretins, who might just about be able to manage buying and selling things but can't cope with anything higher] (*Stolitsa*, No. 3, 1992).

NOTE 2: The verb *dumat'* has a substandard meaning close to the one under consideration here: 'to suspect, consider guilty of smth.'. This meaning manifests itself in the construction *dumat' na kogo-libo*, as in *Neuzhto ty do sikh por ne znal, kto na tebia dones?—Net, ia vse na brata dumal* [Did you really not know until now who informed on you?—No, I suspected my brother all the time.]

NOTE 3: Verbs signifying intellectual activity such as *ponimat'*, *reshat'*, *prinimat'*, etc. have a wide range of meanings similar to the one under consideration here, e.g. *A. Solzhenitsyn slovno ne dopuskaet, chto te, kto ponimaet sud'by otechestva i zadachi literatury inache, chem on, mogut byt' khot' skol'ko-nibud' pravy, khot' skol'ko-nibud' dostoiny uvazheniia* [A. Solzhenitsyn appears not to allow that those who have a different understanding from his of the destiny of their country and the purpose of literature may be in any degree right or deserving of the smallest degree of respect] (V. Vozdvizhenskii); *S chego eto vy reshili, chto ia na nei zhenius'?* [what makes you so sure I'm going to marry her?]; *Oni prinimaiut menia ne za togo, kto ia est'* [they don't take me for what I am] (A. Kabakov).

In the series *zhalovat'sia, setovat', roptat', plakat'sia, nyt', skulit', khnykat'* [to complain] the following notes are provided:

NOTE 1: In the nineteenth century and early twentieth the verb *peniat'* belonged in this series; see outdated uses such as *S svoei storony on na pomeshchenie ne zhalovalsia, a tol'ko penial ne edu* [He for his part did not complain about his accommodation, only about the food] (M. E. Saltykov-Shchedrin); *Oni peniali na svoiu sud'bu i govorili, chto vot tri nochi podriad kabany traviat pashni i ogorody* [They reproached their fate and said that for three nights running wild boar had been damaging their arable land and market gardens] (V. K. Arsen'ev). In the modern language *peniat'* is used mostly in the imperative (often in the expression *peniai[te] na sebia*) [blame yourself] or modal constructions of equivalent meaning, in the sense 'it must be accepted that the culprit is X and X alone'; e.g. *Esli slova svoego ne sderzhit, pust' na sebia peniaet!* [if he doesn't keep his word he'll have only himself to blame!]; *Nechego na zerkalo peniat', koli rozha kriva* [if your mug looks crooked it's no good blaming the mirror] (proverb); *Sobstvenno, reshaete svoiu sud'bu vy: poslushaete narkoma—vy spaseny, ne poslushaete—peniaite na sebia!* [strictly speaking, you yourself decide your future: if you take the People's Commissar's advice you'll be saved; if you don't you'll have only yourself to blame!] (A. Avtorkhanov); *Rasskazhi, s kakoi tsel'iu agitiruesh' naselenie? . . . Skazhesh'—prostit. Net—peniai na sebia* [Tell him why you've been stirring up the population. If you do tell you'll be forgiven. . . . If you don't it's your own look-out] (Iu. Dombrovskii).

NOTE 2: The verb *zhalovat'sia* has a special medical use close to the one at issue: 'communicate to a doctor the symptoms of a possible illness': e.g. *On [doktor] menia vyslushival, vzdykhal i zatem sprosil: na chto vy zhaluetes'?—Ni na chto,—otvetil ia* [He (the doctor) examined me, sighed and then said, 'What are you complaining of?' 'Nothing,' I replied] (G. Gazdanov). This could be paraphrased by the conversive of *zhalovat'sia*, the verb *bespokoit'* [to worry]: *Na chto vy zhaluetes'? = Chto vas bespokoit?* [what's troubling you?].

In addition, *zhalovat'sia* has the following closely related meaning: 'to report to a person in authority the reprehensible behaviour of a third party with the aim of having justice restored by the addressee': *zhalovat'sia v direktsiiu na samoupravstvo glavnogo inzhenera* [to complain to the management about the chief engineer taking the law into his own hands]; *zhalovat'sia nachal'niku aeroporta na plokhoe obsluzhivanie* [to complain to the airport director about poor service]; *[Lenskii] zhalovalsia moei materi, chto my s bratom—inostrantsy, barchuki i snoby, i patologicheski ravnodushny k Goncharovu, Grigorovichu, Maminu-Sibiriaku* [(Lenskii) complained to my mother that my brother and I were foreigners, lordlings, and snobs who were pathologically indifferent to Goncharov, Grigorovich, and Mamin-Sibiriak] (V. Nabokov).

If the valency of the topic in the construction *zhalovat'sia (komu-libo) na chto-libo* is a word denoting an action, the meaning of the verb depends on the interpretation of the valency of the addressee. In *Uchitel'nitsa zhalovalas' na povedenie novichka* [the teacher (f.) complained about the new boy's behaviour], for example, the verb has one sense if the addressee is a colleague, but another if the addressee is the headmaster or a parent of the pupil. Similar ambiguity may occur in real texts. Note the example *Pravda, nakhodilis' i zavistniki, kotorye zhalovalis', chto genial'nye eksperimenty velikogo cheloveka nikto ne mozhet povtorit'. Zhalobshchikam vpolne rezonno otvechali, chto eksperimenty potomu-to i genial'nye, chto ikh nikto ne mozhet povtorit'* [There were, it is true, envious voices who complained that nobody could repeat the great man's brilliant experiments. They received the perfectly sensible reply that the experiments were brilliant precisely because nobody could repeat them] (F. Iskander).

The verbs *nyt'*, *khnykat'* and to a lesser extent *skulit'* may, especially in direct speech, signify not only complaints but also other speech acts, such as requests: *'Kupi morozhenoe, kupi morozhenoe,' nyl/khnykal mal'chik* ['Buy me an ice-cream, buy me an ice-cream,' whined the boy]. In the verb *khnykat'* the sense of 'complain' is difficult to separate from the sense 'weep', for example *Razve zhenshchina umeet liubit'. . .? V liubvi ona umeet tol'ko khnykat' i raspuskat' niuni!* [Is a woman really capable of love. . .? In love all she can do is whimper and snivel!] (A. P. Chekhov), where both interpretations are equally possible.

NOTE 3. The verb *peniat'* in the perfective (*popeniat'*) has a meaning close to the one at issue: 'express to smb. mild displeasure with regard to that person's actions or nature', for example *Zinochka popeniala emu za to, chto on ostavil ee odnu* [Zinochka rebuked him for leaving her all alone] (B. Polevoi).

## 3. The Form Zone

Synonyms may differ from one another in the range of forms (grammemes), the range of grammatical meanings of a single form, the varied semantic, pragmatic, stylistic, syntactic, combinatorial, or other specializations of a given form, and lastly in whether a given form is a proper form of the given lexeme or a non-proper one. All these features of synonyms are described in the form zone. Some of them are illustrated below.

### 3.1. DISTINCTIONS IN THE SET OF GRAMMATICAL FORMS

For verbs this means (in descending order of probability) differences in the forms for aspect, mood, representation (personal forms, infinitive, gerund and participle), voice, tense, person, and number. Noun synonyms usually differ from one another in their number forms, adjectives by long and short forms and degrees of comparison, and adverbs by degrees of comparison.

In the series *zhdat'—ozhidat', dozhidat'sia*, etc. [to wait] there are three synonyms which possess both aspectual forms (*dozhidat'sia—dozhdat'sia', vyzhidat' —vyzhdat'* and *perezhidat'—perezhdat'*); three with only an imperfective form (*zhdat', ozhidat', podzhidat'*); and three which have only a perfective form (*podozhdat', obozhdat', prozhdat'*).

The synonyms *khotet' —zhelat', zhazhdat', mechtat'* [to want], which denote a state rather than an action, are essentially deprived of any imperative form in affirmative sentences. It is impossible for *khotet'* and *zhazhdat'* and unnatural for *zhelat'* and *mechtat'*. For the last two synonyms, however, a negative imperative is possible: *Ne zhelai drugomu togo, chego ne khochesh', chtoby sdelali tebe* [don't wish anybody else anything you wouldn't want done to you]; *Ni o kakikh kvartirakh v Moskve ne mechtai* [Don't even dream of any Moscow flats].

For all synonyms in this series except *zhazhdat'* the subjunctive form is typical: *Ia by khotel vyslushat' i druguiu storonu* [I would like to hear the other side too]; *Kto zhelal by vystupit'?* [who would like to speak?]; *Liubaia zhenshchina v mire, mogu vas uverit', mechtala by ob etom* [I can assure you that any woman in the world would dream of this] (M. Bulgakov).

For the verb *sovetovat'* [to advise], unlike its synonym *rekomendovat'* [to recommend], the passive form is impossible: compare *Ne rekomenduetsia vkliuchat' sistemu signalizatsii bez nadobnosti* [it is not recommended that the alarm system be switched on unnecessarily] and the impossible *\*Ne sovetuetsia vkliuchat' sistemu signalizatsii bez nadobnosti*.

The verb *zhazhdat'* has no gerund and, moreover, there is no means of compensating for this paradigmatic defect (see § 3.4 for compensation in defective paradigms). On the other hand, participles are typical with this verb to a greater extent than with any other member of the series: *zhestokie mal'chishki, zhazhdushchie krovavykh igr* [cruel boys who yearn for bloodthirsty games]; *polaiavshis' s sosedom, zhazhdushchim utrennei opokhmelki* [having had a shouting match with a neighbour who was thirsting for his morning hair of the dog] (G. Vishnevskaia); *K desiati chasam utra ochered' zhazhdushchikh biletov do togo vspukhla, chto o nei doshli slukhi do militsii* [by ten in the morning the queue of those wanting tickets had grown so long that word of it had reached the police] (M. Bulgakov).

3.2. DISTINCTIONS IN THE SET OF GRAMMATICAL MEANINGS OF A SINGLE FORM

As noted above, in addition to differences in the set of forms (or grammemes), synonyms may differ from one another in the set of grammatical meanings belonging to one and the same form.

In the series *videt'—zamechat', vidat', litsezret', zret'* the verb *vidat'* differs from the dominant in that it usually signifies an already completed act of visual perception. On account of the resultative nature of its lexical meaning, *vidat'* is most commonly used in the past with general-factual, resultative, or iterative meaning: *Uzhel' ty ne vidal, | Skol' chasto grom ognekrylatyi | Razit chelo vysokikh skal?* [Surely you have seen | How often thunderbolts on wings of fire | Lash the brow of the high cliffs?] (F. I. Tiutchev); *Spiridon, po-raznomu nakloniaia ee [fotografiiu] k svetu okna, stal vodit' mimo levogo glaza, kak by rassmatrivaia po chastiam.—Ne,—oblegchenno vzdokhnul on, ne vidal* [Spiridon turned it (the photograph) this way and that towards the light from the window and started passing it before his left eye, as if examining it section by section. 'No,' he said with a sigh of relief. 'I haven't seen it.'] (A. Solzhenitsyn). The progressive-durative and other durative meanings of the imperfective are uncharacteristic of *vidat'*: ?*My dolgo vidali parus na gorizonte* is noticeably worse than *My dolgo videli parus na gorizonte* [for a long time we could see the sail on the horizon].

The verb *zamechat'*, which forms part of this series and denotes a momentary action, totally excludes the possibility of the use of the imperfective in the progressive-durative and other durative meanings.

3.3. SEMANTIC, SYNTACTIC, STYLISTIC, AND OTHER SPECIALIZATIONS OF FORMS

In certain grammatical forms some synonyms may acquire semantic, pragmatic, syntactic, combinatorial, and other features which are not characteristic of them in the forms in which they are listed in the series.

In the series *dumat'—schitat', polagat', nakhodit', rassmatrivat', smotret', usmatrivat'*, *videt'* [to think, consider] only *rassmatrivat'* and *smotret'* are used perfectly freely in the imperative with their full meaning intact: *Rassmatrivai eto kak svoe pervoe ser'eznoe poruchenie*; *Smotri na eto kak na svoe pervoe ser'eznoe poruchenie* [consider this your first serious mission]. The synonyms *dumat'* and *schitat'* formally permit use in the imperative (*dumat'* mainly in the expression *dumai chto khochesh'* [think what you like]), but in this form their meaning is slightly altered. *Dumai chto khochesh'* is equivalent to 'you can think whatever you like; it makes no difference to me what you think'; *Schitai, chto tebe povezlo/ chto my dogovorilis'* [consider yourself lucky/consider it agreed] is equivalent to 'in spite of certain reservations that I have, you may consider yourself lucky/ you may consider it agreed'; *Esli ugodno, schitaite eto propagandoi v pol'zu venetsianskikh lavok, ch'i dela idut ozhivlennee pri nizkikh temperaturakh* [if you like, regard this as propaganda for Venetian stalls, which do better business when the temperature is low] (I. Brodskii).

*Schitat'* in the imperative is also used as a parenthetic word, having the meaning 'mozhno schitat'', which is stylistically substandard: *Trofim, schitai, vsiu zhizn' prozhil tut, a ne znaet, gde konchaetsia eta top'* [Trofim has lived all his life here, you could say, and he doesn't know how far this marsh reaches] (V. Tendriakov).

The perfective of this verb *schest'* stands in clear contrast to the perfective of the other synonyms because of the suggestion of will in a mental act: compare *Prokuror schel, chto sobrannykh ulik dostatochno dlia pred"iavleniia obvineniia*, meaning 'the prosecutor decided that the evidence in his possession was sufficient to support pressing charges' and *Prokuror podumal, chto sobrannykh ulik dostatochno dlia pred"iavleniia obvineniia*, meaning 'the prosecutor had such an idea, perhaps without having solid grounds for it'; *Voidia v konflikt s sovetskoi vlast'iu, etot chisteishii, kristal'noi dushevnoi chistoty chelovek* [A. D. Sakharov] *schel nuzhnym vernut' gosudarstvu zarabotannye im 150 tysiach rublei— sberezheniia vsei zhizni!* [when he came into conflict with the Soviet state, this purest of men with a crystal-clear soul deemed it necessary to pay back the 150,000 roubles he had earned—all his life's savings!] (G. Vishnevskaia).

In performative use the synonyms *sovetovat'* [to advise] and *rekomendovat'* [to recommend] permit, besides the present indicative imperfective in the first person, which is the normal form for performatives, a number of less usual forms. These are: (1) the subjunctive: *Ia sovetoval by tebe, igemon, ostavit' na vremia dvorets, i poguliat' gde-nibud' v okrestnostiakh* [I would advise you, Hegemon, to leave the palace for a while and take a stroll somewhere in the grounds] (M. Bulgakov); *Slovom, ia by tebe posovetoval vziat' vse eto delo na sebia, provesti samomu vse sledstvie, vsem pokazat', chto ty nastoiashchii rytsar' revoliutsii* [in brief I would advise you to take over the whole matter, conduct the whole investigation yourself and demonstrate that you are a true knight of the revolution] (V. Aksenov); *I kak shturman ia rekomendoval by vam eshche raz prochitat' instruktsii o poriadke razgruzki* [and as navigator I would recommend that you read the unloading instructions again] (A. and B. Strugatskii); (2) the future perfective indicative, first person; *Posovetuiu vam proverit' eti dannye* [I shall advise you to check the data]; *Porekomenduiu vam na uzhin iazyk v zhele i salat* [I shall recommend that you have tongue in jelly and salad for supper]. In addition, the verb *rekomendovat'* permits performative use in the forms of (3) the passive: *Do vkliucheniia pribora rekomenduetsia proverit' sistemu signalizatsii* [before switching on the appliance it is advisable to check the alarm system] and (4) the infinitive: *Rekomendovat' chlenam profsoiuza vozderzhat'sia ot uchastiia v zabastovke* [it is to be recommended that union members refrain from taking part in the strike]. In the last example the recommendation acquires the status of an order which should be obeyed.

The past tense form of the verb *khotet'* [to want] has an interesting pragmatic specialization: in interrogative sentences it may be used as part of a standardized address to a customer: *Chego/chto vy khoteli?* Here it acquires the features of a substandard or vulgar register.

The verb *dozhidat'sia*, as opposed to *zhdat'* [to wait] has a stylistic specialization in the imperfective. In the modern language (unlike that of the nineteenth century or the first half of the twentieth) *dozhidat'sia* is being replaced by the dominant of the series and limited to the informal register, but in the perfective, where *zhdat'* cannot compete with it, this verb preserves its stylistic neutrality. Compare the lower-style *Chto eto za liudi?—Vas dozhidaiutsia* [Who are those people?—They're waiting for you] and the neutral *Nakonets vsekh priglasili k stolu. Redaktor dozhdalsia polnoi tishiny i skazal* [At last all were invited to the table. The editor waited until there was complete silence, then spoke] (S. Dovlatov).

The verb *vidat'*, evidently for similar reasons, has the same stylistic specialization. In the imperfective *vidat'*, unlike its closest synonym *videt'*, belongs to the informal register, whereas the perfective becomes stylistically neutral: *Ivan uvidal, chto u nego sovsem molodye, veselye, ozornye glaza* [Ivan saw that he had young, merry and mischievous eyes].

The perfective form of the verb *smotret'* in the sense 'to consider' has morphological, syntactic, and lexical co-occurrence constraints all at once. It occurs usually in the future in interrogative utterances or statements expressing doubt, mostly with adverbs such as *kak* [how], *plokho* [badly], *khorosho* [well], when a whole situation is being considered: *Kak on posmotrit na otsrochku zashchity dissertatsii?* [how will he regard the postponement of the defence of your dissertation?]; *Boius', on plokho na eto posmotrit* [I'm afraid he'll take a dim view of it]. Utterances such as *?On plokho posmotrel na otsrochku zashchity dissertatsii* are less natural. The verb *dumat'*, from the same series, has a perfective which in similar collocations is used to appraise not a situation but an object, usually a person: *On mozhet plokho o vas podumat'* [he may think badly of you].

The verb *dozhidat'sia*, from the series *zhdat'*, has an interesting semantic accretion in the imperfective gerund in negative contexts: the expression *ne dozhidaias'* tends towards the sense of a preposition with the meaning 'before':

*uekhali, ne dozhidaias' zvonka* [they left before the telephone call]; *on vstal, ne dozhidaias' otveta* [he stood up before he received an answer]. In similar circumstances the other synonyms, like *dozhidat'sia* itself in the perfective, fully preserve their usual meaning: *On vstal, ne ozhidaia otveta* [not expecting an answer, he stood up] (indicating that the process of expectation did not take place); *Ranenykh vyvezli na mashinakh, ne dozhdavshis' sanitarnogo poezda* [they evacuated the casualties by road, having waited in vain for a while for the hospital train]. The greater shift of the imperfective form (*ne*) *dozhidaias'* towards prepositional meaning is confirmed both by the material provided by other words (cf. *smotria, gliadia, nevziraia/nesmotria na* and the like), and by the fact that the expression is gradually losing the fundamental property of a gerund—the requirement that its subject be co-referential with the subject of the main clause: compare the dubious *?Ranenye byli vyvezeny, ne dozhidaias' komandy* [the wounded were evacuated before the order was issued] and the totally ungrammatical *\*Ranenye byli vyvezeny, ne dozhdavshis' komandy* [the wounded were evacuated without waiting for the order]. For more detail on this see Itskovich (1982: 131–2).

### 3.4. PROPER AND NON-PROPER FORMS

In addition to the forms of a lexeme which are part of its own grammatical paradigm and the linguistic system, account is sometimes taken of so-called non-proper forms, appropriated in usage from the nearest synonym. For example, the verbs *mesti* (*pol*) [to sweep (a floor)] and *bezhat'* in the meaning 'to boil over' are grammatically defective in the linguistic system. They lack a perfective form of their own. If, however, a need arises to express a particular grammatical meaning, the missing forms are easily borrowed from the synonymous verbs *podmetat'* and *ubegat'*: *Chto ty delaesh'?—Metu pol.—Kogda podmetesh', vymoi posudu.* [What are you doing?—Sweeping the floor.—When you've finished sweeping it, do the washing up.]; *U tebia moloko ne bezhit?—Uzhe ubezhalo.* [Is the milk boiling over?—It has already.] Note a similar situation among nouns, where, for example, the missing genitive plural of the noun *mechta* [day-dream] is replaced by the form *mechtanii*, borrowed from the synonym *mechtanie*.

The verb *zhdat'*, unlike most other synonyms in its series, lacks a gerund. When one is needed, *zhdat'* is replaced by *ozhidat'* or *dozhidat'sia*: *Ozhidaia/dozhidaias' ego zvonka, Varia bestsel'no brodila po komnate* [while waiting for him to call, Varia wandered aimlessly about the room].

In the literary language, *khotet'* [to want] lacks a present participle and present gerund. When there is a need to express these senses, the non-proper forms *zhelaiushchii* and *zhelaia* are used.[5]

---

[5] The distribution of finite and non-finite forms in the paradigms of *khotet'* and *zhelat'* is interesting in other respects too. In *khotet'* the finite forms are strong, while the non-finite forms are practically

## 4. The Syntax Zone

The principal concerns of this zone are the differences in the range of syntactic constructions peculiar to the elements of the synonym series. More specifically, consideration is given to differences in government, in the syntactic functions and types of sentence characteristic of them, in word order and other syntactic features.

Here too, in addition to describing the aforementioned types of syntactic difference, we attempt to answer the question: can syntax, like forms, cause any semantic, pragmatic, stylistic, combinatorial, or other specialization in synonyms?

### 4.1. DIFFERENCES IN GOVERNMENT

We shall exemplify these with the series *dumat'*—*schitat'*, etc. [to think, consider].

With the verb *dumat'* the most typical governed form is a whole clause introduced by the conjunction *chto* [that]. There is also a qualifying construction with evaluative adverbs of the type *khorosho* [well] and *plokho* [badly] which is specific to it: *On stal khorosho/plokho o vas dumat'* [He's begun to think well/badly of you].

The syntactic features of the synonyms *schitat'*, *polagat'*, and *nakhodit'* are more varied. Like *dumat'*, they govern a subordinate statement, introduced by the conjunction *chto* [that]. However, they are also used in qualifying constructions of the type *schitat' kogo-libo kakim-libo* [to consider smb. smth.], in which *polagat'* acquires an extremely bookish flavour: *Ran'she prezident ne schital vozmozhnym govorit' ob etom otkryto* [previously the president did not deem it possible to speak openly of this]; *Chto kasaetsia irano-irakskogo konflikta, to Egipet polagaet neobkhodimym nemedlenno prekratit' voennye deistviia i pereiti k ego mirnomu uregulirovaniiu* (*Pravda*, 12 June 1984) [as for the Iran–Iraq conflict, Egypt deems it essential to cease military operations at once and proceed to a peaceful settlement]; *Kstati, pisal ia, esli koe-kogo sluchaino vstretish' na ulitse, mozhesh' soobshchit' ob etom, razumeetsia, esli naidesh' umestnym* (F. Iskander) [by the way, I wrote, if you happen to bump into somebody in the street you can tell them about it, if it seems appropriate, of course].

---

absent, except for the infinitive and the past active participle (*khotevshii*). Its positions are rendered weaker still by the fact that it has no derivative nouns or adjectives. In *zhelat'*, by contrast, the non-finite forms *zhelaia, zhelaiushchii, zhelavshii, et al.* are stronger. They are stylistically neutral, whereas the finite forms *zhelaiu, zhelaete, zhelal*, etc. have clear stylistic marking and are therefore weaker. The positions of *zhelat'* are also strengthened by the fact that it forms such important derivatives as *zhelanie* [wish, desire], *zhelatel'nyi* [desirable] and the substantivized participle *zhelaiushchii* [one who wishes, desires]. In this connection it is possible to advance a cautious hypothesis of a tendency operating in modern Russian towards the merging of the two main wishing verbs into one with a stylistically homogeneous suppletive paradigm which comprises the finite forms of *khotet'* and the non-finite forms of *zhelat'*. It remains unclear how the infinitive should be presented in this paradigm.

For all three synonyms, variations of this construction are possible, when an infinitive or a whole subordinate clause replaces the accusative case (on condition that an adjective of the type *nuzhnyi* [necessary], *pravil'nyi* [correct], *somnitel'nyi* [doubtful], *vozmozhnyi* [possible], *iasnyi* [clear], etc. occupies the instrumental position): *Direktor polagal (ne schital, ne nakhodil) nuzhnym proverit' eti svedeniia* [the director assumed (did not think/find) it necessary to check these facts]; *Ia schitaiu v vysshei stepeni somnitel'nym, chto on soglasitsia na eto predlozhenie* [I think it extremely doubtful that he will agree to this proposal]. *Schitat'* may have a variation of this construction, with nouns such as *chest'* [honour], *udacha* [luck, success], *radost'* [joy], *oshibka* [mistake], and a number of others in the instrumental case: *Ia schitaiu dlia sebia bol'shoi chest'iu razgovarivat' s vami (bol'shoi udachei, chto ia vstretil vas zdes')* [I consider it a great honour to talk to you (very lucky that I met you here)].

The syntactic possibilities of the synonyms in the second group in this series—*rassmatrivat'*, *smotret'*, *usmatrivat'*, *videt'* [to regard, look upon, see]—are much more limited. They are fixed in usage with a single construction, rarely more. *Rassmatrivat'* and *smotret'* have three-member qualifying constructions with the conjunction *kak* or its equivalents (*rassmatrivat' kogo-chto-libo kak kogo-chto-libo* [to regard smb./smth. as smb./smth.]; *smotret' na kogo-chto-libo kak na kogo-chto-libo* [to look upon smb./smth. as smb./smth.]), while *usmatrivat'* and *videt'* have a prepositional construction *usmatrivat'/videt' chto-libo v kom-chem-libo* [to see smth. in smb./smth.].

Apart from government proper, this zone describes two further types of syntactic feature: a word's ability to be used in a so-called absolute construction and its ability to subordinate certain characteristic types of circumstances.

When used in the absolute construction a lexeme will usually undergo a slight modification of its lexical meaning, in a clearly defined way. For example, the verb *zhdat'* [to wait]—the only one in its series which may be used completely freely in this construction—may additionally express the senses of an extended period of waiting, of impatience or displeasure (especially in the first person, present tense), etc.: *Ia zhdu* [I'm waiting] (e.g. when my interlocutor is slow to reply to my question); *Est' groznyi sudiia, on zhdet* [there is an awe-inspiring arbiter, he waits] (M. Iu. Lermontov); *To li dozhd' idet, to li deva zhdet. | Zapriagai konei da poedem k nei* [Either it's raining or a girl is waiting. | Let's harness the horses and drive to see her] (I. Brodskii).

The same feature constitutes the syntactic specifics of the lexeme *videt'* from the series *videt'*—*zamechat'*, *vidat'* [to see], etc. In the absolute construction this verb usually acquires potential meaning: *Posle etoi operatsii ty snova budesh' videt'* [after this operation you will be able to see again].

The same lexeme is used more freely than the others in its series with certain circumstances which are typical of the situation of visual perception. These may indicate (*a*) the position of the observer (*videt' chto-libo s balkona/iz mashiny* [to see smth. from a balcony/a car]); (*b*) an aperture or an optical instrument aiding the perception (*videt' sobravshikhsia gostei v poluotkrytuiu dver'/cherez okno/skvoz' zamochnuiu skvazhinu* [to see the assembled guests through a half-open door/ through a window/a keyhole]; *videt' v elektronnyi mikroskop mel'chaishie mikroorganizmy* [to see minute micro-organisms through an electron microscope]); (*c*) a surface on which the object of perception is placed (*videt' chto-libo na snimke/ portrete/chertezhe* [to see smth. in a photograph/portrait/drawing]); (*d*) the organ of sight (*videt' vse sobstvennymi glazami* [to see everything with one's own eyes]).

## 4.2. DIFFERENCES IN SYNTACTIC TYPES OF SENTENCE

Negative, interrogative, and 'dubious' sentences, in addition to various types of parenthetic constructions, are the most sensitive to different features of lexical semantics.

In the series *privyknut', priuchit'sia, vtianut'sia, priokhotit'sia, pristrastit'sia, povadit'sia* [to grow accustomed] none of the synonyms can normally be used in the imperfective in neutral negative sentences. Sentences such as *"Ia ne privykal/priuchalsia rabotat' so slovariami* [I have not got used to working with dictionaries] and *"Ia ne vtiagivalsia v zaniatiia muzykoi* [I have not been absorbed into musical studies] are semantically odd, to say the least.

In the perfective, of all the synonyms in the given series only *privyknut'* is used with complete freedom in this construction: *Ia ne privyk razgovarivat' v takom tone* [I am not used to conversing in this tone]; *On ne privyk rabotat' so slovariami* [he is not used to working with dictionaries]. Moreover, in many cases a shift in the scope of negation is possible: *Ia ne privyk razgovarivat' v takom tone* = *Ia privyk razgovarivat' ne v takom tone* = *Ia privyk razgovarivat' v drugom tone* [I am used to conversing in a different tone].

In the case of the other synonyms, owing to their great semantic specificity, co-occurrence with neutral negation even in the perfective is to some extent restricted if not impossible. *Priuchit'sia* and *vtianut'sia* permit use in negative sentences if intensifying particles such as *eshche, tak i*, etc. are present: *On tak i ne priuchilsia rabotat' so slovarem* [he never did get used to working with a dictionary]; *On eshche ne vtianulsia v rabotu* [he still hasn't got involved in the job]. For *priokhotit'sia* and especially *pristrastit'sia* even this use is hardly possible, and *povadit'sia* precludes any negative constructions.

For the verb *videt'* in the sense 'to think, believe', negative constructions with the construction *chtoby* are characteristic: *Ne vizhu, chtoby vam chto-nibud' ugrozhalo* [I don't see that there's any threat to you]. The synonym *polagat'*, on the other hand, does not permit use in negative sentences. Cf. the incorrect *\*Prezident ne polagal, chto eti svedeniia nuzhno proverit'* [the president did not suppose that that information should be verified].

*Dumat', schitat'*, and *polagat'*, from the same series, are used in various types of parenthetic construction: *Vy, ia dumaiu, zabyli menia* [I think you have forgotten me]; *Osetrovye ryby, schitaiut znatoki, utratili svoi byloi vkus* [connoisseurs believe that fish of the sturgeon family have lost their former flavour]; *Ob etom, ia polagaiu, nuzhno sprosit' direktora* [I suppose we should ask the director about that]; *Polagaiu, nashe sochinenie dvizhetsia k finalu* [I assume our work (composition) is approaching completion] (S. Dovlatov).

The synonyms *dumat'* and *polagat'* may occur in a parenthetic construction with the modal *nado*: *Ego sem'ia, nado dumat', priekhala nadolgo* [it must be assumed that his family have come for a long stay]; *Udivlennaia Margarita Nikolaevna povernulas' i uvidela na skameike grazhdanina, kotoryi, ochevidno, besshumno podsel v to vremia, kogda Margarita zagliadelas' na protsessiiu i, nado polagat', v rasseiannosti vslukh zadala svoi vopros* [Margarita Nikolaevna turned round in surprise and saw a man sitting on the bench who had evidently sat down silently while she was gazing at the procession, when she had—it must be supposed—absent-mindedly asked her question aloud] (M. Bulgakov). The synonym *schitat'* with the word *nado* is avoided: *?Ego sem'ia, nado schitat', priekhala nadolgo* [it must be assumed that his family have come for a long stay].

In parenthetic constructions the verb *dumat'* in colloquial speech is freely employed without the first- and second-person pronouns: *Dumaiu, eto reshenie eshche ne okonchatel'noe* [I don't believe this is the final decision yet]; *A on, dumaete ⟨dumaesh'⟩, soglasitsia?* [but do you think he'll agree?]. The omission of the subject, especially in the second person, is less usual with *schitat'* and *polagat'*.

With the synonym *nakhodit'* [to find] all parenthetic constructions are restricted if not impossible: *\*Ob etom, ia nakhozhu, nado sprosit' direktora* [*\*about that I find I should ask the director]; *\*Ego sem'ia, nado nakhodit', priekhala nadolgo* [*\*his family, it must be found, has come for a long stay]; *\*Nakhozhu, eto reshenie eshche ne okonchatel'noe* [*\*I find, this decision is not yet final].


## 4.3. WORD ORDER

With *povadit'sia* [to take to], from the series *privyknut', priuchit'sia, priokhotit'sia,* etc. normal usage is to place the verb before the subject: *Povadilis' soldaty na rynok khodit'* [the soldiers took to going to the market]; *Povadilis' kozy na ogorod* [the goats took to going to the kitchen garden]; *Povadilsia medved' na paseku* [the bear took to visiting the beehives]. With all the other verbs in this series such order is stylistically marked.

For verbs of the type *vit'sia* [to wind], *goret'* [to burn], *dut'* [to blow], *idti'* [to fall (of rain, etc.)], *stoiat'* [to stand], *tech'* [to flow], and others, when used as values of the lexical function FUNC$_0$, the typical position is before the grammatical subject: *V temnote v'etsia tropka* [the pathway winds along in the darkness], *Gorit svet* [a light is burning], *Duet veter* [a wind is blowing], *Idet dozhd'* [rain is falling], *Stoiat morozy* [the weather is frosty], *Tekut ruch'i* [the streams are flowing]. The meaning of these verbs is almost exhausted by the idea of existence. It is uninformative compared with the meaning of the key nouns, which are semantically much richer. If one knows that there is light, rain, wind, or a stream, it follows that it burns, falls, blows, or flows respectively. The reverse deduction, however, is less certain: a fire may also burn; a draught can also blow under a door; snow may also fall and a river may flow, and so on. Thus the information communicated by the full sentence is concentrated in a single constituent—the noun. This is why it is placed at the end of the sentence, in the position of the rheme, that is, the part of the utterance of greatest communicative importance.[6]

Of course, if such a verb has a synonym which is richer in content, it may occupy the verb's rightful place—after the grammatical subject. There then arises a contrast in word order between two synonyms. In this respect the synonyms *vit'sia* and *viliat'* [to wind (intrans.)] are of interest. The latter is usually placed after its subject: compare *Tropa viliala mezhdu kamnei* [the path wound between the rocks]; *Doroga viliala mezhdu kholmov* [the road wound through the hills] and the purely existential *\*V temnote viliala doroga* [the road wound in the darkness], which is impossible. The difference lies in the substantially greater semantic and pragmatic weight of *viliat'* compared to *vit'sia*. As noted in § 2.2, *viliat'* is used to express a negative utilitarian evaluation of spatially elongated objects such as roads: the speaker or observer notes that the road he is travelling along has an excessive number of bends on short sectors along the route, thus making movement along it more difficult. The meaning of *viliat'* is thus not only semantically richer than that of *vit'sia*, but also of much greater pragmatic import. It is for this reason that it shifts to the position after the subject—the position of the rheme.

## 4.4. SEMANTIC, SYNTACTIC, STYLISTIC, AND OTHER SPECIALIZATIONS OF CONSTRUCTIONS

In many cases syntactic distinctions are accompanied by differences in the range of accompanying forms or in co-occurrence, as well as by the semantic specialization of synonyms. Here the verb *vidat'*, from the series *videt'*, *zamechat'*, etc. [to see, notice], which we have mentioned several times before, is of interest.

First, it has varying degrees of semantic freedom in the imperfective and perfective aspects (*uvidat'*). As stated previously, the former has a peculiarity of tense and aspect. In the personal forms it has only the past tense with resultative or iterative general-factual meaning. This explains the fact that *vidat'* tends to be fixed in negative and interrogative sentences, which on the whole favour the general-factual meaning (see Glovinskaia 1982): *Ia etogo pis'ma ne vidal* [I haven't seen that letter]; *Ty ne vidal moego portfelia?* [You haven't seen my briefcase, have you?].

On the other hand it hardly ever co-occurs with the types of predicates and adverbial modifiers listed above. As for the perfective *uvidat'*, it has no noticeable tense or aspect specifics and therefore is hardly distinguished from *videt'* in its degree of semantic freedom. In particular, it may be used in all the constructions characteristic of *videt'* (see above), except for the parenthetic and

---

[6] This rule was formulated by V. Apresjan (1995b) independently of the author and at the same time.

absolutive. Secondly, the verb *vidat'* has semantic peculiarities in the infinitive. In this form it is used mainly in negative set expressions with *ne*, indicating the impossibility of visual perception: *Takaia temen', chto nichego ne vidat'* [it's so dark you can't see a thing].

In the series *zhdat'* [to wait] the dominant of the series and its closest synonym *ozhidat'* acquire semantic specifics in negative sentences. In most cases these two synonyms acquire the sense of a supposition: *On vas ne zhdal* [he wasn't expecting you] (you appeared unexpectedly); *On ne ozhidal aresta* [he wasn't expecting to be arrested] (his arrest came as a surprise to him). The sense of waiting proper in a negative context becomes possible when the subject is unspecified (*Nikto menia tam ne zhdal/ozhidal* [Nobody was expecting me there]), or when we negate not the fact of waiting itself but some accompanying circumstance cited in the phrase subordinate to the verb (*On nikogda ne zhdal (ne ozhidal) menia na uslovlennom meste* [he never waited for me at the appointed spot]), or when the meaning of refutation rather than mere negation is intended (*Prostite, chto zastavil vas zhdat'.—Ia sovsem ne zhdal vas, ia sam tol'ko chto voshel* [Forgive me for keeping you waiting.—I haven't been waiting at all. I've just got here myself.])

All the synonyms in this series except *perezhidat'* and *vyzhidat'* may govern a noun denoting the object of waiting—a person, some means of transport, an event, or a moment in time. If the object of waiting is animate the synonyms *zhdat'*, *dozhidat'sia*, *ozhidat'* govern a noun in the accusative: *zhdat' zhenu* [to wait for one's wife], *ozhidat' delegatsiiu* [to expect a delegation], *dozhidat'sia zhenu* [to wait for one's wife] (e.g. *Chto ty zdes' delaesh'?—Dozhidaius' zhenu* [What are you doing here?—Waiting for my wife]). If the thing awaited is an object, an action, or an event the genitive is more usual: *zhdat' poezda* [to wait for a train], *ozhidat' voskhoda solntsa (chtoby nachat' rabotu)* [to wait for sunrise (before starting work)], *dozhidat'sia priezda gostei* [to await the arrival of guests].

To be more precise, the verb *zhdat'* when combined with nouns denoting events, actions, etc. admits both these forms, with the following distinction of sense: *zhdat'* + acc. means that what is expected is known, that is, previously mentioned, promised or made definite in some other way (*zhdat' pis'mo* [to expect the letter]), while *zhdat'* + gen. means that the object is an unknown, unspecified member of the same category (*zhdat' pis'ma* [to expect a letter]). When combined with nouns denoting humans, the opposition remains, even when the accusative and genitive forms coincide.

## 5. The Co-occurrence Zone

This zone describes the similarities and differences between synonyms in semantic, lexical, morphological, syntactic, communicative, prosodic, and other forms of co-occurrence. We shall speak of the semantic co-occurrence (or of semantic constraints on the co-occurrence) of lexeme X if it co-occurs with any lexeme $Y_1, Y_2, \ldots, Y_n$, whose explication includes the semantic component S. Further, we shall speak of lexical co-occurrence if lexemes $Y_1, Y_2 \ldots Y_n$, with which X co-occurs, can only be listed. Lastly, we shall speak of the morphological, syntactic, prosodic, or other co-occurrence properties of lexeme X if it co-occurs with any lexeme $Y_1, Y_2, \ldots, Y_n$, which has a morphological, syntactic, prosodic, or other feature F respectively.

It is possible to suggest at least two more bases for the classification of types of co-occurrence: (*a*) the syntactic relation between X and Y from the standpoint of which of them is the main element of the respective syntactic construction; (*b*) the syntactic function of the co-occurring element with regard to the key word (synonyms may differ in the types of possible grammatical subjects, direct, indirect, and prepositional objects and so on).

However, a strict classification, taking account of all possible bases, will actually complicate rather than facilitate the task of surveying the material. For this reason in what follows we shall use the aforementioned features of lexeme $Y_i$ as the sole basis for the systematization of the material. Under each of the rubrics obtained, however, we shall try to demonstrate as fully as possible the whole range of data supplied in the dictionary on the co-occurrence of synonyms.

Since in many cases it would be unnatural to separate semantic constraints on co-occurrence from lexical constraints, they will be considered together under the rubric 'lexico-semantic co-occurrence'. It is equally natural to subsume under a single title prosodic and communicative constraints on co-occurrence.

## 5.1. LEXICO-SEMANTIC CO-OCCURRENCE

In the series *dumat'—schitat', videt', rassmatrivat'*, etc. [to think, consider] the synonyms differ from one another in co-occurrence with regard to the valency of the subject. *Schitat', videt'*, and *rassmatrivat'* freely occur with the name of a collective (a state, a country, a government, etc.) as their subject: *komissiia vidit zalog uspekha v gotovnosti vsekh stran regiona k kompromissam* [the commission sees in the readiness of all countries of the region to make compromises a guarantee of success]; *Respubliki schitaiut, chto sleduet iskat' politicheskoe reshenie vsekh voznikaiushchikh problem* [the republics deem it necessary to seek a political solution to all problems which arise]; *Indiia vsegda rassmatrivala Kashmir kak svoiu neot"emlemuiu chast'* [India has always regarded Kashmir as an inalienable part of itself]. With the other synonyms of the series, including *dumat'*, these structures are untypical.

The subject of *radovat'sia* [to be glad] may be a human or a higher animal; *Sobaka raduetsia, uvidev khoziaina* [the dog is glad to see its master]. The subject of the feelings denoted by the synonyms *likovat'* and *torzhestvovat'* [to rejoice] may be only a human.

In the series *risovat'—zarisovyvat', pisat', malevat'* [to draw, paint], the distinctions in co-occurrence with regard to the valency of object are of interest. The verb *zarisovyvat'* implies that there must be a real-world object (i.e. an object which exists outside the artist's mind) which he tries to depict as accurately as he can. For this reason, *zarisovyvat'* can hardly co-occur with the names of objects denoting a typical product of the artist's work: *'On zarisovyval kartinu/ portret* [he depicted a picture/portrait]. All the other synonyms in this series are freely applicable to the situation when someone depicts objects from memory or even creates images having no prototype in reality: *narisovyvat' (napisat', namalevat') bol'shuiu kartinu (chei-libo portret)* [to sketch (draw, paint) a big picture (smb.'s portrait)].

When combined with the names of the products of the artist's work, the verb *risovat'* [to draw], being the most neutral semantically, displays the broadest co-occurrence possibilities. Absolutely anything may be 'drawn' [*risovat'*]: a still life, a picture, a sketch, an emblem, stars, diagrams, graphs, arrows, and even lines in sand. The verb *pisat'* [to draw, paint, lit. to write], the most 'artistic' in the series, presupposes the intention of creating an artistic image and therefore requires that the object be of the type 'picture, portrait, sketch, still life', etc. It cannot, of course, co-occur with diagrams, graphs, arrows, etc.

The content valency of the putative verbs *schitat', polagat', nakhodit'* [to consider, suppose, find] is variously filled in the typical qualifying construction *schitat' kogo-chto-libo kakim-libo* [to consider smb./smth. smth.]. The general co-occurrence constraint is that the instrumental-case position must be filled with an adjective denoting a property (not a state), or having a modal meaning. We may say *Ia schital ego zlym chelovekom* [I considered him a wicked man], but not *\*Ia schital ego rasserzhennym/razdosadovannym* [I considered him angry/ irritated]. In this the putative verbs differ from those of perception, for example, which may co-occur with the names of states: *Ia ne raz videl ego rasserzhennym/ razdosadovannym* [I often saw him angry/irritated].

Moreover, *schitat'* and *nakhodit'* co-occur equally freely with both semantic classes of adjectives, while *polagat'* co-occurs mostly with the modal type *nuzhnyi, neobkhodimyi, obiazatel'nyi* [necessary, essential, compulsory]: *Redaktsiia schitala (polagala, ne nakhodila) nuzhnym pomeshchat' oproverzhenie* [the editors deemed (thought, did not find) it necessary to publish a rebuttal], but only *Ego schitali (nakhodili) khladnokrovnym i muzhestvennym* [they considered (found) him cool and courageous]. Collocations such as *'Ego polagali (nakhodili) khladnokrovnym i muzhestvennym* or *'Neuzheli prezident polagal demokraticheskie sily stol' slabymi i bespomoshchnymi* [surely the president did not suppose the democratic forces so weak and helpless], which may be encountered in print, are either extremely bookish or deviations from the contemporary norm.

From the interesting lexical co-occurrence properties of the synonyms in this series we shall single out the following two: (*a*) co-occurrence with the adverbs *kak* [how], *tak* [thus], *inache* [otherwise], etc., denoting the content of a thought or opinion: *Ia tozhe tak dumaiu/polagaiu, a on schitaet inache* [I think/believe so too, but he thinks differently]; *Kak vy smotrite na poslednie sobytiia v nashei strane?* [how do you view recent events in our country?]; *Kak v SShA rassmatrivaiut obrazovanie SNG?* [how is the formation of the CIS regarded in the USA?]. In the case of *nakhodit'*, of all the aforementioned combinations, co-occurrence is possible only with *kak* (*Kak vy menia nakhodite posle sanatoriia?* [how do you find me after my stay at the sanatorium?]), while no such combinations are possible with *usmatrivat'* or *videt'*; (*b*) co-occurrence with adverbs and adverbial phrases such as *verno, pravil'no, spravedlivo* [rightly] and their inexact antonyms *naprasno* and *zria* [in vain]: *Vy verno (pravil'no, spravedlivo) schitaete (dumaete, polagaete), chto khudshee eshche vperedi* [you quite rightly consider that the worst is yet to come]; *Vy sovershenno spravedlivo rassmatrivaete ego deistviia kak dolzhnostnoe prestuplenie* [you quite rightly regard his actions as constituting malfeasance in office]; *On spravedlivo usmatrival (videl) v etom pokushenie na svoiu svobodu* [he rightly saw in this an attempt to restrict his freedom]; *Vy naprasno dumaete (schitaete), chto liberalizatsiia tsen mozhet chemu-to pomoch'* [you are wrong to think that freeing prices can do any good]. Collocations of this type are impossible with *nakhodit'*: *\*Vy verno (pravil'no, spravedlivo, naprasno) nakhodite, chto khudshee eshche vperedi* [*you rightly (correctly, wrongly) find that the worst is yet to come].

## 5.2. MORPHOLOGICAL CO-OCCURRENCE

A synonym of the conjunction *kak tol'ko* [as soon as] is the verb *stoit'* in one of its senses: compare *Kak tol'ko on vkhodil, vse vstavali* [as soon as he came in, everybody would stand up] and *Stoilo emu voiti, kak vse vstavali* [he had only to come in, and everybody would stand up]. Besides minor distinctions in meaning, they display an interesting difference in morphological co-occurrence. *Kak tol'ko* may combine with either aspectual form of the verb in the dependent clause: note a further example, *Kak tol'ko on voshel, vse vstali* [as soon as he came in, everybody stood up]. *Stoit'*, on the other hand, requires that the infinitive in the dependent clause be in the perfective (see the example above). A sentence such as *\*Stoilo emu vkhodit', kak vse vstavali* is incorrect.

## 5.3. PROSODIC AND COMMUNICATIVE CO-OCCURRENCE

Let us consider the phrase *chto kasaetsia* [as for] in sentences such as *Chto kasaetsia ↑↑ Einshteina, to on otnosilsia k kvantovoi mekhanike s ostorozhnost'iu* [as for Einstein, he took a cautious view of quantum mechanics]. As is known, it marks the noun phrase to its right, on which it is syntactically dependent, as a contrasted theme. The purpose of the utterance cited is to contrast the sceptically inclined Einstein with other physicists who readily embraced quantum mechanics.

The communicative function of the noun phrase is marked prosodically as well: it bears the logical phrasal stress.

This peculiarity of the expression *chto kasaetsia* may be described as a property of its communicative and prosodic co-occurrence: its syntagmatic context is a noun phrase which bears the logical stress and fulfils the function of a contrasted theme.

It is interesting to compare *chto kasaetsia* with the synonymous pronoun *sam 1* (the synonymy is inexact, of course, as the meaning of *sam 1* includes the semantic component 'male person'). This pronoun has the same communicative co-occurrence constraint: the noun phrase on which it is dependent fulfils the function of a contrasted theme. However, *sam 1* is prosodically diametrically opposed to *chto kasaetsia*: it itself bears the logical (contrastive) stress, leaving the top node of the noun phrase phrasally unstressed. Compare, ↑↑ *Sam Einshtein otnosilsia k kvantovoi mekhanike s ostorozhnost'iu* [As for Einstein, he took a cautious view of quantum mechanics].

The word *sam* has another lexical sense, in which, as in the instance we have considered, it is prosodically opposed to its closest synonym, although it has the same communicative function. We shall designate this *sam 2* and compare it with the adverb *lichno* [personally] in the sense 'even a person as important as X did so and so'. The pronoun *sam 2* marks the noun phrase to its right as the rheme of the utterance bearing the main phrasal stress: *Sam ↓ patriarkh prisutstvoval na tseremonii* [the patriarch himself was present at the ceremony]. The adverb *lichno* performs exactly the same communicative function, or, to put it differently, has exactly the same communicative co-occurrence constraint. However, being post-posed to its noun phrase, *lichno* itself bears the main phrasal stress, leaving the top node of the noun phrase phrasally unstressed: *Patriarkh ↓ lichno prisutstvoval na tseremonii*. Thus the prosodic co-occurrence features of the two synonyms are again diametrically opposed.

## 5.4. THE SEMANTIC SPECIALIZATION OF TYPES OF CO-OCCURRENCE

In the field of co-occurrence, a phenomenon parallel to the semantic specialization of forms and constructions described in § 3.3 and 4.4 is of interest. We shall consider it using the material of the putative words *dumat'*, *schitat'*, *polagat'* [to think, consider], etc. It makes it possible to illustrate another type of co-occurrence which has already been mentioned—the co-occurrence of X as a subordinate element in a syntactic construction with Y as its dominant node.

The synonyms *dumat'* and *schitat'* combine with the phasal verb *nachinat'* [to begin] (only in the imperfective, mostly with a first person pronoun, or when the speaker adopts the viewpoint of the subject of the thought), forming relatively stable expressions: *Ia nachinaiu dumat'/schitat', chto on ne tak prost, kak kazhetsia* [I'm beginning to think he's not as dim as he seems]. These expressions do not denote simply the commencement of a mental state, the first occurrence of an opinion, but an act of will which has already taken place—the revision of former opinions induced in the speaker by certain new circumstances.

The same two synonyms combined with the phasal verb *prodolzhat'* [to continue] (*Ia prodolzhaiu dumat'/schitat', chto vy nepravy* [I still think you're wrong]) also describe not simply the continuation of a mental state but an act of will performed on the basis of the evidence available to the speaker and in defiance of some other countervailing circumstances, as in, *Eta [rossiiskaia] tsivilizatsiia schitala (da i prodolzhaet schitat'), chto neset v sebe nekii svet i nadezhdu dlia vsego chelovechestva, nekii palladii, bud' to pravoslavie, krest'ianskaia obshchina ili marksizm-leninizm* (*Nezavisimaia gazeta*, 28 Nov. 1991) [this civilization considered (and still considers) that it bears within itself some light and hope for the rest of humanity, some Palladium, be it Orthodoxy, the peasant commune or Marxism-Leninism]. With the other synonyms of the series such collocations would be either untypical (*Ia nachinaiu/prodolzhaiu usmatrivat' v etom zloi umysel* [I'm beginning/continuing to discern ill intent in this]), or highly doubtful (*?Ia nachinaiu/prodolzhaiu polagat', chto vy nepravy* [I'm beginning/continuing to presume you're wrong]), while with *nakhodit'* [to find] they are impossible.

A similar modification of the sense of the whole collocation occurs when synonyms from this series are combined with the predicative word *sklonen* [inclined, apt]. Generally speaking, *sklonen* indicates that the subject is ready to select one action from a range of possibilities, but has not as yet undertaken this action: *Ia sklonen nemnogo porabotat' (poiti v kino)* [I'm inclined to do a bit of work (to go to the cinema)]. However, when *sklonen* is combined with putative verbs it denotes not a forthcoming choice but a definite intellectual position already selected from among a number of possible positions: *Ia sklonen schitat' (dumat', polagat') chto eto—obychnaia khalatnost'* [I'm inclined to think this is simple negligence]; *Ia sklonen rassmatrivat' eto kak proiavlenie khalatnosti, a ne kak akt sabotazha (smotret' na eto kak na obychnoe proiavlenie khalatnosti)* [I'm inclined to view this as a manifestation of negligence rather than an act of sabotage (regard this as a simple manifestation of negligence)]; *Ia ne sklonen videt' (usmatrivat') v etom chto-libo predosuditel'noe* [I am disinclined to see anything prejudicial in this]. Of all the putatives which make up this series of synonyms, only *nakhodit'* lacks the feature in question.

With *schitat'* there is another typical construction indicating choice, formed by the verb in the future tense: *Budem schitat', chto summa uglov treugol'nika ne ravna 180 gradusam* [we shall assume that the sum of the angles of a triangle is not equal to 180 degrees]; *Budem schitat', chto etogo ne bylo (chto v etom nikto ne vinovat)* [we shall assume that that did not happen (that nobody is to blame for that)]. In these instances *budem schitat'* is not a form of the future but a special idiom indicating an assumption of good will.

The verb *dumat'* in its perfective form is typically found in the collocation *mozhno podumat'* [one might think], which, contrary to expectations, does not mean 'there are grounds for thinking' but 'in reality one should not suppose': *Mozhno podumat', chto vy ne ustali* [Don't pretend, I can see you are tired]. Compare this with the same collocation with the verb in the imperfective, where the meaning is 'there are grounds for thinking': *Mozhno dumat', chto eksperimenty zakonchatsia uspeshno* [there are grounds for expecting that the experiments will be successfully completed].

## 6. The Illustration Zone

The illustration zone performs two basic functions in our dictionary. On the one hand, the material provided forms the research base and the basis for conclusions regarding the various properties of the synonyms. This explains the large number of examples (sometimes up to ten or twelve) for the most widely used synonyms in each series: the conclusions must be supported by a substantial amount of material. On the other hand, this zone also serves a purely illustrative purpose, showing the real semantic (and other) potential of a lexeme in modern Russian.

The illustration zone is based on a machine corpus of texts and the authors' files. The main principle in forming this lexicographical data base was to draw on modern Russian texts, that is, the language of the second half of the twentieth century. As a rule only such examples are taken from the classics of the nineteenth century and the first half of the twentieth, mostly from the 'Silver Age', as fully conform to contemporary norms of usage and may be recommended to the user as models to be emulated. This in large measure defines the range of our sources. It excludes ornamental and experimental prose (it is impossible, for example, to cite books as refined as Sasha Sokolov's *Shkola dlia durakov* [School for Fools] or *Mezhdu sobakoi i volkom* [Between Dog and Wolf]) and any texts marked by an excess of linguistic individuality.

Examples are considered ideal when the words being illustrated are highlighted, that is, where the context provides maximum 'definition' and shows their fundamental properties. This is a purely intuitive concept, which can be elucidated only by the illustrations themselves. In the sentence *I khotia schitatetsia, chto povtoriaetsia istoriia uzhe ne kak tragediia, a kak fars, vozmozhnosti vozvysit' fars do tragediii v nashem obshchestve poka est'* [and although some think that history repeats itself not as tragedy but as farce, in our society there are still opportunities to elevate farce to the level of tragedy] (*Izvestiia*, 11 Oct. 1990) the words *tragediia, fars*, and *vozvysit'* [elevate] are highlighted, while the words *istoriia* [history], *vozmozhnosti* [opportunities], *obshchestvo* [society], *schitatetsia* [think], *povtoriaetsia* [repeats itself] and *est'* [there are] are not. The example will serve well to illustrate any one of the first three words, but badly to illustrate any of the last six.

Many quotations are drawn from poetic texts. Of course, the poetic use of a word has a number of special features. The first of these is that in poetry we typically find a shift away from prototypical usage, so that the dictionary meaning of a word may not always be recognizable. Often a word will fluctuate between two or more senses, as in the following examples of the verb *videt'*: *Ia vizhu iz perednei | V okno, kak vsiakii god, | Svoei pory poslednei | Otsrochennyi prikhod* [through the hall window, as every year, I see the delayed approach of my last days] (B. Pasternak); *Vot my i vstali v krestakh i nashivkakh, | V snezhnom dymu. | Smotrim i vidim, chto vyshla oshibka, . . . | i my—ni k chemu!* [and so we rise up, wearing our crosses and ribbons in a haze of snow, and look about us, and see that there's been a mistake, . . . and we count for nothing] (A. Galich). In the example from Pasternak the governed forms *iz perednei, v okno* allow us to interpret *videt'* as a verb of perception while the direct object *otsrochennyi prikhod* displaces this purely physical sense towards the mental interpretation of 'imagining'. In the example from Galich the context of the verb *smotret'* creates the conditions for the physical meaning *videt'* [to see], while the propositional predicate creates those for the mental sense 'to understand'.

## 7. The Auxiliary Zones

The auxiliary zones perform three basic functions.

First, it is their function to indicate as many semantic links as possible between the elements of the synonym series under consideration and other categories of lexeme. The picture thus obtained may be well described by a spatial metaphor: from the given series it is possible to go out by various routes into the semantic space of the whole Russian language and make purposeful journeys in it.

Second, as a rule the material selected for these zones (analogues, conversives, antonyms, and semantic derivatives) may be used in rules of precise and imprecise periphrasis of utterances containing the elements of a given synonym series (see below). Thus these zones describe at least part of the periphrastic resources and the periphrastic system of Russian as defined in I. A. Mel'čuk's 'Meaning ⇔ Text' model.

Third, these zones indicate the areas in which it is planned to work in the near future. In the final analysis, a dictionary of Russian synonyms must be self-contained: all the lexemes mentioned in it will sooner or later be the subject of detailed description. From this viewpoint, the auxiliary zones may be seen as latent, abridged synonym series, represented in the current version of the dictionary either by a list of some elements of a future series (like the analogue and derivative zones) or by an indication of only the key element (like the conversive and antonym zones).

Generally speaking, the auxiliary zones should adhere to the principle of strict economy and confine themselves to noting only such 'derived' semantic information as is exactly one step away from the material of the original series. Indeed, if, for example, some analogue is entered for the given synonym series, this renders a list of synonyms and conversives of the analogue redundant. It may be assumed that they will be cited in the dictionary entry for that analogue. The same logic applies in the case of derivatives and other words which are in some way semantically connected with the material of the given synonym series.

However, in the published dictionary entries we quite often permitted ourselves a departure from the principle of strict economy. This is because for some years to come, owing to the immense amount of work that remains to be done, the dictionary will remain incomplete. Being unable to offer the reader a finished product at this stage, we wished to compensate for the absence of complete synonyms series in it by a small surplus of abridged series in the auxiliary zones.

A brief description is given below of the contents of each auxiliary zone.

### 7.1. PHRASEOLOGICAL SYNONYMS

In the overwhelming majority of cases the current version of the dictionary describes single-lexeme synonyms. Exception to this rule is made in only a few instances (cf. *obeshchat'/davat' slovo* [to promise, give one's word]; *godit'sia—byt' godnym* [to suit, be fitting], etc.), where a set expression or syntactic construction is introduced into a series.

This is not a strategic principle but a convenient practical way of ranking the material: phraseological synonyms will be more extensively represented in the dictionary at a more advanced stage of the work.

By way of preparation for this, the dictionary at its present stage includes a zone of phraseological synonyms. This covers the more current phraseological units which are synonymous with some element in the series, for example: *voobrazhat': risovat' v voobrazhenii* [to imagine: to picture in one's imagination]; *zhalovat'sia: plakat'sia v zhiletku (komu-libo)* [to complain: to cry on smb.'s shoulder]; *zhdat': schitat' dni, zhdat' ne dozhdat'sia* [to wait: to count the days, to be unable to wait any longer]; *ispol'zovat': puskat' v khod, puskat' v delo* [to utilize: to make use of, to bring into play]; *nadeiat'sia: vozlagat' nadezhdy* [to hope: to set store (by)]; *obeshchat': davat' obeshchanie, sviazat' sebia slovom, brat' (prinimat') na sebia obiazatel'stvo, davat' zarok* [to promise: to give a promise, give one's word, to take on an obligation, to give a pledge]; *rugat': pominat' nedobrym slovom* [to curse: to speak ill of].

### 7.2. ANALOGUES

In accordance with existing lexicographical tradition, 'analogue' is the term applied to words of the same part of speech as the dominant, whose meaning intersects substantially with the general meaning of the given synonym series, while not attaining the degree of closeness which constitutes synonymy proper. Hyperonyms, co-hyponyms and hyponyms of the key word are often counted as analogues, but in most cases the semantic links between the analogue and the key word are less rigid.

Different series of analogues may correspond to various components of meaning. For this reason the analogue zone opens up a number of pathways for travels in the lexico-semantic cosmos of the whole Russian language. Some examples follow.

*Voobrazhat'* [to imagine]: *grezit', mechtat'; fantazirovat'; pridumyvat', vymyshliat'; risovat'; vspominat'; myslit'; dumat'.*

*Zhdat'* [to wait]; *pogodit'; ottiagivat', tianut', medlit'; ozhidat', predpolagat', dumat'; predvidet'; nadeiat'sia, polagat'sia, rasschityvat'; vstrechat'; khotet', vybrat', uluchit'* [for *vyzhidat'*]; *(pod)karaulit'* [for *podzhidat'*].

*Izpol'zovat'* [to utilize]; *raskhodovat', tratit', potrebliat'; ekspluatirovat'; privlekat', podkliuchat'* [*K rassledovaniiu etogo prestupleniia byli privlecheny* ⟨*podkliucheny*⟩ *luchshie spetsialisty* (the best specialists were assigned to investigate this crime)]; *perekhodit' na chto-libo* [*Vse zhenshchiny pereshli na kolgotki* (all the women went over to tights)]; *prilazhivat', prisposobliat'; realizovat'; praktikovat'* [*praktikovat' sdel'nuiu oplatu raboty* (to apply piecework rates)]; *rasporiazhat'sia* [*Vlast' nesposobna rasporiadit'sia khotia by desiatoi dolei resursov i vozmozhnostei strany na blago naroda* (the authorities are unable to exploit so much as one tenth of the country's potential and resources for the good of the people)] (*Nezavisimaia gazeta*, 2 June 1992); *vyezzhat' na kom-chem-libo; manipulirovat' kem-libo; sygrat' na chem-libo.*

*Nadeiat'sia* [to hope]: *ozhidat'; dumat'* [*Vot uzh nikak ne dumala, chto uvizhu vas zdes'* (I had no idea I'd see you here)], coll. *chaiat'* [mostly in negative sentences: *ia uzh ne chaiala uvidet' ego zhivym* (I didn't expect to see him alive)], *gadat'* [*Ne dumala, ne gadala, chto dovedetsia vstretit'sia* (I never guessed we'd have occasion to meet)]; *mechtat'; radovat'sia; predvkushat'; dai Bog.*

*Obeshchat'* [to promise]: *zaveriat'; davat' podpisku o chem-libo* (*o nevyezde, etc.*); *obnadezhivat'; poruchat'sia; garantirovat', ruchat'sia; obespechivat'; prisiagat'; predskazyvat'; ugrozhat'; zarekat'sia, zakliuchat' dogovor; brat'sia* [*On vzialsia perevesti tekst za nedeliu* (he undertook to translate the text in a week)], *podriadit'sia; predlagat'; (s)derzhat' slovo.*

*Rugat'* [to curse]: *rugat'sia, branit'sia; odergivat'; vygovarivat', otchityvat', raspekat', chitat' notatsiiu; uprekat', korit', ukoriat', zhurit', peniat'; sovestit', stydit'; sramit'; vorchat', briuzzhat'; shpyniat'; razrugat', raznesti, raspushit', propesochit', raschikhvostit'; kritikovat', gromit', bichevat', prorabatyvat'; obviniat', ulichat'; osuzhdat', poritsat'; vozmushchat'sia; razoblachat', oblichat', razvenchivat'; obzyvat', obkladyvat'; liagat'* [*V svoei novoi knige Diuamel' liagaet svoikh zhe uchitelei* (in his new book Duhamel lashes his own teachers)] (O. Mandel'shtam); *oskorbliat'; beschestit', oslavliat', porochit', shel'movat'; kliast', proklinat'* [*On klial na chem svet stoit bestalannuiu svoiu sud'bu* (he cursed his ill-starred fate for all he was worth) (B. Pasternak); *Neponiatno, za chto my klianem inkvizitsiiu* (why we curse the inquisition is incomprehensible) (A. Solzhenitsyn)]; *krichat' (na kogo-libo), rychat'; nakazyvat'; presledovat', travit'.*

*Khvastat'sia* [to boast]: *risovat'sia, shchegoliat', forsit', bravirovat', kozyriat', vystavliat' napokaz, koketnichat'* (*svoei naivnost'iu*); *pozirovat'*; *krasovat'sia*; *gordit'sia, kichit'sia, zadavat'sia; privirat'; fanfaronit'; reklamirovat', raspisyvat'; blistat'.*

*Chudit'sia* [to seem]: *risovat'sia; kazat'sia; mechtat'sia; grezit'sia; chuvstvovat'sia; videt'sia, slyshat'sia,* [*Ona* (*pesenka*) *eshche ochen' nespetaia,* | *Ona zelena, kak trava,* | *No slyshitsia muzyka svetlaia,* | *I rovno lozhatsia slova* (The song is still far from sung, | It is as green as the grass, | But the bright music rings out, | And the words fall evenly into place) (B. Okudzhava)]; *poslyshat'sia* [*poslyshalos', chto kto-to idet* (it sounded as if somebody was coming); cf. the factive *Poslyshalis' shagi* (footsteps were heard)]; *prisnit'sia; pribredit'sia* [*My—uzhe na predele: pribredilis' vot krasnopogonniki* (we were already at the limit, already imagining the red epaulettes) (A. Solzhenitsyn)].

### 7.3. EXACT AND INEXACT CONVERSIVES

As is well known, 'conversive' is the term applied to predicate words denoting the same situation and having at least two valencies, which are filled by swapping actants:

*Butyl' vmeshchaet 10 litrov* [the container holds 10 litres]—*v butyl' vkhodit 10 litrov* [10 litres go into the container];

*Sneg pokryl polia* [snow covered the fields]—*Polia pokrylis' snegom* [the fields became covered in snow];

*Voda zapolnila bochku do kraev* [water filled the barrel to the brim]—*Bochka zapolnilas' vodoi do kraev* [the barrel filled with water to the brim];

*My znaem nemalo sluchaev takogo roda* [we know many such cases]—*Nam izvestno nemalo sluchaev takogo roda* [many such cases are known to us];

*Ia schitaiu vashi vyvody vpolne obosnovannymi* [I consider your conclusions fully justified]—*vashi vyvody predstavliaiutsia mne vpolne obosnovannymi* [your conclusions seem to me fully justified];

*On zanial u ottsa desiat' tysiach* [he borrowed ten thousand from his father]—*otets odolzhil emu desiat' tysiach* [his father lent him ten thousand];

*On peredal mne dokumentatsiiu* [he passed me the documentation]—*Ia poluchil ot nego dokumentatsiiu* [I received the documentation from him];

*On snimal komnatu v kvartire svoei tetki* [he rented a room in his aunt's flat]—*Tetka sdavala emu komnatu v svoei kvartire* [his aunt rented a room in her flat to him];

*On zarazil menia grippom* [he infected me with flu]—*Ia zarazilsia ot nego grippom* [I caught flu from him].

Discovered by Aristotle, they were introduced into broad linguistic practice several decades ago. The lexicographical assimilation of this material is now beginning. Lexical conversives are obviously of interest in a dictionary of synonyms: they are one of the main sources of synonymy of whole utterances.

Exact conversives are almost as rare as exact synomyms. Inexact conversives are more widely represented:

*Y zaruchilsia podderzhkoi* ⟨*soglasiem*⟩ *X-a* [Y secured the support ⟨agreement⟩ of X] ≈ *X zaveril Y-a v svoei podderzhke* ⟨*soglasii*⟩ [X assured Y of his support ⟨agreement⟩];

*Y vzial s X-a slovo* ⟨*obeshchanie*⟩, *chto P* [Y obtained X's word ⟨promise⟩, that P] ≈ *X obeshchal Y-u, chto P* [X promised Y that P];

*On ispol'zoval divan v kachestve posteli* [he used the couch as a bed]—*Postel'iu emu sluzhil divan* [the couch served him as a bed];

*Otets menia otrugal* [my father berated me]—*mne dostalos'* ⟨*vletelo, popalo*⟩ *ot ottsa* [I caught it from my father];

*Pylkaia molodezh' videla v mechtakh vozrozhdennuiu stranu* [ardent young people dreamed of a reborn country]—*Pylkoi molodezhi predstavlialas' v mechtakh vozrozhdennaia strana* [a reborn country appeared in the dreams of ardent young people].

## 7.4. CONVERSIVES TO ANALOGUES

The meaning of this concept can easily be deduced from the structure of the term itself. Although, as may be seen, this zone is completely redundant, for the reasons given above it has temporarily been accorded independent status in the published dictionary entries:

*Voobrazhat'* [to imagine]: *chudit'sia*; *mereshchit'sia*; *vsplyvat'*; *stoiat' pered glazami*; *stoiat' pered umstvennym* ⟨*myslennym*⟩ *vzorom* [to seem, appear].

*Zhdat'* 1 [to wait]: *zhdat'* 2, *ozhidat'* [to await] [*Chto zhdet menia?* (what awaits me?); *Shkhunu zhdet neizbezhnaia gibel'* (inevitable shipwreck awaits the schooner); *Ego ozhidala blestiashchaia kar'era* (a brilliant career awaited him); *Tridtsat' let nazad ia dazhe ne predstavlial, kakaia zhizn' ozhidaet menia vperedi* (thirty years ago I couldn't even imagine what kind of life awaited me)], *predstoiat'*.

*Ispol'zovat'* [to use]: *funktsionirovat'* [to function, serve] [*My ispol'zuem gruzovoi lift v kachestve passazhirskogo* (we use the goods lift as a passenger lift)—*gruzovoi lift funktsioniruet* (*u nas*) *v kachestve passazhirskogo* (our goods lift serves as a passenger lift)]; *prednaznachat'sia*.

*Chudit'sia* [to seem]: *obmanyvat'* [to deceive] [*Emu chudilos'* ≈ *slukh obmanyval ego* (it seemed to him ≈ his hearing was playing tricks on him).

## 7.5. EXACT AND INEXACT ANTONYMS

Lexemes whose explications when reduced to the level of semantic primitives differ by negation or 'more–less' or 'good–bad' components form antonymous relations. In the case of exact antonymy the difference is reduced to these components alone. In the case of inexact antonymy other minor distinctions appear:

*sobliudat'* [to observe, comply]—*narushat'* [to violate, infringe] (≈ *ne sobliudat'*);
*prisutstvovat'* [to be present]—*otsutstvovat'* [to be absent] (≈ *ne prisutstvovat'*);
*vysokii* [high]—*nizkii* [low] (more-less);
*bystro* [quickly]—*medlenno* [slowly] (more-less);
*vozrastat'* [to increase]—*sokrashchat'sia* [to decrease] (more-less);
*gordit'sia* [to be proud] (= 'to experience the agreeable sensation which occurs
    when a person has done or possesses something very good and when he
    thinks that because of this others will think the better of him')—*stydit'sia* [to
    be ashamed] ('to experience the disagreeable sensation which occurs when a
    person has done something bad or possesses something bad and thinks that
    because of this others will think the worse of him');
*nadeiat'sia* [to hope] (≈ 'to experience the feeling which occurs when a person
    expects something good to happen to him')—*boiat'sia* [to fear] (≈ 'to experi-
    ence the feeling which occurs when a person expects something bad to hap-
    pen to him which he cannot prevent');
*khvastat'sia* [to boast] (≈ 'the subject says that he has done something good or
    possesses something good in the belief that because of this others will think
    the better of him')—*skromnichat'* [to be modest] (≈ 'the subject says that he
    has done nothing particularly good or possesses nothing particularly good, in
    the belief that because of this others will think the better of him').

Since antonymous senses have a large area in common with each other, antonyms may also serve as a means of paraphrasing utterances:

*otsutstvovat'* [to be absent]—*ne prisutstvovat'* [not to be present];
*zapreshchat'* [to forbid]—*ne razreshat'* [not to permit];
*vsegda opazdyvat'* [to always be late]—*nikogda ne prikhodit' vovremia* [to never
    come on time];
*ne ispol'zovat' kalkuliatora pri raschetakh* [not to use a calculator for calcula-
    tions]—*oboitis' bez kalkuliatora pri raschetakh* [to do without a calculator for
    calculations].

## 7.6. DERIVATIVES

This zone, like the analogue zone, is formed quite freely. Besides true derivatives
it includes lexemes which are linked by semantic relations similar to those of
word-formation and provide the same opportunities for paraphrase. Yet formally
the words adduced there may be derived not from any members of the series
but from some other word. Take, for example, the derivative *oshibochno* [mistak-
enly] from the series *oshibat'sia* [to be mistaken]:

   *Oshibochno dumaet intelligentsiia, chtoby russkoe prosveshchenie i russkaia kul'-
tura mogli byt' postroeny na ateizme kak dukhovnom osnovanii* [the intelligentsia

mistakenly believes that a Russian enlightenment and a Russian culture may have atheism as their spiritual foundation] (S. N. Bulgakov)—*Intelligentsiia oshibaetsia, dumaia, chto russkoe prosveshchenie i russkaia kul'tura mogut byt' postroeny na ateizme kak dukhovnom osnovanii* [the intelligentsia is mistaken in believing that a Russian enlightenment and a Russian culture may have atheism as their spiritual foundation].

It is clear that, formally speaking, the adverb *oshibochno* is derived from the adjective *oshibochnyi*, which in turn is derived from the noun *oshibka*. Compare the more distant relationship in the pairs *lechit'* [to heal, treat]—*vrach* [doctor]; *operirovat'* [to operate]—*khirurg* [surgeon]; *lechit'* [to heal]—*medikamenty* [medications]; *streliat'* [to shoot]—*oruzhie* [firearm]; *voobrazhat'* [to imagine]—*mnimyi* [imaginary], which, however, does not prevent the existence of periphrastic relations between the original lexeme and a semantic relative of this kind:

*Kto vas lechil?* [who treated you?] ≈ *kto byl vashim (lechashchim) vrachom?* [who was your doctor?];
*Chem lechat ot anginy?* [with what do they treat tonsillitis?] ≈ *kakie medikamenty ispol'zuiut pri angine?* [what medications are used for tonsillitis?];
*Iz chego strelial prestupnik?* [what did the criminal shoot with?] ≈ *Kakim oruzhiem pol'zovalsia prestupnik?* [what sort of firearm did the criminal use?], etc.

Further examples of semantic (and formal) derivatives follow:

*Voobrazhat'* [to imagine]: *obraz* [image], *kartina* [picture]; *fantaziia* [fantasy]; *khimera* [chimera]; *fantom* [phantom], *mirazh* [mirage], *illiuziia* [illusion]; *galliutsinatsiia* [hallucination]; *voobrazhaemyi* [imagined], *myslennyi* [mental]; *mnimyi* [imaginary].
*Zhdat'* [to wait (for)]: *ozhidanie* [from *ozhidat'* (expectation)]; *vyzhidanie* [temporizing], *vyzhidatel'nyi* [from *vyzhidat'*; temporizing]; *dolgozhdannyi* [long-awaited]; *zazhdat'sia* ('the subject waited for smb. a very long time and with mounting impatience, reaching its peak at the moment the person appeared').
*Ispol'zovat'* [to use]: *(is)pol'zovanie* [use], *primenenie* [application], *upotreblenie* [use], *ekspluatatsiia* [exploitation], *utilizatsiia* [utilization]; *pol'zovatel'* [user]; *klient* [client]; *syr'e* [raw material]; *util'* [salvage]; *sredstvo* [means]; *orudie* [tool]; *funktsiia* [function].
*Nadeiat'sia* [to hope]: *nadezhda* [hope] (*On moia posledniaia nadezhda*—he is my last hope); *optimizm*; *shans* [chance]; *avos'* [maybe] (see the explication by V. V. Vinogradov: 'with a suggestion of insufficiently grounded hope', Vinogradov 1974: 738).
*Obeshchat'* [to promise]: *obeshchanie* [promise]; *obet* [vow]; *posuly* [promises]; *naobeshchat'* [to promise much].
*Khvastat'sia* [to boast]: *khvastovstvo* [boasting], *pokhval'ba, bakhval'stvo* [bragging]; *samovoskhvalenie* [self-praise]; *neskromnost'* [immodesty]; *samoreklama*

[self-advertisement]; *khvastun, bakhval* [braggart]; *khvastlivyi* [boastful]; *raskhva-stat'sia* [to boast extravagantly], *prikhvastnut'* [to boast a little].

*Chudit'sia* [to seem, appear]; *obman zreniia* [optical illusion]; *mirazh* [mirage], *galliutsinatsiia* [hallucination], *fantom* [phantom]; *mnimyi* [imaginary], *voobrazhaemyi* [imagined]; *primereshchit'sia* [to seem; to haunt]. In connection with the last example, it should be noted that the same lexemes may be considered semantic derivatives of various headwords, especially when these stand in relations of exact or inexact conversivity (see *voobrazhat'* and *chudit'sia*).

Prefixed verb derivatives, including the so-called *Aktionsarten*, deserve particular mention. In the series *kopat'—ryt'*, compare the following derivatives:

*vkopat'—vryt'* [to dig in, bury],
*dokopat'—doryt'* [to dig as far as],
*zakopat'—zaryt'* [to bury],
*nakopat'—naryt'* [to dig (up) (a quantity)],
*otkopat'—otryt'* [to dig up, unearth],
*perekopat'—pereryt'* [to dig over],
*podkopat'—podryt'* [to dig under, undermine],
*prokopat'—proryt'* [to dig through],
*raskopat'—razryt'* [to dig up, excavate].

Since all the word-formational types shown here are entirely regular (each prefix contributes the same semantic accretion to the lexical meaning of both *kopat'* and *ryt'*), a basis is created for the description of a further nine synonym series. In order to obtain a clear picture of these series, it is sufficient to have a rudimentary knowledge of the Russian word-formation system and of the meaning conveyed in the synonym series *kopat'—ryt'*.

### 7.7. BIBLIOGRAPHY

Each dictionary entry concludes with a bibliographical note showing theoretical works dealing with one or more of the synonyms considered in drafting the given synonym series.

# 3

# The Picture of Man as Reconstructed from Linguistic Data: An Attempt at a Systematic Description

## 1. Introductory

For hundreds of years the human being has been the subject of study of physiologists, psychologists, philosophers and linguists, to say nothing of sociologists. In the last two to three decades alone dozens of books and hundreds of articles have appeared dealing with human thoughts, desires, feelings, and speech acts. In this chapter it is not possible to take account of all the relevant literature, or even to mention it. We must perforce limit ourselves to references to the following books (Arutiunova 1976: 93–111; Arutiunova 1988: 101–99; Wierzbicka 1987*b*, 1992; Zalizniak 1992) and the survey by V. Apresjan (1995*a*), all containing extensive bibliographies.

From earlier studies we will mention only a few of those closest to this theme, above all the early works of the Moscow semantic school (Zholkovsky 1964*a*; Martem'ianov 1964; Shcheglov 1964; Mel'čuk 1974*a*; Mel'čuk and Zholkovsky 1984; J. Apresjan 1974) and the books by Anna Wierzbicka and N. D. Arutiunova which have already been mentioned. In particular, the ideas set forth here about the 'human make-up' have much in common with what was said by Arutiunova (1988) about the perceptual, mental, emotional, and volitional 'modes', their subtypes and their interpenetration. It would be impossible in the space available here, however, to register all the similarities or all the equally numerous differences both in general ideas and in the specific assessments of linguistic facts. It is more practical to explain why yet another essay is needed on a matter on which there is already a vast body of literature, and how this work differs from the others. I shall cite four differences.

1. The 'picture of man' is reconstructed exclusively on the basis of linguistic data. We have made the greatest effort to ensure that this should be a specifically 'linguistic' picture of man (not, for example, a literary, general-semiotic, cultural, or philosophical one).

2. The reconstruction of each fragment of the picture was regarded as motivated only when the reconstructed fragment was confirmed not by unconnected data (as in Pertsova 1990: 101 ff., for example), but by a large body of facts which made

it possible to construct an integrated and non-contradictory image of the object.

3. The language in which the image of man is recorded is to a greater or lesser degree the language of the explications. This was deemed the clearest and most formalized language of contemporary semantics (see Chapter 8 in this volume on the latest version of this language).

4. All the work was undertaken with one aim in view—to provide a theoretical foundation for systematic lexicography and, more specifically, for the *New Explanatory Dictionary of Russian Synonyms* (see J. Apresjan 1992*b*; J. Apresjan *et al.* 1992; cf. also Chapters 1 and 2) being compiled under the author's guidance at the Institute of the Russian Language of the Russian Academy of Sciences (RAN). The central concept of systematic lexicography is that of the lexicographic type, a group of lexemes with at least one common property (semantic, pragmatic, communicative, syntactic, combinatorial, morphological, prosodic, etc.), to which the same rules of linguistic description (of 'grammar' in the broad sense) refer and which therefore requires a homogeneous description in a dictionary. It is scarcely possible to offer an inventory of lexicographic types for the whole of the Russian language. We have therefore decided to begin this work at the most important sector, the vocabulary used to describe the human being.

We start by considering the general idea of a 'naïve', or linguistic, picture of the world (Section 2). Then a reconstruction is offered of the picture of man as the most important fragment of this picture (Section 3) and a more detailed survey is given of one of the eight systems of the human 'make-up', the emotional system (Section 4). In the fifth and last section an outline is supplied of a general format for describing the human being as the foundation of systematic lexicography. On the basis of this material an attempt is made to demonstrate the connection between the postulates of linguistic theory and the principles of description of lexicographic types in explanatory and synonym dictionaries.

## 2. A Naïve Picture of the World

Without venturing into the history of this issue (W. von Humboldt and the neo-Humboldtians, American ethnolinguistics, the Sapir-Whorf hypothesis of linguistic relativity, the theory of semantic fields, etc.), we may briefly describe the present situation.

Research into the naïve picture of the world is developing in two main directions.

First, certain concepts characteristic of a particular language, linguistic and cultural isoglosses *sui generis* and clusters of such isoglosses are investigated (see for example Vinogradov 1946; Bartmiński 1980; Bartmiński 1984; Tolstoi 1984; Wierzbicka 1990*a*; Sukalenko 1992; Likhachev 1993; Iakovleva 1993). This pertains above all to 'stereotypes' of linguistic and broader cultural mentality, e.g. the typically Russian concepts *dusha* [soul], *toska* [yearning], *sud'ba* [fate] (see

Wierzbicka 1990*a*), *zadushevnost'* [cordiality], *udal'* [dash, élan], *volia* (*vol'naia*) [will, freedom (free)], *pole* (*chistoe*) [field (open)], *dal'* [distance, vista], *avos'* [perhaps] (Sukalenko 1992: 117ff.). Another concern of this type of research is the specific connotations of non-specific concepts, such as the often-described symbolism of colour designations in various cultures.[1]

Second, research is being conducted to reconstruct an integrated, though 'naïve', pre-scientific, view of the world which is in-built in language. Extending the metaphor of linguistic geography, we might say that it is not individual isoglosses or clusters of isoglosses that are the subject of this research but dialect as a whole. While even here national specifics are given the fullest possible consideration, the emphasis is placed on an integrated linguistic picture of the world. A point-by-point summary is given below of the basic propositions in this approach, as this approach will be the sole subject of interest further on.

1. Each natural language reflects a specific way of perceiving and organizing (i.e. conceptualizing) the world about us. The meanings expressed in natural language form a unified system of views, a kind of collective philosophy which becomes obligatory for all speakers of that language. At one time grammatical meanings were seen in contrast to lexical as subject to obligatory expression, irrespective of whether they were relevant to a specific statement or not. In recent decades it has been established that many elements of lexical meaning also have to be expressed, irrespective of the speaker's intentions.

2. The way of conceptualizing reality (the world-view) inherent in a given language is partly universal and partly national-specific, such that speakers of different languages may view the world in slightly different ways, through the prism of their languages.

3. On the other hand, this view is 'naïve' in the sense that it differs in many important particulars from a scientific picture of the world. Not that the 'naïve' notions are in any way primitive. In many cases they are no less complex or interesting than scientific notions. Take, for example, naïve notions of man's inner world. These reflect the experience of introspection over scores of generations through many millennia, and may serve as a reliable guide to this world.

4. In the naïve world picture we may identify a naïve geometry and physics

---

[1] In Greenwood (1993: 17), some interesting data, obtained experimentally by using computers with colour monitors, is adduced on the differences in cultural associations and reactions to colours. In the USA, red is danger, in France aristocracy, in Egypt death, in India life and creativity, in Japan anger and danger, in China happiness. In the USA, blue is courage, in France peace and freedom, in Egypt faith, virtue, and truth, in Japan baseness, in China the sky and clouds; in the USA green is safety, in France crime, in Egypt fertility and strength, in India fertility and prosperity, in Japan the future, youth, and energy, in China the Ming dynasty, the sky and clouds; in the USA yellow is cowardice, in France transience, in Egypt happiness and prosperity, in India success, in Japan grace and nobility, in China birth, wealth, and power; in the USA white is purity, in France neutrality, in Egypt joy, in India death and purity, in Japan death, in China death and purity. These cultural differences in reactions to colours are so important that they have to be considered in designing computer screens intended for use in various Eastern and Western societies.

of space and time (for example, the utterly relativistic, pre-scientific, concepts of the speaker's space and time and the concept of the observer, see J. Apresjan 1986*a*), a naïve ethics, a naïve psychology, etc. From an analysis of pairs of the type *khvalit'* [to praise] and *l'stit'* [to flatter], *khvalit'* and *khvalit'sia* [to boast], *obeshchat'* [to promise] and *sulit'* [to promise the earth], *smotret'* [to look] and *podsmatrivat'* [to peek, spy], *slushat'* [to listen to] and *podslushivat'* [to eaves-drop], *smeiat'sia (nad kem-libo)* [to laugh at] and *glumit'sia* [to mock], *svidetel'* [witness] and *sogliadatai* [spy], *liuboznatel'nost'* [love of knowledge] and *liubopytstvo* [curiosity], *rasporiazhat'sia* [to give orders] and *pomykat'* [to order around], *predupreditel'nyi* [obliging, courteous] and *podobostrastnyi* [servile], *gordit'sia* [to be proud] and *kichit'sia* [to preen oneself], *kritikovat'* [to criticize] and *chernit'* [to defame], *dobivat'sia* [to try to obtain, strive after] and *domogat'sia* [to covet, solicit], *pokazyvat' (svoiu khrabrost')* [to give proof of (one's courage)] and *risovat'sia (svoei khrabrost'iu)* [to make a show of (one's courage)], *zhalovat'sia* [to complain] and *iabednichat'* [to tell on] and others like them it is possible to form an idea of the underlying commandments of Russian naïve-linguistic ethics. Here are some of them: 'it is bad to pursue ends of narrow personal gain' (*domagat'sia, l'stit', sulit'*); 'it is bad to interfere in other people's private lives' (*podsmatrivat', podslushivat', sogliadatai, liubopytstvo*); 'it is bad to belittle the worth of other people' (*pomykat', glumit'sia*); 'it is bad to lose sight of one's own honour and dignity' (*presmykat'sia* [to grovel], *podobostrastnyi*); 'it is bad to exaggerate one's own worth and the shortcomings of others' (*khvastat'sia* [to boast], *risovat'sia* [to show off], *kichit'sia* [to preen oneself], *chernit'* [to de-fame]); 'it is bad to tell third parties what we dislike about the behaviour of those close to us' (*iabednichat', fiskalit'* [to bear tales]); and so on. Of course all these commandments are the merest truisms, but it is curious that they have been fixed in the meanings of words. Certain positive commandments of naïve ethics are also reflected in language.

The primary task of systematic lexicography is to reflect the naïve world-view which a given language embodies—its naïve geometry, physics, ethics, psychology, and so forth. The naïve pictures of each of these areas are not chaotic but form definite systems and should therefore receive a homogeneous description in a dictionary. For this purpose, generally speaking, we should first reconstruct the corresponding fragment of the naïve picture of the world on the basis of lexical and grammatical meanings. In practice, however, in this case and others like it, the reconstruction and the (lexicographical) description go hand in hand and constantly provide each other with correctives.

### 3. A Naïve Picture of the Human Being

At the basis of the reconstructions set forth below lies a single general scheme of the human make-up. In the Russian linguistic picture of the world (which is all we are dealing with, although we may presume that it contains many universal features), man is viewed above all as a dynamic, active being. He performs three different types of action—physical actions, intellectual actions, and speech acts. On the other hand, he is also characterized by certain states: perception, desires, knowledge, opinions, emotions, and so on. Lastly, he reacts in certain ways to external and internal stimuli.

Each form of activity, each type of state, and each reaction is controlled by its own system and each system has its seat in a particular organ, which performs a certain function, switches to a particular state and shapes the required reaction. Sometimes the same organ serves more than one system and the same system is served by several organs. It is interesting, for example, that not only emotions but certain desires are located in the soul.

In most cases the functioning of each system is described by a semantic primitive or primitives, if the system can be broken down into subsystems.

Besides these systems and independently of them, two specific forces, or capabilities, operate in human beings. Usually, in human beings as in other living organisms, there may be several such forces, but at least two must be present: one of these activates a particular system while the other holds it in check.

Section 3.1 is given over to a consideration of these forces. In § 3.2 we consider the systems of human beings as well as the features of their constitution and operation.

## 3.1. WILL AND CONSCIENCE—ACTIVATING AND CHECKING A SYSTEM

The main stimulus for human activity is desires. We implement our desires with the aid of a force termed 'will' [*volia 1*],[2] which is the capacity to realize our wishes. In the Russian linguistic system, *volia* is associated with firmness, pressure, intransigence, and possibly even aggression: *sila voli* [strength of will], *sil'naia ⟨zheleznaia⟩ volia* [strong ⟨iron⟩ will], *nepreklonnaia ⟨nesgibaemaia, nepokolebimaia⟩ volia* [unbending ⟨inflexible, unflinching⟩ will], *vsesokrushaiushchaia volia* [all-conquering will], *volia k pobede ⟨k zhizni, k podvigu⟩* [will to conquer ⟨to live, accomplish great deeds⟩], *volevoi napor* [drive], *volevoi chelovek* [a man of great will-power], *sil'naia lichnost'* [a strong personality] (one whose will is so strong that he can alter the course of events).

Desires may be either rational and moral or irrational and amoral. The will

[2] The notion of the will as a force (rather than an organ) is taken from an early but very interesting work (Shcheglov 1964: 56–60) devoted to the 'vocabulary of the will'. However, in certain important details our picture of the will differs from that offered by Shcheglov. Shcheglov uses the concept of the 'apparatus of the will', which consists of reason, feelings, the will proper, and other organs, which implement a certain behavioural programme. It seems to us that the relationship is rather the reverse: the will forms part of the 'apparatus of reason' (if we are to preserve this metaphor). Moreover, in the picture presented by Shcheglov there is no mention of conscience, although it too has a role—as a moral regulator—in shaping human behaviour.

itself stands outside morality: it may be 'good' or 'ill'. Hence the operation of the will is counterbalanced by that of another force, known as 'conscience' [*sovest'*]. If desires and the will are the initiators of human action, in the Russian linguistic world-view (as well as in some others) conscience is seen as a moral brake which prevents the implementation of immoral desires or impulses: *Sovest' ne pozvoliaet ⟨sovestno⟩ (delat' chto-libo)* [(my) conscience won't let me (do smth.)]; *Esli u nego est' khot' kaplia sovesti, on etogo ne sdelaet* [if he has so much as a shred of conscience he won't do that]; *Sovest' vosstaet (protiv chego-libo)* [(my) conscience rebels (against smth.)].

Generally speaking, conscience, unlike the will, is seen not only as a force, if a potential one (i.e. a capacity); at the same time it appears as a kind of being within us. It is a strict inner judge (*otvechat' za chto-libo pered svoei sovest'iu* [to answer for smth. to one's conscience]; *byt' chistym pered sobstvennoi sovest'iu* [to be at ease with one's own conscience]), always oriented towards good, possessing an innate and unerring sense of supreme justice (*golos sovesti* [the voice of conscience]; *velenie sovesti* [the dictates of conscience]) and giving certain prescripts which are directly based on an understanding of what true goodness is in a given situation.

Like any other judge, conscience may punish or pardon. If we 'hear the voice of conscience', 'heed it' and 'act according to our conscience (as our conscience urges)', the reward is a 'clear conscience'. If we do not 'hear the voice of conscience', 'stifle this voice' to satisfy our desires or 'act against our conscience' we are punished by it: it 'torments' us, 'gives us no peace', 'nags' or 'gnaws' at us; a wrongful act 'weighs heavy on our conscience', we experience 'pangs of conscience' (torments of conscience), etc. Conscience is an indestructible authority and if we succeed in 'stifling its voice within ourselves' it may 'awaken' or 'find new voice' in us again a little while later.

A remarkable property of this inner judge is its complete impartiality: to all people in identical situations it dictates the same decision, the only correct one. Paradoxically this inner voice is the shared inheritance of all. It is for this reason that we may regard a person who is known for moral courage as 'our conscience'. For the same reason we can 'appeal to the conscience' of another person, confident that he will in the end be guided by the same moral truths as we ourselves. Thus conscience transports a person's perception of the world beyond the limits of his own interests and compels him to weigh his actions and those of others on the scales of supreme justice.[3]

---

[3] The reconstruction offered here, which gives an integrated picture of 'conscience', is based exclusively on linguistic data. This naïve-linguistic picture turns out to be unexpectedly close to the concept developed in Russian religious philosophy. Note the following: 'Side by side with everything that man himself *wants* and *is capable of*, side by side with all the aspirations which flow from the empirical nature of man and the component parts of that nature, an ideal force of *duty*, the voice of conscience, also acts upon him,—a call which he perceives as emanating from a higher level, transcending and transforming his empirical nature; and only in acting on this call, in transcending the limits of his empirical being, does man see the true fulfilment of his destiny, of his true inner self' (Frank

From this it follows that conscience acts as a unifying and altruistic principle, whereas the will tends to be an individualizing, egoistic, and capricious one: for example *svoevolie* [self-will], *voleiu sudeb* (*po prikhoti sudeb*) [by the will (whim) of fate], as well as *volia 2* [freedom acknowledging only one's own will]. On the other hand, 'conscience' is a less active principle than 'will', lacking the latter's drive. This is why it is possible to 'stifle its voice' and 'do a deal with it'.

If the primary function of *volia* is creative, active, that of *sovest'* is restraining, blocking. Of course, following the dictates of one's reason, *volia* may be used as a restraining or blocking mechanism, by which a person curbs his irrational desires, and *sovest'* can act as a moral stimulus urging a person to an active defence of justice, irrespective of where he sees it being violated—in his own thoughts and actions or in those of others. These, however, are secondary functions of the will and conscience.

The asymmetry of these two principles is interesting: according to the Russian linguistic picture (as well as some others), there is more good in man than bad, as on the other side of neutral will there is no evil principle to oppose *sovest'*.

## 3.2. THE MAIN HUMAN SYSTEMS

Below are named the main systems which make up a human being; the organs which house them, produce certain states, and perform certain functions; and the semantic primitives which correspond to these systems, organs, states, or functions. We may note that almost all our primitives correspond directly to those in A. Wierzbicka's list (Wierzbicka 1992: 10); see Chapter 8 in this volume on the way primitives are understood in the present work.

(1) Physical perception (sight, hearing, sense of smell, taste, touch). This has its seat in the organs of perception (eyes, ears, nose, tongue, skin). The semantic primitive is 'vosprinimat'' [to perceive].

(2) Physiological states (hunger, thirst, desire—in the sense of 'carnal longing' —calls of nature, pain, etc.). These have their seat in various parts of the body. The semantic primitive is 'oshchushchat'' [to sense].

(3) Physiological reactions to various external and internal stimuli (pallor, cold, shivering, colour, fever, perspiration, heartbeat, grimaces, etc.). Various parts of

1991: 331–2). Cf. the fundamentally different reconstruction of the concept of 'conscience' on the basis of linguistic data and that of literary texts in Arutiunova (1976: 95–7): 'a picture of conscience as a sharp-clawed and sharp-toothed being hostile to human desires and feelings', 'a small rodent', an image of conscience as a 'tedious interlocutor', 'the image of conscience as the enemy, persecutor and tormentor of man', 'a picture of conscience as a kind of surface, a sort of *tabula rasa*', leading to the following conclusion: 'It is clear that the co-occurrence behaviour of the word *sovest'* is not modelled on the basis of an integrated picture. It arises through the amalgamation and intersection of a number of images which are incompatible from the standpoint of the natural laws of imagery' (p. 97). Let us note the national specificity of the concept of *sovest'*. There is a similar concept in German (Gewissen) but not, for example, in French: 'la conscience' denotes something in between *sovest'* and *soznatel'nost'* [consciousness].

the body (face, heart, throat) react, or the body as a whole. There is no semantic primitive. The sense of the verb *reagirovat'* [to react], in particular, can have no claim to this role, as it is indisputable that the meaning can be represented via the following simpler meanings: *A reacts to B* = 'Factor B at moment $t_1$ acted upon organism A [presupposition]; A received this stimulus and at moment $t_2$, later than $t_1$, in some way changed its properties or behaviour; the fact of perceiving the stimulus was the sole cause for the changing properties and behaviour of A'.

(4) Physical actions (to work, rest, go, stand up, lie down, throw, draw, weave, chop, cut, hew, break, etc.). These are performed by the extremities and the body. The semantic primitive is 'delat'' [to do].

(5) Desires (to want, to strive, to feel an urge, to be impatient, to refrain, to compel, to tempt, to entice, to prefer, etc.). They are located either in the body or the soul. The primary, simplest desires, connected with the satisfaction of physiological needs, such as 'to be hungry, thirsty, tired', are located in the body. These are clearly common to humans and animals. Culturally conditioned wishes, connected with the satisfaction of spiritual needs, are located in the soul: e.g. *V dushe ei khotelos' kakoi-to neobyknovennoi liubvi* [her soul longed for some unusual romance]; *Ot vsei dushi zhelaiu, chtoby oni [prazdniki] skoree konchilis'* [I wish with all my soul that the holidays would end very soon] (M. Bulgakov). The latter type, which undoubtedly make up the majority of wishes, are realized with the aid of *volia* [will], whose operation is regulated by *sovest'* [conscience]. The semantic primitive is 'khotet'' [to want].

(6) Thought, intellectual activity (to imagine, picture; to think, suppose; to understand, realize; intuition, illumination; to get through to, to dawn on; to know; to believe; to guess, suspect; to remember, to commit to memory, to recollect, to forget; etc.). Intellectual activity is located in the mind (head) and is performed by these. The semantic primitives are 'znat'' [to know], 'schitat'' [to think] and possibly a few others. 'To understand' and 'to believe' are not primitives; see Chapter 8 in this volume for the explication of these verbs. A more precise explication of *ponimat'* [to understand] will be found in Chapter 5 in this volume.

(7) The emotions (to fear, rejoice, be angry, love, hate, hope, despair, etc.). These too are divided into primary emotions, common to animals and humans (fear, rage), and culturally conditioned emotions (hope, despair, surprise, indignation, admiration, etc.). In man all emotions are located in the soul, heart, or breast. The semantic primitive is 'chuvstvovat'' [to feel].

(8) Speech (to tell, promise, ask, demand, order, forbid, warn, advise, declare, curse, praise, boast, complain, etc.). It is served by the tongue. The semantic primitive is 'govorit'' (komu-to chto P) [to say to smb. that P]. Attempts to explicate this verb in the meaning indicated turn out to be circular.[4]

---

[4] See e.g. the following explication: *X govorit 1 Y-u Z* [X says Z to Y] = 'person X utters a text created by him containing meaning Z so that Y should receive meaning Z' (Zalizniak 1991b: 71). If 'text' in this explication is a metalanguage word its meaning should include an indication of language: 'text' is above all a sequence of signs in some language. 'Language' in its turn should be

The structure and functioning of the systems listed here have the following features: each system has a specific inner organization (§ 3.2.1); the systems form a hierarchy (§ 3.2.2.); the organs of these systems also form a hierarchy (§ 3.2.3); the systems interact with one another (§ 3.2.4); the systems can be divided into subsystems (§ 3.2.5.); on the other hand they amalgamate into larger classes and subclasses on the basis of the principle of duplication (§ 3.2.6).

### 3.2.1. The Internal Organization of Systems

Owing to limitations of space this question can be considered using only one system—perception—as an example. Our choice is determined, first, by the relative simplicity of the system and, secondly, by the fact that it is quite well organized and provides an opportunity to demonstrate the inner connection between a particular way of conceptualizing reality and a lexicographic type (LT).

A primary perception situation includes two main participants. The first is the one who perceives and the second the thing perceived. It is therefore possible to predict the existence of at least two series of verbs (or other predicate words) designating the states of the first and second actants respectively. One is formed by verbs whose first semantic valency is filled in by the name of the subject of perception, and the second by the name of the thing perceived: *iz transhei my videli uzkuiu polosku berega* [from the trench we could see a narrow strip of shoreline].[5] The other is formed by verbs or verbal expressions which are conversive to the first and whose first semantic valency is filled by the name of the thing perceived and the second by the name of the subject of perception: *iz transhei nam byla vidna uzkaia poloska berega* [from the trench a narrow strip of shoreline was visible to us].

defined as the means by which people talk [*govorit'* 2] to one another. Lastly, the two-directional exchange process 'to talk to each other' may naturally be defined via a simpler one-directional process of communicating one's thoughts to another, i.e. by means of *govorit'* 1 [to tell, say]. The result is circular. On the other hand, we may allow that 'text' in this explication is a lexeme denoting 'that which is written'. But even then within one or two steps the same meaning *govorit'* 1 will be revealed in it: that which is written is another, culturally more complex form of what may be 'said'.

[5] The subject of a state, an event or process, etc. is sometimes referred to as the 'object', in sentences such as *Okhotnik vidit lisu* [the huntsman sees the fox], *On boitsia etogo cheloveka* [he is afraid of that man], *On poskol'znulsia i upal* [he slipped and fell], *On dolgo bolel* [he was ill for a long time], *On vyzdorovel* [he recovered], etc. In Otto Jespersen's view, in the example 'he is afraid of that man', 'the grammatical nominative denotes the thing subjected to the action and the accusative the source of the stimulus' (Jespersen 1958). See also similar ideas in Fillmore (1968), Lyons (1968), and other contemporary works. Strictly speaking, there is no object in any of these examples because there is no action by any force on the person. In fact, to describe the semantic roles of the actants in the range of situations under consideration, four different concepts are needed: the agent (the active participant, like the grammatical subject in the phrase 'He chops wood'), the experiencer (the passive recipient, like the grammatical subject in the phrase 'He saw a dog'), the object (that which experiences the real stimulus, like the wood in the above example) and the object of thought (the thing to which the speaker attributes certain properties, like the grammatical subject in the phrase 'the coat costs 500 roubles'). Here, however, we cannot undertake such a profound revision of semantic roles and will therefore use more or less traditional terminology.

The subject of perception may not only passively perceive some object, but also actively use the corresponding organ of perception to obtain information about the world. Theoretically, therefore, another series of verbs is possible: the *smotret'* type [to look]. A ternary opposition of senses results: 'to perceive'—'to be perceived'—'to employ the faculty of perception'. Theoretically it is possible to conceive of the need for a fourth series of verbs denoting the active influence of the object on the sensory organ: *brosat'sia v glaza* [to leap into view] for sight, *donosit'sia* [to resound] for hearing, *shibat'* (*v nos*) [to hit] for the sense of smell. However, this series is less regular in all respects than the first three, so we shall not consider it for the moment.

As there are five subsystems of perception (sight, hearing, sense of smell, taste and touch), each of which may ideally be served by a set of three verbs (not counting their synonyms, of course), perception as a whole may be presented in the form of a table (a semantic paradigm): $3 \times 5 = 15$. This is what provides the basic lexicographic type in the sphere of the vocabulary of perception.

In Russian this LT is represented by the following five triples of verbs:

*videt'* [to see]—*byt' vidnym (komu-libo)*—[to be visible (to smb.)]—*smotret'* [to look];

*slyshat'* [to hear]—*byt' slyshnym (komu-libo)*—[to be audible (to smb.)]—*slushat'* [to listen];

*oboniat'* (*chuiat'*) [to scent, smell (trans.)]—*pakhnut'* [to smell (intrans.)] —*niukhat'* [to sniff];

*oshchushchat' vkus* [to taste (trans.)]—*byt' na vkus* [to taste (intrans.)]— *probovat'* [to try, taste];

*osiazat'* [to feel (trans.)]—*byt' na oshchup'* [to feel (intrans.)]—*oshchupyvat'* [to touch], e.g. *Kogda zhe mal'chik oshchupyval ego litso, to oshchushchal svoimi chutkimi pal'tsami ego glubokie morshchiny* [when the boy touched (the man's) face his sensitive fingers felt its deep wrinkles] (V. Korolenko).

One of the features of this LT is that the boxes in the table are not always filled in the same way. Theoretically all fifteen boxes should be served by verbs. However, in Russian this is only the case with the sense of smell (see above), and even here there is no neutral word meaning 'to perceive with the nose': *oboniat'* is too scientific, while *chuiat'* is markedly substandard. The series *vosprinimat'sia* [to be perceived] is served worst of all: it has only one verb (*pakhnut'*).

In Russian all boxes of the semantic paradigm which lack one-word versions may be filled by free or semi-free collocations. In order to appreciate the peculiar nature of this paradigm it is useful to compare it with the corresponding paradigm in English. Here the dearth of verbal material to fill the boxes in the table is made good not so much by collocations as by polysemy:

to see—to be visible—to look;

to hear—to sound—to listen;

to smell—to smell—to smell ('I can smell apples'—'Apples smell good'—'He bent over to smell a flower');

to taste—to taste—to taste ('I can taste something very spicy in the food'—'The meat tastes delicious'—'He raised the glass to his mouth to taste the wine');

to feel—to feel—to feel ('I could feel the rough surface of the table'—'The water feels warm'—'Feel the bump on my head').

As it is not possible to give a full description of this complex LT, we shall confine ourselves to listing certain features of the verbs of the main series (*videt'*, *slyshat'*, *oboniat'*, *osiazat'*). (*a*) They belong to the class of statives and have all the diagnostic morphological, syntactic, and semantic features of statives (see Chapter 8 in this volume), which, naturally, must be reflected in a dictionary. (*b*) They have the property of being semi-factive, in particular, the capacity to bear the main phrasal stress and to govern clauses introduced by conjunctive words of the type *kto* [who], *chto* [what], *gde* [where], *kuda* [whither], *otkuda* [whence], *skol'ko* [how much/many], *kak* [how], etc. For example: *Ia videl, kto otkryl dver'* ⟨*chtó on prines, kuda on poshel, gde prizemlilsia samolet, skol'ko vina on vypil*⟩ [I saw who opened the door ⟨what he brought, where he went, where the plane landed, how much wine he drank⟩]; *Ia slyshal, kto ego zval* ⟨*chtó on govoril, otkuda donessia zvuk, kak on na tebia krichal*⟩ [I heard who called him ⟨what he said, where the sound came from, him shouting at you⟩]. It is interesting that the variety of means of introducing a subordinate clause decreases between *videt'* and *slyshat'* and further between *slyshat'* and *oboniat'* and *osiazat'*. (*c*) They are able to govern clauses introduced by the conjunctions *chto* [that] and *kak* [how] with the characteristic contrast between event (fact) and action. To N. D. Arutiunova's observations (1988: 115–17) on this topic we should add that the first of these describes an event, even if the verb in the subordinate clause is in the imperfective: *Ia videl, chto on perekhodil na tu storonu ulitsy* [I saw him cross the street] (registering only the fact of the crossing). The second (*kak*) describes the process, even if the verb in the subordinate clause is in the perfective: *Ia videl, kak on pereshel na tu storonu ulitsy* [I saw him crossing the street; lit. I saw how he crossed the street] (even in the perfective, this registers certain phases in the process of crossing).

All the features indicated of the perception verbs and many other features should be considered if we are to obtain a homogeneous description of the given LT in the dictionary.

### 3.2.2. The Hierarchy of Systems

The aforementioned eight systems form a hierarchy according to their complexity. (They are set out above in ascending order of complexity.) The simplest is perception, which humans have in common with all the rest of the living world. Even plants perceive such stimuli as light and warmth, since they react to these.

The most complex is speech, which distinguishes humans from all other organisms.

The relative complexity of a system is determined linguistically by several factors.

The first factor is the number of lexemes and grammatical units which serve it. The more there are, the more complex the system. We have no precise figures, but the order of systems given above roughly corresponds to a priori linguistic estimates. The only exception is the system of physical actions, whose vocabulary exceeds all other systems in richness. However, the four 'spiritual' systems (desires, intellectual activity, emotions, and speech) greatly exceed the system of physical actions in the number of grammatical units serving them. Note the deictic morphological categories (e.g. tense, specified with reference to the moment of speech), as well as such syntactic structures as the imperative and the optative (desires), conditional and hypothetical clauses (intellect), numerous expressive structures in minor type sentences (desires and emotions), and parenthetic structures (whose meaning always contains an implicit reference to the speaker, and therefore to speech).

Secondly, the complexity of System $C_i$ compared with System $C_j$ is determined by the number of lexemes belonging to $C_i$, whose explications include units of System $C_j$. The greater the number of such units, the more complex $C_i$ is in relation to $C_j$. In this respect emotions and speech are substantially more complex than, say, perception and even desires, because the explications of most emotional states and speech acts contain references to perception and desires, whereas the reverse is not true.

Thirdly, the complexity of a system is determined by the role of its concepts in the organization of an utterance. In this respect, speech has no rivals. It is sufficient to point to the central role of the speaker as the figure who organizes the deictic space of the utterance.[6]

### 3.2.3. The Hierarchy of Organs

The organs of these systems may also be ranked in a hierarchy, but according to a different feature, their role in organizing human behaviour. The apex of this hierarchy is the mind. In the naïve world picture the mind is seen as having the key role in regulating human physical, emotional, and speech behaviour. Aided by the power of will and conscience, it keeps behaviour within normal limits, even when the other systems are functioning with increased or maximum inten-

---

[6] The semantic structure itself of speech acts, as described in e.g. Wierzbicka (1987*b*) and Glovinskaia (1993), testifies to the exceptional complexity of speech. In particular, this material gave grounds for identifying an important new layer of meaning: motivation (along with presupposition and assertion). Motivation may be defined as the explanation of the purpose for which a given speech act is undertaken. It binds the assertion, as the result, with one of the presuppositions, as the cause of the speech act. Motivation must evidently be included in the explication of all lexemes which denote fairly complex purposeful acts, not only speech acts.

sity. The mind is a monitoring agency, capable of observing human behaviour from outside (note the expressions *videt' sebia so storony* [to see oneself from the side]; *popytaisia posmotret' na sebia so storony* [try and take a look at yourself from the side]). If, for example, the mind finds signs of irrational behaviour, it gives instructions to the will, which re-establishes normal behaviour (as long as the will is still able to function effectively, of course): *On ponial, chto boitsia, i usiliem voli popytalsia podavit' svoi strakh* [he realized that he was afraid and tried by an effort of will to overcome his fear].

The foregoing may also be confirmed by such pairs of lexical units as *isstuplenie* [frenzy] and *vozbuzhdenie* [agitation], *ekstaz* [ecstasy] and *vostorg* [delight], *panika* [panic] and *strakh* [fear], *poteriat' golovu* [to lose one's head] and *rasteriat'sia* [to become confused], *vzorvat'(sia)* [to explode] and *vozmutit'(sia)* [to make/get indignant]. In existing explanatory dictionaries the distinctions between the members of these pairs are often reduced to the degree of intensity: *frenzy* = 'extreme excitement', *ecstasy* = 'great joy or happiness', *to lose one's head* = 'to become utterly confused', etc. In fact the elements on the left in all these pairs differ from those on the right not only in bearing an indication of greater intensity in the process or state. It is also important that the inner state of the person attains such intensity that the subject's behaviour escapes his control and ceases to be subject to his will. For the sake of comparison, note the pair *iarost'* [rage] and *gnev* [anger] (*On s trudom sderzhival svoiu iarost' ⟨svoi gnev⟩* [he could hardly contain his rage ⟨his anger⟩]), in which the first emotion does indeed differ from the second by being of the utmost intensity, but not by loss of self-control.

Thus the semantic component which is repeated in the meanings of the lexical units *isstuplenie, ekstaz, panika, teriat' golovu, vzorvat'(sia)* turns out to be fairly regular (systematic). The idea of complete loss of control as the natural limit in the development of certain inner states is therefore indeed a characteristic of the naïve representation of the human psyche.

Further evidence of this may be seen in the fact that a similar semantic opposition emerges in the field of so-called symptomatic vocabulary—the expressions describing the outward manifestations of a person's emotional state. See such series as *otsepenet' (ot strakha)* [to go numb (with fear)], *ostolbenet' (ot udivleniia)* [to be struck dumb (with surprise)], *okamenet' (ot uzhasa)* [to be petrified (with horror)] on the one hand, and *zameret' (ot sladkogo ozhidaniia)* [to stand rooted to the spot (with sweet anticipation)] and *zameret' (v voskhishchenii pered kartinoi)* [to stand rooted to the spot (in admiration of a picture)] on the other. The last verb means 'to stand absolutely still' and contains no information as to whether the subject loses his self-control or not. The reaction may be in greater or lesser measure spontaneous, yet fully controllable when used outside collocations with the names of emotions: *uvidev olenia, okhotnik zamer* [on seeing the deer, the hunter stopped in his tracks]. As for the first three verbs, their meaning is not simply 'to freeze into immobility under the stimulus of some powerful emotion', as some dictionaries would have it. *Otsepenet'*, for example, is to become immobile as a result of paralysis of the will, which occurs when the will is no longer controlled by the mind, which in turn is purely the result of the subject's state of terror: *chto s nim tvorilos'—konechno, i voobrazit' nevozmozhno, udivitel'no, kak on ne umer tut zhe na stsene. Za kulisami i v zale vse otsepeneli* [of course what was going on inside him (the opera-singer Selivanov, who was so terror-stricken that he could not perform his aria in the presence of Stalin) is quite beyond all imagination. It is surprising that he did not fall down dead on the stage. Behind the scenes and in the house everybody froze] (G. Vishnevskaia). The verb *zastyt'* [to become still], which occupies an intermediate position between *zameret'* and *otsepenet'*, should also be mentioned: *On v voskhishchenii zastyl pered kartinoi* [lost in admiration, he stood stock still before the painting].

An indication of complete loss of control as a result of shock, excessive physical activity, etc. is included in the meaning of many other words and expressions: *poteria samoobladaniia* [loss of self-possession], *neistovstvo* [fury], *konvul'sii* [convulsions], *prostratsiia* [prostration], *trans* [trance], *stupor* [stupor] and substandard *otkliuchka* [state of being 'switched off', 'out of it'].

### 3.2.4. The Interdependence of Systems

The various human systems and subsystems have varying degrees of autonomy and interact with one another in varying degree. The simpler the system, the greater its autonomy. The more complex the system, the less autonomy it has, i.e. the greater the number of other systems which it activates or whose data it exploits.

The most autonomous system is perception. Perception proper takes place independently, irrespective of the functioning of other systems. We may see or hear something while in a completely immobile state, wanting nothing, not thinking of anything, feeling nothing and not speaking. The exception is those cases in which we wish to perceive something and by an act of will bring the relevant organ into a state in which it may help us perceive: *smotret'* [to look], *slushat'* [to listen], *niukhat'* [to sniff], *probovat'* [to taste], *shchupat'* [to palpate].

Physical activity and desires are less autonomous. It is possible, of course, to stand somewhere, go somewhere, or want something in silence and without experiencing any emotion. There are, however, more complex forms of physical activity, especially purposeful activity, which are impossible without the participation of desires, as they provide the aim and the motivation (*stroit' most* [to build a bridge], *zhdat' kogo-libo* [to wait for smb.], *reshat' zadachu* [to solve a problem]). As for the desires themselves, even the simplest of them may be based on the indications of some sensory organs: *khotet' est'* [to be hungry, lit. to want to eat], for example, means to feel (with the body) a need for food.

The functioning of the mind is even less autonomous. It is impossible without the perception of certain facts as a point of departure for thought processes. Besides this, certain intellectual processes and states presuppose the operation of the will. In this respect opinions are particularly interesting. Prototypical opinions presuppose a preceding act of will by which they are directed into the mind and constituted as opinions. Compare *Sledovatel' schel, chto sobrannykh ulik uzhe dostatochno* [the investigator concluded/considered that enough evidence had been collected] (by an act of will a thought is transposed into the category of an opinion which a person is prepared to uphold as correct) and *Sledovatel' podumal, chto sobrannykh ulik uzhe dostatochno* [the investigator thought that enough evidence had been collected] (a certain supposition arises in his mind without the participation of his will). For more detail on *schitat'* and *dumat'* see Mel'čuk and Zholkovsky (1984: 867); Dmitrovskaia (1988*b*); Zalizniak (1991*a*); J. Apresjan (1993: Chapter 4 in this volume).

The least autonomous systems are the emotions and speech. These interact most with the other human systems.

Emotions mostly occur following the perception or mental contemplation of some situation and an intellectual appraisal of it as probable or improbable, or good or bad for the subject. Here one may recall the following description of hope, fear, confidence, and despair offered by Spinoza: 'If we know about some future thing that it is good and that it may happen, the soul assumes the form which we know as hope . . . If, on the other hand, we suppose that the thing which may arise is bad, the soul assumes the form which we know as fear. If we believe that the thing is good and will certainly come, the soul is filled with the calm that we know as confidence . . . When we believe that the thing is bad and certain to come, the soul is filled with despair' (Spinoza 1957: 128–9). Physiological reactions (*pobagrovet' ot gneva* ⟨*ot iarosti*⟩ [to turn purple/crimson with anger /rage]), physical actions (*prygat' ot radosti* [to jump for joy]) and speech (*gromko vostorgat'sia* [to rejoice loudly]) may also play a part in the manifestation of emotion.

Basic speech acts must entail the parallel action of at least three other systems: the mind, desires, and physical activity. Indeed, most speech acts are preceded by some assessment on the part of the speaker of the informational state of the listener. Furthermore, every speech act presupposes motivation—a reason why the speaker wishes to alter in some way the informational state of his listener. Finally, any speech act is a form of physical activity—for the simple reason that the operation of the organs of speech is an inalienable component of speech. Besides this, very many speech acts are dictated by various emotions (*umoliat'* [to beg, plead], *kleimit'* [to brand, stigmatize], *bakhvalit'sia* [to brag], *skulit'* [to whimper, whine] (in the sense 'to complain'), etc.) or by a wish to evoke certain emotions in the listener (*stydit'* [to shame], *umoliat'* [to beg, plead], *uprekat'* [to rebuke], etc.) For a more detailed treatment of aspects of the speech acts described here see Wierzbicka (1987*b*) and Glovinskaia (1993).

## 3.2.5. The System and its Subsystems

Each system may be broken down into a number of subsystems: *zrenie* [vision], *slukh* [hearing], *obonianie* [sense of smell], etc. form part of perception; *znanie* [knowledge], *vera* [belief], *uverennost'* [confidence], *ponimanie* [understanding], *mnenie* [opinion], *voobrazhenie* [imagination], *pamiat'* [memory] and many others form part of intellect; various speech acts make up speech.

These subsystems may be served by their own organs: the subsystem we call *pamiat'* [memory] (*zritel'naia* ⟨*slukhovaia*⟩ *pamiat'* [visual ⟨auditory⟩ memory], *obraznaia pamiat'* [pictorial memory], *tsepkaia* ⟨*fotograficheskaia*⟩ *pamiat'* [retentive ⟨photographic⟩ memory], *korotkaia* ⟨*devich'ia*⟩ *pamiat'* [short memory], *pamiat' sdaet* [(his/her/my, etc.) memory is going], etc.) is served by an organ which is also known as *pamiat'* (*vrezat'sia v pamiat'* [to become etched in the memory], *khranit' v pamiati* [to hold in one's memory], *vosstanovit' v pamiati* [to restore in one's memory], *izvlech' iz pamiati* [to drag out of one's memory], etc.). For more detail see Mel'čuk and Zholkovsky (1984: 559 ff.) and Uryson (1995a).

The subsystems of one system may sometimes also form a hierarchy. We shall demonstrate this using the example of the system of perception, whose subsystems are ranked in importance according to the volume of information which passes through them into the human mind. From this angle, all investigators regard vision as the most important subsystem. It is followed by hearing, then by the senses of smell, taste, and touch, although the relative order of the last three subsystems is less clear and apparent than that of the first two.

Two arguments may be adduced to support the case that this principle of ranking is not imposed upon language from outside, owing to some abstract logical considerations, but flows directly from the linguistic facts and processes occurring within language itself.

First, the place of any given subsystem in the hierarchy, in accordance with the aforementioned principle, depends directly upon the number of lexemes serving it. Clearly, visual perception is served by the richest and most varied vocabulary. It is followed, with substantially less volume, by the vocabulary of hearing. Smell, taste, and touch, with fewer lexemes to serve them than 'hearing', do not differ so markedly from one another. To rank them it is therefore necessary to apply a second, purely linguistic argument: the processes of metaphorization in language.

As far back as the early 1950s S. Ullmann (1951) formulated the following statistical law: approximately 80 per cent of intersensory (kinesthetic) metaphorical transfers move strictly from the lower levels of the hierarchy of perception to the higher and only slightly over 20 per cent move in the opposite direction. This means that metaphors of the type *teplye* ⟨*kholodnye*⟩ *kraski* [warm ⟨cold⟩ colours], *miagkie tona* [soft tones], *koliuchii vzgliad* [barbed look], *teplyi* ⟨*kholodnyi*⟩ *golos* [warm ⟨cold⟩ voice], *zhestkie zvuki* [harsh sounds], *krichashche odeta* [garishly attired], *glukhie tona* [muted hues], *sladkie rechi* [sweet words], *ostrye zvuki* [shrill sounds], *sladkii* ⟨*solenyi, kislyi, gor'kii*⟩ *zapakh* [sweet ⟨salty, sour, bitter⟩ smell], *ostrye zapakhi* [pungent smells], *ostrye pripravy* ⟨*bliuda*⟩ [piquant sauces ⟨dishes⟩], *miagkii vkus* [mild taste], etc. are much more likely (and natural) than those of the type *tusklyi zvuk* [dim sound], *nosatyi golos* [large-nosed voice] (Z. Shakhovskaia), *iarkie* ⟨*tusklye*⟩ *zvuki* [bright ⟨dim⟩ sounds], *krasnye zvuki* [red sounds], *glukhie zapakhi* [deaf smells], *sladkaia na oshchup' tkan'* [fabric sweet to the touch], etc. From this it follows that visual perception and to a lesser extent auditory perception are the ones always in need of new means of expression. It is the vocabulary of these systems which serves the greatest number of communicative situations and is most quickly worn out by constant use.

All this is directly related to the anthropocentric nature of language: humans can distinguish a larger number of visual and auditory images (the latter evidently owing to the auditory nature of language) than any other living creature. The human sense of smell, on the other hand, is far less developed than that of dogs, for example, which can distinguish, as we know, up to 300,000 smells. The relative poverty of the corresponding class of lexemes is linked to this less acute sense of smell. In 'cynocentric' language, if there were such a thing, smell would occupy first place in the hierarchy.

### 3.2.6. Classes and Subclasses of Systems

In certain aspects the systems set out in § 3.2 draw close to one another and sometimes even unite to form larger classes. The two largest classes consist of those systems linked mostly with the activity of the human body (the first four) and those linked mostly with that of the human spirit (the last four).

On the other hand, certain bodily systems draw close to certain spiritual systems,[7] so that each bodily system is reflected, duplicated, imitated in the matching spiritual system, and vice versa. Mental states and activity correspond to perception; desires correspond to physiological states (needs); emotions to physiological reactions; and speech to physical activity.

The principle of paired bodily and spiritual systems flows directly from the well-known 'body vs. spirit' dichotomy which is characteristic of the naïve world-view (and not only the naïve view). (Note also the variant 'body vs. soul'.)

Such similarities, though the basis for them varies in different cases, are linguistically interesting in that they make it possible to see the underlying similarity of outwardly different lexical units and thus create an additional basis for the systematization and unification of semantic descriptions of them. We shall use the material of four of the above-mentioned paired classes to support this.

(1) Perception and intellect. In the naïve world picture, as in the scientific one, a human being acquires via his perception system all the information which is sent to the mind for processing and on the basis of which he apprehends reality, obtains knowledge, develops opinions, plans his actions, etc. It was observed long ago that perception and thought are so similar to each other and so closely interlocked that the main verb of perception *videt'* [to see] develops mental meanings (see e.g. Arutiunova 1988: 110 ff. and Arutiunova 1989). We shall list all the mental meanings which this verb has developed in Russian and demon-

---

[7] Note the following observation by Arutiunova (1976: 95): 'Since man's inner world is modelled on the outer, material world, the main source of psychological vocabulary is 'physical' vocabulary used in secondary, figurative senses.'

strate that the next most important perception verb *slyshat'* [to hear] has analogous meanings or uses.

In the verb *videt'* the following four mental meanings may be distinguished: (1) 'to picture, imagine' (*Ia vizhu, tochno eto bylo vchera, kak my bezhim po kosogoru* [I can see us running down the slope as if it were yesterday]); (2) 'to consider, think' (*Ne vizhu v etom nichego durnogo* [I see nothing bad about this]; *Mnogie vozderzhivalis' ot khudozhestvennogo i filosofskogo tvorchestva, tak kak schitali eto delom beznravstvennym s tochki zreniia interesov naroda, videli v etom izmenu narodnomu blagu* [many refrained from artistic or philosophical work, regarding it as immoral from the standpoint of the interests of the people and seeing in it a betrayal of the general good] (N. Berdiaev)); this transfer of sense is well represented in the cluster of verbs with the meaning *smotret'* [to look]: *rassmatrivat' etot demarsh kak proiavlenie slabosti* [to regard this move as an indication of weakness], *usmatrivat' v chem-libo sostav prestupleniia* [to see something as a criminal offence], etc.; (3) 'to understand' (*Vy vidite ⟨ponimaete⟩ svoiu oshibku?* [do you see ⟨understand⟩ your error?]); (4) 'to know' (*ne videt' putei vykhoda iz krizisa* [to see no way out of the crisis]).

Similar mental meanings or usages may be found in the verb *slyshat'* [to hear], although in this case they are less detached from their bodily trappings and associations: (1) 'to picture, imagine' (*Gliadiashchii na etu kartinu ('Futbolist') uzhe slyshal svist kozhanogo snariada, uzhe videl otchaiannyi brosok vrataria* [anybody who looked at the picture ('The Footballer') could hear the whistle of the leather projectile and see the goalkeeper's desperate dive] (V. Nabokov)); (2) 'to consider, think' (*V vashikh slovakh ia slyshu skrytuiu ugrozu* [in your words I hear a veiled threat] = 'hearing your words, I believe they contain a veiled threat'); (3) 'to understand' (*Da ne sobiraetsia on vas uvol'niat', slyshite?* [but he's not planning to sack you, do you hear?]); (4) 'to know' (*Ia slyshal ot kogo-to, chto match otlozhen* [I heard from somebody that the match has been postponed]).

Note also the mental meanings of the verbs *chuiat'* [to scent] in the meaning 'to suspect, sense' (*Chuiu, chto on zatevaet chto-to nedobroe* [I can sense that he's up to no good]), and *oshchushchat'* [to feel, sense] in the meaning 'to understand' (*Ia oshchushchaiu nekotoruiu nelovkost' etoi situatsii* [I sense a certain awkwardness in this situation]), etc.

(2) *Physiological states and desires.* It was stated earlier that there are two types of desires: the simplest, linked with the satisfaction of bodily needs (hunger = a feeling of a desire to eat; thirst = a feeling of a desire to drink), and more complex desires linked with the satisfaction of spiritual needs (to want to go to an exhibition, study at the Sorbonne; to dream of heroism). In the former case the person feels that he lacks something which is necessary for his bodily comfort; in the latter, that he lacks something which is necessary for his spiritual comfort. Thus, in accordance with the general rule of metaphorical transfer,

which moves from concrete to abstract, words denoting bodily needs (*golod* [hunger], *zhazhda* [thirst]) regularly develop meanings of intellectual or other spiritual needs: *dukhovnyi golod* [spiritual hunger], *zhazhda znanii* [thirst for knowledge], *zhazhdat' podviga* [to yearn for heroism].

(3) Physiological reactions and emotions. Physiological states such as pallor, accelerated heartbeat and perspiration are reactions to external or internal irritants. Emotions are also reactions, the reactions of the soul to external or internal stimuli. Here there is a deep-seated similarity between emotions and physical states (see Chapter 7 in this volume). For example, in a state of fear the soul experiences something similar to what the body experiences when it is cold, and the body reacts to fear as it does to cold. Note the following expressions: *drozhat' ot strakha ⟨kholoda⟩* [to shiver with fear ⟨cold⟩]; *murashki begut po spine ot strakha ⟨kholoda⟩* [shivers run down one's spine from fear ⟨cold⟩]; *otsepenet' ot strakha ⟨kholoda⟩* [to go numb with fear ⟨cold⟩]; *strakh ⟨kholod⟩ skoval ego telo* [fear ⟨cold⟩ gripped/paralysed his body], etc.

There is another, more fundamental aspect to their similarity: physiological states such as hunger, thirst, sleepiness, etc. always have their causes—lack of food, liquids or sleep for some period of time. Emotions also have their causes. Therefore, in a systematic description of both physiological states and emotions there must be an indication of the cause which gives rise to the given physiological state or emotion.

(4) Physical and speech acts. Their closeness is based mainly on the fact that both are forms of purposeful activity, and all purposeful activity has its motivation. We drive into the city because we need to do something there; we ride a bicycle because we enjoy the ride; we ask a neighbour to do something because we want him to do it; we give advice to a friend because we wish him well (the latter formulation is from Glovinskaia 1993: 184). An indication of motivation in a semantic description of physical and speech acts is a condition as necessary as an indication of cause in describing physiological reactions and emotions.

The principle of pairing (duplication, imitation) operates in some degree not only at the level of systems but also at the deeper level of subsystems. Thus in the perception system the 'lower' subsystem of taste is metaphorically projected onto the hierarchically higher subsystem of smell. Essentially, the smell subsystem lacks a nomenclature of its own. To denote the basic smells the metaphorically reinterpreted nomenclature of basic tastes is applied: *sladkii ⟨gor'kii, kislyi, solenyi⟩ zapakh* [a sweet ⟨bitter, sour, salty⟩ smell]. More complex smells, especially strong ones, are described either by the corresponding taste terms (*terpkii ⟨prianyi⟩ zapakh* [a tart ⟨spicy⟩ smell]; *pritornyi zapakh* [a sickly smell]), or by reference to an object with a characteristic scent (*gribnoi zapakh* [a smell of mushrooms], *zapakh gor'kogo mindalia* [a scent of bitter almonds], *khvoinyi zapakh* [a smell of pine needles], etc.). Only the evaluative adjectives of the type *voniuchii* [stinking], *aromatnyi* [fragrant], *dushistyi* [sweet-scented], etc. are truly peculiar to smells and not borrowed. Compare some similar considerations in a different theoretical context (Arutiunova 1988; Sukalenko 1992: 44–5).

## 4. The Emotional System

This is one of the most complex human systems (only the speech system seems more complex), since practically all the other systems—perception, physiological reactions, intellect, physical systems (especially the various motor systems, including facial expression) and even speech—participate in causing, developing, and manifesting emotions. The emotions have been thoroughly studied in their linguistic, psychological, and physiological aspects, and the results obtained by various methods show a large measure of agreement; (Arutiunova 1976: 93 ff.; Arutiunova 1988: 129 ff.; Wierzbicka 1992; Zalizniak 1992; V. Apresjan 1995*a*; Mel′čuk and Zholkovsky 1984; J. Apresjan 1992*b*; Chapter 1 in this volume; Wierzbicka 1990*a*; Wierzbicka 1969: 39 ff.; Wierzbicka 1972: 67–70; Wierzbicka 1980: 142–57; Wierzbicka 1990*b*; Iordanskaja 1970; Iordanskaja 1972; Iordanskaja 1984; Iordanskaja and Mel′čuk 1990; Uspensky 1979; Lakoff and Johnson 1980; Ekman 1984; Shaver *et al.* 1987; Ortony, Clore, Collins 1988; Kövecses 1990; Pajdzińska 1990*a*; J. Apresjan 1992*c*; Fries 1992; Oatley 1992; Swanepoel 1992; V. Apresjan 1997*b*; J. Apresjan *et al.* 1979; Uryson 1995*b*, and many other works).

We shall confine ourselves to a purely linguistic study of a few facts from Russian, but must emphasize that in the most varied of European languages the language of emotions has many points of similarity and a description of it requires a similar lexicographic methodology. In the description offered below material and ideas from a previously published work (J. Apresjan 1992*b*) are utilized, but these are substantially expanded and refined.

The basic vocabulary of this type includes the synonym series of the verbs *bespokoit′sia, boiat′sia, serdit′sia, stydit′sia, gordit′sia, udivliat′sia, voskhishchat′sia, liubit′, nadeiat′sia, radovat′sia, grustit′* [to worry, to fear, to get angry, to be ashamed, to be proud, to be surprised, to admire, to love, to hope, to be glad, to be sad] and many others; and the series of corresponding nouns, adjectives, adverbs, etc. (*bespokoistvo, radost′, rad, trevozhno, s trevogoi, v trevoge, boiazno, so strakhom, v strakhe,* etc. [worry, joy, glad, worried, with alarm, in alarm, fearfully, with terror, in terror]).

In addition to this basic vocabulary it is necessary to take account of words which, while not denoting emotions in the strict sense, include in their meaning an indication of the subject's emotional state at the moment of performing some action or being in a certain state. Such a series is *liubovat′sia* [to admire], *zagliadet′sia* [to be lost in admiration], *zasmotret′sia* [to be lost in admiration].

Lastly, it is necessary to consider another group of words which do not intrinsically denote emotions but are very closely connected to the expression of emotion. These are metaphors denoting a certain physical symptom of a feeling.

They were first studied in Iordanskaja (1972); see also Chapter 7 in this volume. We shall henceforth be concerned only with light and colour metaphors of the type *glaza goriat* ⟨*sverkaiut, blestiat*⟩ *ot vostorga* ⟨*ot gneva*⟩ [his eyes blaze ⟨flash, sparkle⟩ with delight ⟨anger⟩], *ee shcheki porozoveli ot udovol'stviia* [her cheeks flushed with pleasure], *on pobagrovel ot styda* [he turned crimson with shame], etc. This group manifests the richest synonymy of figurative meanings: note the series *blestet', sverkat'* [to glint, to flash]; *zagoret'sia, zazhech'sia* [to light up]; *siiat', svetit'sia* [to shine]; *zasiiat', zasvetit'sia, ozarit'sia* [to light up, start shining]; *potemnet', pogasnut', potukhnut'* [to become dark, to fade, die down]; *pokrasnet', pobagrovet', zarumianit'sia, zardet'sia* [to turn red, turn purple/crimson, blush, flush]; and many others.

All these series provide us with a point of departure in the attempt to reconstruct a naïve picture of the world of emotions as reflected and conceptualized in the Russian language. In view of limitations of space we can give only a few characteristic details of the naïve picture or model of man's emotional world. Nevertheless, even these few details are instructive, and only by making use of these can we provide a systematic description of the specific synonym series in the dictionary.

1. In the development of emotions as they are represented in language the following five phases may be singled out:

(1) The primary cause of the emotion—usually a physical *perception* or mental *contemplation* of a certain state of affairs. Things that we directly perceive may *anger* us [*zlit'*], while certain facts or information that we obtain at second hand may *arouse our indignation* [*vozmushchat'*] (for example, outrages committed by extremists in Haiti). Compare also the verbs *liubovat'sia* [to admire], *zagliadet'sia, zasmotret'sia* [to be lost in admiration], which presuppose visual perception of an object at the moment the feeling is experienced, and the inexact conversive *nravit'sia* [to please], which does not.

(2) The direct cause of the emotion—usually an intellectual *appraisal* of a state of affairs as probable, unexpected, desirable, or undesirable for the subject. The role of this factor in the evocation of emotions was first pointed out by Spinoza and has since been noted by all researchers (see the works cited above). The cause of positive emotions (joy, happiness, love, admiration, hope, etc.) is our intellectual appraisal of certain events as desirable and the cause of negative emotions (sadness, grief, hatred, indignation, despair, etc.) is our appraisal of them as undesirable. Within each of these classes a more finely graded differentiation of causes takes place. An important role in the evocation of some emotions is played, of course, by the subject's appraisal of his own actions. *Torzhestvovat'* [to exult, triumph] differs from *radovat'sia* [to be glad] in denoting joy as a result of the subject's successful actions, his being proved right, etc., while it is possible to *be gladdened* by an event whose cause has nothing to do with the subject. A similar distinction is found in the series *grustit', pechalit'sia* [to be sad], *sokrushat'sia* [to regret]. *Grustit'* may apply whatever the cause, while

*sokrushat'sia* relates principally to one's own not very successful actions.

(3) The emotion itself, a state of the soul brought about by a state of affairs perceived or contemplated, and by an intellectual appraisal of this state of affairs. A. Wierzbicka describes the emotion itself by means of the semantic components 'to feel good' and 'to feel bad'. In the explication of emotions in Iordanskaja (1970) these same semantic components are termed 'positive emotional state' and 'negative emotional state'.

V. Apresjan (1997a) points out that the positive and negative states may themselves differ substantially in the case of different emotions. In a state of hatred [*nenavist'*] a person experiences one unpleasant or negative feeling, in a state of fear [*strakh*] another, in a state of sadness [*toska*] a third. In view of this it was suggested that emotions proper might be differentiated with the aid of the metaphors of the bodily states associated with them (Chapter 7). As stated above, the unpleasant feeling which arises when a person is afraid is akin to the unpleasant bodily state when he is cold (note the following: *drozhat' ot strakha* [to shiver with fear], *pokholodet' ot strakha* [to turn cold with fear], *otsepenet' ot strakha* [to go numb with fear], *strakh ledenit dushu* [fear freezes the soul], *strakh skovyvaet cheloveka* [fear grips/paralyses a person], etc.). The unpleasant feeling in the case of disgust recalls the unpleasant physical sensations one feels when affected by a nasty taste or smell (Chapter 7).

Comparisons like these as a way of more closely defining the strictly emotional component in the explication of an emotion may be justified by the pairing principle mentioned above.

(4) A desire, brought about by the intellectual appraisal or by the emotion proper, to prolong or terminate the existence of the cause which elicited the emotion. In a state of fear a person tries to cut short the effects of the undesirable stimulus by attempting to hide or shrink, etc. In a state of joy, on the other hand, his wish is that the positive stimulus should last as long as possible and his whole being seems to expand. Compare *ego raspiraet ot radosti* [he is bursting with joy], *on razduvaetsia ot gordosti* [he swells up with pride] and the impossible \**ego raspiraet ot toski* ⟨*ot strakha*⟩ [he is bursting with sadness ⟨fear⟩], \**on razduvaetsia ot styda* [he swells up with shame].

(5) The outward manifestation of the emotion, in two main forms: (*a*) uncontrollable physiological reactions to the cause of the emotion or to the emotion itself; raised eyebrows (eyes widening) in the case of surprise, eyes narrowing in the case of malice or anger, pallor in the case of fear, perspiration in the case of embarrassment, blushing in the case of shame, etc.; (*b*) controlled motor and speech reactions by the subject to the emotion-inducing factor or to an intellectual appraisal of the emotion; retreat in the case of fear, attack in the case of anger, exclamation in the case of rejoicing, snarling in the case of rage, etc.

As a generalizing example we may take the words *nenavist'* [hatred], *otvrashchenie* [disgust], and *strakh* [fear], which denote emotions of one class. *Nenavist'* is an unpleasant feeling induced by the perception or at least the thought of an object or situation which we appraise as highly unpleasant and hostile to ourselves and which we would so fervently like to remove that we are prepared to undertake the most destructive of actions including the physical annihilation of the object. Outwardly hatred, like other aggressive feelings (anger, fury, etc.) may manifest itself in blazing eyes. Disgust is an unpleasant feeling like the sensation produced by a vile taste or smell; it is induced by the perception of some object which we appraise as highly unpleasant, though not necessarily hostile, and with which we would like to terminate contact. It may manifest itself outwardly in an involuntary grimace on the face of the person experiencing the disgust. Fear is an unpleasant feeling similar to the sensation we experience from cold; it occurs when a person (or other living being) perceives an object which he appraises as dangerous to himself and with which he wishes to have no contact. In a state of fear a person turns pale, his heart rate increases, his voice fails, and he wishes to hide, shrink, or flee from the danger.[8]

This scenario for the development of emotions should be borne in mind in drawing up the appropriate synonym series. In a synonym dictionary which purports to be systematic in the presentation of lexical material, the general plan of the description should be the same for all series and for all members of a series. In particular, for each emotion the following should be given: the perceived or contemplated stimulus which induces it; the intellectual appraisal of this stimulus by the subject of the emotion; the type of feeling experienced; the desires accompanying the emotion; the outward manifestations of that emotion, including the physiological reactions of the body, movements, gestures, facial expression, and speech.

2. In different emotions the proportion of feeling proper and intellectual appraisal may vary. In some there will be a preponderance of direct feeling (experience), in others appraisal will predominate. Accordingly, emotions are conceptualized by language as being primary or basic (biologically induced), and secondary or culturally conditioned. This division is confirmed by data from a number of physiological studies (see the survey by V. Apresjan 1995*a*). The primary emotions, for example fear, rage, pleasure, and joy, presuppose less intellectual appraisal of some state of affairs as good or bad for the subject than an unmediated feeling that this is so. For this reason the primary emotions are accessible not only to humans but also to higher animals. It is clear, for example, that a dog which, on seeing its master rushes to him, jumps, wags its tail, licks his face ⟨puts its tail between its legs and runs away⟩ is glad ⟨afraid⟩ in the literal sense of the word: *Tiun'ka radovalas' by. Ona liubit videt' srazu vmeste vsekh svoikh* [Tiun'ka (a dog) would have been glad. She likes to see all her family together

---

[8] See a similar description of *strakh* [fear] and emotions generally in the dictionary (J. Apresjan *et al.* 1979: 30–1, 175–7 and elsewhere), and in Zalizniak (1992), Wierzbicka (1990*b*), Iordanskaja and Mel'čuk (1990), V. Apresjan (1997*b*), Uryson (1995*b*). It is easy to see a similarity between this type of description, proposed as far back as 1979 (see also Chapter 1 in this volume) and what C. Fillmore later (1982, 1985, Fillmore and Atkins 1992) termed 'frame semantics'.

at once] (E. Korotkova); *edinstvenno, chego boialsia khrabryi pes, eto grozy* [the only thing the brave dog was afraid of was thunderstorms] (M. Bulgakov). Secondary, culturally conditioned emotions such as hope, anger, indignation, despair, etc. are motivated by an intellectual appraisal of a situation as desirable or undesirable to the subject and are therefore normally only attributed to humans. This distinction between biologically induced and culturally conditioned emotions is quite regular and should be taken into account in the corresponding synonym series.

A similar opposition lies at the basis of the division of emotions into the more and less elemental, having respectively a greater proportion of feeling proper and a greater proportion of intellectual appraisal. It is of interest that the more elemental emotions, such as fear, panic, anxiety, sadness [*toska*], horror, envy, jealousy, etc., are conceptualized as hostile forces assailing us from outside: *Strakh ovladevaet chelovekom, okhvatyvaet ego, zapolzaet emu v dushu* [fear overwhelms a person, grips him, steals into his soul]; *chelovek nakhoditsia tselikom vo vlasti strakha* [a person finds himself totally in the power of fear]; *zavist' pozhiraet ⟨snedaet⟩ cheloveka* [envy devours ⟨consumes⟩ a person]; *revnost' ego gryzet* [he is gnawed by jealousy]; *toska ego beret ⟨navalivaetsia na nego⟩* [sadness takes hold of him ⟨descends upon him⟩]. The smaller the proportion of appraisal and the greater the proportion of unmediated feeling, the more likely it is that the name of the emotion will form a collocation with a verb of this kind. It is precisely this, and in no sense the intensity of the emotion, as may be thought at first glance, that provides the motivation for the possibility or impossibility of the corresponding collocations. *Izumlenie* [astonishment] is clearly a strong feeling, but it cannot 'grip' a person because it is too rational. On the other hand, *trevoga* [alarm] and *grust'* [sadness] may 'grip' one, although they are far less intense, because their intellectual component is insignificant. It is no accident that they may be 'inexplicable', which is completely out of the question with *izumlenie* [astonishment].

3. Emotions differ from one another in intensity and depth. *Likovat'* [to exult] is more intense than *radovat'sia* [to be glad]; *strast'* [passion] is more intense than *liubov'* [love]; *vostorg* [rapture] is more intense than *voskhishchenie* [admiration]. On the other hand, *radovat'sia* is more profound than *likovat'*; *liubov'* is deeper than *strast'*; *voskhishchenie* is deeper than *vostorg*.

Of these two features, intensity merits further comment as it manifests itself in more varied and interesting ways than depth.

When classifying emotions according to intensity it is essential to bear in mind that the scale of intensity for emotions is assymetrical: normal intensity is well represented (*udivlenie* [surprise], *nepriiazn'* [dislike], *voskhishchenie* [admiration], *strakh* [fear], *grust'* [sadness], *radost'* [joy], *zlost'* [anger] and other prototypical emotions), as is the greater degree of intensity (*izumlenie* [astonishment], *nenavist'* [hatred], *vostorg* [rapture], *uzhas* [horror], *gore* [grief], *likovanie* [exultation], *iarost'* [fury]). Weaker emotions, however, (if we exclude a few scattered and clearly peripheral lexemes), which are antonyms to the strong ones are absent from the Russian linguistic picture.

In fact, if the weaker emotions were represented in the scale, the corresponding lexemes could not form collocations with adjectives denoting the upper extreme of the scale of intensity. But the names of all emotions, including those like *grust'* [sadness], *dosada* [irritation], *nepriiazn'* [dislike], etc., combine with adjectives like *sil'nyi* [strong] and even *sil'neishii* [strongest]. Contrast these with the strong emotions such as *iarost'* [fury], *nenavist'* [hatred], *izumlenie* [astonishment], *vostorg* [rapture], etc., which cannot and do not combine with adjectives denoting a low degree of intensity, such as *slabyi* [weak].

It is clear that the greater degree of intensity should be treated as a semantic constant which must be included in the description of all strong emotions. However, existing lexicographical practice is inconsistent here. In those cases where a language has a minimal pair consisting of the name of a strong emotion and its prototype (*izumlenie—udivlenie* [astonishment—surprise], *iarost'—zlost'* [fury —anger], *uzhas—strakh* [horror—fear], *vostorg—voskhishchenie* [rapture—admiration], etc.), the stronger emotion is defined as 'intense X' or 'strong X', where X is the name of the prototype. If there is no minimal pair, the component 'strong' is absent from the explication of the emotion in question. This is the case with *otchaianie* [despair], for example, which has no neutral prototype.

This undermines the basis for a logical account of the fact that the co-occurrence potential of the names of all strong emotions including *despair* coincides. In fact all strong emotions can be graded with the aid of adjectives meaning the superlative degree of the given feature: *slepaia iarost'* [blind fury], *polneishee* ⟨*krainee*⟩ *izumlenie* [utter ⟨extreme⟩ astonishment], *nevyrazimyi uzhas* [inexpressible horror], *polnyi vostorg* [absolute rapture], etc. Similar combinations are possible with the lexeme *otchaianie* too: *v polnom otchaianii* [in absolute despair]. On the other hand, as stated above, no strong emotion can combine with adjectives denoting a small degree of the feature. This constraint naturally applies to *despair* as well.

A systematic description of these facts may be given only if it includes the crucial component 'strong' in the explication of all such lexemes, whether or not they form minimal pairs.

4. As noted above, emotions may manifest themselves outwardly and may differ considerably in these manifestations. *Likovanie* [exultation], *obozhanie* [adoration], *izumlenie* [astonishment], *vostorg* [rapture], and *beshenstvo* [rage] have a far greater need for outlets in speech, behaviour, actions, gestures, or facial expression than *radost'* [joy], *liubov'* [love], *udivlenie* [surprise], *voskhishchenie* [admiration], and *zlost'* [anger] respectively. In general, the last five may be experienced without any outward sign betraying these feelings.

The importance which, in the naïve picture of emotions, is given to the possibility of their outward expression is emphasized by the fact that language often develops two series of devices to express the emotion proper and the fact of its outward expression. These devices include polysemy, various affixes and lexico-syntactic structures. Thus the words *grustno* [sadly], *veselo* [happily], and some others each have two distinct senses: 'being in a certain emotional state' and 'expressing a certain emotion'. In these senses they are included in separate synonym series which differ from each other lexically: compare the predicative usage *emu bylo grustno* [he felt sad], which is synonymous with *on grustil*, and the adverbial *On grustno posmotrel na menia* [he looked at me sadly], which is synonymous with *on pechal'no ⟨s grust'iu⟩ posmotrel na menia* [he looked at me with sadness]. In the case of *styd* [shame], the same distinction is expressed by words with different suffixes: *stydno* expresses the meaning 'feeling shame', while *stydlivo* means 'expressing shame'. Compare also the preposition-and-noun phrases *v iarosti* [in fury], *v gneve* [in anger], *v vostorge* [in raptures], *v toske* [in sadness], etc. which signify only the state, and *s vostorgom* [with rapture], *s grust'iu* [with sadness], *s trevogoi* [with alarm], *s radost'iu* [with joy], *s toskoi* [with sadness], which express the meaning of the manifestation.

5. An important aspect of the conceptualization of emotions is their relation to the idea of light. On the whole the positive emotions, like *love, joy, happiness*, and *rapture* are conceptualized as bright, while the negative emotions, such as *hatred, sadness, despair, anger, rage, fury, fear*, and *horror* are seen as dark. It is striking how consistent language is in its adherence to these ideas. We speak of *svet liubvi* [the light of love], *glaza svetiatsia ⟨siiaiut⟩ ot radosti ⟨liubvi⟩* [one's eyes shine ⟨sparkle⟩ with joy ⟨love⟩], *glaza svetiatsia liubov'iu* [one's eyes are alight with love], *ee litso ozarilos' ot radosti* [her face lit up with joy], *radost' osvetila ee litso* [joy lit up her face], but *glaza potemneli ot gneva* [(his, her, etc.) eyes darkened with anger], *on pochernel ot goria* [lit.: he turned black with grief], *chernyi ot goria* [black with grief], etc. It is impossible to say *\*potemnet' ot radosti* [to turn black with joy] or *\*ozarit'sia ot gneva* [to light up with anger].

In the colour metaphors even a slight admixture of dark becomes an obstacle in describing a positive emotion. One may *zarumianit'sia ⟨zardet'sia⟩ ot radosti* [blush or flush with joy] or *pobagrovet' ot gneva ⟨ot zloby⟩* [turn purple/crimson with rage ⟨spite⟩], but not *\*pobagrovet' ot radosti* [turn purple/crimson with joy] or *⁇zarumianit'sia ⟨zardet'sia⟩ ot gneva* [blush ⟨flush⟩ with anger]. The behaviour of the synonyms *styd* [shame] and *smushchenie* [embarrassment, confusion] throws additional light on the problem. The former denotes a disagreeable feeling induced by a sense of guilt. There is nothing bright about it. One may therefore *pobagrovet' ot styda* [turn purple/crimson with shame] but not *⁇zardet'sia ot styda* [be flushed with shame]. The latter synonym denotes a disagreeable feeling which, however, is not induced by any sense of true guilt but by a fear of failure, an inability to conduct oneself in society and other similar factors. These factors usually have more to do with the modesty of the subject than his real shortcomings. *Smushchenie* therefore has an ambivalent nature: both *pobagrovet'* and *zardet'sia* are possible, depending on the speaker's view of the inner state of the subject.

On the other hand the Russian language has a large group of verbs in which the idea of light combines with the idea of effulgence: *goret'* [to burn], *sverkat'* [to flash], *blestet'* [to gleam], *vspykhivat'* [to flare up, blaze], etc. These verbs are completely neutral with regard to the contrast between bright and dark emotions: *ee glaza vspykhnuli ot radosti* ⟨*ot gneva*⟩ [her eyes blazed with joy ⟨anger⟩], *ego glaza goreli liubov'iu* ⟨*nenavist'iu*⟩ [his eyes burned with love ⟨hatred⟩].

It is interesting to note that in all these cases we are dealing with pure conceptualization with no palpable physical reality behind it. Contrast this with the 'symptomatic' expressions, which reflect fully objective changes of appearance as a result of an emotion: *ego glaza rasshirilis' ot udivleniia* ⟨*suzilis' ot gneva*⟩ [his eyes widened with surprise ⟨narrowed with anger⟩].

Even this scant material demonstrates that when investigating series of synonyms denoting emotion it is essential to try in equal measure to discover the specifics of each series and to reveal the presumably homogeneous naïve model of the world which underlies all series and motivates the choice of synonyms to describe any specific situation.

It is clear that by reflecting all these facts in a dictionary of synonyms we shall enhance the systematic presentation of the material and take a serious step towards the lexicographer's ultimate goal.


## 5. A General Schematic Description of the Human Being

On the basis of the ideas set forth in § 2–4 we may propose a general format for a description of various human states, of the processes which occur in the human soul or mind, and of intellectual or speech acts (purely physical actions are practically left out of account here, owing to the vast range of material). This format is merely a hierarchically ordered list of features relevant to a description of those states, processes and actions; compare its predecessor (Chapter 1 in this volume).

All the terminal features of the hierarchy listed below are general, that is, suited to the description of several or many lexemes and groups of lexemes. We do not assert, however, that the whole outline in its present form takes account of all such features, that is, that the hierarchy is complete. All groups of actant and non-actant concepts represented in it require further detailed study and unification. In this sense it is mainly illustrative in nature.

The terminal features of the hierarchy are briefly illustrated by material from entries drafted by the author for the *New Explanatory Dictionary of Russian Synonyms*. The examples bearing on the series *zhalovat'sia, setovat', roptat'*, etc. [to complain], *obeshchat', sulit'*, etc. [to promise] and *rugat', ponosit', pilit'*, etc. [to curse] are taken from entries written jointly by M. Ia. Glovinskaia and the author; the examples bearing on the series *boiat'sia* are taken from V. Apresjan (1997*b*).

## 5.1. THE SUBJECT OF THE STATE, PROCESS OR ACTION

### 5.1.1. Physical Characteristics

#### 5.1.1.1. *Numerical Characteristics*

In the case of *rasstat'sia* and *razoitis'* [to part company] there may be several parties: *komanda rasstavalas' do vstrechi v Madride* [the team members went their separate ways before the Madrid meeting]; *k momentu vstrechi chleny kruzhka okonchatel'no razoshlis' vo vzgliadakh* [by the time of the meeting the members of the group had adopted widely differing views]. In the case of *razluchit'sia* there are only two parties, irrespective of the number of participants in each party: *mat' ne khotela razluchat'sia s det'mi* [the mother did not want to be parted from her children]. Only an individual can *rasserdit'sia* [get angry], while a group of people considered as a single unit may *raz"iarit'sia* [become furious]. In the case of *roptat'* the subject may be collective; in that of *setovat'* the complaint is ascribed to individuals: *armiia ropshchet* [the army is restive] but not *\*armiia setuet* [the army is lamenting].[9]

#### 5.1.1.2. *Humans versus Animals*

Only humans may *likovat'* [exult] and *torzhestvovat'* [be triumphant], while higher animals may *radovat'sia* [be glad]. Only humans *opasaiutsia* [are apprehensive] (as observed in V. Apresjan 1997*b*), while all higher animals may *boiat'sia* [fear]. In the naïve world-view, not only humans may experience desire in the form of *khotet'* [to want], while desire in the form *mechtat'* [to dream of, e.g. going to Paris] and *zhazhdat'* [to thirst, e.g. for revenge] is confined to humans. Only a human may *vozmutit'sia* [get indignant] and *rasserdit'sia* [lose his temper], while animals too may *razozlit'sia* [become enraged] and *raz"iarit'sia* [fly into a fury].

#### 5.1.1.3. *The Whole Person versus the Organ*

Dreaming (*mechtat'*) is an attribute of a human being, while the state of

---

[9] The importance of the idea of the collective subject in Russian is further substantiated by the fact that the language possesses grammaticalized means to express it: the circumfixes *raz-sia, s-sia* in verbs of the type *razbezhat'sia—sbezhat'sia* [to disperse, run away in different directions—to converge, run to the same spot from different points], *razletet'sia—sletet'sia* [to disperse, fly away in different directions—to converge, fly to the same spot from different points, flock in], the prefix *pere-* in verbs of the type *perebyvat'* [to visit—of many visitors], *perebolet'* [to get over an illness—of many patients] (*Vse moi deti perebyvali v Parizhe* ⟨*pereboleli kor'iu*⟩ [all my children have been in Paris ⟨down with measles⟩]) and the like. Moreover, the idea of a collective object is expressed in Russian with no less regularity; note the prefixes *raz-* and *s-* with causative verbs of the type *razognat'* —*sognat'* [to scatter (trans.), chase away in various directions—to muster, drive together], *razobrat'* (*knigi*) [each of a certain set of persons takes one book until no books are left]—*sobrat'* (*knigi*) [to collect, put together all the books that have previously been left in different places], and *pere-* again in sentences such as *Ona perechitala vse frantsuzskie romany v biblioteke ottsa* [she has read all the French novels in her father's library]; *Moi syn perebolel vsemi detskimi bolezniami* [my son has had all the childhood illnesses], and the prefix *ob-* with verbs of the type *obshivat'* ⟨*obstiryvat'*⟩ *vsiu brigadu* [to make clothes for ⟨do the laundry for⟩ the whole team], etc.

*zhazhdat'* [to thirst, yearn] may be ascribed to his soul or heart as well. Exactly the same distinction may be seen in the pair *torzhestvovat'* [to triumph, exult] —*radovat'sia* [to rejoice, be glad]: compare *serdtse ⟨dusha⟩ raduetsia* [one's heart ⟨soul⟩ rejoices] but not *?serdtse ⟨dusha⟩ torzhestvuet* [one's heart ⟨soul⟩ triumphs].

## 5.1.2. Non-Physical Characteristics

### 5.1.2.1. *Intentions*

*Lgat'* [to lie] always implies an intention to deceive, while *vvesti v zabluzhdenie* [to mislead] need not be deliberate. In a similar way *pritvoriat'sia (bol'nym)*, *prikidyvat'sia (bol'nym)*, *simulirovat' (bolezn')* [to feign illness], on the one hand, differ from *kazat'sia (bol'nym)* [to look ill]. *Voobrazhat'* and *predstavliat' (sebe) chto-libo* [to imagine smth.] entail an act of will: *Voobrazite, chto za kazhdyi dobrodetel'nyi postupok chelovek poluchal by voznagrazhdenie v vide kakogo-libo mirskogo blaga* [imagine that for every virtuous deed a person might be rewarded by some form of earthly blessing]; *i etogo sekretar' predstavit' sebe ne mog, khotia i khorosho znal prokuratora* [the secretary could not imagine this, although he knew the Procurator well] (M. Bulgakov). The synonymous verb *videt'* presupposes the spontaneous appearance of images in the mind: *vizhu, kak na kartine, ego nebol'shuiu, tonkuiu, akkuratnuiu figuru* [as in a picture, I see his small, slim, tidy figure] (V. Nabokov).

### 5.1.2.2. *Aims*

**5.1.2.2.1. *The Presence of an Aim*.**   *Prinorovit'sia, priladit'sia, primenit'sia* [to adjust (intrans.)] presuppose purposeful efforts to bring one's behaviour, work, or mode of life into accord with some external circumstances. *Szhit'sia, adaptirovat'sia, akklimatizirovat'sia* [to adapt, acclimatize] describe a natural, and in the last case even biological, process of gradual adaptation by the subject to new conditions.

**5.1.2.2.2. *The Nature of the Aim*.**   The synonymous verbs *poseshchat', naveshchat', provedat', navedat'sia* [to visit] differ from one another especially in what concerns the purpose of the visit. If the aim is to acquaint oneself with cultural objects, perform official duties or make use of something, *poseshchat'* is preferred; if the aim is to maintain human contact, *naveshchat'* is preferred; if the aim is to obtain information about the state of the object, *provedat'* is preferred; if people come visiting or on business, *navedyvat'sia* is preferred. *Pisat' kartinu* [to paint a picture, etc.] implies an intention of creating a work of art, whereas one may *risovat'* [sketch] for one's own amusement. *Kritikovat'* [to criticize] and *vygovarivat'* [to rebuke] imply that the purpose is to remove shortcomings; *oblichat'* [to expose] implies that the purpose is to demonstrate to all that the object of censure has fundamental and, furthermore, incorrigible shortcomings;

*porochit'* [to discredit] has the unseemly aim of undermining a person's reputation while having insufficient evidence for this.

### 5.1.2.3. *Motivation*

The motivation of *setovat'* is a wish to share with somebody some unpleasant information in the hope of obtaining understanding, and without expecting any definite result. *Skulit'* and *khnykat'* [to whimper, whinge] imply a wish to have an undesirable state of affairs set right. People *khvastaiutsia* [boast] when they wish to be seen to best advantage by the person they are speaking to; they *bakhvaliatsia* [brag] when unable to restrain a gush of self-satisfaction. A person *pytaetsia* [tries] to do something when he has an interest in the action itself being performed. He may *probovat'* [attempt] to do something when he merely wishes to see whether the action may in principle be performed, whether it will result satisfactorily, etc. Compare *on pytalsia napisat' stikhotvorenie* [he tried to write a poem] and *on proboval pisat' stikhi* [he tried to write poetry]. A person *obeshchaet* [promises] or *daet slovo* [gives his word] that he will do something because he wishes to be believed. He *sulit* [promises] to do something because he wants the addressee to believe him and do something for him.

### 5.1.2.4. *Features of Character, Personality and Social Role*

Any individual may *radovat'sia* [be glad, rejoice], but only those given to gloating *torzhestvuiut* [triumph, crow] (on being proved right). Any person may *voskhishchat'sia* [admire something], but those of excitable temperament may *vostorgat'sia* [go into raptures]. People with professional training *pishut* (*kartiny*) [paint (pictures)] whereas anybody can sketch. Anybody can *stydit'sia* [feel ashamed], but it is mostly timid, self-conscious or shy people who *smushchaiutsia* and *konfuziatsia* [get embarrassed].

### 5.2. THE OBJECT OF THE STATE, PROCESS, OR ACTION

### 5.2.1. The Presence of an Object

The verb *zarisovyvat'* [to draw, sketch] requires the presence of an outward object (a model) at the moment of the action and a large measure of similarity between the image (the result of the action) and the object being reproduced. With *risovat'* [to draw, sketch] neither is essential. With *kopirovat'* [to copy] there must be a model or original, whereas one may *vosproizvodit'* [reproduce] from memory.

### 5.2.2. Physical Attributes

### 5.2.2.1. *Properties of the Object*

In the case of *risovat'* attention is directed towards the shapes and contours, while in the case of *pisat'* and *malevat'* [to paint] it is focused on the colour.

*Pilit'* and *gryzt'* (in the sense of 'to nag') must have a human as their object, while one may *ponosit'* [abuse], *kryt'* [revile], and *kritikovat'* [criticize] people and social institutions, and one may *rugat'* and *branit'* [curse] people, social institutions, and even natural phenomena (the weather, for example). *Upotrebliat'* [to use] is said of relatively simple tools and means, while *primeniat'* [to apply] is said of more complex instruments, including the apparatus needed in scientific experiments. *Pol'zovat'sia* [to use, make use of] is said of freely manipulated and stationary objects alike: *razvedchiki umelo pol'zovalis' skladkami mestnosti, chtoby nezametno podoiti k storozhevym postam protivnika* [the scouts made skilful use of the relief to approach the enemy guard posts unobserved]. Neither *upotrebliat'* nor *primeniat'* can be said of immovable objects (such as topography).

### 5.2.2.2. *Part of the Object (a Feature or Property) versus the Whole*

*Uprekat'* and *vygovarivat'* [to rebuke] differ from *rugat'* and *branit'* in placing the focus of attention not on a person but on a specific action by that person which displeases the subject. We may *dorozhit'* [prize] the object as a whole and we may *tsenit'* [value] its individual qualities: *ia tseniu vashe uporstvo* [I value your persistence], *on tsenit v liudiakh uporstvo* [he values persistence in people], *my tsenim ego za ego znaniia* [we value him for his knowledge]. Compare these with the impossible *\*ia dorozhu vashim uporstvom* [I prize your persistence], *\*on dorozhit v liudiakh uporstvom* [he prizes persistence in people], *\*my dorozhim im za uporstvo* [we prize him for his persistence].

### 5.2.3. Non-Physical Attributes

### 5.2.3.1. *Properties of the Object*

We may *nadeiat'sia* [rely on] ordinary people and ordinary circumstances, while we *upovaem na* [place our trust in] powerful people or higher powers. People *voskhishchaiutsia* [admire] the deeper qualities of the object which do not catch the eye, while *vostorgat'sia* [go into raptures] is applied to what is on the surface, what attracts attention by being unusual, what captures the imagination.

### 5.2.3.2. *The Designation or Function of the Object*

The verbs *videt'* [to see] and *slyshat'* [to hear] are used in sentences such as *ia videl 'Zerkalo'* ⟨*'Gerniku', ego posledniuiu knigu*⟩ [I've seen 'The Mirror' ⟨'Guernica', his latest book⟩]; *ia slyshal Vishnevskuiu v 'Katerine Izmailovoi'* ⟨*ego vystuplenie na vcherashnem sobranii*⟩ [I heard Vishnevskaia in 'Katerina Izmailova' ⟨his speech at yesterday's meeting⟩], in which their meaning differs from that of mere perception. This meaning may be formulated as follows: 'Person A has formed a mental picture of an object or situation B designed to give people pleasure or communicate information to them, as a result of visual ⟨aural⟩ perception of B.' In other words, *videt'* and *slyshat'* denote the use of 'informational' objects in accordance with their function. The homonymy of sentences of the type *ia videl etu kartinu* [I saw that picture] (either 'visually perceived it', like any other physical object, or 'mentally took in its information content') is a testimony of the autonomous status of the 'informational' meaning: *ia slyshal razgovor za dver'iu* (either 'I heard the sound of some conversation behind the door' or ' I mentally took in the information content of the conversation taking place behind the door'). The contrast between 'simply perceive' and 'perceive, while extracting from the object the information which it is designed to supply' is present in the active verbs *smotret'* [to look, watch] and *slushat'* [to listen]: *my smotreli etot fil'm* [we watched that film] and *my slushali etu operu* [we listened to that opera]. Compare the homonymy of purely physical and 'informational' meanings, confirming this contrast, in *ia posmotrel na chasy* [I looked at the clock], meaning either that I simply directed my eyes towards it (it was an antique clock, a present, etc.) or that I glanced at it to check the time, that is, to satisfy a need for information. A remarkable feature of the passive-ability verbs *videt'* and *slyshat'* is that their 'informational' meaning is realized exclusively in the past tense and imperfective aspect in the general-factual meaning. The dynamic verbs *smotret'* and *slushat'* have no such constraints, that is to say they have a complete formal and semantic tense-aspect paradigm. (See J. Apresjan 1980: 68 on this point.)

## 5.3. THE ADDRESSEE

### 5.3.1. The Presence of a Specific Addressee

*Zhalovat'sia* [to complain] has one, while *roptat'* [to grumble] usually does not. *Velet'* [to order] always has a specific addressee, while *rasporiadit'sia* [to give orders] hardly ever does: *on rasporiadilsia, chtoby vse dokumenty byli unichto-zheny* [he gave orders to have all the documents destroyed].

### 5.3.2. The Nature of the Addressee

*Zhalovat'sia* and *plakat'sia* are normally used to signify complaining to somebody who is in a better position, while *setovat'* may be used of a lament addressed to a companion in misfortune. *Sovetovat'* [to give advice] may have any kind of addressee, while *konsul'tirovat'* [to provide consultancy] is usually applied to a specialist giving advice to a non-specialist. The same distinction is present in the pair *sovetovat'sia* and *konsul'tirovat'sia* [to seek advice], with the difference that with these verbs the addressee (the seeker of advice) has the first valency. The distinction between *sovetovat'* and *rekomendovat'* is similar: the subject of the latter is usually a person with some special knowledge or information.

### 5.3.3. Addressee and Audience

*Obeshchat'* [to promise] has a specific addressee, who is indicated by a noun in the dative. *Prisiagat'* [to vow, swear] implies a larger audience whose name is shown by the preposition-and-noun group *pered kem-libo* [before smb.]. The same distinction is present in *khvastat'sia, khvalit'sia* [to boast] (usually to a specific addressee) and *pozirovat', risovat'sia, shchegoliat'* [to strike attitudes, show off] (usually before an audience).

## 5.4. RELATIONS BETWEEN SUBJECT, OBJECT AND ADDRESSEE

### 5.4.1. Closeness

One may *obizhat'sia* [take offence] at a person one is close to. Anybody may *oskorbit'* [offend] another person. *Razluchat'sia* [to part, separate (intrans.)] is used of parting from somebody close, often somebody one loves, while *raskhodit'sia* [to part, separate (intrans.)] is applied to friends, companions in some common cause, etc. *Rasproshchat'sia* [to take one's leave] may be used to signify parting with one's subordinates.

### 5.4.2. Status

The subject of *otchityvat'* [to rebuke] has a higher social position than the addressee/object. *Ponosit'* and *kryt'* [to abuse, curse] contain no information regarding the status of the subject or object. One may *videt'* [see] anybody or anything, but *litsezret'* [behold] (when not used ironically) will usually apply to an important person. The object of *serdit'* [to annoy] is usually someone with a higher status in the social or age hierarchy: *vnuk serdit babushku* [the grandson annoys his grandmother], but not *\*babushka serdit vnuka* [the grandmother annoys her grandson], while the object of *zlit'* [to vex] is unrestricted.

### 5.4.3. Reciprocal Evaluation

*Kichit'sia* [to preen oneself], compared to *gordit'sia* [to be proud], implies that the subject has a greater sense of his own superiority over his potential audience. On the other hand, *ugodnichat', zaiskivat', lebezit'* [to grovel, fawn] imply a subject whose whole bearing demonstrates to the addressee that the former is of lower standing and hopes in this way to gain favour or achieve his ends.

### 5.4.4. Interaction of Subject and Object

The verbs *adaptirovat'sia* [to adapt (intrans.)] and *akklimatizirovat'sia* [to acclimatize] signify a unilateral process of adaptation by the subject to an inert and unalterable environment; the verb *priteret'sia* signifies change by both participants in some activity as a result of their mutual and active interaction.

### 5.4.5. Coincidence of Object and Addressee

In *pilit'* and *gryzt'* (in the sense 'to nag') the object of disapproval is always the addressee of the speech act at the same time. On the other hand, *rugat'* and *branit'* [to curse] are possible when the object of censure is not present and thus does not coincide with the addressee of the speech act: *on rugal ⟨branil⟩ mne svoego nachal'nika* [lit. he cursed his boss to me]. Similar distinctions may be seen in the group *l'stit'* [to flatter] (usually to somebody's face, that is, when the object of praise and the addressee of the speech act coincide) and *khvalit'* [to praise] (a person who may or may not be present).

## 5.5. TOOL AND MEANS

In order to *pisat'* [paint], a tool (a brush) and a means (paint) are essential, while to *risovat'* [draw] the tool alone suffices: *risovat' palochkoi na peske* [to draw with a stick in the sand]. One may *pribivat'* [nail something up], using a tool (such as a hammer) and a means (nails); for *prikleivat'* and *prilepliat'* [stick, paste on] the means (glue, for example) is sufficient; lastly, one may *prikrepliat'* [attach something] without either tool or means. For *strel'ba* [shooting] a tool is needed (a gun or bow), as well as the means (artillery shells, bullets, or arrows); for *bombardirovka* [bombardment] and *bombezhka* [bombing] the means is sufficient. One cannot *rubit'* [chop, hew] without a special tool, but one may *kolot'* [crack, split] nuts or lumps of sugar without one.

## 5.6. PLACE

*Pokazat'sia* and *poiavit'sia* in the sense 'to move into one's field of vision' have a valency for place: *pokazat'sia ⟨poiavit'sia⟩ v dveriakh ⟨na doroge, na poliane⟩* [to appear in the doorway ⟨on the road, in the clearing⟩]. With *mel'knut'* and *promel'knut'* [to flicker, flit] this is optional, while with *vyvernut'sia* [to emerge, appear] in a comparable sense there is none: *iz tolpy vyvernulsia kakoi-to mal'chishka i brosilsia nautek* [a boy emerged from the crowd and fled]. *Dozhidat'sia* and *podzhidat'* stress that the subject is in a certain place (*dozhidat'sia v prikhozhei* [to wait in the hall], *podzhidat' v podvorotne* [to wait in a gateway]), *ozhidat'*—that the subject is in a certain mental or emotional state (*neterpelivo ozhidat' otkrytiia bara* [to wait impatiently for the bar to open]).

## 5.7. CAUSES OF A STATE, PROCESS, OR ACTION

### 5.7.1. Presence of a Cause

*Proistekat'* always presupposes a very specific cause (*Pozhar proistek iz-za neostorozhnogo obrashcheniia s ognem* [the fire occurred because of carelessness]), whereas *proiskhodit'*, *sluchat'sia*, *poluchat'sia*, *vykhodit'* [to happen] register only the fact that a certain event took place.

### 5.7.2. The Nature of the Cause

We are 'vexed' or 'annoyed' [*nas zlit*] by things that we directly perceive ourselves, but we may be 'made indignant' [*vozmushcheny*] by things we have not ourselves perceived but know of only at second hand. Compare *menia zlit, chto ona menia ignoriruet* [it annoys me that she ignores me] and *menia vozmush-chaet, kogda terroristov vypuskaiut beznakazanno na svobodu* [it makes me indignant when they let terrorists go without punishing them]. We 'rely on' [*polagaemsia na*] a person because we have prior experience of dealing with that person and consequently trust him. We 'place our trust in' [*upovaem na*] a person or divinity regardless of prior experience, solely because we have faith in that person's power. People who have been on close terms may 'part' [*razluchat'sia*] owing to circumstances beyond their control, 'go their separate ways' [*razkhodit'sia*] owing to mutual incompatibility and 'take leave of each other' [*rasproshchat'sia*] on the initiative of either one because he is dissatisfied with the other.

### 5.7.3. The Temporal Relation between the Cause of a State and the State Itself

In the case of *stesniat'sia, smushchat'sia, konfuzit'sia* [to get embarrassed] the emotion and the cause are more or less synchronic, while in the case of *stydit'sia* [to be ashamed] the feeling may occur on remembering some misdeed long after it was committed.

### 5.8. CONSEQUENCES

In the case of a broken promise [*obeshchanie*] a loss of trust ensues, while if an obligation [*obiazatel'stvo*] is not kept the consequence may be punishment. The breaking of a vow [*kliatva*] normally leads to punishment by a higher power (see Glovinskaia 1993: 176–8). If a person is accused of something [*obviniat'*] (insincerity, ingratitude) he may expect a different kind of punishment, in the form of public censure, for example. If he is blamed [*vinit'*] for something, there may be no consequences for him; at best (or at worst) he may recognize that he is responsible for an unfavourable state of affairs which has arisen because of him.

### 5.9. MANNER

*Ponosit'* [to abuse] and *kryt'* [to curse] imply harsh language that pulls no punches, *zhurit'* [to scold, tick off] is a milder form of reproof. *Prisiagat'* [to swear an oath] is always oral, with use of ritual objects. *Obiazyvat'sia* [to take on an obligation; to undertake] may be performed in writing. *Podlizyvat'sia* [to crawl, grovel, lick someone's boots] usually entails the use of words, movements and actions; *podol'shchat'sia* [to gain favour] entails flattering utterances. *Sozyvat'* [to convene, convoke] involves an announcement of a forthcoming event; *sgoniat'* [to round up] involves coercive measures.

5.10. QUANTITATIVE PARAMETERS OF THE STATE, PROCESS, OR ACTION

5.10.1. Frequency of Performance in Relation to a Perceived Norm

In the case of *povadit'sia* the frequency of visits to a place is presented as exceeding the norm; compare this with the neutral (normal) *poseshchat'* and *naveshchat'* [all meaning 'to visit']. *Posylat'* [to send] may be used to describe sending someone somewhere in accordance with frequency norms, while *goniat'* usually implies frequency in excess of that norm: *nepreryvno ⟨ves' den', to i delo⟩ goniat' kogo-libo na pochtu* [endlessly ⟨all day, constantly⟩ to send someone to the post office].

5.10.2. Intensity

*Mechtat'* [to dream of, in the sense of 'to wish'] is more intense than *khotet'* [to want], and *zhazhdat'* [to yearn for] is more intense than *mechtat'*. *Likovat'* [to exult] is more intense than *radovat'sia* [to be glad]; *strast'* [passion] is more intense than *liubov'* [love]; *vostorg* [rapture] is more intense than *voskhishchenie* [admiration]. In the case of *pristrastit'sia* [to take a liking to, to become addicted to] the desire to do something is more intense than in the case of *priokhotit'sia* [to develop a taste for].

5.10.3. Depth

*Radovat'sia* [to be glad] is deeper than *likovat'* [to exult]; *liubov'* [love] is more profound than *strast'* [passion]; *voskhishchenie* [admiration] is deeper than *vostorg* [rapture]. *Oshibka* [error, mistake] can concern something insignificant and be trivial and superficial; *zabluzhdenie* [error, delusion] concerns more serious matters and implies a more profound departure from the truth.

5.10.4. Range, Scale, Amplitude

A single event which is agreeable or desirable to the subject is sufficient to produce *radost'* [joy]. All the subject's wishes, or at least his most important wishes must come true to produce *schast'e* [happiness]. *Obdumyvat'* [to consider, reflect on] implies a wider span of phenomena to be considered; *produmyvat'* [to think over] implies greater depth of analysis.

5.10.5. Temporal Attributes of a State, Process, or Action

5.10.5.1. *Duration of Existence, Number of Periods of Observation*

A wish expressed by *mechtat'* [to dream] usually lasts longer than one expressed by *zhazhdat'* [to thirst]: compare *ia mechtal uvidet' vas* [I dreamed of seeing you] (which may mean all the speaker's life) and *ia zhazhdal uvidet' vas* [I was longing to see you] (we might have seen each other an hour ago). *Zhdat'* [to wait] may include many periods of observation, even covering one's whole life, while *podzhidat', podozhdat'* [to wait] usually imply a single period of observation: compare *tselykh desiat' let ona zhdala vozvrashcheniia muzha iz lageria* [for ten whole years she waited for her husband to return from the camp], and *u dverei prokhodnoi zhenshchiny podzhidali svoikh muzhei* [the women waited for their husbands by the entrance], *podozhdi menia u prokhodnoi* [wait for me by the entrance]. *Prinorovit'sia* may signify adaptation in the course of a single period of observation (*on postepenno prinorovilsia k moemu shagu* [he gradually adapted to my pace]). *Adaptirovat'sia* [to adapt (intrans.)] signifies a longer process, extended over several or many such periods. See also T. V. Bulygina's examples (in a slightly different terminological framework): *nravit'sia* [to please] (may imply a single period of observation: *vam nravitsia eto vino?* [do you like this wine?]) and *liubit'* [to like, love] (there are always several or many periods: *vy liubite eto vino?* [do you like this wine? (i.e. are you fond of it?)]); *est'* versus *pitat'sia* [to eat] (Bulygina 1982: 29, 55).

### 5.10.5.2. *Speed*

The process *ponimat'* [to understand] implies normal speed, while *skhvatyvat'* [to grasp] implies acceleration and *dokhodit'* and *dopirat'* suggest delay (*Nu kak, doshlo, nakonets?* [well, has it finally sunk in?]; *Doper?* [Got it now?]); compare also *govorit'* [to talk] and *taratorit'* [to chatter, babble]; *pisat' pis'mo* [to write a letter] and *strochit' pis'mo* [to dash off a letter].

### 5.10.5.3. *Retrospect versus Prospect*

*Ruchat'sia* [to vouch] and *garantirovat'* [to guarantee] may be used retrospectively: *ruchaius' ⟨garantiruiu⟩, chto on uzhe prishel* [I guarantee he has already arrived]. *Obeshchat'* [to promise] and *obiazat'sia* [to undertake] can only apply to the future: compare *obeshchaiu ⟨obiazuius'⟩ zakonchit' rabotu v srok* [I promise ⟨undertake⟩ to complete the job on time] and the impossibility of these two verbs in the preceding context. *Nadeiat'sia* [to hope] may be retrospective (*Nadeius', chto pal'to tebe ponravilos' ⟨chto rasskaz prishelsia tebe po vkusu⟩* [I hope you liked the coat ⟨that the story was to your liking⟩]), while *upovat'* [to place one's trust in] refers only to the future.

## 5.11. CONNECTIONS BETWEEN THE GIVEN STATE, PROCESS, OR ACTION AND OTHER STATES, PROCESSES, OR ACTIONS

### 5.11.1. Connection with Perception

#### 5.11.1.1. *The Choice of a Specific Subsystem of Perception*

*Chudit'sia* [to seem] denotes an impression which is connected in the subject's mind above all with auditory perception, although visual and other forms of perception are not excluded. *Mereshchit'sia* [to appear, seem] denotes an impression which the subject links above all with visual perception, although auditory perception is also possible. *Vygliadet'* [to seem, look, appear] implies perception primarily of the visible attributes of the object, while *kazat'sia* [to seem] implies that of less obvious, more varied and deep-seated attributes: compare *mal'chik vygliadel umnym* [the boy looked bright] (judging by his eyes, high forehead, etc.) and *mal'chik pokazalsia umnym* [the boy seemed bright] (judging by the way he answered questions, his speed of understanding, etc.).

### 5.11.1.2. *The Reality of the Perception*

Something which does not in fact exist, which a person does not perceive physically, may *mereshchit'sia*, while *chudit'sia* may apply to something that actually does exist: compare *I dvazhdy opiat'-taki pochudilos' findirektoru, chto potianulo po polu gniloi maliariinoi syrost'iu* [and twice more it seemed to the financial director as if a mouldy malarial dampness was wafting over the floor] (it really was) (M. Bulgakov). *Donosit'sia* [to be heard] is used only of real sounds reaching one's ears, while in the case of *(po)slyshat'sia* there may be no actual sound at all.

### 5.11.2. Connection with the Motor System

### 5.11.2.1. *Movement*

*Likovanie* [exultation] is usually accompanied by energetic motion: a person may jump about, wave his arms, etc. *Radost'* [joy] may be experienced in silence, internally, with no outward manifestations. Compare the similar contrast in the pairs *panika* [panic]—*strakh* [fear], *iarost'* [rage]—*gnev* [anger], *beshenstvo* [fury]—*vozmushchenie* [indignation]. (The left-hand elements in the pairs are more likely to be coupled with energetic motion than those on the right.)

### 5.11.2.2. *Facial Expression*

One may *obizhat'sia* [take offence] without any outward manifestation, while *dut'sia* (to sulk) usually suggests pouting. When a person is angry [*serditsia*] he may frown; if he is annoyed (*dosaduet*) he may make a wry face.

### 5.11.2.3. *Gestures and Voice*

*Preduprezhdat'* and *predosteregat'* [to warn] usually signify a verbal warning pronounced in neutral tones. A threat (*ugroza*) may be accompanied by an appropriate gesture—the ritualized motion of the raised finger or clenched fist—and a raising of the voice. *Prosit'* (to request) may be unaccompanied by gestures and pronounced in a normal tone of voice; *umoliat'* [to plead, entreat] involves clasped hands extended towards the addressee and speaking in a special pleading voice or giving other signals of our helplessness and faith in the power of the addressee.

### 5.11.3. Connection with Involuntary Physical Reactions

When a person *boitsia, pugaetsia, trusit* [is fearful, cowardly] he may turn cold or pale and may begin to shiver. When a person is ashamed or embarrassed (*styditsia, smushchaetsia, konfuzitsia*) he may feel hot, his movements become clumsy, he may go red in the face and he may start perspiring.

### 5.11.4. Connection with Desires

#### 5.11.4.1. *The Presence of a Wish*

*Vtianut'sia* [to get involved], *priokhotit'sia* [to develop a taste for], *pristrastit'sia* [to take a liking to, to become addicted to], and *povadit'sia* [to take to visiting] presuppose a wish to do something, whereas *privyknut'* [to get into a habit] and *priuchit'sia* [to get accustomed to] do not express any wish. People may *rasstat'sia* [part] at the wish of one or both parties, while *razluka* [separation] is usually imposed by circumstances. *Zlit'* [to annoy, vex] may be either intentional (*perestan' zlit' sobaku!* [stop teasing the dog!]) or unintentional, while *vozmushchat'* [to anger, make indignant] is usually unintentional.

#### 5.11.4.2. *Specific Wishes*

*Nenavist'* [hatred] engenders a wish to destroy the object; *otvrashchenie* [disgust]—a wish to get away from it. *Strakh* [fear] produces a wish to run away; *styd* [shame] a wish to hide.

### 5.11.5. Connection with the Intellect

#### 5.11.5.1. *The Presence of Some State of Mind*

In *rasschityvat'* and *polagat'sia* [to count on, rely on] the intellect is dominant (logical calculation or reliance on previous experience) and feeling plays no part. On the other hand, in *nadeiat'sia* [to hope; to rely] and especially *upovat'* (*na*) [to put one's trust in] there is a large measure of feeling. In *stydit'sia* [to be ashamed] a rational assessment of one's actions or qualities as deviating from the norm is predominant; in *smushchat'sia* and *konfuzit'sia* [to be embarrassed] an immediate emotional reaction to a situation plays a substantial role. A similar pattern can be seen in the pairs *voskhishchat'sia* [to admire] (in which a rational evaluation predominates)—*vostorgat'sia* [to be in raptures] (in which an immediate emotional reaction plays a substantial role) and *opasat'sia* [to be apprehensive]—*boiat'sia* [to fear] (this last observation is due to V. Apresjan).

#### 5.11.5.2. *A Specific State of Mind or Mental Activity (Imagining, Recollecting, Thinking, Understanding, Knowing)*

*Voobrazhat'* [to imagine] presupposes reliance on the imagination, *predstavliat'* [to picture] on thought, *videt'* [to see, in the comparable mental sense] often on the memory: *uchenye, ne vidia, nakhodiat zvezdy i mikroby* [scientists can locate stars and microbes without seeing them]; *tot, kto voobrazil polet cheloveka, byl predtechei aviatsii* [the person who imagined manned flight was the forerunner of aviation] (M. Slonim); *predstaviv vsiu slozhnost' zadachi, on neskol'ko priunyl* [picturing to himself the complexity of the task he became slightly despondent]; *ia predstavil sebe . . . net, ne predstavil, a voobrazil vid Urala s vysoty neskol'kikh kilometrov* [I pictured . . . no, I didn't picture, I imagined the view of the Urals from a height of several kilometres] (V. Kataev).

### 5.11.5.3. *Source of Knowledge or Understanding*

Compare the purely rational *znat'* and *ponimat'*, on the one hand, with *oseniat'* (to occur to; understanding comes in an irrational, suprasensory way) and *ozarenie* (to see the light; understanding is inspired by a higher power), on the other. *Vera* [faith] in a person has no explanation, while *doverie* [trust] is usually based on previous knowledge of that person.

### 5.11.6. Connection with Emotions

### 5.11.6.1. *The Presence of an Emotion*

*Zhazhdat'* [to thirst, yearn] differs from *khotet'* [to want] in that it presupposes a strong emotion, whereas emotion is by no means essential with *khotet'*. In *smushchat'sia* and *konfuzit'sia* [to get embarrassed], as noted above, the immediate emotional reaction to a situation plays a major role; in *stesniat'sia* there is an indication of a desire restrained or of the undesirable necessity of doing something.

### 5.11.6.2. *Specific Emotions*

*Radost'* [joy] may be accompanied by slight sadness, while *likovanie* [exultation] leaves no room for any other emotion. If close friends are obliged to *razluchit'sia* [part] they may feel sad about this; if they *rasproshchalis'* [have taken leave of each other, gone their separate ways] they may feel bitterness. If a person *obmanulsia v kom-to* [is mistaken in smb.] he may be disappointed; if he *proschitalsia* [miscalculated] he may be annoyed. In *setovat'* [to lament] there is regret that reality is what it is; in *roptat'* [to grumble] there is indignation about that reality; in *plakat'sia* [moaning] there is self-pity.

### 5.11.7. Connection with Speech

The act of condemnation present in *rugat', branit', uprekat', ukoriat', vygovarivat', otchityvat', kritikovat', bichevat'* [to curse; to rebuke, reprove, reprimand, criticize] is always expressed in speech, while in *osuzhdat'* [to hold in the wrong] and *poritsat'* [to blame] one may keep it to oneself. In exactly the same way *obviniat'* [to accuse] (always a speech act) differs from *vinit'* [to blame] (not necessarily a speech act). *Vostorg* [rapture] requires an outlet in speech more than *voskhishchenie* [admiration]. In the case of *vzorvat'* (in the sense 'to exasperate, make indignant') a verbal reaction is certain, while in the case of *vozmu-tit'* [to make indignant] such a reaction is possible, but not essential.

## 5.12. THE SPEAKER'S ASSESSMENT

### 5.12.1. General Assessment

In the case of *plakat'sia, nyt', khnykat', skulit'* [to moan, whinge, gripe, bellyache] the complaint is deemed to be unfounded or exaggerated and the subject is seen as lacking steadfastness and excessively given to self-pity. In the case of *pilit'* and *gryzt'* [to nag] the speaker dislikes the unmotivated persistence and constant repetition of the same thing.

### 5.12.2. Aesthetic Assessment

*Malevat'* [to paint, daub], compared to neutral *pisat'* [to paint] and *mazila* [dauber] compared to neutral *khudozhnik, zhivopisets* [painter, artist] express an unfavourable aesthetic judgement on the product of the art; *shedevr* [master-piece], compared to neutral *proizvedenie* [work of art], expresses a favourable aesthetic judgement. Utterances such as *peschanaia doroga izvivalas' ⟨zmeilas', petliala⟩ mezhdu kustami* [the sandy track wound ⟨snaked, zigzagged⟩ through the bushes] contain no aesthetic assessment of the road. A statement such as *tropinka vilas' po sklonu gory* [the path wound its way up/down/along the hill-side] contains a favourable aesthetic assessment of the path—it is presented as beautiful, picturesque, etc.

### 5.12.3. Ethical Assessment

*Chernit'* [to blacken, censure] implies a dishonest attempt to present the object as bereft of any virtues, while *lakirovat'* [to varnish] implies an equally dishonest attempt to present it as lacking any defects. Both of these elicit the speaker's negative ethical judgement. By describing a speech act as an *insinuatsiia* [insinu-ation], the speaker attributes to the subject the ill intent of using an intricately disguised falsehood to discredit someone, an act which is naturally judged to be ethically unworthy. The same judgement is present in the meaning of *zamazyvat'* [to gloss over] and, to a lesser extent, *zamalchivat'* [to hush up]; cf. the neutral *skryvat'* [to conceal].

### 5.12.4. Utilitarian Assessment

The statement *doroga postoianno viliala* [the road kept twisting and turning] expresses a negative utilitarian judgement of the object. Cf. *raiskogo v prirode tam ne nakhodit* [. . .]. *To tropinka 'podlovato viliaet', to v Novoi Anglii 'kislaia vesna'* [he finds nothing Eden-like about the countryside there [. . .]. Either 'the path is meanly crooked' or the New England spring is 'sour'] (Z. Shakhovskaia).

Compare this with *tropinka vilas'* above, which contains a favourable aesthetic judgement.

### 5.12.5. The Truth Value of the Assessment

A confident *schitat'* [to consider, believe] makes a stronger claim to veracity than the less confident *polagat'* [to suppose] and the tentative *dumat'* [to think]. *Kazat'sia* [to seem] contains more readiness to accept that an impression may be false than *predstavliat'sia* and *sdavat'sia* [to appear]. In rheme position, when appraising the addressee's impression, *kazat'sia* always categorizes it as false: *tebe eto tol'ko ↓ kazhetsia* [that's only the way it seems to you] (This observation is due to Anna Zalizniak 1992: 142; note however, that in a statement about oneself in the present tense the suggestion of falsehood is absent even in rheme position: *mne tak kazhetsia* [that's how I see it].) *Predstavliat'sia* and *sdavat'sia* are not found in this position so the idea of the veracity or falsity of the impression is left unexpressed. Both verbs indicate only hypothesis: *mne sdaetsia ⟨predstav-liaetsia⟩, chto ia ego gde-to videl* [it seems to me I've seen him somewhere].

### 5.13. THE OBSERVER

### 5.13.1. The Presence of an Observer

*Silit'sia* [to make an effort] (*silit'sia podniat'sia ⟨otkryt' glaza, skazat' chto-to⟩* [to make an attempt to get up ⟨open one's eyes, say smth.⟩]) presupposes an ob-server (someone who sees a person making unsuccessful efforts), while *pytat'sia* and *probovat'* do not (*neskol'ko raz on pytalsia ⟨proboval⟩ pisat' stikhi* [he tried several times to write poetry]). *Pokazat'sia* (*na doroge*) [to appear, show oneself (on the road)] also presupposes an observer, while *vyiti* (*na dorogu*) [to set out] does not. Similarly, the putative verb *nakhodit'* [to find] in many contexts pre-supposes direct observation or contemplation of the object. For example, if a woman is looking at her reflection in the mirror it is quite normal for her to say *ia nakhozhu sebia privlekatel'noi* [I find myself attractive]. In this situation it is impossible to replace *nakhodit'* with its synonym *schitat'* [to consider, believe], although in other respects the latter is far more universal. *Schitat'* describes opinions formed as a result of thorough processing of information and weighing of all the pros and cons, not during the direct visual observation of the object. Cf. *mne stol'ko govorili o moei krasote, chto ia stala schitat' sebia privlekatel'noi* [I've heard so much about my own beauty that I've started to believe I'm attrac-tive], in which the verb *schitat'* cannot be replaced by *nakhodit'*.

### 5.13.2. The Position of the Observer

The preposition *pered* [in front of] in sentences such as *pered derevom stoial mototsikl* [in front of the tree stood a motorcycle] places the motorcycle between the observer and the tree and considerably closer to the tree. The preposition *za* in sentences such as *za derevom stoial mototsikl* [behind the tree stood a motorcycle] places the tree between the observer and the motorcycle, with less distance between the tree and the motorcycle than between the observer and the tree. The verb *viliat'* (in sentences such as *doroga nepreryvno viliala* [the road kept winding]) places the observer directly upon the object he is travelling along (often by some means of transport); in the situation described by the verb *vit'sia* (*tropa zhivopisno vilas' po sklonu gory* [the path wound its picturesque way up/ down/along the hillside]) the observer is looking at the object from afar, or seeming to see it from afar.

# 4

# The Synonymy of Mental Predicates: *schitat'* [to consider] and its Synonyms

## 1. Preliminary Remarks

This chapter is essentially a dictionary entry I wrote for the *New Explanatory Dictionary of Russian Synonyms* which is being compiled at the Russian Language Institute of the Russian Academy of Sciences by a small team of lexicographers (J. D. Apresjan, O. Iu. Boguslavskaia, I. V. Levontina, and E. V. Uryson) headed by the present author. It is a synonym series of putative verbs *dumat'*, *schitat'*, *polagat'*, *nakhodit'*, *rassmatrivat'*, *smotret'*, *usmatrivat'*, *videt'* [to think, consider, suppose, find, regard, look upon, regard, see].

The concept of the dictionary was set forth in J. Apresjan (1992*b*); see also Chapters 1 and 2 of this volume; and it is assumed that the reader is familiar with it. By way of preamble to the main theme, on the basis of the author's previously published works, some points about systematic lexicography which the author would like to implement in the synonym dictionary are here set forth in summary form.

(1) The lexical stock of any language, or of its core at least, may be broken down into lexicographic types. 'Lexicographic type' (LT) is the term applied to a group of lexemes with a number of shared properties, to which the same grammatical and other fairly general linguistic rules are sensitive, including semantic, pragmatic, communicative, prosodic, and co-occurrence rules. The concept of a lexicographic type is thus substantially different from that of a (lexico-) semantic class or semantic field. On the one hand, it need not be based on the semantic similarity of lexemes. On the other, it is defined via grammatical and other rules and therefore becomes meaningful only within the framework of an integrated description of language (see Chapter 10).

(2) The main principle of systematic lexicography is that it should describe each lexeme as an element of a lexicographic type, that is, it should identify the recurrent features of the lexical units and present them homogeneously in the dictionary.

(3) The body of lexicographic types in any given language is determined above all by the way in which that language arranges its conceptual material to produce the so-called 'naïve' world picture. The vocabulary which is thematically

related to a single fragment of this picture will usually have many features in common, and these must be consistently reflected in the dictionary (see the 'naïve geometry' underlying words denoting linear parameters in Chapter 9, or the 'naïve psychology' underlying the vocabulary of the emotions in J. Apresjan 1992b; see also Chapter 3 in this volume). Most of these features are apparently universal in their nature, that is, common to human language as a whole, and only a few features of the 'naïve' world picture are language-specific.

(4) On the other hand, the body of the lexicographic types in any given language is determined by the way that language is formally organized, for example, by the peculiarities of its word-formation models (Chapter 10). Lexicographic types determined by the formal features of a language, on the other hand, are in most cases language-specific, although they too may exhibit interesting universal features. An example of these is the polysemy of the main verbs of locomotion, whose structure exhibits a combination of three meanings typical of copulas—a classifying meaning (or rather a copula meaning), a locative, and an existential meaning—see Chapter 10.

(5) An important principle of systematic lexicography is that in the explication of lexical meanings it should consistently reduce complex meanings to simpler ones, until the level of so-called semantic primitives, or indefinability, is reached. This explicatory strategy, which is characteristic of the works of the Moscow semantic school (Mel'čuk and Zholkovsky 1984), makes it possible to present clearly all semantic links between individual lexemes and large groups of lexemes.

In connection with the concept of semantic primitives, it is useful to note that they do not necessarily possess the property of being fundamentally non-decomposable. *Khotet'* [to want], for example, is undoubtedly a semantic primitive, although theoretically a simpler element may be isolated within it which is common to the verbs *khotet'*, *khotet'sia* [to feel like], *zhelat'* [to wish]. *Khotet'* must be accepted as a primitive because this shared element cannot be verbalized within Russian. The point is that each of the three verbs has features which distinguish it from the other two. *Khotet'sia* signifies a less well defined wish than *khotet'*, which is felt to be less a condition of one's own will than a bodily condition. It is curious that unlike *khotet'*, *khotet'sia* never signifies an intention (on the intention present in *khotet'* see Zalizniak (1984: 87)). *Zhelat'*, like *khotet'*, describes a condition of the will. However, *khotet'* implies that the implementation of the will is linked above all with the actions of the subject himself, whereas *zhelat'* to a significantly greater extent implies the possible actions of other people.

It is worth noting that in other languages—as a direct result of the characteristic features of their conceptualization of the world—words describing roughly the same fragment of extralinguistic reality may differ from one another in completely different ways. Thus in English states of will are described by the verbs *want*, *wish*, *desire*. The last two are close to Russian *zhelat'*, but there is no equivalent to the very Russian verb *khotet'sia*, while the main verb—*want*—which is comparable to *khotet'*, differs from it in additionally suggesting not the intentions of the subject but his needs.

From this it follows, incidentally, that semantic primitives are language-specific; that since only 'foreground words', which are very finely honed in any language and its whole national culture, may claim to be primitives, there can be no primitives proper (the simplest senses, which can be expressed in one word in all human languages); and that the task of constructing a universal semantic language is therefore postponed into the indefinite future.

(6) Systematic lexicography entails active-type dictionaries. An active dictionary should contain full information about a lexeme, not only that which is necessary to understand it correctly in any context, but also that which is needed to use it correctly in one's own speech. Dictionaries of this type store a smaller number of words than traditional passive dictionaries, but they should surpass them greatly in the amount of information assigned to every lexeme. Thus the lexicographic type turns out to be only one of the mainstays of systematic lexicography. Another is the concept of the lexicographic portrait (Chapters 9, 10) —an exhaustive and non-redundant account of the linguistically relevant features of a given lexeme within the framework of an integrated description of a language. Only an active dictionary permits us to cope adequately with the two central tasks facing every lexicographer, that of unification (lexicographic types) and that of individualization (lexicographic portraits).

After these preliminary remarks we may proceed to the presentation of the synonym series of the main Russian putative verbs. From the large body of literature on the subject the following works were taken into account: (J. Apresjan 1986c; Arutiunova 1989; Dmitrovskaia 1988b; Zalizniak 1991a; Mel'čuk and Zholkovsky 1984; Ruwet, 1981). However, the problem required a new analysis, reinterpretation, and a new description of a substantial body of material. Some details of the description were refined following critical observations from O. Iu. Boguslavskaia, M. Ia. Glovinskaia, I. B. Levontina, and E. V. Uryson during discussion of the series at a working meeting of the Theoretical Semantics Section of the RAN Russian Language Institute. I am also deeply indebted to the members of N. D. Arutiunova's seminar, at which this series was presented.

Considerations of space dictate that the synonym series be set forth in abridged form. In particular, the illustration zone and bibliography zone are not given and the number of examples has been reduced to a minimum in the Syntax and Co-occurrence zones. The structure of the dictionary entry and the technical methods of presenting the material are not explained. The reader will find some information on this topic in Chapter 2.

## 2. The Synonym Series

### 2.1. THE HEADING

*Schitat'* (~ pf. *schest', poschitat'*) [to consider], *dumat'* (~ pf. *podumat'*) [to think], *polagat'* (bookish) (no pf.) [to suppose], *nakhodit'* (bookish) (pf. *naiti*) [to find], *rassmatrivat'* (no pf.) [to regard], *smotret'* (pf. *posmotret'*) [to look upon], *usmatrivat'* (bookish) (pf. *usmotret'*) [to regard], *videt'* (pf. *uvidet'*) [to see]. The dominant of the series is a semantic primitive.

## 2.2. THE SEMANTIC FEATURES FOR THE *SCHITAT'* SERIES

The synonyms differ by the following semantic features:

(1) the presence of a qualification (judgement, interpretation, classification) of the object by the subject (*dumat'* mostly introduces a simple statement, while *rassmatrivat'* always introduces a qualifying judgement);

(2) the participation of the will in forming an opinion (*schitat'*, particularly in the form *schest'*, presupposes the role of the will in forming an opinion, while *dumat'* does not);

(3) the proportion of certainty versus supposition in somebody's opinion (certainty is highest in the case of *schitat'*);

(4) the presence or absence of direct perception of the situation at issue (*dumat'*, *schitat'*, and *polagat'* may apply to something not directly observed, while *nakhodit'* implies direct observation or contemplation of the object);

(5) the possibility of an outside observer (for *nakhodit'* an outside observer is more necessary than for *polagat'*);

(6) the extent and precision of the intellectual effort applied in forming the opinion (in the case of *schitat'* this is greater than in that of *nakhodit'*);

(7) the possibility of viewing the given mental state as an intellectual process (in *rassmatrivat'* and *smotret'* the element of process is more prominent than in *usmatrivat'* and especially *videt'*);

(8) the relation between the thought and the individual's overall system of views (in the case of *smotret'* a particular judgement may be based on the whole system of views, while in the case of *usmatrivat'* it is usually the product of the analysis of the current situation);

(9) the nature of the situation under consideration (a *fait accompli* vs. an event still to come; compare *usmatrivat'*, which introduces judgements about facts, and *videt'*, which is possible in statements about future situations).

## 2.3. SEMANTIC SIMILARITIES AND DIFFERENCES BETWEEN SYNONYMS

Depending on the proportion of interpretation or evaluation, the whole series may be divided into two large groups (compare the simple judgement *Ia schital, chto on uzhe priekhal* [I thought he had already arrived] and the distinctly evaluative or interpretive *Ia schitaiu eto nedorazumeniem* [I regard this as a misunderstanding]): *schitat'*, *dumat'*, *polagat'* and *nakhodit'*, on the one hand, and *rassmatrivat'*, *smotret'*, *usmatrivat'*, and *videt'* on the other.

The synonyms in the first group may introduce simple statements about states of affairs and evaluative judgements alike. Simple statements: *kazhdyi tretii zhitel'*

*Moskvy schitaet, chto v sushchestvuiushchikh usloviiakh Rossiia ne dolzhna poddzerhivat' politiku Fidel'ia Kastro* [one in three Moscow residents considers that in present conditions Russia should not support the policies of Fidel Castro] (*Moskovskie novosti*, 8 Dec. 1991); *Sofa pila naravne so vsemi i, kogda dumala, chto ia ne vizhu, ukradkoi kosila na menia bol'shimi svetlymi glazami* [Sofa drank with the best of them, and when she thought I wasn't looking she glanced sidelong at me with her big bright eyes] (Iu. Dombrovskii); *ia ne nauchilsia liubit' svoiu rodinu s zakrytymi glazami, s preklonennoi golovoi, s zapertymi ustami. Ia nakhozhu, chto chelovek mozhet byt' polezen svoei strane tol'ko v tom sluchae, esli iasno vidit ee* [I did not learn to love my homeland with closed eyes, bowed head, and lips shut tight. I believe that a person can be of use to his country only if he sees it clearly] (P. Ia. Chaadaev). Evaluative judgements: *vy chereschur plokho o nei dumaete, ona ne soglasitsia na etu sdelku* [you think too badly of her; she won't agree to that deal]; *pust' sochtut priznanie* [M. Zoshchenko] *nedostatochnym, nevazhno, mery priniaty, mozhno dolozhit'* [let them think the confession (by M. Zoshchenko) inadequate; it doesn't matter; we can report that measures have been taken] (D. Granin); *prezident polagal neobkhodimym provesti reformu ispolnitel'noi vlasti* [the president deemed it essential to carry out a reform of executive power]; *voennaia prokuratura provodila rassledovanie v otnoshenii S. Matevosiana i ne nashla ego povedenie v period plena predosuditel'- nym* [the military prosecutor conducted an investigation of S. Matevosian and did not find his behaviour during captivity reprehensible] (K. Smirnov).

The synonyms in the second group, i.e. *rassmatrivat', smotret', usmatrivat',* and *videt',* always introduce only evaluative judgements in which some object is appraised, interpreted, or classified in some particular way. This is borne out by the fact that none of the synonyms in the second group is used in the prototypical construction for simple statements, with the conjunction *chto* [that]: *ia rassmatrivaiu intellektual'nuiu svobodu kak neobkhodimoe uslovie nauchnogo tvorchestva* [I regard intellectual freedom as an essential precondition for creative scholarly work]; *vladel'tsy doma—starik i starukha—izgolodalis' i smotreli na kvartirantov kak na edinstvennyi istochnik propitaniia* [the owners of the house—an old man and an old woman—were starving and looked on their tenants as their sole source of nourishment] (A. Popov); *nikto ne usmatrivaet v etom zlogo umysla* [nobody sees in this any ill intent]; *my videli v nem nastoiashchego druga* [we saw in him a true friend].

In the first group, *dumat'* less than all the others implies a judgement of the object and is used mainly in the construction *dumat', chto P* [to think that P]. Evaluation is possible only in the construction *khorosho ⟨plokho⟩ dumat' o kom-l.* [to think well ⟨ill⟩ of smb.]. The latter introduces purely evaluative judgements, usually with a person as their object: *ty chereschur plokho dumaesh' o svoikh kollegakh* [you think too badly of your colleagues] but not *\*ty chereschur plokho dumaesh' o svoikh knigakh* [you think too badly of your books]. *Nakhodit',* on the other hand, in most contexts introduces evaluative statements and is therefore more often used in constructions of the type which serve such judgements: *nakhodit' kogo-chto-libo strannym* [to find smb./sth. odd]. *Schitat'* occupies an intermediate position between these two poles. As for *polagat'*, in modern Russian it is closest in this respect to *dumat'*, although highly bookish or archaic qualifying uses in the construction *polagat' kogo-chto-libo strannym* [to think smb./sth. odd] remain typical in the press (see the foregoing and following examples).

*Dumat'* contrasts with *schitat'* above all in the degree of supposition versus certainty. Statements like *ia dumaiu, chto zavtra vse vyiasnitsia* [I think everything will become clear tomorrow]; *druz'ia bol'nogo dumali, chto krizis pozadi* [the patient's friends thought the crisis had passed] represent suppositions. Usually the subject himself is aware of their hypothetical nature. Statements like *ia schitaiu, chto zavtra vse vyiasnitsia* [I believe everything will become clear tomorrow]; *vrachi schitali, chto krizis pozadi* [the doctors believed the crisis had passed] represent certainty that the situation is exactly as seen. These statements are appropriate in situations in which the subject has no contradictory facts in his field of view. Unreliable or incomplete knowledge may underlie a thought, but not an opinion. To the question *vy ne znaete, na kakoi put' prikhodit poezd iz Varshavy?* [do you know which platform the train from Warsaw arrives at?] I may reply *Dumaiu, chto na pervyi* [number one, I think], but not *ia schitaiu, chto na pervyi* [number one, I consider].

This distinction is related to the fact that a thought (the product of thinking) may occur in the mind without any effort of will, given a single brief perception of some object. We may test the bath water and say, *dumaiu, chto gradusov tridtsat' piat' budet* [I think it's about thirty-five degrees]. *Schitat'* is less appropriate in this context because more serious conditions are required to develop an opinion (that which we *schitaem* [consider]). An opinion is usually the result of a fairly long and thorough process of consideration of all observable facts (note the original idea of *schet* [counting] which is present in *schitat'*), weighing up other possible interpretations of them and selecting the interpretation which best accords with the accumulated personal experience of the subject and which he is prepared to uphold as correct. See the sentence *Dlia SShA, Anglii i Frantsii vriad li budet dostatochno idushchikh iz Tripoli obeshchanii, chtoby schitat', chto Liviia otvergaet terrorizm* [for the USA, Britain, and France the promises emanating from Tripoli will hardly suffice to make them believe that Libya is renouncing terrorism] (*Izvestiia*, 29 Nov. 1991). Here the promises are considered insufficient because the countries concerned have the results of long and thorough investigations showing beyond doubt that Libya has been responsible for terrorist acts.

Generally speaking, the more complex a situation is, the greater the number of possible interpretations, and the harder it is to establish the truth, the more justification there is for the use of *schitat'*. And the simpler, the more obvious and trivial it is, the greater the justification for using *dumat'*. Consider the following: *Kak vy znaete, Shalamov schitaet lagernyi opyt—polnost'iu negativnym. Ia nemnogo znal Varlama Tikhonovicha. Eto byl porazitel'nyi chelovek. I vse-taki ia ne soglasen* [As you know, Shalamov considered the prison camp experience utterly negative. I knew Varlam Tikhonovich slightly. He was an amazing man. But nevertheless I disagree] (S. Dovlatov). *Dumat′* would be less appropriate here.

We may say *ia schitaiu, chto on podobrel* [I believe he has become kinder], *ia schitaiu ego kumirom molodezhi* [I regard him as an idol of young people], *ia schitaiu, chto on liubit svoiu zhenu* [I believe he loves his wife], because other opinions are also possible. Far less likely are sentences such as *?ia schitaiu, chto on pokrasnel* [I consider that he has turned red], *?ia schitaiu ego svoim kumirom* [I believe he is my idol], *?ia schitaiu, chto ia liubliu svoiu zhenu* [I believe I love my wife]. The fact that somebody has turned red in the face is a directly observable phenomenon, and the fact that somebody is my idol or that I love my wife is an element of knowledge which I have about myself. No intellectual calculations are required to reach these conclusions; any other judgements on these matters are out of the question. The sentences cited above could be correct only in a somewhat unusual sense: 'I believe it is acceptable to use the words *pokrasnet′, kumir,* and *liubit′* to describe what I see in reality or in myself.'

For these reasons, what a person *schitaet* may be part of his world-view, his system of beliefs: compare *Platon schital, chto dusha bessmertna* [Plato believed that the soul was immortal], in which Plato's philosophy is set forth, and *Platon dumal, chto dusha bessmertna* [Plato thought that the soul was immortal], in which one of his hypotheses, in the speaker's view most likely a mistaken one, is set forth. When we say, *on nikogda ne schital, chto spory mozhno razreshat′ siloi* [he never believed that arguments could be resolved by force] we are most likely to be talking about a person's convictions and saying that in his view, the present argument was not or would not be resolved. When we say, *on nikogda ne dumal, chto spory mozhno razreshat′ siloi* [he never thought that arguments could be resolved by force] we are most likely to be talking about that person's expectations and the fact that to his surprise the argument was resolved by force.

Another feature by which *dumat′* contrasts with *schitat′* is the possibility of having in mind the process of reflection at the same time as its result. The clearest syntactic contexts in which this component of meaning is made explicit are the following: (*a*) the pseudo-co-ordinative construction with words of the type *stoiat′* [to stand (and)], *sidet′* [to sit (and)], *lezhat′* [to lie (and)], etc.: *lezhu i dumaiu, chto mne nado iskat′ novuiu rabotu* [I lay there thinking I'd have to look for a new job]; *stoit i dumaet, chto kolbasy na nashu doliu ne khvatit* [he stands and thinks there won't be enough sausage for us]; (*b*) the parenthetic construction with the verb *dumat′* in a finite form and the subject not expressed: *Nu, dumaiu, seichas ia tebia udivliu* [right, I thought, now I'll surprise you]; (*c*) the parenthetic construction with the verb *dumat′* in a finite form and the subject post-posed: *Net, dumal ia, mir, v kotorom sozdana takaia pesnia, imeet pravo na schast′e i budet schastliv* [well, I thought, a world in which a song like that can be created has the right to happiness and will be happy] (F. Iskander). In the parenthetic construction with the subject pre-posed before *dumat′* the meaning of 'state proper' and therefore supposition, is restored: *vy, ia dumaiu, zabyli menia, Vera?—sprosil on* [I think you've forgotten me, Vera, haven't you? he asked] (I. A. Goncharov).

In the uses of *dumat'* considered above we see a kind of direct reportage on what is happening in the subject's mind. The object of this reportage can be only a 'thought proper', in the process of taking shape, and not a supposition because a supposition is an instantaneous event. The verb *schitat'* in such cases is either impossible or, as before, signifies a mental state: *\*lezhu i schitaiu, chto mne nado iskat' novuiu rabotu* [I lay there considering I'd have to look for a new job]; *\*nu, schitaiu, seichas ia tebia udivliu* [right, I considered, now I'll surprise you]; *mir, v kotorom sozdana takaia pesnia, schital ia, imeet pravo na schast'e* [a world in which a song like that can be created, I believed, has the right to happiness] (*schital* represents a state).

On the 'supposition-certainty' axis, *polagat'* [to suppose] is closer to *dumat'* and *nakhodit'* [to find] closer to *schitat'*. The first two synonyms may signify such a large element of guesswork that often their truth value is in question the moment the thought is stated: *on dumaet, budto vse im voskhishchaiutsia* [he thinks everybody admires him]; *eti liudi polagaiut, budto oni mogut chego-to dobit'sia, deistvuia porozn'* [these people imagine they can achieve something by their separate actions]. The use of *schitat'* in such contexts is on the verge of the permissible, while *nakhodit'* would be impossible: *?on schitaet, budto vse im voskhishchaiutsia* [he considers that everybody admires him]; *\*on nakhodit, budto vse im voskhishchaiutsia* [he finds everybody admires him].

On the other hand, *polagat'* approaches *schitat'* in presupposing a certain intellectual effort before an opinion results: *I ty, Anna Savishna, polagaesh', chto u tebia byl sam Dubrovskii* [and you, Anna Savishna, suppose that it was Dubrovskii himself who called on you] (A. S. Pushkin). The difference between it and *schitat'* lies primarily in the pragmatic position of the subject with reference to a potential interlocutor and stands out clearly in first-person statements. In the case of *schitat'* the subject is more categorical, less tentative, less inclined to allow that the other party may be right. The subject of *polagat'* is more modest, perhaps more polite in stating his point of view, more prepared to accept that the other party's view may be closer to the truth than his own. It is easy to imagine a situation in which it is natural to say *ia schitaiu, chto vy lzhete* [I believe you're lying]. The statement *?ia polagaiu, chto vy lzhete* [I suppose you're lying] would sound far less natural in the same situation, owing to the mis-match between the force of the assertion and the indecisive manner in which it is stated.

*Dumat', schitat',* and *polagat'* on the one hand and *nakhodit'* on the other are contrasted above all on the axis of the necessity or otherwise of directly perceiving an object or situation. *Dumat', schitat',* and *polagat'* are possible on the basis of somebody else's information about the object of thought, while with *nakhodit'*, direct perception or contemplation of that object, either before an opinion is formed or concurrent with the process of forming one, is essential. We may say *kogda mne soobshchili ob otkaze firmy predostavit' nam komp'iuter, ia schel eto narusheniem nashego dzhentl'menskogo soglasheniia* [when I was told the firm had refused to supply a computer I regarded this as a breach of our gentleman's agreement] but not \**kogda mne soobshchili ob otkaze firmy predostavit' nam komp'iuter, ia nashel eto narusheniem nashego dzhentl'menskogo soglasheniia* [when I was told the firm had refused to supply a computer I found this a breach of our gentleman's agreement]. The indication of the immediacy of the perception is especially strong in the perfective: *a kak vy nashli nashego gubernatora? —sprosila Manilova.—Ne pravda li, chto prepochtenneishii i preliubeznyi chelovek?* [and how did you find our governor? asked Manilova.—A most estimable and obliging man, is he not?] (N. V. Gogol'); *kak vy nashli Andreia?—sprosila ona.— Doktor skazal, chto on dolzhen ekhat' lechit'sia* [how did you find Andrei? she asked.—The doctor said he should go and take a cure] (L. N. Tolstoi). Both these examples deal with impressions received during meetings.

The indication of immediacy of perception contained in the meaning of the synonym *nakhodit'* militates against its use in describing situations which are difficult to observe. This particularly affects the imperfective form. We may say *ia schitaiu ego chuzhim* [I consider him alien], *ia schitaiu ego chelovekom ne nashego kruga* [I don't consider him one of our circle] but not <sup>??</sup>*ia nakhozhu ego chuzhim* [I find him alien], <sup>??</sup>*ia nakhozhu ego chelovekom ne nashego kruga* [I don't find him one of our circle].

For the same reason *nakhodit'* in the imperfective usually signifies an opinion about a situation which is an actual fact. *Nakhodit'* cannot therefore govern a clause in the future or one containing modality of possibility: *ia dumal ⟨schital, polagal⟩, chto on vam pomozhet ⟨chto ia sumeiu vam pomoch'⟩* [I thought he would help you ⟨that I would be able to help you⟩], but not \**ia nakhodil, chto on vam pomozhet ⟨chto ia sumeiu vam pomoch'⟩* [I found he would help you ⟨that I would be able to help you⟩]. Modality of obligation, which is semantically closer to fact than the modality of possibility, is more acceptable in the context of *nakhodit'*: *ia nakhozhu, chto vy dolzhny emu pomoch'* [I find you should help him] is better than <sup>??</sup>*ia nakhozhu, chto vy mozhete emu pomoch'* [I find you can help him].

Another difference between *nakhodit'* and the other synonyms in this group is connected with the presence of an outside observer. We can say *ia schitaiu sebia skuchnym* [I consider myself boring], *ia schitaiu ⟨dumaiu, polagaiu⟩, chto ne lishen sposobnostei* [I consider that I am not without ability], but not \**ia nakhozhu sebia skuchnym* [I find myself boring], \**ia nakhozhu, chto ne lishen sposobnostei* [I find that I am not without ability]. Compare this with the correct utterances *ia nakhozhu ego skuchnym* [I find him boring], *ia nakhozhu, chto on ne lishen sposobnostei* [I find that he is not without ability]. This is explained by the fact that *nakhodit'* always requires the presence of an outside observer. This is why, when one looks at oneself in the mirror (that is, from outside), one may say, *ia nakhozhu, chto segodnia ia vygliazhu neplokho ⟨chto eto plat'e mne idet⟩* [I find that I look all right today ⟨that this dress becomes me⟩].

In some contexts, when certain semantic components are suppressed, a significant though not total neutralization of the semantic distinctions between synonyms takes place.

The 'supposition' component in the meaning of *dumat'* is suppressed in evaluative syntactic constructions such as *dumat' kak-libo o kom-libo* [to think somehow of smb.] or *dumat' chto-libo o kom-libo* [to think smth. of smb.]: *ne dumaite obo mne plokho ⟨khuzhe, chem ia zasluzhivaiu⟩* [don't think badly of me ⟨worse of me than I deserve⟩]; *chto ty dumaesh' o nashem direktore ⟨ob etoi knige⟩?* [what do you think of our director ⟨of this book⟩?]. In these contexts *dumat'* is semantically interchangeable with *schitat'*, although the syntactic structure must be changed: *ne schitaite menia khuzhe, chem ia est'* [don't regard me as worse than I am].

The formal and semantic conditions favouring the neutralization of semantic distinctions between all synonyms of the first group are the imperfective aspect and a context of modal judgement or judgement concerning the presence or absence of something: *Ia dumaiu ⟨schitaiu, polagaiu⟩, chto pora ⟨nado, mozhno, nevozmozhno, trudno, neobiazatel'no⟩ prinimat' okonchatel'nye resheniia* [I think ⟨consider, believe⟩ it is time ⟨necessary, possible, impossible, difficult, not essential⟩ to take final decisions]; *ia dumaiu ⟨schitaiu, polagaiu, nakhozhu⟩, chto ne stoilo ⟨ne sledovalo⟩ etogo delat'* [I don't think ⟨believe, consider⟩ that should have been done]; *vash rukovoditel' nakhodit ⟨dumaet, schitaet, polagaet⟩, chto u vas est' talant* [your supervisor finds ⟨thinks, considers, believes⟩ you have talent].

In the second group of synonyms the main division is between *rassmatrivat'* and *smotret'* on the one hand and *usmatrivat'* and *videt'* on the other. The first two (especially the second of these) place the object of the reflections in a wider context and imply an attempt to interpret it against the background of the general system of the subject's views. It is precisely this fundamental position, adopted 'off stage', or some broader approach, which serves as the basis for the development of an attitude to a specific fact or large class of phenomena: *zapadnaia Evropa rassmatrivala agressiiu Iraka protiv Kuveita kak priamoi vyzov mirovomu soobshchestvu* [Western Europe viewed Iraq's aggression against Kuwait as a direct challenge to the world community]; *kak vy smotrite na narushenie supruzheskoi vernosti* [how do you view marital infidelity?]. The last two synonyms imply more spontaneous judgements motivated to a lesser extent or not at all by the subject's system of views: *gazety usmotreli v poslednem vystuplenii prezidenta priznaki gotovnosti k kompromissu* [the newspapers saw in the president's latest speech signs that he was prepared to compromise]; *ne vizhu v etom bol'shoi poteri* [I see no great loss in this].

Besides this, *rassmatrivat'* and *smotret'* to a greater extent than *usmatrivat'* and especially *videt'* make it possible to view an opinion or appraisal as the process of arriving at them. In other words they preserve, though in attenuated form, the procedural component which is present in their basic meanings. This is attested by the fact that *rassmatrivat'* and *smotret'* are used with complete freedom in the imperative, in which they preserve their meaning in full: *rassmatrivai eto kak svoe pervoe poruchenie* [consider this your first assignment], *smotri na veshchi proshche* [look at things more simply]. With *usmatrivat'* there are constraints on the formation of the imperative and in the case of *videt'* it is completely impossible.

In the first pair of synonyms *rassmatrivat'* describes a more objective and dispassionate judgement than *smotret'*; in *smotret'* the element of personal opinion and personal interest is greater. For this reason *rassmatrivat'* may have as its subject large groups of people, newspapers, or even society as a whole, so there is often no need to mention it, while the usual subject of *smotret'* is an individual: *Ne tol'ko posle revoliutsii, no i zadolgo do nee tserkov' v Rossii rassmatrivalas' kak priamoi instrument gosudarstvennogo vmeshatel'stva v zhizn' obshchestva* [not only after the Revolution but long before it the Church in Russia was seen as a direct instrument of state intervention in the life of society]; *uchenye rassmatrivaiut Vselennuiu kak rezul'tat dlitel'noi evoliutsii* [scientists see the universe as the result of prolonged evolution]; *ia smotriu na rannie braki prosto ⟨bez vsiakoi predvziatosti⟩* [I regard early marriages simply ⟨without prejudice⟩].

In the subgroup *usmatrivat'* and *videt'* the synonyms differ above all in that they highlight different components of meaning. *Usmatrivat'* focuses attention on the intellectual effort required to produce an opinion, while *videt'* focuses on the opinion itself. For this reason it is appropriate to use *usmatrivat'* when it is necessary to stress the considerable amount of intellectual effort applied, or the difficulty of it, or even that this effort was made quickly, that is, concurrently with the contemplation or perception of some specific situation: *Skol'ko ia ni dumaiu ob etom, ia ne mogu usmotret' zdes' nikakogo podvokha* [however much I think about it, I can see no catch here]; *ia usmatrivaiu v ego deistviiakh popytku uiti ot otvetstvennosti* [in his actions I see an attempt to evade responsibility]. *Videt'* is preferred when we are dealing with opinions already formed on the most general matters: *v rabote on videl smysl zhizni* [he regarded work as the purpose of life]; *v iskusstve ⟨v vospitanii detei⟩ ona videla svoe prizvanie* [she regarded art ⟨raising children⟩ as her vocation]; *chtoby ne bylo tak obidno zhit', my zaranee teshim sebia smert'iu i chut' chto—govorim: 'Pust' ia umru, plevat'!' Veroiatno, za etu derzost', kotoraia vidit v smerti vykhod iz igry, s nas krepko sprositsia* [to make life less painful we make light of death in advance and at the slightest excuse say, 'So I'll die. What do I care?' For this impudence in regarding death as a way out we shall probably pay dearly] (A. Siniavskii).

Another difference between *usmatrivat'* and *videt'* lies in the fact that the first introduces judgements about facts, that is, situations which have already occurred or events which are occurring at the moment of speech, while the second is possible in statements about future situations, for example *ia vizhu vykhod v nemedlennoi privatizatsii* [I see immediate privatization as a way out] where *usmatrivat'* would be less appropriate.

In texts dealing with specific facts a partial neutralization of the semantic distinctions between *videt'* and *usmatrivat'* occurs: *ia ne vizhu ⟨ne usmatrivaiu⟩ v etom sostava prestupleniia* [I can't see a corpus delicti in this]; *v chem vy usmatrivaete* 〈*vidite*〉 *svoeobrazie khudozhestvennogo metoda Nabokova* 〈*noviznu etoi dissertatsii*〉? [what do you see as the distinctive feature of Nabokov's method 〈the original feature of this dissertation〉?].

None of the synonyms in this series may bear the main phrasal stress in any position other than the end of a sentence. However, *dumat'* and *schitat'* easily acquire contrasting (logical) stress, especially in contexts where supposition and knowledge are contrasted: *vy* ↓↓ *dumaete* 〈↓↓ *schitaete*〉, *chto Irak razrabatyvaet khimicheskoe oruzhie, ili vy eto* ↓ *znaete?* [do you think Iraq is developing chemical weapons or do you know it?].

### 2.4. NOTES ON THE SEMANTIC ZONE

NOTE 1: In the nineteenth century and early twentieth century the now obsolete verbs *pochitat'* and *myslit'* were synonymous with *schitat'*: *odni pochitaiut menia khuzhe, drugie luchshe, chem ia v samom dele* [some think me worse, some better than I really am] (M. Iu. Lermontov); *Gleb Mironych, Kak myslish' ty?—Sprosi- ka Vasil'ka; pust' skazhet on, a ia potom otvechu* [Gleb Mironych, what do you think? Ask Vasilii; let him say, then I'll answer] (A. K. Tolstoi).

In the nineteenth century the verb *mnit'* was used in a related sense, 'to suppose wrongly': *Ne to, chto mnite vy, priroda,* | *Ne slepok, ne bezdushnyi lik* [Nature is not what you suppose it to be, | not a mould, not a soulless face] (F. I. Tiutchev).

In modern substandard and slang speech the verb *derzhat'* [to hold] is used as a synonym of *schitat'* in an evaluative sense—mostly in collocations of the type *derzhat' kogo-libo za duraka* 〈*za polnogo idiota*〉 [to regard smb. as a fool 〈a complete idiot〉].

A sense exactly synonymous with *smotret'* [to look] is indicated in dictionaries for the verb *gliadet'*: *gliadi na veshchi prosto* [look at things simply] (A. P. Chekhov); *inzhenery i studenty-praktikanty gliadeli na dom Zinenko kak na gostinitsu* [engineers and trainees looked upon the Zinenko building as a hotel] (A. I. Kuprin). However, this use of *gliadet'* is more potential than real, and due to an analogy with *smotret'*. It is not found in contemporary usage.

NOTE 2: The verb *dumat'* has a substandard meaning close to the one at issue here, 'to suspect, to consider guilty of smth.'. It takes the construction *dumat' na kogo-libo: neuzhto ty do sikh por ne znal, kto na tebia dones?—Net, ia vse na brata dumal* [surely you must have known by now who told on you?—No, I always thought it was my brother (suspected my brother)].

### 2.5. GRAMMATICAL FORMS

In the past tense *schitat'* does not necessarily mean 'on the basis of observations and reflection': *vsiu zhizn' Sergei schital ego svoim ottsom* [all his life Sergei regarded him as his father].

The perfective *schest'* of *schitat'* contrasts sharply with the perfective of the other synonyms in that it suggests a much greater degree of participation of the will in a mental act. Compare *prokuror schel, chto sobrannykh ulik dostatochno dlia pred"iavleniia obvineniia* [the prosecutor considered that enough evidence had been collected to press charges, i.e. he decided to press charges on the basis of the available evidence] and *prokuror podumal, chto sobrannykh ulik dostatochno . . .* [i.e. the prosecutor had this idea, perhaps without sufficient grounds].

The perfective *posmotret'* of *smotret'* is grammatically, lexically, and syntactically restricted: it is usually found in the future in interrogative or 'hypothetical' utterances, mostly combined with the adverbs *kak* [how] and *plokho* [badly] when the object of thought is a whole situation: *kak on posmotrit na otsrochku zashchity dissertatsii?* [how will he regard the postponement of the defence of your thesis?]; *boius', on plokho na eto posmotrit* [I'm afraid he'll take a dim view of that]. (Compare the similar collocation *on mozhet plokho o vas podumat'* with a fundamentally different meaning [he may think badly of you], see above.)

Of all the synonyms in this series, only *rassmatrivat'* and *smotret'* are used with complete freedom in the imperative while fully preserving their meaning (see above for examples and an explanation). *Dumat'* and *schitat'* formally admit use in the imperative (*dumat'* mainly in the set expression *dumai, chto khochesh'* [think what you like]), but with a slight change of meaning: *dumai, chto khochesh'* [ ~ you may think whatever you please, it's all the same to me]; *schitai, chto tebe povezlo ⟨chto my dogovorilis'⟩* [think yourself lucky ⟨consider it a deal⟩; i.e. despite one or two reservations on my part, you may count yourself lucky ⟨consider that we are in agreement⟩]; note *esli ugodno, schitaite eto propagandoi v pol'zu venetsianskikh lavok, ch'i dela idut ozhivlennee pri nizkikh temperaturakh* [if you like you may regard this as propaganda for Venetian shops, which do a more lively trade when the temperature is low] (I. Brodskii). *Schitat'* in the imperative is also used as a parenthetic word, with the sense 'you may consider' and belonging stylistically to the substandard register. *Pro nego nado by skazat' osobo, potomu chto on v etoi istorii, schitai, glavnyi chelovek* [he should be mentioned specially because you could say he's the most important person in this story] (V. Chivilikhin). For the other synonyms in the series there are constraints on the use of the imperative (*polagat', usmatrivat'*), or else it is quite impossible (*nakhodit', videt'*).


## 2.6. SYNTACTIC CONSTRUCTIONS

The syntactic properties of the synonyms *schitat'*, *polagat'*, and *nakhodit'* are the most varied. Like the verb *dumat'*, they govern a subordinate statement introduced by the conjunction *chto* [that] (see above and below). At the same time they are used in qualifying constructions of the type *schitat' kogo-libo kakim-libo* [to consider smb. smth.], in which *polagat'* acquires an extremely bookish overtone (see above).

With all three verbs, variations on this construction are possible when an infinitive or a whole subordinate clause appears in place of the accusative (as long as the position of the instrumental case is occupied by an adjective of the type *nuzhnyi* [necessary], *pravil'nyi* [correct], *somnitel'nyi* [dubious], *vozmozhnyi* [possible], *iasnyi* [clear], etc.): *direktor polagal ⟨ne schital, ne nakhodil⟩ nuzhnym proverit' eti svedeniia* [the director thought ⟨did not consider, did not deem⟩ it necessary to check this information]; *ia schitaiu v vysshei stepeni somnitel'nym, chto on soglasitsia na eto predlozhenie* [I consider it doubtful in the extreme that he will agree to this proposal]. With *schitat'* a variant of this construction is possible in which the position of the instrumental case is occupied by a noun of the type *chest'* [honour], *udacha* [success, luck], *radost'* [pleasure, delight], *oshibka* [mistake], and a number of others: *ia schitaiu dlia sebia bol'shoi chest'iu razgovarivat' s vami ⟨bol'shoi udachei, chto ia vstretil vas zdes'⟩* [I consider it a great honour for me to talk to you ⟨great good fortune that I met you here⟩].

The three synonyms of the first group—*schitat'*, *dumat'*, *polagat'*—are used in various kinds of parenthetic construction: *vy, ia dumaiu, zabyli menia* [I think you've forgotten me]; *osetrovye ryby, schitaiut znatoki, utratili svoi byloi vkus* [fish of the sturgeon family, so the connoisseurs believe, have lost their former flavour]; *ob etom, ia polagaiu, nuzhno sprosit' direktora* [I think we should ask the director about that]; *polagaiu, nashe sochinenie dvizhetsia k finalu* [I think our work is nearing completion] (S. Dovlatov). With *dumat'* and *polagat'* a parenthetic construction with the modal *nado* [one must] is possible: *ego sem'ia, nado polagat' ⟨dumat'⟩, priekhala nadolgo* [we have grounds to presume that his family have come to stay]. The synonym *schitat'* is avoided in the context of *nado*: *⁇ego sem'ia, nado schitat', priekhala nadolgo.* Moreover the verb *dumat'* is freely used in colloquial speech without its subject in the first and second persons: *dumaiu, eto reshenie eshche ne okonchatel'noe* [I don't think this decision is final yet]; *a on, dumaete ⟨dumaesh'⟩, soglasitsia?* [but do you think he'll agree?]. With *schitat'* and *polagat'* the dropping of the subject is less typical, especially in the second person. With *nakhodit'* all parenthetic constructions are restricted or impossible: *\*ob etom, ia nakhozhu, nado sprosit' direktora* [I find we should ask the director about that]; *\*ego sem'ia, nado nakhodit', priekhala nadolgo* [we must find that his family have come to stay]; *\*nakhozhu, eto reshenie eshche ne okonchatel'noe* [I don't find this decision is final yet].

The syntactic potential of the synonyms of the second group—*rassmatrivat'*, *smotret'*, *usmatrivat'* and *videt'*—is much more limited. With them a single type, rarely more, of construction has become the fixed norm. In the case of *rassmatrivat'* and *smotret'* this is a three-member construction with the conjunction *kak* [as, like] or its equivalents (*rassmatrivat' kogo-chto-libo kak kogo-chto-libo* [to regard smb./smth. as smb./smth.], *smotret' na kogo-chto-libo kak na kogo-chto-libo* [to look upon smb./smth. as on smb./smth.]). In the case of *usmatrivat'* and *videt'* it is the prepositional construction *usmatrivat' ⟨videt'⟩ chto-libo v kom-chem-libo* [to see smth. in smb./smth.]. *Smotret'* is also used in the construction *smotret' na kogo-chto-libo kak-libo* [to look at smb./smth. in a certain way] (see above and below).

Some synonyms may be used in constructions which are untypical of other members of the series.

The verb *dumat'* has constructions of the type *dumat' chto o kom-chem-libo* [to think smth. of smb./smth.] and *dumat' khorosho* ⟨*plokho*⟩ *o kom-libo* [to think well ⟨badly⟩ of smb.]. The latter construction is also characteristic of the verb *smotret'*, but with a broader range of evaluative or qualifying adverbs and adverbial phrases: *smotri na veshchi prosto* [take a simple view of things]; *samaia eta missiia mozhet pokazat'sia delom nestoiashchim. No Belyi smotrel inache, a nam vazhna psikhologiia Belogo* [this mission itself may appear trivial. But Belyi saw it differently, and we are concerned with Belyi's psychology] (V. Khodasevich). The verb *schitat'* occurs in the construction *schitat' kogo-chto-libo za kogo-chto-libo* [to regard smb./smth. as smb./smth.], which is semantically very close to *schitat' kogo-chto-libo kakim-libo*, but lexically and stylistically far more restricted: *schitat' za chest'* (*byt' priglashennym*) (bookish) [to consider it an honour (to be invited)]; *ne schitat' kogo-libo za cheloveka* [not to consider smb. a human being]; *schitat' kogo-libo za duraka* (coll.) [to regard smb. as a fool].

The group *schitat'*, *nakhodit'* and *rassmatrivat'* allows a passive construction, but for the first two synonyms this is possible only in the perfective: *ego rabota byla sochtena* ⟨*naidena*⟩ *vpolne udovletvoritel'noi* [his work was deemed ⟨found⟩ quite satisfactory]; *khotia formal'no tserkov' byla otdelena ot gosudarstva, fakticheski ona rassmatrivalas' kak ego organ* [although formally the Church was separated from the State, in practice it was seen as its organ]. Finally, the verb *videt'* governs a negative clause with the conjunction *chtoby: ne vizhu, chtoby vam chto-nibud' ugrozhalo* [I don't see that anything threatens you].

The verb *polagat'* does not admit use in negative sentences: \**sud'ia ne polagal, chto eti svedeniia nuzhno proverit'* [the judge did not suppose that the information should be verified].

2.7. LEXICO-SEMANTIC CO-OCCURRENCE

The synonyms *schitat'*, *videt'*, and *rassmatrivat'* co-occur freely with collective nouns (a state, a country, a government, etc.) as the grammatical subject of an opinion: *Komissiia vidit zalog uspekha v gotovnosti vsekh stran regiona k kompromissam* [the commission sees an earnest of success in the readiness of all the countries of the region to make compromises]; *respubliki schitaiut, chto sleduet iskat' politicheskoe reshenie vsekh voznikaiushchikh problem* [the republics consider it necessary to seek a political resolution to all problems which arise]; *Indiia vsegda rassmatrivala Kashmir kak svoiu neot"emlemuiu chast'* [India has always regarded Kashmir as an inalienable part of itself]. With the other synonyms of the series such collocations are untypical.

In a construction such as *schitat' kogo-chto-libo kakim-libo*, which is characteristic of *schitat'*, *polagat'*, and *nakhodit'*, the position of the instrumental case may be occupied by an adjective denoting a property or one with modal meaning, but not one denoting a state. We may say *ia schitaiu ego zlym* [I consider him evil], *ia schitaiu eto vozmozhnym* [I consider that possible] but not *\*ia schitaiu ego zlym na vas* [I consider him angry with you]. Whereas *schitat'* and *nakhodit'* combine equally freely with both semantic classes of adjective, *polagat'* combines mainly with modal adjectives of the type *nuzhnyi* [necessary], *neobkhodimyi* [essential], *obiazatel'nyi* [compulsory]. Compare *redaktsiia schitala* ⟨*polagala, ne nakhodila*⟩ *nuzhnym pomeshchat' oproverzhenie* [the editors considered ⟨presumed, did not find⟩ it necessary to publish a denial], but only *ego schitali* ⟨*nakhodili*⟩ *khladnokrovnym i muzhestvennym* [they considered ⟨found⟩ him cool and courageous]. Collocations of the type ⁇*ego polagali khladnokrovnym i muzhestvennym* [they presumed him cool and courageous], ⁇*neuzheli prezident polagal demokraticheskie sily stol' slabymi i bespomoshchnymi* [surely the president did not suppose the democratic forces to be so feeble and helpless] (A. Gel'man), which may occur in texts, are departures from the norm.

Most synonyms in the series combine with the adverbs *kak, tak, inache*, etc., denoting the content of the thought or the opinion (see examples above). With *nakhodit'*, of all the collocations shown only that with *kak* is possible (*Kak vy menia nakhodite posle sanatoriia?* [how do you find me after the sanatorium?]). With *usmatrivat'* and *videt'* such collocations are impossible.

All the synonyms in the series except *nakhodit'* combine with adverbs and adverbial phrases of the type *verno, pravil'no, spravedlivo* [correctly] and their inexact antonyms *naprasno, zria* [wrongly] which have truth-functional meanings: *vy verno* ⟨*pravil'no*⟩ *schitaete* ⟨*dumaete, polagaete*⟩, *chto khudshee eshche vperedi* [you are right to believe ⟨think, suppose⟩ that the worst is yet to come]; *vy sovershenno spravedlivo rassmatrivaete ego deistviia kak dolzhnostnoe prestuplenie* [you are quite right to view his actions as malfeasance in office]; *on spravedlivo usmatrival* ⟨*videl*⟩ *v etom pokushenie na svoiu svobodu* [he rightly saw in this an assault on his freedom]; *vy naprasno dumaete* ⟨*schitaete*⟩, *chto liberalizatsiia tsen mozhet chemu-to pomoch'* [you are wrong to think ⟨believe⟩ that freeing prices can do any good]. With *nakhodit'* these collocations are impossible: *\*vy verno* ⟨*pravil'no, spravedlivo, naprasno*⟩ *nakhodite, chto khudshee eshche vperedi* [you are ⟨right, correct, wrong⟩ to find that the worst is yet to come].

*Schitat', polagat'*, and *dumat'* co-occur with words and expressions indicating the factual basis for the judgement which is introduced: *chto daet mne osnovaniia schitat'* ⟨*polagat', dumat'*⟩, *chto oni otkazhutsia ot svoikh namerenii?* [what gives me grounds to believe ⟨suppose, think⟩ they will renounce their intentions?]; *pochemu on dumaet* ⟨*schitaet*⟩, *chto ego vse boiatsia?* [why does he think ⟨believe⟩ everyone is afraid of him?]. With the other synonyms of this series such collocations are either untypical or impossible.

*Dumat'* and *schitat'* combine with the phasal verb *nachinat'* [to begin] (only in the imperfective, mainly with a first person pronoun or when the speaker adopts the viewpoint of the subject of the opinion), forming relatively fixed expressions: *ia nachinaiu dumat'* ⟨*schitat'*⟩, *chto on ne tak prost kak kazhetsia* [I'm beginning to think he's not as simple as he looks]. These expressions indicate not simply the beginning of a mental state, that is, not the inception of an opinion, but an act of will which has already taken place to review one's previous opinions, as new circumstances have forced this upon the speaker. Collocations comprising the same two synonyms and the phasal verb *prodolzhat'* [to continue] (*ia prodolzhaiu dumat'* ⟨*schitat'*⟩, *chto vy nepravy*) also signify not simply the continuation of a mental state but an act of will undertaken on the basis of facts in the possession of the speaker and in spite of some countervailing circumstances. With the other synonyms in the series such collocations are untypical (*ia nachinaiu* ⟨*prodolzhaiu*⟩ *usmatrivat' v etom zloi umysel* [I'm beginning ⟨I continue⟩ to see malicious intent in this]) or dubious (*?ia nachinaiu* ⟨*prodolzhaiu*⟩ *polagat', chto vy nepravy* [I'm beginning ⟨I continue⟩ to suppose, that you are wrong]), while with *nakhodit'* they are impossible.

All the synonyms in this series except *nakhodit'* combine with the predicative word *sklonen* [inclined, apt], which signifies the choice of a definite intellectual position from among a number of possible positions: *ia sklonen schitat'* ⟨*dumat', polagat'*⟩, *chto eto—obychnaia khalatnost'* [I'm inclined to believe ⟨think, suppose⟩ that it was plain negligence]; *ia sklonen rassmatrivat' eto kak proiavlenie khalatnosti, a ne kak akt sabotazha* ⟨*smotret' na eto kak na obychnoe proiavlenie khalatnosti*⟩ [I'm inclined to view it as negligence rather than sabotage ⟨to look upon it as plain negligence⟩]; *ia ne sklonen videt'* ⟨*usmatrivat'*⟩ *v etom chto-libo predosuditel'noe* [I am not inclined to see anything prejudicial in this].

With *schitat'* there is another typical construction which signifies choice, formed by the verb in the future tense: *budem schitat', chto summa uglov treugol'nika ne ravna 180 gradusam* [we shall assume that the sum of the angles of a triangle is not equal to 180 degrees]; *budem schitat', chto etogo ne bylo* ⟨*chto v etom nikto ne vinovat* [we shall consider that it didn't happen ⟨that nobody is to blame for this⟩]. In all these cases the collocation *budem schitat'* is not simply a future form but a special expression signifying either supposition or good will.

With some synonyms, lexically or semantically specific collocations are possible.

With the verb *dumat'* in the perfective a specific construction is *mozhno podumat'* [one might think], which despite appearances does not mean 'there is reason to believe' but 'in fact it should not be thought': *mozhno podumat', chto vy ne ustali* [anyone might erroneously think you weren't tired]. With *smotret'* such a specific construction is the collocation with the word *glaza* [eyes] in the instrumental case and with an epithet: *teper' ia sovershenno drugimi glazami smotriu na eto* [now I see this with completely different eyes].

### 2.8. PARADIGMATIC SEMANTIC LINKS

Phraseological synonyms: *derzhat'sia mneniia* [to hold to a view], *imet' mnenie* [to have an opinion]; *imet' takoi-to vzgliad na veshchi* [to have a certain view of things].

Analogues: *verit′* [to believe]; *dopuskat′, predpolagat′* [to assume]; *podozrevat′* [to suspect]; *predstavliat′, voobrazhat′* [to picture, imagine]; *znat′* [to know]; *ponimat′* [to understand]; *reshit′* [to decide] (*dver′ khlopnula, i ia reshila, chto on ushel* [the door slammed and I decided he had left]); *zhdat′* [to wait] (*on zhdal, chto na seminare ego doklad raznesut v pukh i prakh* [he expected that his paper would be torn to shreds at the seminar]), *ozhidat′* [to expect] (*vot uzh nikak ne ozhidal, chto vy pozovete takikh neinteresnykh gostei* [I never expected you to invite such dull guests]); *dumat′* (*o chem-libo*) [to think (about smth.)], *razmyshliat′* (*o chem-libo*) [to reflect (on smth.)]; *otsenivat′* (*kak-libo*) [to appraise (in a certain way)], *rastsenivat′* (*kak-libo*) [to regard (in a certain way)]; *sudit′* (*o kom-libo kak-libo*) [to judge (smb. in a certain way)], *otzyvat′sia* (*o kom-libo kak-libo*) [to speak (of smb. in a certain way)], *kvalifitsirovat′* (*kak-libo*) [to describe (in a certain way)], *kharakterizovat′* (*kak-libo*) [to describe, characterize (in a certain way)]; *otnosit′sia* (*kak-libo*) [to have a (certain) attitude, view]; *priznavat′* [to acknowledge], *prinimat′* [to accept]; *somnevat′sia* [to doubt]; *predvidet′* [to foresee] (*predvizhu, chto on budet vozrazhat′* [I foresee that he will object]).

Inexact conversives: *schitat′sia* [to be considered], *slyt′* [to have a reputation]; *kazat′sia* [to seem], *predstavliat′sia* [to appear].

Derivatives: *mysl′* [thought]; *mnenie* [opinion]; *vzgliad* [view]; *tochka zreniia* [point of view]; *vozzreniia* [outlook].

# 5

## The Problem of Factivity: *znat'*
## [to know] and its Synonyms

*For Anna Wierzbicka,*
*to mark the 35th anniversary of the*
*beginning of her scholarly career.*

### 1. Preliminary Remarks

This chapter is based on the material of the synonym series *znat'* and *vedat'* [to know], written by the author for the *New Explanatory Dictionary of Russian Synonyms*. The general concept of this dictionary was set forth in J. Apresjan 1992*b* and J. Apresjan 1995*b*; see also Chapter 2 in this volume. Sample synonym series have also been published; see, for example, J. Apresjan *et al.* 1992, J. Apresjan *et al.* 1995 and Chapter 4 in this volume. The present chapter follows on directly from Chapter 4, on the verb *schitat'* and its synonyms, and is in a sense a continuation of it.

We shall begin with two preliminary remarks. The first concerns the lexemes selected for analysis and the second—systematic lexicography and the concept of the lexicographic type, which is fundamental to it.

#### 1.1. THE VERB *ZNAT'*

It is customary to distinguish at least three different senses for the epistemic class of verbs of the *znat'* [to know] type (see for example Wierzbicka 1969: 21; Lyons 1979: 113–16; cf. Yokoyama 1986: 6–24, distinguishing as many as 'seven types of knowledge'): (*a*) 'propositional knowledge' (*znat', chto P* [to know that P]); (*b*) acquaintance (*znat' vsekh sobravshikhsia ⟨Moskvu⟩* [to know all those assembled ⟨Moscow⟩]; *znat' matematiku ⟨avtomobil'⟩* [to know mathematics ⟨a car⟩]; *znat' liudei ⟨zhizn'⟩* [to know people ⟨life⟩]); (*c*) skill (note the obsolete constructions *znat' po-frantsuzski ⟨po-pol'ski⟩* [to know French ⟨Polish⟩]; *znat' chitat' ⟨pisat'⟩* [to know how to read ⟨write⟩], and the obsolete phraseme *znat' gramote* [to be literate]). Only the first of these senses concerns us here.

The Russian lexeme *znat'* has recently been fairly well studied, especially in its logical and syntactic aspects. Among recent works we may cite Arutiunova 1988: 123 ff.; Dmitrovskaia 1988*a*, 1988*b*; Ioanesian 1988*a*, 1988*b*; Shatunovskii 1988*a*,

1988*b*; Bulygina and Shmelev 1988; Paducheva 1988; Zalizniak 1992; Shmelev 1993, Bogusławski 1994*b*—each with a further bibliography. See also some general works on words with the meaning 'to know' and the concept of knowledge itself: Moore 1959; Hintikka 1962; Malcolm 1963; Chisholm 1966, 1982; Wittgenstein 1969; Vendler 1972 (especially Chapter 5); Griffiths 1976; Lyons 1979; Ziff 1983; Cohen 1986; Borillo 1982; Bogusławski 1981, 1994*a*, 1994*c*, *et al.*

A standard dictionary which claims to be comprehensive, as the *New Explanatory Dictionary of Russian Synonyms* is in its design, should of course incorporate all accumulated knowledge of words. It will therefore inevitably contain a body of more or less well-known facts. In the present work they have been included in the discussion, in order not to detract from the integrated lexicographic portrait of *znat'* and to give at least a general idea of the dictionary itself. At the same time it should be stated that the problems of this semantically straightforward verb (and its counterparts in other languages) are so profound that the summary of even its most important features is still far from complete. We are, of course, interested only in the lexicographical problems and aspects of the description of *znat'* and *vedat'*.

A few words are needed to explain why the synonym series *znat'* was selected. First, because the propositional *znat'* is one of the most fundamental meanings expressed in natural language; it occurs as a component in hundreds of other, more complex lexical and grammatical meanings. Second, because it abuts closely, though in different ways, on a number of other fundamental senses, such as *vosprinimat'* [to perceive], *khotet'* [to want], *schitat'* [to believe], *chuvstvovat'* [to feel], *govorit'* [to say], which together form the basis for one of the most important fragments of the lexical system of language—the vocabulary linked to man's inner world. Third, because it is convenient to use the material of this series of verbs to illustrate the lexicographer's central problem—that of combining a description of the generic features of a word (unification) with a description of its individual features (individualization), or the problem of combining a lexicographic type with a lexicographic portrait.

## 1.2. ON SYSTEMATIC LEXICOGRAPHY AND LEXICOGRAPHIC TYPES

The *New Explanatory Dictionary of Russian Synonyms* is being compiled within the framework of the ideas of systematic lexicography. The four central principles of systematic lexicography are that the dictionary should be geared to active production (oriented towards use in speech); it should be integrated (the lexicographic description of the language should be harmonized with its grammatical description, taking account, in particular, of the differing grammatical conditions of use); it should be systematic (taking account of the different lexicographic types to which the lexeme at issue belongs); and it should aim to reflect the 'naïve' picture of the world. All these principles have been considered in detail in a number of published works by the author (J. Apresjan, 1986*b*, 1992*c*, 1995*b*, 1995*c*, and also Chapters 4, 9, and 10 in this volume). For this reason only the third, the most important in the context of this chapter, receives a brief commentary.

The key concept in systematic lexicography is that of the lexicographic type (LT). By this term we mean a group of lexemes with at least one property in common, to which certain general rules of the given language (its 'grammar' in the broadest sense, including semantic, pragmatic, prosodic, and some other types of rules) are sensitive. Such a group requires unified treatment in a dictionary.

The peculiarities of an LT are determined by two main factors: the specifics of the conceptual organization of the language ('the naïve picture of the world') and the specifics of its formal organization (especially noticeable in the area of morphology, word-formation, and syntax).

The concept of the LT differs in three respects from the more traditional concepts of the semantic field, semantic class and lexico-semantic group of words, etc.

(1) The basis for an LT is provided by any shared properties of lexemes (for example prosodic or syntactic), not only semantic.

(2) It follows from the definition that an LT is meaningful only within the framework of an integrated description of language, that is, a concerted account of grammar and lexis. In an 'integrated' dictionary every lexeme is assigned all properties relevant for 'grammar', i.e. all sufficiently general linguistic rules. The constitution of an LT is thus determined with reference to linguistic rules, whereas a division into semantic classes (fields, etc.) is determined solely by ideographic considerations. Semantic classes which lie far outside the scope of any linguistic rules are fully possible (for example 'tropical plants', 'freshwater fish', 'minerals', etc.).

(3) Unlike semantic fields as presented, for example, in an ideographic dictionary or thesaurus, LTs do not form a strict hierarchy but classes which repeatedly intersect, since one and the same lexeme may appear in various classes on the strength of each one of its various properties or any lexicographically interesting cluster of properties.

The main principle of systematic lexicography requires that each lexeme be described first and foremost as an element of one or several intersecting LTs.

The systematic properties of the lexemes *znat'* and *vedat'* are determined by the fact that they lie at the intersection point of two large LTs: those of the factive and stative verbs. Each of these classes of verbs possesses a number of semantically motivated properties, partly described previously in the large body of literature dealing with them. To some degree or other, these properties are characteristic of both *znat'* and *vedat'*. Since we wish only to illustrate here the general strategy of lexicographical description (unification + individualization), it will suffice to mention one typical manifestation of factivity and stativity respectively.

Factivity is responsible, for example, for the ability of these verbs to govern not only subordinate clauses introduced by *chto* [that] (hereafter *chto* clauses) but also clauses with interrogatives such as *chto* [what], *kto* [who], *kakoi* [which], *gde* [where], *kuda* [whither], *otkuda* [whence], *kogda* [when], *pochemu*

[why], *zachem* [what for], etc., and including the interrogative particle *li* [whether] (hereafter interrogative clauses): *on znal, chem eto grozit emu ⟨gde iskat' oshibku, pochemu molchat ego druz'ia, otkuda mozhno zhdat' podderzhki⟩* [he knew what risks he was running ⟨where to seek the error, why his friends were silent, where he could find support⟩]; *postoi-ka, Volk skazal: sperva mne vedat' nado,* | *Kakov pastukh u stada?* [wait a moment, said the wolf: first I must know what kind of shepherd tends the flock] (I. A. Krylov). This feature has been described in Vendler 1972 and, on the basis of Russian material, in Arutiunova 1988: 123–8, Bulygina and Shmelev 1988, Paducheva 1988, and other works.

The stativity of *znat'* and *vedat'* is responsible, for example, for their inability to co-occur with verbs of the type *zanimat'sia* and *delat'* [to do]; note the incorrect *\*on zanimalsia tem ⟨delal to⟩, chto znal ⟨vedal⟩, pochemu ego nedoliublivaiut* [\*he was busy knowing why he was disliked] (for more detail see Melig [Mehlig] 1985).

Of course the properties discussed here do not exhaust the interesting general manifestations of factivity and stativity. They will be considered more fully and in more detail below. It is important to stress here that both these properties are absolutely regular and, on the other hand, lexicographically valuable. It is clear, for example, that the ability to govern *chto* [that] clauses and interrogative clauses has more claim to a place in a dictionary than the transitiveness of knowledge. The latter is of more interest from a logical point of view than a linguistic one.[1]

The properties mentioned here of the lexemes *znat'* and *vedat'*, making them members of the lexicographic types of stative and factive verbs, are common to most stative and factive verbs. They should be uniformly represented in the dictionary entries for all statives and factives, including *znat'* and *vedat'*. However, it would be insufficient simply to ascribe to all such lexemes the properties of stativity and factivity, leaving the deduction of their specific manifestations to some general rules. Stativity and factivity in themselves, like any other properties of this kind, give slightly differing reflexes in the material of different lexemes. For this reason, after describing the basic manifestations of stativity and factivity in the respective linguistic rules, it is best to duplicate the relevant part of the information for each lexeme in its dictionary entry. This method will best meet the lexicographic requirement that each entry be relatively self-sufficient.

Of late, especially in theoretical literature unconnected with actual lexicographic practice, a tendency to reduce the description of a lexeme to a list comprising only its generic properties is becoming increasingly apparent. In reality the task of the lexicographer does not end here. Above and beyond its generic properties, each lexeme almost always has a number of unique features which give it its individuality. This is particularly true of such foregrounded lexemes

---

[1] Transitiveness of knowledge is given by the formula: From *A znaet, chto B znaet, chto P* [A knows, that B knows that P] it follows that *A znaet, chto P* [A knows that P]. It is clear, moreover, that from *A schitaet ⟨dumaet, podozrevaet, somnevaetsia, govorit i t.p.⟩, chto B znaet, chto P* [A believes ⟨thinks, suspects, doubts, says, etc.⟩ that B knows that P] then *A znaet, chto P* [A knows that P].

as *znat'*. The principles of systematic lexicography require that the individual properties of a lexeme be just as meticulously recorded as its prototypical ones.

An inventory of the individual features of *znat'* and *vedat'* leads to the conclusion that 'naïve' knowledge differs substantially from logical knowledge. Consideration will be given below, in one form or another, to three types of difference between naïve and logical knowledge: (*a*) indistinct boundaries between knowledge proper and mental states close to it; (*b*) gradual shading of one into the other; (*c*) transcendence; the possible absence of an empirical or theoretical source (see particularly a series of words such as *prozrenie, ozarenie, naitie, znat' napered, znat' zaranee, oseniat', ozariat'* [insight, seeing the light, intuition, to know ahead of time, to know in advance, to dawn upon, to strike], etc.; to some degree this is also a feature of the lexeme *vedat'*).

## 2. A Lexicographic Description of the Synonyms *Znat'* and *Vedat'*

Here we shall focus our attention on the verb *znat'*, a basic factive lexeme in Russian, and its closest synonym *vedat'* in the sense shown in sentences of the type *ona ne znala ⟨ne vedala⟩, chto sud'ba ee uzhe reshena* [she did not know that her fate had already been decided]. The obsolete lexeme *vedat'*, once an almost exact synonym of *znat'*, has in modern Russian been pushed to the periphery, to a bookish and poetic form of speech, where it is used mostly for stylistic effect. In ordinary speech it is preserved mainly in a number of syntactic clichés and phrasemes. Nevertheless it displays a number of interesting and important features which justify its inclusion in the synonym series under consideration.[2]

Following the general scheme of presentation adopted in the *New Explanatory Dictionary of Russian Synonyms*, we shall consider (1) the place of *znat'* and *vedat'* amongst other mental predicates; (2) the semantics of these lexemes; (3) those other senses of *znat'* and *vedat'* which are closest to the meaning of the given series; (4) their grammatical forms; (5) syntactic constructions characteristic of them; (6) their co-occurrence features; (7) their systematic paradigmatic links with semantically related lexemes. In all these cases we shall attempt to trace the way in which the deep semantic feature of factivity manifests itself in the outward behaviour of the lexemes.

### 2.1. THE PLACE OF *ZNAT'* AND *VEDAT'* AMONG OTHER MENTAL PREDICATES

The meaning and usage of verbs with the factive sense of *znat'* is determined by the contrast between them and two classes of putative verbs—those meaning 'to think' and those meaning 'to believe, to have faith in'. On the other hand they

---

[2] In some uses the verbs *videt'* [to see] and *slyshat'* [to hear] draw close to *znat'* and *vedat'*: *khotelos' by videt'* [~ *znat'*], *kuda idut vse eti den'gi* [I'd like to see (~ know) where all that money is going]; *ot kogo vy eto slyshali* [~ *znaete*]? [who did you hear that from (~ do you know it from)?].

contrast with factive verbs meaning 'to understand'. These four senses—'znat'' [to know], 'schitat'' [to consider], 'verit'' [to believe, to have faith in], and 'ponimat'' [to understand]—are internally so close to one another that their actual lexical incarnations in various uses slide with relative ease from one sense to another. In particular, as we shall demonstrate below (§ 2.2.2), the verb *znat'* in its principal uses covers the entire semantic area sketched out above.

## 2.1.1. Knowledge and Opinion

The factive sense of *znat'*, although closely related to the putative sense of *schitat'*, is nevertheless most sharply opposed to it semantically, communicatively, prosodically, and syntactically.

Words with the sense 'to know' (*znat'*, *izvestno* [known], *dogadyvat'sia* [to guess] and other factives) serve to make assertions about the presence in the subject's consciousness of true information about something, that is, information about a fact. Words with the sense 'to consider' (*schitat'*, *dumat'* [to think], *polagat'* [to suppose], *nakhodit'* [to find] and other putatives) serve to make assertions about the presence in the subject's consciousness of certain opinions, about whose relation to reality nothing is known in advance. Knowledge has a source but no cause; hence *otkuda ty eto znaesh'?* [lit. where do you know that from?] but not *\*pochemu ty eto znaesh'?* [why do you know that?]. An opinion has a cause but no source; hence *pochemu ty tak schitaesh'?* [why do you think that?] but not *\*otkuda ty tak schitaesh'?* [whence do you think that?]. (On *otkuda* [whence] and *pochemu* [why] in connection with *znat'* see for example Seleznev 1988 and Bogusławski 1994*a*).

The semantic property of factivity is manifested in a so-called presupposition of the truth of knowledge: if someone does not possess certain knowledge, that knowledge does not cease being true. The sentences *on znal, chto za nim ustanovleno neglasnoe nabliudenie* [he knew that he was under secret surveillance] and *on ne znal, chto za nim ustanovleno neglasnoe nabliudenie* [he did not know that he was under secret surveillance] equally presuppose that secret surveillance was taking place.

Opinions, unlike knowledge, may be either true or false. Hence neither from the statement *on schital, chto za nim ustanovleno neglasnoe nabliudenie* [he believed that he was under secret surveillance], nor from the statement *on ne schital, chto za nim ustanovleno neglasnoe nabliudenie* [he did not believe that he was under secret surveillance] may we draw any conclusions as to whether secret surveillance was taking place or not.

The presupposition of the truth of knowledge is manifested in an interesting manner in questions. A question with a factive word and a subordinate *chto* clause differs from an ordinary question in that it does not presuppose the absence of any knowledge in the speaker or its presence in the addressee. Indeed a question such as *ty znaesh', chto na tebia kto-to dones?* [do you know that somebody has denounced you?] (with the phrasal stress on *znaesh'* [do you know?] and falling pitch on *dones* [denounced]) is impossible in a situation in which the speaker knows nothing about the addressee being denounced and wants to obtain this information. It is appropriate only when the speaker himself is in possession of this information and wishes only to find out whether it is known to the addressee (for more detail on this meaning see § 2.4 and § 2.5).

Putative words, on the other hand, when they introduce a similar question, always assume that the subject has no information on the issue he is asking about. Sentences such as *ty schitaesh', chto na tebia kto-to dones?* [do you think somebody has denounced you?] (with no stress on *schitaesh'* and with rising pitch on *dones*) are appropriate only when the speaker is genuinely interested in somebody's opinion and has no prior knowledge of that opinion.

Communicatively and prosodically, factivity manifests itself in the fact that words meaning 'to know' may bear the main phrasal stress and therefore be the rheme of the sentence: *on ↓ znaet, kto na nego dones* [he knows who denounced him]. This is natural: it is pragmatically useful and psychologically justified to draw the addressee's attention to what is known to be true by accenting the relevant word. On this feature see J. Apresjan 1990*c*: 103; 1992*b*: 21–2; see also Zalizniak 1992: 141–2.

Putative words differ from factive words in this respect too. In neutral statements they cannot bear the main phrasal stress and therefore usually appear in the thematic part. However important somebody's opinion might be, it is valued less than information known to be true. The only kind of phrasal stress which may be allocated to a putative word is contrastive (logical) stress: *vy ↓↓ schitaete, chto on vas predal (ili vy eto znaete)?* [do you believe that he betrayed you (or do you know it)?]

The property of factivity manifests itself syntactically in the fact that words with the sense 'to know' govern not only *chto* clauses but also interrogative clauses: *mozhet byt', nachal'nik vokzala znaet, kogda otpravliaetsia poslednii poezd ⟨pochemu my tak dolgo stoim, skol'ko stoit bilet do Veny⟩ i t.p.* [perhaps the station-master knows when the last train leaves ⟨why we're waiting all this time, how much a ticket to Vienna costs⟩, etc.]. The opposition of two types of government—*znat', chto P* [to know that P] vs. *znat' gde ⟨kuda, kogda, kto, pochemu i t.p.⟩ P* [to know where P is ⟨where P is going/when/who/why P is⟩, etc.] is semantically charged and embraces all the properties of the verbs, including their morphological, syntactic, and co-occurrence properties (see below).

Putative words do not govern interrogative clauses; note incorrect sentences such as *\*on schital, kogda otpravliaetsia poslednii poezd ⟨pochemu my tak dolgo stoim, skol'ko stoit bilet do Veny⟩ i t.p.* [he thought when the last train leaves ⟨why we're waiting all this time, how much a ticket to Vienna costs⟩, etc.].

### 2.1.2. Knowledge and Belief

Another important and much-discussed opposition is that between knowledge and belief (see for example Seleznev 1988, Bulygina and Shmelev 1989, Shmelev 1993). Note the following typical passage: *chto vlast' bol'shevikov konchitsia, my ne tol'ko verim, my eto znaem, khotia nikto ne mozhet predskazat', kogda i v kakoi forme eto proizoidet* [we not only believe, we know that Bolshevik rule will end, although nobody can predict when or how this will happen] (V. Khodasevich).

There are instances when knowledge and belief draw close to each other: e.g. *no tut vmeshivaetsia serdtse:—Net. Ia ne veriu etomu, kak ne veriu i nikogda ne poveriu v smert', v unichtozhenie. Luchshe skazhi: ne znaiu. I neznanie tvoe—tozhe taina* [but here the heart intervenes:—No. I don't believe this, just as I don't believe and never will believe in death, in annihilation. You'd do better to say: I don't know. And your not knowing is also a mystery] (I. Bunin); *no spokoino-blagogoveino ona [M. Tsvetaeva] verit, chto on [muzh] zhiv, i zhdet ego, kak ne-vesta zhdet zhenikha. Ee serdtse znalo verno. Ona dozhdalas' svidan'ia i soedinilas' s liubimym* [but she (M. Tsvetaeva) calmly and piously believes that he (her husband) is alive and she waits for him, like a bride for her bridegroom. Her heart knew it for sure. The reunion came and she was united with her beloved] (K. Bal'mont).

However, in protoypical cases knowledge presupposes the existence of some rational source of reliable information: *Otkuda ty eto znaesh'?—Vchera po radio peredali ⟨Ob etom napisano vo vsekh gazetakh, Druz'ia skazali i t.p.⟩* [how do you know that?—It was on the radio yesterday ⟨it was in all the papers, friends told me, etc.⟩].

Belief does not presuppose any external source of reliable information. It is the mental state of a person, motivated less by facts than by the integral world picture in his mind, in which the object of his belief simply cannot fail to exist. See the following typical passages: *pust' veriat legkovernye i poshliaki, chto vse skorbi lechatsia ezhednevnym prikladyvaniem k detorodnym organam drevne-grecheskikh mifov. Mne vse ravno* [let the gullible and the vulgar believe that all ills may be cured by daily obeisances before the organs of generation of the ancient Greek myths. I don't care] (V. Nabokov); *U nego [Nil'sa Bora] sprosili; 'Neuzheli vy verite, chto podkova prinosit schast'e?', na chto on otvetil: 'Net, ne veriu. Eto predrassudok. No, govoriat, ona prinosit schast'e dazhe tem, kto ne verit'* [(Nils Bohr) was asked, 'Do you really believe that a horseshoe brings good luck?', to which he replied, 'No, I don't. It's a superstition. But they say it brings luck even to those who don't believe in it'] (M. Bessarab); *Iz Sibiri dokhodiat vesti, | Chto Vtoroe Prishestvie blizko. | Kto gadaet, kto verit, kto ne verit* [Word comes to us from Siberia | that the Second Coming is nigh. | Some speculate, some believe, some do not believe] (G. Ivanov).

On the basis of these passages we may posit the following explication of the verb *verit'* [to believe] in its basic meaning: X *verit*, *chto* P = 'X thinks that P; X does not know why he thinks this; X will think this even if there are circum-stances or opinions which contradict this because he wants P to exist'.

It should be emphasized that this meaning usually requires varying intona-tions in various personal forms. In the first person *verit'* is normally pronounced with rising intonation (*ia* ↑ *veriu, chto ego zhena vernetsia* [I believe his wife will come back]), and in the third person with falling pitch (*on* ↓ *verit, chto ego zhena vernetsia* [he believes his wife will come back]). If *veriu* is pronounced with falling pitch (*ia* ↓ *veriu, chto ego zhena vernetsia*) or if *verit* has rising pitch (*on* ↑ *verit, chto ego zhena vernetsia*), this usually expresses either indifference or doubt as to the grounds for some other person's belief.[3]

We may emphasize the following substantive features of the explication offered above: (*a*) it reflects the fundamentally putative (not factive) nature of *verit'*: the top node of the explication is the sense of '*dumat'*', which explains, in particular, why *verit'* does not co-occur with interrogative clauses (note the incorrect *\*ona verila, kogda vernetsia muzh* [she believed when her husband would come back]); (*b*) it reflects the irrationality of belief: the subject does not know why he thinks this; (*c*) it reflects the emotional nature and the arbitrary principle of faith: a person thinks that P because he wants P to be.[4] Thus *verit'* includes three basic predicates (to think, to know, and to want) which describe man's inner world.

### 2.1.3. Knowledge and Understanding

Besides putative predicates with the meaning 'to think' and 'to believe', predicates of the *znat'* class form an interesting semantic contrast with factive predicates of the *ponimat'* [to understand] class, partially described in Bulygina and Shmelev 1989: 41. *Ponimat'* (*chto P*) [to understand that P] is semantically more complex than *znat'*, just as *verit'* is more complex than *schitat'* and to the same degree, although the nature of the contrast is different here.

A typical situation involving understanding is shown by the following examples: *ne ponimaiu ⟨ne mogu poniat'⟩, kak emu udalos' voiti v kvartiru* [I can't understand how he managed to get into the flat]; *o tom, chto vse bedy Rossii poshli ot ateizma, ia znal davno, znal ot Dostoevskogo, a vot ponial okonchatel'no tol'ko nedavno* [I had long known that all Russia's disasters stemmed from atheism; I knew it from Dostoevskii, but I came to understand it fully only recently] (Iu. Kariakin); *prosto s godami ia stal ponimat', chto smert' est' chast' zhizni, i roptat' na nee mozhno ne v bol'shei mere, chem na zhizn'* [over the years I simply came to understand that death was part of life and that there was no more point complaining about it than about life] (Iu. Daniel'); *segodniashnii den' nel'zia poniat' vne sviazi s vcherashnim, i sledovatel'no, s davno proshedshim; to, chto est' zdes' i teper', postizhimo lish' v sviazi s tem, chto est' vezde i vsegda* [the present day cannot be understood outside its connection with yesterday, and consequently with the distant past; that which exists here and now is comprehensible only in connection with what exists everywhere and always] (S. Frank); *i mozhet*

---

[3] M. G. Seleznev (1988: 251–2; see also Shmelev 1993: 167) links the distinction between these two senses, which he calls (not quite accurately) those of 'cosmic optimism' and 'condescending disdain for someone's error', with the difference between the first and third persons respectively. As is clear from the foregoing, the real picture is more nuanced and cannot be described without taking account of prosody.

[4] The presence of the sense 'to want' (or the similar sense of 'good') in the predicate *verit'* has been noted in the literature (see Seleznev 1988: 247 ff., Bulygina and Shmelev 1989: 48, Shmelev 1993: 167).

*byt' velichaishim triumfom chelovecheskogo geniia iavliaetsia to, chto chelovek sposoben poniat' veshchi, kotorye on uzhe ne v silakh voobrazit'* [and perhaps the greatest triumph of the human spirit is the fact that man is able to understand things that he is incapable of imagining] (L. Landau, quoted by M. Bessarab); [*Nekhliudov*] *znal nesomnenno, chto nuzhno bylo izuchit', razobrat', uiasnit' sebe, poniat' vse eti dela sudov i nakazanii* [(Nekhliudov) knew beyond any doubt that it was necessary to study, examine, clarify to himself and understand all these matters of courts and punishments] (L. N. Tolstoi).

These examples show that at the basis of understanding lies knowledge or imagination[5] comprising fairly complex facts or situations. For this reason understanding requires a certain deductive effort which relies on the subject's prior experience. The knowledge or notion obtained in this way makes it possible to predict how the situation will develop further (the 'predictive' aspect of understanding was noted in Martem'ianov 1964: 126).

We shall attempt to condense these ideas into an explication. *A ponimaet, chto Q* [A understands that Q] = 'at moment $t_0$ A knows or imagines that Q; this knowledge or notion arose as a result of the fact that before $t_0$ A knew something about situations related to Q and thought of something related to Q; the knowledge of Q makes it possible to know or imagine what may happen after $t_0$'. Thus understanding is threefold knowledge (past, present, future) based upon reflection and deduction. Compared with simple knowledge it has far-reaching retrospective and prospective components.[6]

## 2.2. THE SEMANTICS OF *ZNAT'* AND *VEDAT'*

### 2.2.1. The Question of Explications

As noted above, the dominant of the series *znat'* is a semantic primitive and therefore cannot be explicated. Attempts to explicate this lexeme, as well as its synonyms or analogues in other languages, cannot be counted as successful. Let us consider briefly the best known of these, which have already been discussed in the literature of the subject (see, for example, Wierzbicka 1969: 21ff., Bogusławski 1994c).

---

[5] Strictly speaking, the meaning here is that of *predstavit'* [to imagine, picture] = 'to have in one's consciousness an image of an object or situation which is not directly perceived by the sense organs at the time'. This meaning is needed to explicate *ponimat'* in many modal contexts, where the sense 'to know' is impossible. Thus, *X ne mozhet poniat' P* [X cannot understand P] = 'X cannot imagine P', rather than 'X cannot know P'.

[6] It is not difficult to observe the similarities and differences between our explication and that of I. M. Boguslavsky, which is designed to cover three kinds of construction: (1) *ponimat', chto P* [to understand that P]; (2) *ponimat'* + interrogative; (3) *ponimat' muzyku/detei* [to understand music/children]: *X ponimaet Y* [X understands Y] = 'the fact that X has processed or usually processes with a component of his psyche W, usually his mind, certain facts connected with Y has resulted in X (*a*) having or (*b*) beginning to have in his consciousness reliable information Z about the substantive features of Y' (Boguslavsky 1984: 623). The differences between the two explications can, it seems, be explained by the fact that Boguslavsky's explication effectively serves only the third type of construction, in which it is more natural to see a separate lexical meaning of *ponimat'*.

The idea most frequently elaborated is that *znat' P* means 'to think that P and P is true'. The explications of the sense of this verb offered in Scheffler 1965, Chisholm 1966, Lehrer 1974, Stelzner 1984, Shatunovskii 1988a, and a number of other works are constructed along these lines. The explications of K. Lehrer and W. Stelzner are analysed in detail in Bogusławski's article 1994c: 261–6 and we shall not repeat this here. We shall concentrate on H. Scheffler's and R. Chisholm's explications as typical examples of the implementation of the scheme shown here and try to demonstrate that it creates insurmountable difficulties.

Scheffler's and Chisholm's explications are as follows: 'X knows that Q if and only if (i) X believes that Q, (ii) X has adequate evidence that Q, (iii) Q' (Scheffler 1965: 21); 'S knows at t that h is true, provided: (1) S believes h at t; (2) h is true; and (3) h is evident at t for S' (Chisholm 1966: 23).

The explications cited give rise to the following objections:

(1) An explication of 'to know' by way of 'to believe' lacks the most important feature of any correct definition—the feature of substitutability. An attempt to replace 'to know' with any of the definitions given above, even in the simplest contexts, makes the utterance grammatically incorrect or at least pragmatically dubious, or else substantially changes its meaning.

Consider the following situation. A certain person, Sergei, wishes to get into a watchmaker's workshop but is unable to do so because it is shut. His resulting mental state may be described by the sentence: 'Sergei knows that the watchmaker's workshop is shut'. Replacing 'to know' with the first definition gives the following statement: ?'Sergei believes that the watchmaker's workshop is shut and has adequate evidence of this and it is (indeed) shut'. With regard to the situation described, this statement is strange, to say the least, if not utterly anomalous. The directly observable fact 'the workshop is shut' is too simple to be the subject of the complex intellectual operations which result in the mental state 'to believe'.

On the other hand, if some fact is so well known as to comprise an axiom, placing the relevant statement in the context of a word denoting an opinion has the unexpected pragmatic effect of revising the axiom. Thus the statement *on schitaet, chto Volga vpadaet v Kaspiiskoe more* [he believes the Volga flows into the Caspian] is fully appropriate as a description of somebody's mistaken view, the absurdity of which occasions the speaker's wry surprise. But the statement *on znaet, chto Volga vpadaet v Kaspiiskoe more* [he knows the Volga flows into the Caspian] in no way shakes accepted views of our world.

(2) The right-hand part of both explications contains words which semantically are undoubtedly more complex than 'to know', such as 'evidence' and 'apparent', for example. In particular, 'P is evidence that Q' = 'the presence of P makes it possible to believe that Q is true'; 'Q is apparent' = 'anybody can understand that Q is true without mental effort and without requiring supplementary information.'

We have tried to demonstrate above that the sense 'to know' forms part of the meaning 'to understand', which in its turn underlies the meaning of 'apparent'. If we accept a decomposition of 'understand' based on this idea we find that Chisholm's explication contains a vicious circle as well.

(3) On the basis of the explications at issue it is impossible to make correct predictions about the syntactic, communicative, or co-occurrence features of the verb znat' [to know]. In particular, its main syntactic feature—the ability to govern an interrogative clause—remains unexplained. As we have seen, at the top node of both explications stand putative senses of the schitat' [to believe] type, which completely rule out the possibility of this government pattern. Nor are there any other semantic components in these explications which could motivate the ability of znat' to govern interrogative clauses.

A more interesting decomposition of znat' [to know] (actually of the Polish equivalent wiedzieć) was proposed in one of A. Wierzbicka's early books. In translation this explication runs as follows: 'to know' = 'to be able to tell (the truth)' (Wierzbicka 1969: 22), with the further explication of 'to tell' = 'to utter sounds which make it possible to make a truthful judgement about something', or simply 'to make it possible to make a truthful judgement about something'.

Attractive though the basic idea may be, this explication is vulnerable on two counts.

First, it leaves aside instances of knowledge in higher animals, which of course cannot tell the truth or make a truthful judgement about anything. The use of the predicates 'speak' and 'judgement' even when applied to higher animals can only be metaphorical. And yet, higher animals can know certain things in the literal sense of the word (see similar arguments in Bogusławski 1994c: 259–60, 270).

Second, the explication contains the sense 'truth', which is clearly less simple than that of 'to know'. Without embarking upon a detailed discussion of this matter, we may refer to some recent investigations of the cultural concepts pravda [truth] and istina [verity] (see Logicheskii analiz 1995), which are shown to have a more complex semantic structure and more involved pragmatic features than the verb 'to know'.

Thus znat' cannot be explicated through any simpler senses and must therefore be recognized as a semantic primitive. This treatment of the meaning of znat' dates back to the early works of John Cook Wilson and H. A. Prichard (see Bogusławski 1994c). In contemporary linguistics this case has been persuasively argued by A. Bogusławski in a series of works devoted to epistemic predicates; besides Bogusławski 1994c, see Bogusławski 1981, 1986. From 1980 on, Anna Wierzbicka also began treating znat' as a semantic primitive (see Wierzbicka 1980: 37, 156 and Wierzbicka 1992: 10).

## 2.2.2. The Semantic Similarities and Differences between Znat' and Vedat'

The main distinctions between these synonyms are stylistic (see above). This apart, znat' has a more general meaning and hence a broader range of applications than vedat'.

Although *znat'* is the main factive verb in Russian, it does more than introduce judgements about facts. Its real lexical meaning lies between the poles of 'true knowledge' and 'opinion'. It wholly covers the former pole, intersects with the semantics of such intermediate mental predicates as *ponimat'* [to understand], *byt' uverennym* [to be sure], *verit'* [to believe], and *byt' ubezhdennym* [to be convinced], and reaches the boundaries of the latter pole.

True knowledge. The stock examples of this range of usage are sentences in which *znat'* governs a *chto* clause with the verb in the past or present, describing a real situation, that is, one which exists outside the consciousness of the subject: *ia znaiu ⟨znal⟩, chto on rabotaet v Konservatorii* [I know ⟨knew⟩ that he works at the Conservatory]; *nikto iz nas ne znal, chto v tot moment na nashikh zapadnykh granitsakh nachalis' pervye boi* [none of us knew that at that moment the first battles had begun on our western borders] (G. Lin'kov); *Iura ne znal, chto otets davno brosil ikh, ezdit po raznym gorodam Sibiri i zagranitsy, kutit i razvratnichaet* [Iura did not know that their father had long since deserted them, that he was travelling through various Siberian and foreign towns indulging in revelry and debauchery] (B. Pasternak). An extended clause may be replaced by a phrasal pronoun such as *eto* [this], *to* [that], *chto* [what], *nechto* [something], *vse* [everything], etc.

In less strict use of *znat'*, when its meaning shifts towards understanding, certainty, belief, conviction, or opinion, so that it enters into a relation of synonymy with the corresponding verbs, the following conditions are typical though not binding: (1) a context of future events or any reference to the future in relation to the moment of knowledge: *voditel' znal, chto mashina ego ne podvedet* [the driver knew the vehicle would not let him down]; (2) juxtaposition of knowledge not with any real event in the outside world but with other information present in one's own mind or someone else's: *ia znaiu, chto ia sobiraius' delat'* [I know what I intend to do]; *ia znaiu, o chem vy dumaete* [I know what you're thinking]; (3) any indication that the event, even if real, is being interpreted in some way: *on [Selikhov] znal, chto eto byli slezy po molodosti, po tomu schastlivomu letu, chto vypadaet odnazhdy v zhizni kazhdoi devushki, chto ne v Iordanskom tut delo* [(Selikhov) knew that these tears were for youth, for that happy summer that comes but once in every girl's life, and that it was not to do with Iordanskii] (I. Bunin); *On obidel tebia, ia znaiu, | Khot' i bylo eto lish' snom, | No ia vse-taki umiraiu | Pred tvoim zakrytym oknom* [He hurt you, I know, although it was only a dream. But I am dying all the same under your open window] (N. Gumilev).

Moreover, in the context of a complement clause introduced by the conjunction *chto* or by no conjunction, the sense of *znat'* may shift either towards the putative meanings 'to be certain', 'to believe', 'to be convinced' or towards the factive meaning of 'to understand' (see below). In the context of an interrogative clause the range of possible shifted uses of *znat'* is somewhat smaller: its meaning shifts either towards 'to understand' (*ne znaiu* [~ *ne ponimaiu*], *chto ona v tebe takogo nashla* [I don't know (~ don't understand) what it is she finds in you]) or towards 'to have an opinion' (*ne znaiu* [~ *ne mogu predstavit'* ⟨*ne imeiu mneniia o tom*⟩], *chto on sdelaet v etom sluchae* [I don't know (~ have no idea ⟨I have no opinion⟩) what he might do in that case]). In this situation the meanings 'to be certain', 'to believe' and 'to be convinced' are precluded.

Understanding (especially in reference to relatively complex events or non-apparent connections between events; this usage is treated as an independent sense in Ushakov's dictionary and the large and small Academy dictionaries): *Vez Babushkin transport oruzhiia dlia vosstaniia, s nim* [*ego*] *i rasstreliali. On znal, na chto shel* [Babushkin was carrying a load of weapons for the uprising. With this load he was shot. He knew the risk he was taking] (A. Solzhenitsyn).

Certainty (especially in the affirmative in the context of statements about specific future events which are planned or foreseen): *prokuratoru zakhotelos' podniat'sia, podstavit' visok pod struiu i tak zameret'. No on znal, chto i eto emu ne pomozhet* [the procurator felt a desire to get up, place his temple under the flowing water and freeze into immobility. But he knew that this would not help either] (M. Bulgakov).

Faith, conviction (especially in the affirmative in the context of statements about future events or general judgements about the way life and the world are arranged): *vy ne ponimaete, chto mozhno byt' ateistom, mozhno ne znat', est' li Bog i dlia chego on, i v to zhe vremia znat', chto chelovek zhivet ne v prirode, a v istorii, i chto v nyneshnem ponimanii ona osnovana Khristom* [you don't understand that one may be an atheist, not know if God exists or what he is for, and at the same time know that man exists not in nature but in history, and that in our modern understanding history begins with Christ] (B. Pasternak).

Opinion (especially in negative and interrogative sentences in the context of statements concerning specific future actions or events): *ne znaia* [~ *ne imeia mneniia*], *kak otvetit' na eto, sekretar' schel nuzhnym povtorit' ulybku Pilata* [not knowing how (having no idea as to how) to answer this, the secretary deemed it necessary to imitate Pilate's smile] (M. Bulgakov). The meaning of an opinion is particularly apparent in the phraseme *tak i znat'* (noted in Dmitrovskaia 1985). This phraseme may be explicated as follows: *Ia tak i znal* ~ 'I thought what happened would happen even before it happened'; *Ona vykhodit zamuzh za drugogo.—Ia tak i znal.* [she's getting married to somebody else.—I knew it].

In contemporary usage, the synonym *vedat'* is permissible mainly in negative contexts: *v etu kvartiru* [*vy*] *podnialis',* . . . *ne vedaia ni togo, chto brat zhil tut poslednie mesiatsy, ni togo, chto tut proizoshlo* [you climbed the stairs to this flat . . . not knowing that your brother had lived his last months here or what had happened here] (B. Pasternak). Even in these contexts the word is stylistically coloured: it retains something of an elevated or solemn style, of poetic language, of heated polemics, and other elevated forms of speech. Only in more or less fixed expressions such as *znat' ne znaiu, vedat' ne vedaiu* [I have no idea]; *sami ne vedaem, chto tvorim* [we know not what we do], etc. is this word acceptable in everyday speech. Only in these are the distinctions between them partly neutralized.

In the nineteenth century and early twentieth century *vedat'* was evidently used in colloquial speech too, to judge by its appearance in literature: *moia p'esa podvigaetsia vpered, poka vse idet plavno, a chto budet potom, k kontsu, ne vedaiu* [my play is moving forward; so far everything is going smoothly, but what will happen later, towards the end, I don't know] (A. P. Chekhov).

Semantically speaking, *vedat'* is rather narrower than *znat'*, in the sense that it has only two typical spheres of usage: true knowledge (*da vedaiut potomki pravoslavnykh | Zemli rodnoi minuvshuiu sud'bu* [let the children of the faithful know | the history of their native land] (A. S. Pushkin) and certainty. With the latter meaning, as in the case of *znat'*, the affirmative form in the context of statements about specific forthcoming events is typical: *ia zhit' khochu, chtob myslit' i stradat'; | I vedaiu, mne budut naslazhden'ia* [I want to live in order to think and suffer; | And I know that there are pleasures in store for me] (A. S. Pushkin).

This apart, *vedat'*, owing to its stylistic features, is in some degree preferable to *znat'* in situations where the object of knowledge is something standing above man and beyond his control, or when supernatural knowledge is involved, perhaps inspired by some higher power, or when the subject is a higher power: *itak, vse rukhnulo, po krainei mere na pervoe vremia, pokuda Marina Ivanovna [Tsvetaeva] nichego ne znala o muzhe . . . ne vedala, chto teper' budet s ee ot"ezdom* [thus everything foundered, at least for the moment, as Marina Ivanovna knew nothing about her husband. . . . She did not know what would happen regarding her departure] (A. Saakiants). With *znat'* this use is possible but less typical.

## 2.3. SENSES OF *ZNAT'* AND *VEDAT'* CLOSE TO THOSE UNDER CONSIDERATION

Both synonyms admit of extended figurative use, especially personification: *u tebia zhe, kogda tvorish' milostyniu, pust' levaia ruka tvoia ne znaet, chto delaet pravaia* [but when thou doest alms, let not thy left hand know what thy right hand doeth] (Matthew 6: 3); *Ne vedaet gornyi istochnik, kogda | Potokom on v stepi stremitsia . . . | Pridut li k nemu pastukhi i stada | Struiami ego osvezhit'sia* [The mountain stream as it flows through the steppe knows not whether . . . shepherds with their flocks will come to be refreshed in its currents] (A. K. Tolstoi).

The verb *znat'* has a sense 'to be acquainted with smb./smth.', 'to have information about smb./smth.', which is close to the meaning under consideration: *znat' Moskvu ⟨kazhdyi ugolok parka⟩* [to know Moscow ⟨every corner of the park⟩]; *znat' vsekh sobravshikhsia* [to know all who had gathered]. With *vedat'* this use is possible but not well established and it has a markedly individual character: *I vedali my vse tropinki dorogie | i vsem berezan'kam davali imena* [and we knew all the dear pathways | and gave names to all the little birches] (V. Nabokov).

Both verbs have a sense 'to experience', which is close to the meaning under discussion here: *ne znat' ⟨ne vedat'⟩ kolebanii ⟨somnenii⟩* [to know no hesitation ⟨no doubt⟩]; *ne znat' ⟨ne vedat'⟩ pokoia ⟨ustalosti⟩* [to know no rest ⟨no weariness⟩]; *krepostnogo prava ia ne znal i ne videl, no, pomniu, u tetki Anny Gerasi-*

*movny chuvstvoval ego* [I never knew or witnessed serfdom, but I remember sensing it in the household of my aunt Anna Gerasimovna] (I. Bunin).

*Znat'* and *vedat'* in this meaning are synonymous with the words *ispytyvat'* [to experience], *videt'* [to see], and *izvedat'* [to learn the meaning of]: *kto ispytal naslazhdenie tvorchestva, dlia togo uzhe vse ostal'nye naslazhdeniia ne sush-chestvuiut* [for one who has known the joys of creativity no other joy exists] (A. P. Chekhov).

The verb *znat'*, unlike *vedat'*, has the meaning 'to have knowledge or skill in a certain field', which is close to the meaning under consideration; *znat' muzyku* ⟨*matematiku*⟩ [to know music ⟨mathematics⟩]; *znat' frantsuzskii* ⟨*pol'skii*⟩ [to know French ⟨Polish⟩]; *znat' avtomobil'* ⟨*komp'iutery*⟩ [to be an expert on cars ⟨computers⟩]; *znat' zhizn'* ⟨*liudei*⟩ [to know life ⟨people⟩]; *znat' mnogo* ⟨*malo*⟩ [to have extensive ⟨slight⟩ knowledge in some area or areas]. Collocations such as *znat' mnogo* ⟨*malo*⟩ also express the meaning of this series, but usually in a construction with double government of the type 'something about something'; see § 2.5 below.

## 2.4. GRAMMATICAL FORMS

Being statives, both synonyms lack their own perfective and passive forms.

For the same reason they do not have a normal imperative form in contexts containing a direct object unless it is a pronoun; note the impossibility of *\*znai* ⟨*vedai*⟩ *moi adres* ⟨*telefon, dorogu na Rim*⟩ [know my address ⟨telephone number, the road to Rome⟩].

The verb *znat'*, when co-occurring with a phrasal pronoun *eto* [this], a *chto* [that] clause or its conjunctionless equivalent, may formally have an imperative. However, as with other factives, it does not express the idea of urging, which is the norm for the imperative, but a more complex meaning of sharing knowledge: owing to the presupposition of truth, what is being communicated to the addressee is automatically known to the subject. *Znai, chto P* [know that P] = 'I know that P; I believe you do not know that P; I believe that a knowledge of P is important to you; I want you to know that P and therefore am telling you that P';[7] cf. *eiu* [*zhizn'iu*] *kliast'sia samoe vremia, tak kak ona visit na voloske, znai eto!* [this is the very moment to swear on your life, because it's hanging by a thread—know this!] (M. Bulgakov). Compare the sense of sharing knowledge and senses close to this expressed in interrogative clauses and in some lexico-semantic types of collocation (see § 2.5 and 2.6).

The sense of urging in the imperative is possible in the context of the interrogative clause, but such utterances are marginal with regard to the norm and are met with mostly in poetry: *no ty, khudozhnik, tverdo verui, | V nachala i kontsy.*

---

[7] This explains why sentences such as *\*ne znai, chto P* [do not know that P] are grammatically incorrect. They are 'self-falsifying' (Shmelev 1993: 168).

*Ty znai*, | *Gde steregut nas ad i rai* [but you, artist, have firm faith in beginnings and in ends. Know where heaven and hell lie in wait for us] (A. Blok).[8]

For the same reason *znat'* and *vedat'* are devoid of a number of special aspectual senses of the imperfective, such as the progressive-durative, the present with future meaning or the historical present. Note the incorrect *\*kogda ia voshel, on znal ⟨vedal⟩, chto doma ego nikto ne zhdet* [when I came in he knew that there was nobody waiting for him at home]; *\*zavtra on znaet, chto doma ego nikto ne zhdet* [tomorrow he knows that there is nobody waiting for him at home]; *\*on sidit i znaet, chto doma ego nikto ne zhdet* [he is sitting and knowing that there is nobody waiting for him at home]. Sentences of the type *v etot moment on uzhe znal, chto primirenie nevozmozhno* [at that moment he already knew that reconciliation was impossible] in fact have perfective meaning rather than progressive-durative, while those of the type *idet on i znaet*, | *Chto sneg uzhe smiat*, | *Chto tam dogoraet* | *Poslednii zakat* [he walks along and knows that the snow is already crushed, and that the last sunset is fading there] (A. Blok) represent departures from the norm.

## 2.5. SYNTACTIC CONSTRUCTIONS

Both synonyms have up to four valencies: the subject of the knowledge, the content of the knowledge, its theme, and its source. The means of expressing the second valency are the most varied.

With both synonyms the content of knowledge is expressed above all by a predicate noun in the accusative (genitive in negative contexts): *znat' namereniia protivnika ⟨ch'e-libo mnenie⟩* [to know one's opponent's intentions ⟨someone's opinion⟩]; *znat' dorogu ⟨adres, telefon⟩* [to know the way ⟨an address, telephone number⟩]; *nikto tolkom ne znal prichiny provolochki* [nobody really knew the reason for the delay] (B. Pasternak); *Sudil on i pravil* | *S dubovogo trona*, | *Ne vedaia pravil*, | *Ne znaia zakona* [he ruled and judged from his oaken throne, without knowing the rules, without knowing the law] (S. Marshak). Such substantive complements are in essence condensed transforms of interrogative clauses or of subordinate *chto* clauses formed by an existential or possessive verb: *on znal moi adres* [he knew my address] ~ *on znal, gde ia zhivu* [he knew where I lived]; *on znal dorogu k lesnomu ozeru* [he knew the way to the forest lake] ~ *on znal, kak proiti k lesnomu ozeru* [he knew how to get to the forest lake]; *on ne znal ⟨ne vedal⟩ prichin otkaza* [he didn't know the reasons for the refusal] ~ *on ne znal ⟨ne vedal⟩, pochemu emu otkazali* [he didn't know why he had been refused]; *on znal za soboi etu chertu ⟨takuiu privychku⟩* [he was aware of this feature of his own character ⟨aware of his own habit⟩] ~ *on znal, chto u nego est' eta cherta ⟨takaia privychka⟩* [he knew that he had this feature of character ⟨this habit⟩].

---

[8] For more detail on the specifics of the imperative in various types of stative verb see J. Apresjan 1988: 30–2.

With both synonyms the content of the knowledge may also be expressed by phrasal pronouns such as *chto* [what], *chto-to* [something], *nechto* [something], *nichego* [nothing], *eto* [this], *odno* [one thing], *vse* [everything], and the like in the accusative: *Pod kakimi zhe bugrami kosti babushki, dedushki? A Bog vedaet! Znaesh' tol'ko odno: vot gde-to zdes', blizko* [Where do Grandmother's and Grandfather's bones lie? God alone knows! You know only one thing: they're somewhere here, close by] (I. Bunin); *Nichego-to vy ne znaete, nichego ne vedaete! Chto na svete delaetsia! Kakie veshchi tvoriatsia!* [You know nothing at all about what's going on in the world and what's being done!] (B. Pasternak).

*Znat'* may govern quantitative adverbs such as *mnogo, nemalo* [much], *malo, nemnogo* [little], and others in the same role, but usually combined with a thematic object of the kind *o chem-libo* [about smth.] (see below): *ia sovsem nemnogo ⟨chereschur malo, nichego ne⟩ znaiu o ego planakh ⟨namereniiakh⟩* [I know very little ⟨too little, nothing⟩ about his plans ⟨intentions⟩], *ia koe-chto ob etom znaiu* [I know a bit about that]. With *vedat'* this construction is untypical.

With both words the same function (the content of knowledge) may be served by subordinate clauses introduced by the conjunction *chto* [that] or with no conjunction: *I ne znala ona, ne znala,* | *Chto bessmertnoi v utro stala* [And she didn't know, she didn't know | that that morning she had become immortal](A. Galich).

Both synonyms govern interrogative clauses in the role of content of knowledge: *ia znal, kuda ⟨kogda, pochemu, ot kogo, s kem, za chem⟩ on uekhal* [I knew where ⟨when, why, from whom, with whom, for what⟩ he had gone away].

*Znat'* in the second person typically functions as a parenthetic word within a sentence denoting the content of knowledge: *ia, znaesh' ⟨znaete⟩, reshil zaniat'sia modal'noi logikoi* [you know, I've decided to take up modal logic]. In most instances of this usage, *znat'* has an attenuated sense of 'confidentiality'—'I want to tell you something'. With *vedat'* this construction and its attenuated sense are untypical.

Both synonyms govern prepositional-nominal groups of the type *o chem-libo, pro chto-libo* [about smth.], meaning the topic of the knowledge: *vse na doroge znali o zabastovke* [all the railwaymen knew about the strike] (B. Pasternak).

The verb *znat'*, unlike *vedat'*, governs the prepositional-nominal group *za kem-libo* in the same role: *on [Iura] znal za soboi etu unasledovannuiu chertu i s mnitel'noi nastorozhennost'iu lovil v sebe ee priznaki* [Iura knew this trait he had inherited and with mistrustful wariness detected its symptoms in himself] (B. Pasternak). This construction requires a direct object denoting the content of knowledge and a prepositional object denoting a specific person, never a class of persons, cf. the incorrect *?²my znaem za professorami sklonnost' k rasseiannosti* [*?²we know of professors' tendency to absent-mindedness]. (I. B. Levontina has drawn the author's attention to the concrete referential status of the prepositional object.)

*Znat'*, unlike *vedat'*, may govern words and prepositional-nominal groups such as *otkuda* [whence], *ot kogo-libo* [from smb.], *iz chego-libo* [from smth.], *po chemu-libo* [through/via smth.], and the like, meaning the source of the knowledge: *otkuda vy eto znaete?* [how do you know that?]; *ia znaiu eto ot ottsa* [I know this from my father].

If the source of the knowledge is indicated it is impossible to use *znat'* in a negative clause or in any shifted senses.

In negative sentences both synonyms obey the following rule: if they govern a *chto* [that] clause they cannot be in the first person of the present tense. Sentences such as *\*ia ne znaiu, chto ty chitaesh' ⟨chto on rabotaet⟩* [I don't know that you are reading ⟨that he is working⟩], *\*ia ne znaiu, chto ty ⟨on⟩ rabotal* [I don't know that you ⟨he⟩ were working], *\*ia ne vedaiu, chto uchast' moia uzhe reshena* [I don't know that my fate is already sealed], etc., are incorrect because of the internal contradiction.[9] On the strength of the presupposed truth of the knowledge, your reading ⟨his working, etc.⟩ is presented here as an established fact. But at the moment of speech the speaker cannot fail to know what he himself presents as fact.

Sentences such as these become correct if the subject of ignorance is different from the speaker, or if his ignorance relates to a moment other than the moment of speech, or if *znat'* governs an interrogative clause: *on ne znaet, chto ty chitaesh' ⟨chto ty rabotal⟩* [he doesn't know that you are reading ⟨that you were working⟩]; *ia ne znal, chto ty chitaesh' ⟨chto on rabotaet⟩* [I didn't know that you were reading ⟨that he was working⟩]; *ia ne znaiu, kuda on uekhal* [I don't know where he's gone].[10]

Unlike *vedat'*, *znat'* is freely used in the second person in interrogative sentences, where its presence changes the usual function of the question.

It is usual for a person to ask about something when he himself does not know the answer and presumes that the addressee has the information he seeks. However, a question containing the verb *znat'* does not automatically imply that the subject lacks the information he requires. The meaning of the question depends on the syntactic construction in which *znat'* is used.

If *znat'* governs a *chto* [what] clause the question as a whole always implies that the enquirer has the knowledge at issue and is only interested in whether the addressee possesses it. The question in this case is merely an alternative form of statement. In reality, the subject imparts his knowledge to the addressee. *Vy znaete, chto Olia razvelas' ⟨chto pervyi otdel rasformirovali, chto v institute budet*

---

[9] Sentences such as *ia ne znaiu, chto ty doma* [I don't know that you're at home], as A. D. Shmelev has observed in a private conversation, may be correct in a situation in which the speaker and addressee are conspiring to lie to a third person, if they judge this to be necessary in the interests of one or both of them. However, there is a different propositional purpose here from that which *znat'* ordinarily has.

[10] For an explanation of this property see Arutiunova (1988: 125). An interrogative clause, as is well known, expresses disjunction, creating a situation of ideal semantic concordance: *liubliu li tebia, ia ne znaiu, no kazhetsia mne, chto liubliu* [whether I love you or not, I know not, but it seems to me that I do].

*reorganizatsiia*⟩? [Do you know that Olia has got divorced ⟨that the first department has been disbanded, that the institute will be reorganized⟩?].

If *znat'* governs an interrogative clause, the question as a whole may be used
in two different situations. First, it may have the normal function of a question:
*vy (kazhetsia ⟨mozhet byt'⟩) znaete, kto etot chelovek?* [do you know who that man
is? (perhaps you know . . . you may know . . .)]. Secondly, it is even more appropriate in a situation in which the questioner has some particular knowledge
and is only interested in discovering whether the addressee also has it, while at
the same time expressing his readiness to share it with the addressee if necessary:
*vy znaete, chto zhdet vas?* [. . .] *Vy, v obshchem, zdes' ostanetes' naveki* [do you
know what awaits you? (. . .) You will remain here forever.] (I. Brodskii). This
is especially characteristic of questions in which the subject is omitted (*znaesh',
zachem sledovatel' priekhal ⟨kto na tebia dones⟩?* [do you know why the investigator has come ⟨who denounced you⟩?], when the questioner indicates not only
readiness but a desire to share his knowledge. This meaning is close to that of
shared knowledge (see § 2.4) and the examination question.

The subject's ignorance is assumed in negative sentences with a subordinate
interrogative clause and the main phrasal stress on the negated predicate. Here,
naturally, any sense of shared knowledge is ruled out: *vy ne ↓ znaete, kto etot
chelovek?* [you don't happen to know who that man is, do you?], *vy ne ↓ znaete,
chto tut proiskhodit?* [you don't happen to know what's going on here, do you?]
(the speaker does not know).

In negative questions with a *chto* [that] clause the meaning of the verb *znat'*
shifts towards 'the speaker believes that somebody knows', sometimes lending
the utterance a slightly rude tone or one of irritation: *on chto, ne znaet, chto my
ego zhdem?* [doesn't he know we're waiting for him?]; *ili on ne znaet, chto my ego
zhdem?* [doesn't he know we're waiting for him?].

Both synonyms permit inversion of subject and predicate with phrasal stress
on the predicate, expressing the emphatic meaning 'to know very well': *↓ znaet
koshka, ch'e miaso s"ela* [the cat knows whose meat it's eaten]; *↓ znaet narod
iudeiskii, chto ty nenavidish' ego liutoiu nenavist'iu i mnogo muchenii ty emu
prichinish', no vovse ty ego ne pogubish'!* [the Jewish people know that you hate
them with a passion and that you will cause them much torment, but you will
certainly not be their undoing] (M. Bulgakov); *↓ vedaet tsar', chto protiv nego za-
myshliaiut nedobroe* [the emperor knows that people are conspiring against him].
Essentially, this syntactic inversion fulfils the same reinforcing function as some
adverbs which denote the quality or extent of the knowledge (see § 2.6).

In colloquial speech utterances with this inversion are typical of the verb *znat'*
when used to request that the addressee cease his communication because the
content is already well known: *da ↓ znaiu ia* [I know that already], ~ 'you
needn't tell me'. Similar emphasis with the same meaning can be seen in
reduplications such as *znaiu, znaiu, chto ty ni v chem ne vinovat* [I know, I know
you're in no way to blame]. This reduplication, incidentally, is impossible or

unnatural with putative verbs: note the incorrect or dubious *?schitaiu, schitaiu, cho on ni v chem ne vinovat* [I believe, I believe he's in no way to blame].

## 2.6. LEXICO-SEMANTIC CO-OCCURRENCE

With both synonyms nouns denoting people can appear as the subject; this is self-evident. With *znat'*, the names of collective bodies and animals may also appear as the subject: *derevnia khorosho znala, chto perezhila ona za osen'* [the village well knew what she had endured in the autumn] (I. Bunin); *sobaka znala, chto miaso trogat' nel'zia* [the dog knew it must not touch the meat]. The verb *vedat'*, being bookish and elevated, is more anthropocentric and describes to a greater extent the mental state of the individual, so such combinations are impossible with it.

In contexts dealing with operations performed mechanically, the names of certain parts of the human body, especially the extremities, may be used figuratively as the subject of *znat'*: *mysli ee byli daleko, no ruki sami znali, chto delat', i ni na sekundu ne ostanavlivalis'* [her thoughts were far away, but her hands themselves knew what to do and did not stop for a second]; *on plokho soobrazhal, kuda shagaet, shiroko raskidyvaia nogi, no nogi prekrasno znali, kuda nesli ego* [he had little idea where he was striding, but his legs knew perfectly well where they were taking him] (B. Pasternak). With *vedat'*, for the reasons mentioned above, such combinations are untypical.

*Znat'*, unlike *vedat'*, co-occurs with certain adverbs and adverbial phrases which grade the quality or extent of the knowledge. These are adverbs expressing a positive evaluation such as *tverdo* [firmly], *dostoverno* [reliably], *tochno* [precisely], *khorosho* [well], *otlichno* [perfectly], *prekrasno* [very well], *velikolepno* [splendidly] (but not *zamechatel'no* [remarkably], *udivitel'no* [surprisingly], *potriasaiushche* [stunningly], *vdol' i poperek* [through and through], *kak svoi piat' pal'tsev* [inside out], *nazubok* [by heart], *naperechet* [through and through], *naskvoz'* [through and through], etc., which modify a different sense of *znat'*— 'to possess information') and adverbs expressing a negative evaluation such as *netverdo* [shakily], *netochno* [imprecisely], *priblizitel'no* [roughly], *tolkom ne (znat')* [to have little idea], *plokho* [badly]: *ia tochno ne znaiu,—zhivo otvetil arestovannyi,—ia ne pomniu moikh roditelei* ['I don't know exactly,' replied the arrested man quickly. 'I don't remember my parents'] (M. Bulgakov).

The ability to combine with adverbs of positive and negative evaluation depends on the syntactic construction in which the verb *znat'* is used.

With *chto* [that] clauses, *znat'* normally co-occurs only with adverbs indicating positive evaluation (*khorosho* [well], *otlichno* [perfectly], *prekrasno* [very well], *tochno* [precisely], *tverdo* [firmly], *dostoverno* [reliably], etc.): *oni prekrasno znali, chto ia dolzhen byl bezhat', chtoby predotvratit' utechku* [they knew very well that I had had to run away to prevent a leak] (A. and B. Strugatskii). It is impossible to say *\*oni priblizitel'no* [roughly] ⟨*plokho*⟩ [badly] *znali, chto ia dolzhen byl* *bezhat'* because sure knowledge cannot be imprecise or bad. Even such examples as *razve ty . . . znaesh' nedostatochno khorosho, chto ty, mysl' o tebe i vernost' tebe i domu spasali menia ot smerti i vsekh vidov gibeli v techenie etikh dvukh let voiny?* [do you . . . really know insufficiently well that you, the thought of you and faithfulness to you and our home have saved me from death and all forms of ruin for these two years of war?] (B. Pasternak) diverge from the norm.

In positive evaluation contexts, the adverb in fact has a purely reinforcing effect: the speaker emphatically asserts only the presence of knowledge, without specifying its quality or amplitude. In this respect there is less difference between, for example, *khorosho znat'* [to know well] and *otlichno ⟨prekrasno⟩ znat'* [to know very well] than between *khorosho spravit'sia (s rabotoi)* [to cope well with a job] and *otlichno ⟨prekrasno⟩ spravit'sia s rabotoi* [to cope very well with a job], where a true gradation takes place.

In constructions with an interrogative clause, and in the equivalent construction with nouns of the type *adres* [address], *telefon* [telephone number], *doroga* [the way], etc. as the direct object, *znat'* co-occurs with adverbs expressing both positive and negative evaluation. Both types produce a real gradation of knowledge: *provodnik khorosho ⟨prekrasno, otlichno⟩ znal, kak idti na pereval ⟨dorogu na pereval⟩* [the guide knew well ⟨very well, perfectly⟩ how to get to the pass ⟨the way to the pass⟩]; *pilot vertoleta plokho ⟨lish' priblizitel'no⟩ znal, gde ⟨v kakikh usloviiakh⟩ emu predstoit sazhat' mashinu* [the helicopter pilot had only a rough idea where ⟨in what conditions⟩ he was to land].

The verb *znat'* freely co-occurs with three types of time indication which are not typical with *vedat'*: (1) adverbs and adverbial phrases such as *davno* [for a long time], *s detstva* [from childhood], *s voskresen'ia* [since Sunday], etc.: *on s detstva ⟨s institutskikh let⟩ znal, chto v zhizni mozhet rasschityvat' tol'ko na sebia* [he had known since childhood ⟨since his student days⟩ that in life he could count only on himself]; (2) the adverbs *zaranee, napered, zagodia* [in advance] in statements about the future: *ona zaranee ⟨napered⟩ znala, chto on seichas skazhet* [she knew in advance what he would now say]; (3) adverbs meaning duration, especially extended duration, only in negative contexts: *rodnye godami ne znaiut ⟨ne znali⟩, chto stalo s arestovannym* [the arrested man's relatives did not know for years what had happened to him].

Being statives, *znat'* and *vedat'* do not co-occur with inclusive temporal adverbial modifiers such as *za piat' minut* [in five minutes], *za tri nedeli* [in three weeks], adverbial modifiers of purpose or most adverbial modifiers denoting modes of action: note the incorrect *\*za tri minuty on znal ⟨vedal⟩, chto soprotivlenie bessmyslenno* [in three minutes he knew that resistance was pointless]; *\*s tsel'iu postupit' v universitet, on znal ⟨vedal⟩, chto emu nado mnogo rabotat'* [with the aim of gaining a university place, he knew that he had to work hard]; *\*on uverenno znal ⟨vedal⟩, zachem priezzhal sledovatel'* [he knew confidently why the investigator had come]. Note the breaching of this ban in poetic discourse to create a particular stylistic effect: *O, ia znaiu: ego otrada | Napria-*

*zhenno i strastno znat'*, | *Chto emu nichego ne nado*, | *Chto mne ne v chem emu otkazat'* [Oh, I know: his joy | Is to know tensely and passionately, | That he needs nothing, | That I have nothing that I can deny him] (A. Akhmatova).

In addition to this, neither synonym co-occurs with phasal verbs or modal words denoting possibility or impossibility: note the incorrect *\*on nachal ⟨perestal⟩ znat' ⟨vedat'⟩, kto emu ob etom skazal* [he began ⟨ceased⟩ to know who had told him about that]; *\*on sposoben ⟨nesposoben⟩ eto znat' ⟨vedat'⟩* [he is capable ⟨incapable⟩ of knowing that]; *\*ia ne mogu znat', zachem on eto sdelal* [I cannot know why he did that]. Sentences such as *on mozhet eto znat'* [he can know that] are correct only in the epistemic sense (i.e. denoting probability) or the deontic sense (specifically a 'permitting' sense), but not in the alethic sense of possibility. The collocation *ne mogu znat'* [I cannot know] ~ 'I don't know as I have no source of information' is a phraseme.

Both words have their characteristic series of fixed expressions and phrasemes, for example: *znat' tsenu chemu-libo* [to know the value of smth.]; *dat' znat' komu-libo o chem-libo* [to let smb. know about smth.]; *tol'ko i znat'* [to be unable to do anything else]; *a on znai svoe* [he just won't listen]; *naskol'ko ia znaiu* [as far as I know]; *znaem my vas* [we know your sort]; *Bog ⟨Allakh, chert, shut, kto, obs. chuma⟩ ego znaet ⟨vedaet⟩* [God ⟨Allah, the devil, who, the plague⟩ knows]; *ne znat', kuda glaza devat'* [not to know which way to look]; *znat' ne znaiu, vedat' ne vedaiu* [I have no idea]; *ne vedaem, chto tvorim* [we know not what we do].

## 2.7. PARADIGMATIC SEMANTIC LINKS

Up to now we have been dealing with the properties of the synonyms *znat'* and *vedat'* themselves, that is, their semantic, pragmatic, referential, communicative, prosodic, morphological, syntactic, and co-occurrence similarities and distinctions and the conditions in which the distinctions are neutralized. The design of *The New Russian Synonym Dictionary* also makes provision for the inclusion of information about their paradigmatic semantic links within the entire lexicon. Several zones of each dictionary entry are devoted to these, each one being a list of language units with a specified semantic relation to the key words. The categories dealt with are mostly exact and inexact conversives, conversives of analogues, exact and inexact antonyms and semantic derivatives (broadly understood). The purpose of this information, besides its practical value, is to demonstrate that the semantic space of language is uninterrupted.

Some samples of such information are given below, exclusively for illustrative purposes and only with the commentary which actually appears in the entry for the verb *znat'*.

Analogues: *schitat'* [to believe], *dumat'* [to think]; *verit'* [to believe]; *ponimat'* [to understand]; *predstavliat'* [to imagine]; *dogadyvat'sia* [to guess]; *podozrevat'* [to suspect].

Conversives: *izvestno* [known] (*ia znaiu chto P ~ mne izvestno chto P* [I know that P ~ it is known to me that P]; the range of meanings of *izvestno* is restricted mainly by the meaning of attested knowledge (that is, it does not have the senses of understanding, belief, conviction, certainty or opinion); on the other hand, *izvestno*, to a greater extent than *znat'*, presupposes an external source of knowledge); obs. or high style: *vedomo*.

Antonyms: *byt' v nevedenii* [to be ignorant], *ne imet' poniatiia* [to have no idea], *ne imet' predstavleniia (o chem-libo)* [to have no notion (of smth.)].

Inexact antonyms: *uma ne prilozhu (gde on mozhet skryvat'sia ⟨kuda delis' den'gi, kto k nemu prikhodil i t.p.⟩)* [I can't imagine (where he could be hiding ⟨where the money's got to, who came to see him, etc.⟩)].

Derivatives: *znanie* [knowledge]; *svedeniia* [information]; *istina* [truth]; *providenie* [foresight], *prozrenie* [insight], *ozarenie* [illumination], *intuitsiia* [intuition]; *neznanie, nevedenie* [ignorance]; *izvestnyi* [well known], *obshcheizvestnyi* [generally known], *neizvestnyi* [unknown]; *nevedomo, nevdomek* [unknown] (*a doma nikomu nevdomek, gde ia seichas nakhozhus'* [and nobody at home knows where I am now] (E. Kazakevich)); *vyznat', vyvedat', doznat'sia', proznat', provedat', razuznat', uznat'* [to find out].

# 6

## *Khotet'* [to want] and its Synonyms: Notes about Words

### 1. On the Concept of Systematic Lexicography

Academician V. V. Vinogradov's book, *The History of Words* (Vinogradov 1994), is remarkable in being essentially an extended illustration of two programmatic theses which are formulated in the introductory essay:

1. 'The structure of a language is determined by the interaction of its grammar and lexis' (Vinogradov 1994: 5). Moreover the grammar of a language is constantly being lexicalized (note the idea of the breakdown of the once unified copula verb *byt'* [to be] into the independent words *est'*, *byt'*, *sut'*, *sushchii*, *bude*, originally parts of *byt'*), and its lexis grammaticalized (for example, because the meaning of a word is shaped by, among other things, 'its function in a sentence').

2. 'Just as it is customary to speak of the grammatical structure of a language, so we should speak of its lexical structure', and of the 'lexical system' characteristic of any given period in the development of that language (Vinogradov 1994: 5). The lexical system of a language as a whole is composed of smaller lexical systems—of 'semantically closed' series of words. The elements of these series are united by shared meanings and are therefore subject to the action of the same historical processes.

The notes on words offered below, a product of my work on the *New Explanatory Dictionary of Russian Synonyms*, may be seen as a projection of these two theses onto synchrony (for more detail see J. Apresjan 1992*b*). They are based on the material of the synonym series of the verb *khotet'* [to want] which includes the words *zhelat'* [to wish], *mechtat'* [to yearn], and *zhazhdat'* [to hunger/thirst for], and presented in the spirit of systematic lexicography.[1]

The systematic nature of any synonym series manifests itself in two ways.

First, a substantial proportion of the semantic features by which the elements of a series resemble one another or differ, underlies many other series, other types of semantic relations between words (antonymy, conversivity, etc.), the

[1] This series was discussed at a working meeting of the Theoretical Semantics Section of the RAN Russian Language Institute. I am grateful to the participants, V. Apresjan, O. Iu. Boguslavskaia, M. Ia. Glovinskaia, I. B. Levontina, and E. V. Uryson, for their valuable critical comments.

opposition of meanings in the semantic structure of polysemous words, and, reaching beyond lexis, morphological, derivational, and syntactic oppositions, that is, language as a whole.

Second, owing to a large degree of semantic similarity the elements of a synonym series react in the same or similar ways to the grammar of a language in the broad sense of the word.

Besides such shared properties, stemming from their membership of the same lexicographic type, an explanatory synonym dictionary should take into account their individual properties—everything that makes up the unique character of each lexeme. It is not only the lexicographic type which is important, but also the lexicographic portrait.

Here an attempt is made to show how all these ideas are implemented in a dictionary of synonyms. First, however, it is necessary to explain why the *khotet'* series has been chosen as an illustration.

The vocabulary of wishing is of particular interest in theoretical semantics and lexicography. As is well known, language is to a large degree anthropocentric. A vast proportion of its vocabulary is devoted to the human being—his inner world, his perception of the outer world, his physical and mental activity, his aims, his relations with others, his dealings with them, and his view of events, situations, and circumstances. In very many instances, what a person does, feels, thinks, or says is motivated by what he wants. In linguistic terms this means that the sense of 'khotet'' [to want] (together with such senses as 'znat'' [to know], 'schitat'' [to believe, consider], 'delat'' [to make, do], etc.) constitutes a fundamental stratum in the semantics of the overwhelming majority of anthropocentric classes of words. It is clear how important it is to describe it systematically.

The vocabulary of wishing is extremely rich and varied and has many times been the focus of linguistic attention (Kenny 1963, Shcheglov 1964, J. Apresjan *et al.* 1979, Robinson 1983, Sémon 1989, Wierzbicka 1992, Zalizniak 1992, Kibrik 1987). The verb *khotet'* itself and its analogues in other languages have also been the subject of research (Wierzbicka 1992: 428, Zalizniak 1992: 60–2, Kibrik 1987). To date, however, there is no integrated and full account of the basic verbs of wishing in Russian.

The synonym series of the verb *khotet'*, except for some insubstantial technical details and commentaries, is presented here as it was written for the *New Explanatory Dictionary of Russian Synonyms*. A typical entry in this dictionary comprises the following zones: (1) the heading, in which the elements of the series are listed, together with stylistic and some grammatical markers, and an explication of the common core of their meaning; (2) a synopsis or short guide to the entry—a list of semantic features underlying similarities and differences between the members of the series; (3) a detailed description of semantic similarities and differences between synonyms and conditions for the neutralization of differences; (4) notes to the semantic zone; (5) grammatical forms and their semantic specifics; (6) syntactic constructions and their semantic specifics; (7) lexico-semantic co-occurrence; (8) examples of use from literary sources (omitted in this text); (9) lists of words semantically related to the elements of the series. The full entry also includes a bibliography zone, which is also omitted here.

## 2. A Lexicographical Description of *khotet'* [to want] and its Synonyms

### 2.1. THE HEADING

*Khotet'* 1 [~ pf *zakhotet'*],[2] (formal)[3] *zhelat'* [pf *pozhelat'*], *mechtat'* 2 [no pf], (formal) *zhazhdat'* [~ pf high style or iron. *vozzhazhdat'*]. The dominant of the series is a semantic primitive.

Examples: *rebenok khochet est'* [the child is hungry]; *ne zhelaiu vas videt'* [I have no wish to see you]; *studenty mechtali popast' v ego seminar* [the students dreamed of getting a place in his course]; *on zhazhdal mesti* [he was thirsting for revenge].

Generally speaking, this zone includes an explication of the series, or more precisely, of that part of the meaning which is common to all the elements of the series. In this instance no explication is possible because the Russian language possesses no simpler words with which to represent the meaning of *khotet'*. In this sense *khotet'* is a semantic primitive. (For more detail on this verb as a semantic primitive see Chapter 8 in this volume.) Nor is it possible to use this semantic primitive to explicate the series. Although *khotet'* is the dominant of the series it has its own semantic specificity, just as all its synonyms do (see § 2.2 and 2.3 below). It would be incorrect to ascribe it to all members of the series.

### 2.2. THE SEMANTIC FEATURES FOR THE *KHOTET'* SERIES

The synonyms differ by the following semantic features:[4]

(1) The nature of the object of desire (*khotet'* may be applied to anything one wants for oneself or for others; *mechtat'* is usual for something good that one wants for oneself; *zhazhdat'* is applied to things that appear important and unusual).

(2) The intensity of the desire (*mechtat'* and *zhazhdat'* denote considerably stronger desires than *khotet'* and *zhelat'*).

---

[2] The approximation symbol (~) preceding 'pf' indicates that *zakhotet'* and *vozzhazhdat'* are not regarded as true perfective partners of the given verbs.

[3] Our label 'formal' [*neobikhodnyi*] means that the register of the lexeme is a little higher than the usual literary-colloquial without, however, reaching as high as 'bookish' [*knizhnyi*], 'poetic' [*poeticheskii*], 'high' [*vysokii*], and so on. Round brackets enclosing the label indicate that the status is not obligatory—in this case the fact that the 'formal' register does not apply in all uses of the lexeme; see the meaning and form zones below.

[4] All the features listed below are of a general nature, that is, they are needed to describe many other lexical and grammatical phenomena in Russian.

(3) The relation between wish and intent, the readiness to make an effort to make the wish a reality (this is present in *khotet'* and *zhazhdat'* but not in *zhelat'* or *mechtat'*).

(4) The involvement of mental systems, in particular the imagination (it is implied in *mechtat'*).

(5) The emotional state of the subject (*zhazhdat'*, unlike *khotet'* and *zhelat'*, implies some strong emotion).

(6) The attainability of the desired object (greater in *khotet'* and *zhelat'* than in *mechtat'*).

(7) The duration of the wish (longer in *mechtat'* than in the other members of the series).

(8) The time interval between the moment when the wish is experienced and the moment when it may be achieved (longer in the case of *mechtat'*, which may postpone the moment of achievement into the indefinite future; *zhazhdat'*, on the other hand, requires immediate satisfaction).

(9) The type and status of the subject experiencing the wish (the subject of *zhelat'* tends to be an individual whose status is likely to be higher than that of the people around him).

## 2.3. SEMANTIC SIMILARITIES AND DIFFERENCES BETWEEN SYNONYMS

*Khotet'* and *zhelat'* are the synonyms with the most general meaning, denoting a certain norm in the sphere of wishes. In this they differ from *mechtat'* and *zhazhdat'*, which respectively denote intense and very intense wishes.

The norm in the sphere of wishes permits some fluctuation in the intensity of the wish; significant intensity is possible: *on ochen' khotel est'* [he was very hungry]; *on strastno khotel etogo* [he passionately wanted it]. The lower limit of intensity, however, for normal wishes is not a weak wish, but a wish of medium magnitude. For this reason it is impossible to say *\*on nemnogo ⟨slegka, chut'-chut'⟩ khotel ⟨zhelal⟩ etogo* [he wanted ⟨desired⟩ it somewhat ⟨slightly, a little⟩].[5]

The verb *khotet'* signifies the most typical wish—from medium to high intensity, not mediated by either mind or emotions, realistic (and realizable in the foreseeable future) or fantastic. The object of desire may equally well be an ordinary thing or something unusual or important, while the subject may be either an individual or a group: *vse shakhty Vorkuty khoteli ob"iavit' predupreditel'nuiu zabastovku* [all the Vorkuta pits wanted to declare a warning strike]; *plokh tot*

---

[5] This gradation of the scale of intensity—'normal P vs. strong P' without 'weak P'—is typical of some other inner human states. In particular, the scale of intensity for emotions is graded in exactly the same way: the norm, or prototype, is well represented (*udivliat'sia* [to be surprised], *boiat'sia* [to fear], *radovat'sia* [to be glad], *nadeiat'sia* [to hope; to rely]) as is the greater degree (*izumliat'sia* [to be amazed], *byt' v uzhase* [to be horrified], *likovat'* [to exult], *upovat'* [to hope; to place one's trust in]), while the lesser degree is virtually absent.

*soldat, kotoryi ne khochet stat' generalom* [it's a poor soldier who doesn't want to be a general] (proverb).

The specific feature of *khotet'*, especially when compared to *zhelat'*, is that it points to the involvement of the subject's will. In other words, besides the wish itself it implies a readiness by the subject to make efforts to make it come true: *im [Rudinu i dr.] on protivopolagaet liudei, umeiushchikh ne tol'ko zhelat', no i khotet'* [against these [Rudin et al.] he sets people with the ability not merely to wish but to want] (A. Koni); *on risoval [. . .] polnoe otsutstvie [. . .] voli i vialost' kharaktera, vyrazhaiushchiesia v naklonnosti zhelat' i nesposobnosti khotet'* [he depicted . . . complete absence . . . of will and lack of character which manifested themselves in a tendency to wish and an inability to want] (A. Koni).

Readiness to act is in turn motivated by the subject's feeling that the object of desire is necessary to sustain the normal conditions of his existence, including the most basic, such as food, sleep, etc. This is why it is usual to say *ia khochu est' ⟨pit', spat'⟩* [I want to eat ⟨drink, sleep⟩] rather than *\*ia zhelaiu ⟨mechtaiu⟩ est' ⟨pit', spat'⟩* [I wish to eat ⟨drink, sleep⟩, I dream of eating ⟨drinking, sleeping⟩].

This feature of *khotet'* clearly manifests itself in the fact that the sense of wishing in this verb is closely bound up with the sense of intending (in D. N. Ushakov's dictionary, in *Malyi akademicheskii slovar'* [The Shorter Academy Dictionary] and *Bol'shoi akademicheskii slovar'* [The Great Academy Dictionary] the idea of intention is isolated as a separate sense): for example, *Iurii Andreevich [. . .] khotel sprosit' ee, chto s nei, khotel rasskazat' ei, kak dvazhdy v zhizni videl ee* [Iurii Andreevich (. . .) wanted to ask her what was wrong and wanted to tell her that he'd seen her twice in his life] (B. Pasternak), in which both senses are expressed at once. There are, however, contexts in which one or the other of these is foregrounded.

There are two factors which favour the expression of 'the wish proper'.

The first is the rhematicity of *khotet'*. Rhematicity occurs, by the common rule, when:

(a) *khotet'* bears the main phrasal or emphatic stress: ↑ *khotite vypit' chego-nibud'?* [do you want something to drink?]; *ia ↓↓ khochu poekhat' v Moskvu* [I want to go to Moscow];

(b) *khotet'* is in a negative context: *bol'she ia ne khochu lgat'* [I don't want to tell any more lies] (M. Bulgakov); *ona (. . .) ne khotela plakat' pri postoronnikh* [she . . . did not want to cry in front of strangers] (B. Pasternak).

Second, *khotet'* expresses a wish proper if the subject of the wish and subject of the action are not the same: *khochesh', valenki snimu* [if you like I'll take off my felt boots]. This is natural: intentions always demand that the subjects of the state and of the action be the same.

The expression of intent is theoretically favoured by thematicity and the absence of phrasal stress on the corresponding predicate, as well as an indication of the temporal framework of the state. In the case of *khotet'* this happens in the following contexts:

(a) a context of verbs of physical action in the perfective: *ia khochu po doroge zaekhat' v institut* [I want to call in at the institute on the way].

(b) a context including the particles *uzhe* and *bylo* signifying an action abandoned at the last moment: *on khotel bylo ⟨uzhe khotel⟩ vykliuchit' ratsiiu, no peredumal* [he was about to switch off the walkie-talkie, but changed his mind].

(c) a context including time expressions such as *teper'* [now], *kak raz, tol'ko chto* [just], *pered etim* [just before that], *posle etogo* [after that], *potom* [then] in syntactic constructions expressing the idea of events in sequence. These contexts are typical of situations in which action is planned, as planning inevitably implies an intention to do something: *koe-kakie materialy ia uzhe sobral i teper' khochu poekhat' v Moskvu* [I've collected some material already and now I want to go to Moscow].

The verb *zhelat'* has two main areas of application, with clearly marked stylistic, semantic, and pragmatic specifics in each.

In negative sentences, which are highly typical of *zhelat'*, as well as in the participial, gerundial, and infinitive forms, it is stylistically, semantically, and pragmatically neutral.

Negative sentences: *Ne razdenus'. Ne zhelaiu chasti tela vsem pokazyvat'* [I won't undress. I don't wish to show everybody some parts of my body] (B. Pasternak); *nikto ne zhelaet menia slushat'* [nobody wishes to listen to me] (M. Bulgakov).

Non-finite forms: *soznatel'no zhelat' usnut'—vernaia bessonnitsa* [to consciously wish to fall asleep means certain insomnia] (B. Pasternak); *Radek osen'iu zvonil emu, zhelaia vstretit'sia* [Radek phoned him in the autumn, wishing to meet] (A. Solzhenitsyn).

Since in the case of *khotet'* the non-finite forms (except the infinitive) are either impossible or can hardly be expressed (see § 2.5. below), and since, on the other hand, such important derivatives as the name of the state (cf. *zhelanie*) and the adjectival form (cf. *zhelatel'nyi* [desirable]) are lacking, *zhelat'* and *khotet'* tend to merge into a single verb with suppletive grammatical and word-formation paradigms, in which all members are stylistically neutral.

The second area of application is that of finite forms in affirmative and interrogative sentences. In these contexts *zhelat'* is in most cases stylistically or pragmatically marked and therefore preferred in the narrative or official style, or else sounds ironic or slightly pretentious. Narrative: *Petr Petrovich zhelal pokazat' sebia pered tovarishchem radushnym, shchedrym, bogatym—i delal eto neumelo, po-mal'chisheski* [Petr Petrovich wished to appear hearty, generous, and wealthy before his friend, and he did this in a clumsy, boyish fashion] (I. Bunin). Official: *Itak prokurator zhelaet znat', kogo iz dvukh prestupnikov nameren osvobodit' sinedrion* [so the procurator wishes to know which of the two criminals the Sanhedrin intends to release] (M. Bulgakov). Ironic: *togda on napisal v sovetskoe posol'stvo, chto zhelaet vernut'sia v dorogoe emu otechestvo* [then he wrote to the Soviet embassy to say that he wished to return to his dear motherland] (A. Solzhenitsyn);

or it may be slightly pretentious: *gospoda novobrantsy! Ia zhelaiu pozdravit' vas eshche vo mnogikh drugikh momentakh i otnosheniiakh* [gentleman recruits! I wish to congratulate you on many other points and respects] (B. Pasternak).[6]

On the other hand, it is precisely in the finite forms that *zhelat'* shows the strongest semantic contrast with *khotet'*.

First, unlike *khotet'*, *zhelat'*, especially in the imperfective, signifies a wish proper, with no suggestion of active will: *ot vsei dushi zhelaiu, chtoby prazdniki skoree konchilis'* [I wish with all my heart that the holidays would soon end] (M. Bulgakov). See also the examples from A. Koni, quoted above.

Secondly, in the first and second persons *zhelat'* may indicate a difference in social status between the subject of the wish and his interlocutor. In such contexts *zhelat'* acquires features of 'shopkeeper's usage', of semi-educated, semi-official, or other stylistically marked usage. Compare the neutral *ia khochu poslushat' penie tsygan* [I want to hear the gypsies sing]; *Chto ty khochesh' nadet'—khalat ili pizhamu?* [what do you want to put on? Your dressing gown or your pyjamas?] and the stylistically or pragmatically marked *ia zhelaiu, chtoby tsygane peli vsiu noch'* [I wish to have the gypsies sing all night] (a picture is produced of a tipsy and rather brash merchant); *Chto zhelaete nadet'—khalatik ili pizhamu?* [what do you wish to put on? Your dressing gown or your pyjamas?] (M. Bulgakov); *ne zhelaete li zakazat' obed v nomer?* [do you wish to order lunch in your room?] (respectful, appropriate for one serving a client).

Thirdly and lastly, *zhelat'* differs from *khotet'* in a slightly greater degree of individualization, a stronger sense of a single individual. When dealing with the shared wishes of large groups of people, *khotet'* is more appropriate. *Vse shakhty Vorkuty khotiat ob"iavit' predupreditel'nuiu zabastovku* [all the Vorkuta pits want to declare a warning strike] is not only stylistically but also semantically preferable to *vse shakhty Vorkuty zhelaiut ob"iavit' predupreditel'nuiu zabastovku* [all the Vorkuta pits wish to declare a warning strike].

These distinctions between *khotet'* and *zhelat'* are partially neutralized in the following two situations:

(a) when the potential agent of the intended action is not the subject of the wish but some other person: *Chego vy khotite za to, chto segodnia byli u menia khoziaikoi? Chego zhelaete za to, chto proveli etot vecher nagoi?* [What do you want in return for being my hostess today? What do you wish for in return for spending the evening in the nude?] (M. Bulgakov).

(b) in negative sentences: *ia ne khochu ⟨ne zhelaiu⟩ govorit' na etu temu* [I don't want ⟨don't wish⟩ to talk about that].

Neutralization in negative sentences is not total because *ne zhelaiu, ne zhelaet, ne pozhelal,* etc. signify a more categorical absence of wish than *ne khochu, ne*

---

[6] From this it follows, among other things, that in general the object of stylistic description in the dictionary is not the lexeme (a word in a particular sense) but a smaller unit—the lexeme in a particular grammatical form, a particular syntactic construction, or a particular lexical context.

*khochet, ne zakhotel,* etc. Compare *ia uidu, ia ne khochu ego videt'* [I'm going; I don't want to see him] and *ia uidu, ia ne zhelaiu ego videt'* [I'm going; I don't wish to see him].

The only shared feature of the two other synonyms, *mechtat'* and *zhazhdat'*, is an indication of the intensity of the wish: *neskol'ko sutok zazhatye i shkriuchen-nye v kupe stolypina—kak my mechtali o peresylke!* [after several days of being crammed and contorted in a 'Stolypin carriage', how we dreamed of the transit camp!] (A. Solzhenitsyn); *no iz vsekh okonets, v nego-to moi geroi-izgnanniki muchitel'no zhazhdali posmotret'* [but of all the windows this was the one into which my exiled heroes most agonizingly longed to peer] (V. Nabokov).

On other features they differ substantially, their semantic specificity betraying some characteristics of their basic meanings.

*Mechtat'* in the sense 'to want' is closely linked with its basic meaning 'to think of something unattainable; to dream' and therefore presupposes the operation of the imagination and other human mental systems. This determines the following particular features.

First, *mechtat'* usually points to an appraisal of the desired state of affairs as being very good for the subject or for those close to him: *mechtat' o kruzhechke piva v zharkii den'* [to dream of a mug of beer on a hot day]; *mechtat' uchit'sia v universitete* [to dream of going to university].

More than with the other synonyms, the object of desire in the case of *mechtat'* appears as the only thing capable of delivering satisfaction to the subject: *ty mechtaesh' tol'ko o tom, chtoby prishla tvoia sobaka, edinstvennoe, po-vidi-momu, sushchestvo, k kotoromu ty priviazan* [you dream only of your dog coming, evidently the only creature you are attached to] (M. Bulgakov); *nado zh i o tekh skazat', kto eshche do 41-go ni o chem drugom ne mechtal, kak tol'ko vziat' oruzhie i bit' etim krasnykh komissarov* [mention must also be made of those who even before 1941 dreamed of nothing but taking up arms and using them against the red commissars] (A. Solzhenitsyn). To the extent that this indicates something good which may await the subject in the future, *mechtat'* approaches the meaning of *nadeiat'sia* [to hope] (see § 2.4).

Second, this verb retains the suggestion of the dreamy nature of the subject, his unrealistic attitude to life, his lack of will to act, etc., thanks to which his wish is removed from reality and is probably unrealizable: *glupo mechtat' o Sorbonne, esli vy ne gotovy kak sleduet vyuchit' frantsuzskii iazyk* [it's silly to dream of the Sorbonne if you're not prepared to learn French properly].

Third, *mechtat'* signifies a wish which has existed for some time. It cannot be spontaneous. If I am asked, *Khotite popast' na vystavku rabot Pikasso?* [do you want to go to an exhibition of Picasso's work?] I can reply either *Khochu* [yes, I do want to] or *Mechtaiu* [yes, I've been dreaming of it]. The former answer is possible in a situation in which I have only just learned of the exhibition as well as when I have long known of it and wanted to go. The latter answer is possible only in the second situation.

Fourth, the moment of first occurrence of the wish may be separated from that of its potential realization by a substantial, theoretically unlimited interval: *Kuz'ma vsiu zhizn' mechtal nauchit'sia chitat' i pisat'* [all his life Kuz'ma had dreamed of learning to read and write] (I. Bunin). With retrospective use in the past tense the time interval separating first occurrence and fulfilment is also usually longer with *mechtat'* than with other synonyms: compare the exclamations *ia tak mechtal popast' v Bol'shoi teatr!* [I dreamed so much of going to the Bol'shoi] when the speaker is at the Bol'shoi and *ia tak khotel popast' v Bol'shoi teatr!* [I wanted so much to go to the Bol'shoi] in the same context.

The verb *zhazhdat'* means 'to feel an acute and powerful need for something'. Thus the sense in which it is synonymous with *khotet'* also derives from its basic meaning ('to thirst, feel a need to drink'), although in the modern language this sense is obsolescent.

This synonym also has two areas of usage.

In the first and more typical, *zhazhdat'* retains its semantic specifics to a considerable extent, when compared with both *mechtat'* and *khotet'*.

Above all, *zhazhdat'* is used when the object of desire is or at least appears important or exceptional to the subject: *zhazhdat' pravdy ⟨dobra, novogo, prikliuchenii, reform⟩* [to hunger for truth ⟨goodness, something new, adventures, reform⟩]: *velikodushnoi i shirokoi amnistii zhdali i zhazhdali my!* [we waited and hungered for a broad and generous amnesty!] (A. Solzhenitsyn).

Further, *zhazhdat'* implies an excited emotional state in the subject: *Varenukha razrydalsia i zasheptal* [. . .], *chto on prosit, molit, zhazhdet byt' zapert v bronirovannuiu kameru* [Varenukha burst into sobs and whispered (. . .) that he begged, pleaded and longed to be locked in a padded cell] (M. Bulgakov). In many cases, desire in the form *zhazhdat'* is so closely bound up with some strong emotion that, like passion, it becomes blind; the subject strives to satisfy his desire whatever the cost, heedless of everything and perhaps in defiance of reason: *on zhazhdal ee uvidet' i sovershenno ne dumal ob opasnosti* [he longed to see her and gave no thought at all to the danger].

The third difference between *zhazhdat'* and *mechtat'* is that the former implies more variety in the object of desire. In this respect *zhazhdat'* again approaches *khotet'*. It is most usual, however, in the context of some dark wish, a wish for something bad for oneself or for others: *zhazhdat' ch'ei-libo krovi* [to thirst for smb.'s blood], *zhazhdat' mesti* [to thirst for revenge], *zhazhdat' smerti* [to long for death].

Finally, *zhazhdat'* signifies impatient desires, usually implying a minimal time interval between occurrence and the fulfilment the subject wishes for: *ia okazalas' pered ogromnoi dvuspal'noi krovat'iu i pod obstrelom liubopytnykh glaz devits i molodykh parnei-tekhnikov, zhazhdushchikh uvidet', kak eto uvazhaemaia Galina Pavlovna budet segodnia na glazakh u vsekh i sobstvennogo muzha obnimat'sia i tselovat'sia* [I found myself confronted by an enormous double bed and exposed to the curious gaze of the girls and young technicians who were agog to see the respected Galina Pavlovna today embracing and kissing somebody before everybody's eyes including her own husband's] (G. Vishnevskaia). This feature is related to the fact that *zhazhdat'* suggests a physical need which can totally frustrate the subject if not speedily satisfied. The use of *mechtat'* in such contexts is either inappropriate or alters the temporal perspective; if the wish is close to fulfilment, the moment at which it arose is pushed back far into the past: *oni davno uzhe mechtali uvidet', kak proslavlennaia pevitsa budet na glazakh u vsekh obnimat'sia i tselovat'sia* [they had long dreamed of seeing the famous singer embracing and kissing somebody before everybody's eyes].

In the second area of usage, where *zhazhdat'* signifies everyday situations, it is in many ways close to *khotet'*, differing from it mainly in that it indicates a rather greater intensity of desire: *k desiati chasam utra ochered' zhazhdushchikh biletov do togo vspukhla, chto o nei doshli slukhi do militsii* [by ten in the morning the queue of those wanting tickets had grown so much that word of it had reached the police] (M. Bulgakov).

## 2.4. NOTES TO THE SEMANTIC ZONE

NOTE 1. Two additional little-used synonyms come close to the series under consideration. These are the bookish, archaic or ironic *vozhdelet'* (to experience a passionate desire or a strong carnal attraction) and the obsolete, bookish, or stylized *alkat'* (to wish fervently).[7] In the modern language they are used to produce stylistic effects of various kinds: *kak oni na [bogatuiu amerikanku] gliadeli, kak oni vozhdeleli ee liubvi neverolomnoi i po vozmozhnosti ekskliuzivnoi!* [how they gazed at the rich American woman; how they hungered for her undying and if possible exclusive love!] (S. Chuprinin); *nichego luchshego ne smogu ia skazat' svoemu narodu, kogda alchushchie vlasti obeshchaiut emu skoreishee spasenie Rossii* [I shall have nothing better to say to my fellow-countrymen when the power-hungry promise them the immediate salvation of Russia] (G. Vladimov).

NOTE 2. The verbs *khotet'*, *zhelat'*, and *zhazhdat'* have a sense of carnal attraction which is close to the meaning under consideration: *ia tebia khochu* [I want you]; *kak on zhelal etu zhenshchinu!* [how he desired that woman!]. Here *khotet'* is preferred in direct address and *zhelat'* in third-person reporting.

The verb *zhelat'* has a sense close to that under consideration here: 'to express to smb. a wish that some person may have smth.'; *zhelat' komu-libo schast'ia* ⟨*zdorov'ia, uspekhov*⟩ [to wish smb. happiness ⟨health, success⟩].

The verb *mechtat'* (in absolutive use or in the construction *mechtat' o chem-libo* [to dream of something]) has the sense 'to think of something unattainable, to day-dream', which is close to the meaning under consideration: *ty vse mechtaesh', a nado deistvovat'* [you keep on day-dreaming, while you need to act]; *khotelos' mechtat' i dumat' o budushchem* [one felt like day-dreaming and thinking

---

[7] 'Stylized' is a new label indicating that a lexeme may be used to imitate an old-fashioned style.

about the future] (B. Pasternak); *nikto ne pomeshaet ei dumat' o chem ugodno, mechtat' o tom, chto ei ponravitsia* [nobody will prevent her thinking about whatever she likes or dreaming of whatever she pleases] (M. Bulgakov).

*Mechtat'* has the obsolete sense of 'to hope', which is close to the one at issue: [*Dardanelov*] *imel nekotoroe pravo mechtat', chto on ne sovsem protiven prelestnoi, no uzhe slishkom tselomudrennoi i nezhnoi vdovitse* [(Dardanelov) had some grounds to hope that he was not utterly repugnant to the charming but excessively virtuous and tender widow] (F. M. Dostoevskii). In modern Russian this meaning is preserved mainly in negative sentences of various kinds: *ia ne mechtal vnov' vas uvidet'* [I had no hopes of seeing you again].

A characteristic feature of *khotet'* is the possibility of figurative use, personification, etc.: *veter kak by khotel vyrvat' rastenie tselikom* [the wind seemed to want to uproot the plant completely] (B. Pasternak).


## 2.5. GRAMMATICAL FORMS

*Khotet'* lacks its own perfective. The perfective form *zakhotet'* in affirmative sentences in the indicative often has inchoative meaning: *posle progulki on zakhotel est'* [after his stroll he felt hungry]. In negative sentences and in the subjunctive the meaning of *zakhotet'* shifts towards the purely aspectual, and this form semantically approaches the perfective form *pozhelat'* of imperfective *zhelat'*: *on ne zakhotel* ⟨~ *ne pozhelal*⟩ *razgovarivat' so mnoi* [he did not want ⟨~ did not wish⟩ to talk to me].

The past tense of *khotet'* acquires a pragmatic, semantic, and stylistic specialization in interrogative sentences of the type *Chego* ⟨*chto*⟩ *vy khoteli?* [what did you want?]. In such circumstances it is part of a stock mode of address to a customer, petitioner, etc. It denotes a state contemporaneous with the moment of speech and smacks of substandard or semi-educated style.

Since the synonyms in this series denote not actions but states, the imperative is impossible in affirmative sentences (for *khotet'*, *zhazhdat'*), or at least unnatural (for *zhelat'*, *mechtat'*). With *zhelat'* and *mechtat'*, however, a negative imperative is possible: *ne zhelai drugomu togo, chego ne khochesh', chtoby sdelali tebe* [don't wish another person anything you wouldn't wish to have done to you]; *ni o kakikh kvartirakh v Moskve ne mechtai* [don't dream about any flats in Moscow].

The subjunctive form is characteristic of all these synonyms except *zhazhdat'*: *ia by khotel vyslushat' i druguiu storonu* [I'd like to hear the other side as well]; *kto zhelal by vystupit'?* [who would like to speak?]; *liubaia zhenshchina v mire mechtala by ob etom* [any woman in the world would dream of that] (M. Bulgakov).

In the literary language *khotet'* has no present participle or present gerundial. When there is a need to express these senses, the borrowed forms *zhelaiushchii* and *zhelaia* are therefore employed.

*Zhazhdat'* also lacks a gerundial, but in this case there is no compensation for its absence.

With *zhazhdat'*, participial forms are typical: see the examples given above and below.

## 2.6. SYNTACTIC CONSTRUCTIONS

*Khotet'* and less commonly *zhelat'* govern a direct object expressed by a noun in the accusative which denotes the content of the wish: *khochesh' konfetku?* [do you want a sweet?]; *zhelaete zakusku ili srazu pervoe bliudo?* [would you like to have a starter or shall I serve the first course straightaway?]. The underlying meaning of the collocation is: 'do you want to obtain or consume an object?': *khochesh' kartu goroda?* = 'do you want to acquire a map of the city?'; *khochesh' konfetku?* = 'do you want to eat a sweet?'

All these synonyms except *mechtat'* govern a direct object in the genitive or partitive genitive, also denoting the object of the wish: *khochu sladkogo chaiu* [I want some sweet tea]; *zhelaete chaiu ili kofe?* [would you like tea or coffee?]. In addition, if the complement is expressed by a noun which does not denote a physical object, the collocation as a whole also expresses the idea of existence: *khochu ⟨zhelaiu, zhazhdu⟩ mira v sem'e* [I want ⟨wish for, long for⟩ peace in the family] = 'I want peace to exist in the family'; *khochu ⟨zhelaiu, zhazhdu⟩ peremen* [I want ⟨wish for, long for⟩ change] = 'I want changes to come'.

All the synonyms may govern an infinitive or a subordinate clause introduced by the conjunction *chtoby*, also denoting the content of the wish: *ona khotela ⟨zhelala, mechtala, zhazhdala⟩ uvidet' svoego kumira* [she wanted to ⟨wished to, dreamed of, longed to⟩ see her idol]; *khotet' ⟨zhelat', mechtat', zhazhdat'⟩, chtoby na traditsionnyi sbor priekhali vse vypuskniki shkoly* [to want all school-leavers to come to the traditional gathering ⟨wish that, dream that they would come; long for them to come⟩].

*Khotet'* and *zhelat'* govern the prepositional-nominal group *ot kogo-libo* [from smb.], indicating the potential fulfiller of the subject's wish: *chego vy ot menia khotite?* [what do you want from me?]; *chego tebe eshche ot Boga zhelat'?* [what else do you wish from God?] (I. Bunin). With *zhazhdat'* such constructions are untypical; with *mechtat'* they are impossible.

The verb *zhelat'*, but not the other synonyms in the series, may govern the dative to signify the person whom the subject would like to see in a certain situation or state. Here the extreme states of good and evil are most usual: *ia zhelaiu emu schast'ia* [I wish him happiness] (see Note 2); *ia ved' dobra tebe zhelaiu* [I wish you well, you know]; *razve ia tebe zla zhelaiu?* [do you think I really wish you ill?] (I. Bunin).

*Khotet'*, but not the other members of the series, may govern a complement meaning the terminal point of locomotion, in which the corresponding infinitive is dropped: *khotet' v Moskvu ⟨v derevniu⟩* [to want to go to Moscow ⟨to the country⟩]; *Tsvetaeva khotela v Krym* [Tsvetaeva wanted to go to the Crimea].

Besides this, certain syntactic phrasemes are characteristic only of the verb *khotet'*: *zovi kogo khochesh'* [invite anyone you like], *idi kuda khochesh'* [go where you like], *delai kak khochesh'* [do as you please].

All the synonyms except *mechtat'* have certain semantic peculiarities in negative sentences; *mechtat'* in the sense considered here is not used in negative sentences (see Note 2).

*Khotet'* and *zhelat'*, when combined with stative verbs of the type *znat'* [to know], *videt'* [to see], *slyshat'* [to hear], etc. in negative sentences acquire an additional sense of distaste for something: *ne khochu tebia znat'* [I don't want to know you]; *ne zhelaiu tebia bol'she videt' ⟨slyshat'⟩* [I don't wish to see ⟨hear⟩ you again].

With the verb *zhazhdat'* the negative meaning is softened, so the resulting meaning is 'I have no particular wish to do smth.': *ia ne zhazhdu ego videt'* [I'm not longing to see him].

## 2.7. LEXICO-SEMANTIC CO-OCCURRENCE

All the synonyms combine with the name of an individual as the subject (see above and below). *Khotet'* and *zhazhdat'* combine more easily than *zhelat'* and especially *mechtat'* with the name of a group as the subject: *komissiia khotela otlozhit' rassmotrenie voprosa* [the commission wanted to postpone consideration of the matter]; *tolpa zhazhdala krovi* [the crowd was thirsting for blood].

*Zhazhdat'*, which suggests a connection between the wish and some strong emotion, combines freely with words such as *dusha* [soul], *serdtse* [heart], *vse ee sushchestvo* [her whole being], etc. as the subject of the wish; *odna polovina menia zhazhdet naslazhdeniia* [one half of me longs for pleasure] (A. and B. Strugatskii). Collocations of this kind are less typical of *khotet'* and *zhelat'* and impossible with *mechtat'*, since this synonym signifies a wish rooted in some mental evaluation of things.

All members of the series combine with the adverbs *tak* [so], *kak* [how], *strastno* [passionately], signifying the very great intensity of the wish: *on tak khotel spat'* [he wanted so much to sleep]; *kak my mechtali o peresylke!* [how we dreamed of the transit camp!]; *on strastno khotel ⟨zhelal⟩ popast' v krug etikh liudei* [he passionately wanted ⟨wished⟩ to enter that circle of people].

*Mechtat'* typically combines with the adverb *zhadno* [avidly] in this sense, while *zhazhdat'*, meaning a passionate wish, combines with the adverb *muchitel'no* [agonizingly] (see above).

Only *khotet'* co-occurs with the word *ochen'* [very; very much]: *on ochen' khotel est'* [he was very hungry].

*Khotet'* and *zhelat'* in the second person co-occur with the propositional pronoun *kak* [as], forming the fixed formulae *kak khotite,* ⟨*(po)zhelaete*⟩ with the meaning 'as you please'.

Only *khotet'* co-occurs with the propositional pronoun *tak* [so; thus]: *Zachem eto vam nuzhno?—Ia tak khochu* [Why is this necessary?—I want it this way].

With *zhelat'* this combination is restricted and with the other two synonyms it is impossible.

Only *khotet'* combines with the particles *uzhe* and *bylo*, signifying an action abandoned at the last moment: *ona uzh khotela vygovorit' zavetnye* [. . .] *slova, kak vdrug poblednela* . . . [she was about to utter the cherished (. . .) words, when suddenly she turned pale . . .] (M. Bulgakov); *on khotel bylo prodolzhat', no Aleshka ne vyterpel* . . . [he was about to resume, but Alesha lost his patience . . .] (I. Bunin).

### 2.8. PARADIGMATIC SEMANTIC LINKS

This zone provides lists of lexical units which have paradigmatic semantic links with the elements of the given series. Minimal commentary is supplied. The theoretical purpose of these lists is to demonstrate the continuity of the semantic space within a language. In practical terms they provide journeys of various kinds through this space and the opportunity to take the route which best suits the user's educational or research purposes.

This zone includes phraseological synonyms, analogues (co-hyponyms and other lexemes which are semantically fairly close to the elements of the series, though not synonymous with them), exact and inexact conversives, conversives of analogues, exact and inexact antonyms, and derivatives. The last, in addition to derivatives proper (including suppletive derivatives), includes all lexical units of other parts of speech whose meaning differs in a fairly regular pattern from the meanings exemplified in the given lexeme series.

In the present series the following subzones are relatively well represented:

Phraseological synonyms: *imet' okhotu* [to have a wish], *leleiat' mechtu* [to cherish a dream ⟨wish⟩], *goret' zhelaniem* [to burn with desire]; *spat' i videt'* [to dream of]; *dorogo by dal za chto-libo* [one would pay dearly for smth.]; *otdal by ⟨pravuiu⟩ ruku za chto-libo* [one would give one's right arm for smth.]; *chego izvolite?* (~ *chego by vy khoteli?*) [what would you like?].

Analogues: *nadeiat'sia* [to hope], *upovat'* [to aspire]; *mechtat', grezit'* [to daydream]; *bredit' (morem)* [to be mad about (the sea)]; *zhdat'* [to long to see] (*ia tak zhdal vas!* [I longed so much to see you!]); *pristrastit'sia, priokhotit'sia* [to take to]; *stremit'sia* [to strive]; *namerevat'sia, sobirat'sia, dumat'* [to intend to], *vzdumat'* [to take it into one's head to]; *iskat'* [to seek] (*vy, ia vizhu, ishchete ssory* [I see you're looking for a quarrel]); *prosit'* [to ask for].

Inexact conversives: *khotet'sia* [to feel like], *ne terpet'sia* [to be impatient to], *podmyvat'* [to feel an urge to].

Conversives of analogues: *privlekat', manit', tianut'* [to lure, entice]; *soblazniat'* [to tempt]; *prispichit'* [to be impatient to]; *vzbresti v golovu, vzdumat'sia* [to enter one's head to].

Inexact antonyms: *brezgovat', gnushat'sia* [to have an aversion to]; *raskhotet'* [to cease to want].

Derivatives: *zhelanie, okhota* [wish], *zhazhda (zhazhda prikliuchenii)* [longing, thirst (thirst for adventure)]; *pozyv* [urge, call]; *impul's* [impulse]; *zhelaiushchii (est' zhelaiushchie?)* [interested person (any takers?)]; *predmet zhelanii, predel zhelanii, predel mechtanii* [object of desire, pinnacle of one's desires, limit of one's dreams]; *zhelatel'nyi* [desirable], *zhelannyi* [desired]; *dolgozhdannyi* [long-awaited]; *vozhdelennyi* [longed-for]; *ugodno (kak vam budet ugodno)* [suitable (however suits you best) ~ 'as you please']; *okhotno, neokhotno* [willingly, unwillingly]; *po-moemu ⟨po-tvoemu, po-vashemu⟩*, etc. [as I ⟨you⟩ choose]; *raskhotet'* [to cease to want], *pozhelat'* [to express a wish].

# Part II
# SYSTEMATIC LEXICOGRAPHY

# 7

# Metaphor in the Semantic Representation of Emotions

J. D. APRESJAN, V. J. APRESJAN

## 1. Two Approaches to a Description of Emotional Vocabulary

Until recently the inner world of human beings was the province of psychiatrists, philosophers, and poets, but was of little interest to linguists. The situation began to change with the rise of contemporary linguistic semantics in the 1960s, when the first attempts were made to describe the vocabulary of the emotions lexicographically (Wierzbicka 1969, 1972; Iordanskaja 1970, 1972). Since then there has been a steady growth in interest, both theoretical and lexicographical, in words denoting emotions, as shown by such works as Lakoff and Johnson 1980; Wierzbicka 1980, 1990*b*; J. Apresjan 1979; Uspensky 1979; Zalizniak 1983; Iordanskaja 1984; Pajdzińska 1990*a*; Iordanskaja and Mel'čuk 1990; Wierzbicka 1991; J. Apresjan 1992*b*; V. Apresjan 1997*a*.[1] Data which may be of interest to linguists, among others, can be found in a number of contemporary psychological, physiological, sociological, and other studies, for example Ekman 1984; Ortony *et al.* 1988; Kövecses 1990; Fries 1992; Oatley 1992. A survey of these studies is provided by V. Apresjan (1995*a*). It is to be hoped that the linguistic results of studies of the emotions may also be of value to researchers in other disciplines. Language contains the experience of millennia of psychological and cultural introspection, and its data are every bit as reliable as those provided by experimental research.

Simplifying somewhat the real state of affairs, we may say that in linguistics two approaches to the description of emotions have developed. For convenience we will term these 'meaning-based' and 'metaphorical'. Within the framework of these approaches the central difficulty which confronts the researcher in describing the vocabulary of the emotions is tackled in different ways. As we know, the emotions themselves are not amenable to direct observation. In this respect they resemble other inner states, such as mental states, for example. However, unlike mental states, which can fairly easily be verbalized by the subject himself, emotions are very difficult to translate into words. This ontological difficulty lies at the root of a linguistic difficulty: it is almost impossible to provide a direct lexicographic explication of a word denoting an emotion.

[1] Hereafter the word 'emotions' will take the place of the expression 'words (lexemes) denoting emotions' in all contexts where this does not lead to ambiguity.

In cases where a direct explanation of a phenomenon is for some reason not possible, a speaker generally resorts to various kinds of periphrasis, appealing to knowledge which the listener may be presumed to possess. The following two methods of explanation are the most frequently used, and perhaps the only ones possible: either the speaker indicates a known situation in which the given phenomenon occurs, or he compares the phenomenon with another one which is known to his listener. Essentially these same principles underlie the two linguistic approaches to a description of the emotions.

### 1.1. THE MEANING-BASED APPROACH

This approach was proposed in the early works of A. Wierzbicka and L. N. Iordanskaja, in which emotions were described by means of the prototypical situations in which they occur. Some examples follow. (The first two, using the English vocabulary of emotions, are drawn from Wierzbicka; the Russian example from Iordanskaja.)

*X feels ashamed* = X feels as one does when one thinks that one has done something bad and ridiculous and when one desires that no one know about it.

*X feels proud* = X feels as one does when one thinks that one has done something more than good and when one desires that other people know about it. (Wierzbicka 1972: 63)

*A ogorchaetsia iz-za B* [A feels upset because of B] = A experiences a passively negative emotional state which in the ordinary person 'i' is usually caused by the following appraisal of an event 'j': (1) 'i' is sure that event 'j' has happened or will happen; (2) event 'j' is undesirable to 'i'; this emotional state is caused in A by his appraisal of event B. ( Iordanskaja 1970: 7)

In subsequent works by Wierzbicka and Iordanskaja, as well as those of other authors who adopted the meaning-based approach, these and other explications like them were refined but the principle of reduction to a prototype remained. Compare the following more recent explications:

*Afraid*
    X feels something
    sometimes a person thinks something like this:
        something bad can happen
        I don't want this
        I don't know what I can do
    because of this, this person feels something bad
    X feels like this (Wierzbicka 1990b: 363–4)

BOJAT'SJA I.1a *X boitsja Y-a* 'X is afraid of Y' =
Assertion
Evaluation 'X expects that Y will cause something undesirable for X
        or

Emotion    'X is or has the property of being in

| Characterization | an unpleasant emotional state with respect to Y |
|---|---|
| Cause | which is caused by said X's expectation, |
| Prototyp. conditions | this state being such as is usually caused by the expectation of something being dangerous, |
| Effect | this expectation and/or state causing X to tend to avoid Y'. |

(Iordanskaja and Mel'čuk 1990: 335)

The principle of reduction to a prototype still seems to be thoroughly valid, but on its own it is insufficient for a full and adequate lexicographical description of the vocabulary of the emotions.

First, the nature of the emotion itself (Wierzbicka's 'feeling something good' and 'feeling something bad'; Iordanskaja's and later Iordanskaja's and I. A. Mel'čuk's 'positive [pleasant] state' and 'negative [unpleasant] state') needs to be further defined. In essence, the difference in emotional states as described in the explications cited come down to differences in their causes. We may, however, suppose (and this supposition has been expressed by V. Apresjan (1997a)) that the states of the soul are different, even in the case of two emotions as prototypically close as *strakh* [fear] and *opasenie* [apprehension]. In the same way the negative feelings *gore* [grief] and *skorb'* [mourning] differ, although they also practically coincide in their prototype: both assume a great loss as their usual cause.

Secondly, it would be desirable to offer semantic descriptions of emotions which would make it possible to give a well-founded (semantically motivated) explanation of 'symptomatic' vocabulary, that is, of expressions such as *pokholodet' ot strakha* [to turn cold from fear], *pokrasnet' ot styda* [to blush with shame], *zadokhnut'sia ot vozmushcheniia* [to be stifled by indignation], first subjected to profound and detailed analysis in Iordanskaja (1972, 1984); see also Pajdzińska (1990a).

## 1.2. THE METAPHORICAL APPROACH

G. Lakoff and M. Johnson (1980: 57–8) note that the linguistic means of expressing emotion are metaphorical in the highest degree. Emotion is hardly ever expressed directly, but always compared to something. For this reason the authors regard description via metaphors in which these emotions are conceptualized in language as the most satisfactory linguistic description of emotions. For example, the emotions *schast'e* [happiness] and *grust'* [sadness] are metaphorically contrasted in English as TOP and BOTTOM. On the one hand a physical motivation is given for this metaphor: a person raises his head when he is happy and lowers it when he is sad. On the other hand, a linguistic motivation is offered: the metaphor at issue is an instance of a metaphor of the type 'good—up; bad—down'. Thus Lakoff's and Johnson's description is constructed in the form of a hierarchy of metaphors, in which metaphors of a lower order inherit the structure of 'ancestral' metaphors. For a similar approach to the description of emotions see Kövecses (1990).

One undoubted advantage of this approach is that it permits one to reflect the inner comparative nature of words denoting emotions and to introduce into the description, in addition to the emotion words themselves, large groups of metaphorical expressions related to them.

The disadvantage is that the metaphor is presumed to be the end product of linguistic analysis and a strictly semantic motivation for the association between a given metaphor and a particular emotion is lacking.

Moreover the specificity of metaphors referring to emotions (mainly to 'symptomatic' vocabulary) receives no explanation.

Lastly, some metaphorical comparisons appear to be dictated less by established linguistic practice than by individual usage. For example, on the basis of occasional and marginal utterances about the nature of love as *my na perekrestke* [we are at a crossroads], *my zashli slishkom daleko* [we've gone too far], *ty toropish' sobytiia* [you are hurrying things], *ty edesh' po skorostnoi polose na avtostrade liubvi* [you're travelling in the fast lane of the highway of love] (the last example is taken from an unpublished work by G. Lakoff), Lakoff proposes for love the image of a journey. More precisely, he sees love in the guise of a vehicle in which the lovers move towards their shared destination. Clearly many other forms of human activity (argument, negotiation, decisions, criticism, praise, and others) might no less successfully be compared to a journey or a vehicle, so the value of this metaphor as a specific description of love is diminished.

On this matter some interesting ideas have been put forward by V. A. Uspensky (1979), who examines the behaviour of the abstract nouns *avtoritet* [authority, prestige], *strakh* [fear], *gore* [grief] and *radost'* [joy] in metaphorical expressions such as *prochnyi avtoritet* [secure prestige], *khrupkii avtoritet* [shaky prestige], *dutyi avtoritet* [inflated prestige], *avtoritet lopnul* [(smb.'s) prestige burst] and the like; *strakh napadaet na cheloveka, okhvatyvaet ego, dushit, paralizuet; borot'sia so strakhom; pobedit' v sebe strakh* [fear assails a person, grips him, stifles, paralyses him; to wrestle with fear; to conquer one's fear] and the like; *glubokoe gore* [deep grief], *tiazheloe gore* [heavy grief], *ispit' goria, khlebnut' goria* [to taste grief], *chelovek pridavlen gorem* [a person is oppressed by grief], etc.; *radost' razlivaetsia v cheloveke, burlit, igraet, iskritsia, perepleskivaetsia cherez krai* [one's joy overflows, surges, plays, sparkles, runneth over], etc.

V. A. Uspensky wonders whether beneath these set expressions there are underlying motivating images which might serve as a basis for the coining of new metaphorical expressions with a given key word. He answers this question in the affirmative. In his view, *avtoritet* [authority, prestige] is perceived in Russian as 'a balloon, in the best case large and heavy; in the worst case small and light. False authority is hollow, with walls so thin that they can burst [*lopnut'*]' (Uspensky 1979: 145). 'Fear may be perceived in the form of a hostile organism resembling a giant arthropod or octopus with a sting injecting a paralysing substance' (Uspensky 1979: 146). 'Grief is a viscous liquid' filling 'a vessel with a man on the bottom' (Uspensky 1979: 147). Lastly, joy is 'a light, bright liquid', 'apparently lighter than air' (Uspensky 1979: 147).

The notion that motivating images may be sought for large classes of symptomatic and other metaphorical expressions seems a highly fruitful one. We would like, however, to link the metaphorical description with the purely meaning-based, as proposed in V. Apresjan (1997a), and on the other hand to find independent evidence to support the metaphorical prototypes proposed for the emotions. Without this they may appear arbitrary.

In fact the conclusion that *avtoritet* is conceptualized in Russian as an empty balloon is based essentially on the fact that it may 'burst' [*lopnut'*] and be 'inflated' [*dutyi*]. But first, it is not only spherical physical objects that can burst or be inflated; note also *banka* ⟨*verevka, struna, shina, perchatka*⟩ *lopnula* [a jar ⟨cord, (violin or guitar) string, tyre, glove⟩ burst]; *steklo lopnulo* [the glass (window-pane) burst]; and *dutaia trubka* [blown glass tube]. Co-occurrence with *dutyi* and *lopnut'* therefore provides an insufficient basis for the assertion that *avtoritet* is seen as balloon-like. Secondly, other things may be inflated and may burst in a figurative sense, for example *sudebnoe delo, plan, reputatsiia* [a court case, plan, reputation]; note also *dutye tsifry, dutyi otchet* [inflated figures, inflated report], *firma lopnula, zateia lopnula* [the firm went bankrupt, the plan fell through], etc. If this is taken to be a sufficient basis for the conclusion that speakers of Russian also conceptualize these objects as hollow spheres the resulting picture will be too inconsistent and non-specific for the key words.[2]

## 2. The Explication of Emotions

### 2.1. THE SCENARIO FOR THE EMERGENCE AND DEVELOPMENT OF EMOTIONS

As may easily be seen, the explications adduced in § 1.1 are structured. The following three parts are distinguished: the cause of the emotion (an appraisal by the intellect of a given situation), the emotion itself and its consequences. Similar components, though somewhat differently structured, are distinguished in Zalizniak 1983 and in the works of a number of other researchers.

It is desirable to add some details to amplify this scenario. These are necessitated by certain general considerations regarding the systems whose operation

---

[2] Pertsova (1990) is an illustration of how perilous it may be to draw conclusions regarding the motivating image by simply decoding the linguistic metaphor. The author proposes for the word *vremia* [time] the following connotations: (1) 'a liquid' (*vremia techet*) [time flows by]; (2.1) 'an elastic object' (*vremia tianetsia*) [time stretches]; (2.2) 'a valuable object', 'the equivalent of money' (*vyigrat' vremia, tratit' vremia*) [to gain time, to waste time]; (3) 'a living being' (*vremia idet* ⟨*terpit, zhdet*⟩, *ubivat' vremia*) [time passes ⟨stands still, waits⟩, to kill time]; (3.1) 'a flying object' (*vremia letit*) [time flies]; (3.2) 'a person' (*vremia pokazhet, vremia toropit*) [time will tell, time hastens]. Clearly these interpretations are based on too literal a reading of dead metaphors which have long since lost any connection with the original image.

and interaction make up human behaviour, at least in the 'naïve' picture of the world which is the subject of this description. For each system we will indicate the organ or organs in which it is located, and the semantic primitive which gives a basic description of the way it functions.

In developing the ideas set forth by J. Apresjan (1992b and 1992c), we shall distinguish seven such systems:[3] (1) perception (bodily organs; 'to perceive'; the role of perception in evoking a number of emotions is noted by Arutiunova (1988: 136)); (2) physiology (the body as a whole; 'to sense'); (3) motor functions (parts of the body; 'to do'); (4) wishes (the will; 'to want'); (5) the intellect (the mind; 'to think about'); (6) emotions (the soul; 'to feel'); (7) speech (language; 'to speak').[4] Some systems are served by one and the same organ, or even by the body as a whole, various parts of which may serve as organs of touch; certain other systems seem to have a choice of two organs, for example 'mind' and 'head', 'soul' and 'heart'.

We should note one feature of the configuration of these seven systems. They do not form a homogeneous set, but a hierarchy, in which each one is more complex than the preceding one. The most primitive system is perception, which mankind shares with all the rest of the animal kingdom. The most complex is speech, which separates mankind from the rest of nature.

The emotions are also a highly complex system. First, with the exception of some basic emotions such as fear, rage, and pleasure, they are peculiar to humans.[5] Secondly, almost any emotional experience activates all the other systems.

In order to experience fear, for example, one must (1) perceive or at least imagine a certain situation and (2) appraise it as dangerous to oneself or to something or somebody close. The result is the emotion itself, (3) an unpleasant sensation evoked by (1) or (2). This sensation may manifest itself (4) in certain physiological reactions (pallor, trembling, etc.), over which the subject has no control, and/or (5) in wishes (for example, a wish to hide, shrink, etc.), which may in turn lead (6) to deliberate motor activity or (7) to speech.

This pattern of emergence and development of emotions is one of the factors determining the structure of their explication.


## 2.2. SYMPTOMATIC EXPRESSIONS: PHYSICAL METAPHORS FOR EMOTIONAL STATES

Another factor determining the structure and composition of explications of emotions is purely linguistic and has to do with symptomatic expressions of two types.

---

[3] An eighth system was added later; see Chapter 3 in this volume.

[4] The place of the spirit [*dukh*] in this model remains unclear. There is no doubt, however, that it is situated *above* all the other systems rather than *beside* them.

[5] Views on what constitutes the range of basic (fundamental and genetically conditioned) emotions vary from one work to another, but fear, rage, and pleasure appear as basic in most of them.

To the first belong expressions describing physiological, directly observable human reactions to fear:[6] *belet'* ⟨*blednet'*⟩ *ot strakha* [to turn white ⟨pale⟩ with fear], *drozhat'* ⟨*triastis'*⟩ *ot strakha* [to shiver ⟨tremble⟩ with fear], *szhat'sia ot strakha* [to shrink with fear], *tsepenet'* ⟨*zastyvat', ne moch' dazhe pal'tsem poshevelit'*⟩ *ot strakha* [to go numb ⟨be frozen, be unable to move so much as a finger⟩ with fear], *onemet' ot strakha* [to go rigid with fear]; *iazyk zapletaetsia ot strakha* [to be tongue-tied with fear]; *zuby stuchat ot strakha* [(one's) teeth chatter from fear], *golos drozhit* ⟨*preryvaetsia*⟩ *ot strakha* [(one's) voice quavers ⟨breaks off⟩ from fear], *murashki probegaiut po telu* ⟨*spine, kozhe*⟩ *ot strakha* [shivers run down one's spine ⟨over one's body, skin⟩ from fear], *drozh' probegaet po telu* ⟨*spine, kozhe*⟩ *ot strakha* [shivers run down one's spine ⟨over one's body, skin⟩ from fear] and some others, see Iordanskaja (1984), from which the great majority of these expressions are drawn.

To the second belong metaphorical expressions which reflect not the actual observable effects but the conceptualization of fear by speakers: *kamenet'* ⟨*stolbenet'*⟩ *ot strakha* [to be petrified with fear], *strakh skovyvaet* ⟨*paralizuet*⟩ *kogo-libo* [fear paralyses smb.], *strakh pronizal ego dushu* [fear penetrated his very soul], *strakh ledenit krov' komu-libo* [fear chills smb.'s blood], *krov' stynet* ⟨*ledeneet*⟩ *v zhilakh ot strakha* [the blood freezes in one's veins from fear], etc. There are also expressions which form an intermediate stage between the two groups, classifiable equally as literal or metaphorical, e.g. *kholodet' ot strakha* [to turn cold with fear].

An analysis of this material leads to the following conclusion: the psychological reaction to fear is very similar to the body's reaction to cold. Indeed, almost all the 'symptomatic' verbs used to describe the physical manifestations of fear are also used to describe the effects of cold: *konchik ee nosa pobelel ot kholoda* [the tip of her nose turned white from cold], *drozhat'* ⟨*triastis'*⟩ *ot kholoda* [to shiver ⟨shudder⟩ with cold], *szhat'sia ot kholoda* [to shrink with cold], *tsepenet'* ⟨*zastyvat', ne moch' dazhe pal'tsem poshevelit'*⟩ *ot kholoda* [to go numb ⟨be frozen, be unable to move so much as a finger⟩ with cold], *ruki onemeli ot kholoda* [(one's) hands went stiff with cold]; *zuby stuchat ot kholoda* [(one's) teeth chatter from cold], *drozh' probegaet po telu* ⟨*spine, kozhe*⟩ *ot kholoda* [shivers run down one's spine ⟨over one's body, skin⟩ from cold].

The similarity between fear and cold also extends into the sphere of metaphor. The effects of these two states are metaphorized in the same expressions: *kholod skoval vse ego chleny* [the cold transfixed all his limbs], *kholod paralizuet* [the cold is paralysing], *krov' stynet v zhilakh ot kholoda* [the blood freezes in one's

---

[6] Owing to the well-known anthropocentric factor, language generally reflects the symptoms of emotions characteristic of humans. Expressions such as *sobaka podzhala khvost ot strakha* ⟨*oshchetinilas' ot iarosti*⟩ [the dog put its tail between its legs from fear ⟨bristled with rage⟩], *koshka zashipela ot zlosti* ⟨*murlykala ot udovol'stviia*⟩[the cat hissed with spite ⟨purred with pleasure⟩] are less common and not nearly as varied as the symptomatic expressions which characterize the manifestations of emotions in human beings.

veins from cold], *kholod pronizal ego telo* [the cold penetrated his body].

The question arises: is the identity in collocational range between words denoting psychological and physical states coincidental, or does it demonstrate the presence of some underlying pattern? Certain facts point to the latter conclusion.

Some examples follow of other emotions which are conceptualized in language in the same way as physical states.

*Otvrashchenie* [revulsion, disgust]: *pomorshchit'sia* ⟨*smorshchit'sia, skrivit'sia*⟩ *ot otvrashcheniia* [to grimace ⟨make a face⟩ in disgust], *sdelat' grimasu ot otvrashcheniia* [to grimace in disgust], *peredernut'sia ot otvrashcheniia* [to wince from disgust], *toshnit ot otvrashcheniia* [to feel nauseous with disgust], *plevat'sia ot otvrashcheniia* [to spit in disgust], etc. It can easily be seen that the physiological reaction coincides with that to a very unpleasant (for example, sour or bitter) taste. There is no need to cite obvious examples.

*Zhalost'* [pity]: *zhalost' kol'nula* ⟨*pronzaet, shchemit*⟩ [pity jabbed ⟨pierces, squeezes], *ostraia zhalost'* [sharp pity]; compare the collocations *bol' kol'nula* [pain jabbed], *bol' pronzaet* [pain pierces], *v grudi shchemilo* [there was a tightness in the chest (said of a physical ache)], *ostraia bol'* [sharp pain]. The closeness of the emotion to a physical sensation is so great that pity is often perceived as pain and the word *bol'* acquires the meaning of *zhalost'*: *shchemiashchee chuvstvo zhalosti* [a feeling of pity squeezing one's heart], *serdtse razryvalos' ot zhalosti* [(my/his, etc.) heart was breaking with pity], *v 'Izvestiiakh'* [. . .] *byla opublikovana seriia ocherkov ob etikh izgnannikakh—bol' za nikh, sostradanie k nim—eto byl glavnyi i edinstvennnyi motiv 'Parizhskikh dnevnikov'* [*Izvestiia* . . . published a series of articles about these exiles. Pain on their account and sympathy for them were the central motif, the only motif, of the 'Paris Diaries'] (*Nezavisimaia gazeta*, 23 June 1992), *mne prosto do boli zhalko liudei, kotorye ne vidiat v zhizni khoroshego* [I simply feel painfully sorry for people who can't see the good side of life] (M. Gor'kii).

A large group of emotions (especially passion, fury, anger) is associated with illness or fever: *goriachka strasti, likhoradka strasti* [a fever of passion], *ot strasti sokhnut* ⟨*sgoraiut*⟩ [they wither ⟨are consumed⟩ with passion], *strast'iu goriat* ⟨*pylaiut*⟩ [to burn ⟨blaze⟩ with passion], *strast' ostuzhaiut* [they cool passion], *strast' ostyvaet* [passion cools, dies down], *ot gneva* ⟨*iarosti*⟩ *zakipaiut* ⟨*kipiat*⟩ [they ⟨seethe⟩ flare up with anger ⟨fury⟩], *ot gneva* ⟨*iarosti*⟩ *goriat glaza* [eyes blaze with anger ⟨fury⟩], *iarost' klokochet v kom-to* [fury seethes in smb.].

Note also the conceptualization of *gore* [grief] as a burden, noted by V. A. Uspensky and evidenced by its symptoms *chelovek sognulsia ot goria* [the man was bowed by grief] and by collocations such as *gore davit* ⟨*pridavlivaet*⟩ *kogo-libo* [grief oppresses smb.] and *gore obrushivaetsia na kogo-libo* [grief buries smb. under its weight], etc., see above.

We may summarize the material presented here as follows:

1. The physical analogues proposed for the emotions (fear—cold; revulsion—foul taste; pity—physical pain; passion—fever, etc.) seem more clearly motivated

and less arbitrary than those previously proposed (love—a journey; joy—a light liquid; fear—an octopus, etc.). They allow us to explicate a substantially broader range of symptomatic and other collocations, including metaphorical collocations.

Furthermore, like any other productive model, such as word-formation models, they have predictive force. It is evident, for example, that expressions such as *ego znobilo ot strakha* [he was chilled by fear] and *emu stalo zharko ot gneva* [he grew hot with anger], not encountered in common use, will be more readily accepted and more easily understood than [?]*ego znobilo ot gneva* [he was chilled by anger] or [?]*emu stalo zharko ot strakha* [he grew hot with fear]. The point is that the first two exploit regular images based on general linguistic awareness, while the last two rely on irregular images with nothing behind them except perhaps the personal experience of one individual (see Vladimir Nabokov's *Dar* [The Gift]: *kogda on serdilsia, gnev ego byl kak vnezapno udarivshii moroz* [when he was angry his anger was like a sudden frost]; here, however, what is portrayed is not inner feelings but the effect of this emotion upon others).

2. As potential claimants to a place in the explication, the images 'love—journey', 'joy—light liquid', 'fear—octopus' also give rise to doubt because they refer to an excessively wide range of natural phenomena and human activities. They do not form any unified whole.

The images proposed in this work make up a more consistent system of conceptualization of emotions in language. At the basis of this system lies the unifying principle of comparing that which cannot be observed directly (an emotional reaction) to that which can (a physical reaction). Physical reactions provide the key to what is happening at the emotional level, though perhaps in a limited number of instances.

3. The motivating images outlined above form such a substantial part of the linguistic consciousness of speakers that in some form or other they must be included in explications of the corresponding emotions.

## 2.3. THE STRUCTURE OF EXPLICATIONS

In this section we shall discuss two problems bearing on the structure of explications: the place of metaphor in the explication and the logical structure of the prototypical part of an explication.

First of all, we propose introducing into the explication comparisons of the following nature: 'given emotion X, a person's soul experiences something similar to what the body experiences when exposed to physical stimulus Y or when it is in the physical state of Y'.

The 'body metaphor of the soul' should be included in the explication of just those emotions in which it can be supported by sufficiently typical and consistently organized material. There exist large classes of emotions with their own distinctive symptoms but with no corresponding physical phenomena. One of them is surprise and related feelings: *shiroko raskryt' glaza ot udivleniia; vypuchit' glaza ot udivleniia* [to open one's eyes wide with surprise] (no physical stimulus which forces one to open one's eyes wide can be identified). It is clear that the difference between *surprise* and, for example, *fear* should not be levelled by forcing surprise into the same explicatory mould.

From our observations, it is reasonable to include a metaphor M in the explication of emotion A if at least one of the following two conditions is met: (*a*) the given symptomatic expression, used to describe both the reaction of the soul as well as that of the body, allows unequivocal reconstruction of the type of emotion; *u nego zuby stuchat* [his teeth are chattering], *on pokholodel* [he turned cold] (emotions like fear); (*b*) a metaphorical expression exists which alone, even without the name of the emotion in the nearest context, is capable of designating it; *on po nei sokhnet*—[he's pining (lit. drying up) for her] (emotions like love).

The thesis that lexicographical accounts of words may or should include metaphors is not new. There are large categories of expressions which can only be described metaphorically, such as the well-known example of words denoting changes in time. It is more difficult to resolve the question of how to allocate different types of metaphor between different parts of the lexicographical description of a word.

We cannot now propose an all-embracing resolution of this question. We may point out, however, that given the principle formulated above we should not include in the explication arbitrary metaphors such as 'joy—light liquid' or 'grief—viscous liquid', etc. The linguistic status of these metaphors cannot be more than that of a connotation, and even this status should only be ascribed with the greatest caution to any lexeme (see Note 2). It is evident that the presence in a language of a single set expression, a single derivative, or a single figurative sense in which a hypothetical connotation of a lexeme appears as an element of the former's lexical meaning, is insufficient even to establish a connotation. A series of such facts is needed, all organized after a unifying pattern.

We move on to the question of the logical structure of the prototypical part of the explications.

As is known, in the works of the Moscow Semantic School a propositional form of the type X P Y provides the entry point to the explication of predicate lexemes. Here P is the predicate lexeme to be explicated and X and Y are variables standing for the participants in the situation. In the absence of anything else, it is assumed by default that these variables are bound by an existential quantifier.

The prototypical part of an explication is constructed differently. It contains a reference to a general or at least usual occurrence, that is, to the experience of many people, occasioned by a specific event. This means that in the prototypical part of the explication the subject of the emotion must be bound by something like a universal quantifier ('many people', 'the ordinary person'), and the cause of the emotion must be introduced by a quantifier of singularity or definiteness. From this in turn it follows that to denote the subject and the cause of the emotion in the prototypical part it is essential to use new variables, distinct from X and Y, and then establish a correspondence between these variables on the one hand and the pair (X, Y) on the other.[7]

A relatively rigorous explication taking account of all these nuances could take the form:

XPY = 'a certain feeling caused in X by Y; this feeling usually occurs when person A perceives or imagines object B, which in his estimation possesses a certain property; A's soul feels something akin to what his body experiences when he is in a certain physical state, and A's body reacts to this as it reacts to the respective physical state; A wishes to do certain things when he experiences this feeling; in relation to Y, X experiences the same as A in relation to B'.

Whatever their logical advantages, it is clear that explications of this type are conceptually too complex for a dictionary. Our aim, however, is to elaborate a *lexicographically* acceptable model for an explication of the emotions. In the prototypical part of the explication we therefore employ less rigorous notations. It is not difficult, however, to develop them into formally impeccable notation when we wish to do so.

This goal is also served by the lexicographer's (and general linguist's) natural desire to provide a 'naïve' (linguistic, ethnolinguistic) picture of the world, in this case—a naïve picture of the emotions (see § 2.1 above).

## 2.4. EXPERIMENTAL EXPLICATIONS OF CERTAIN EMOTIONS

Taking account of the above, the following explications are offered for the emotions mentioned. (In the explication of *strakh* [fear] substantial use is made of the considerations set forth in Wierzbicka 1972, Iordanskaja 1984, and V. Apresjan 1997*a*.)

*Strakh X-a pered Y-om* [X's fear of Y] (*on ispytyval strakh pered budushchim* [he experienced fear of the future]) = 'an unpleasant feeling caused in X by Y; this feeling usually occurs when a person perceives or imagines something which in his estimation presents a serious danger to him; his soul feels something akin to what his body experiences when he is cold; his body reacts to this as it reacts to cold; the person experiencing this feeling wishes to become invisible; if the feeling of danger increases in intensity he may lose his self-control and start running or shouting'.

*Otvrashchenie X-a k Y-u* [X's disgust with Y] (*on ispytyval otvrashchenie k takim zabavam* [he experienced disgust with these games]) = 'a very unpleasant feeling caused in X by Y; this feeling usually occurs when a person perceives or imagines something very unpleasant; his soul feels something akin to what his

---

[7] Essentially this is the way in which the explications in the earliest work of L. N. Iordanskaja were structured. See the definition of *ogorchat'sia* cited in § 1.1.

bodily organs experience from a sour or bitter taste, a very pungent odour or the touch of something dirty which can stain; his bodily reaction is the same as his reaction to a sour or bitter taste, a very pungent odour or the touch of something dirty; the person experiencing this feeling wishes to get away or in some other way remove himself from contact with the unpleasant object; it is difficult for him to conceal his feelings if he remains in contact with it or continues to think of it.'

*Zhalost' X-a k Y-u* [X's pity for Y] (*ego zhalost' k bol'nym byla poistine bespredel'noi* [his pity for the patients was truly limitless]) = 'a feeling upsetting X's spiritual equilibrium and caused in X by Y; this feeling usually occurs when a person thinks that somebody is in a bad situation and that this situation is worse than that person deserves; his soul feels something akin to what his body experiences when he is in pain; his body reacts to this as it reacts to pain; the person experiencing this feeling wishes to alleviate the situation of the other person.'

*Strast' X-a k Y-u* [X's passion for Y] (*ego strast' k etoi zhenshchine tolkala ego na bezumnye postupki* [his passion for that woman drove him to acts of insanity]) = 'a very strong feeling upsetting X's spiritual equilibrium and caused in X by Y; this feeling usually occurs when a person experiences an insurmountable carnal longing for another person; he feels something akin to what his body experiences when he is feverish; the feeling has the same effect as an illness has on his body; his body reacts to this as it reacts to fever; if the feeling remains unsatisfied the person suffers deeply; this feeling may deprive the person of the ability to think rationally and impel him to act recklessly.'[8]

[8] Independently of these authors, E. V. Uryson has set forth the idea of the relation between fear and cold, and I. B. Levontina—the idea of the relation between pity and pain; see their entries for *strakh* and *zhalost'* respectively in J. Apresjan *et al.* (1997).

# 8

# On the Language of Explications and Semantic Primitives

Work on an explanatory dictionary of Russian synonyms in progress since 1991 (see J. Apresjan 1992*b*, 1993, Chapters 2–6 in this volume, and J. Apresjan *et al.* 1992, 1995, 1997) has entailed broad theoretical research in the field of semantics, and in particular it has required a new approach to the language of explications in which a description is given of the shared part of the meanings of the synonyms.

The question of the language of explications, or semantic metalanguage, has been discussed over the past thirty to forty years in all the advanced lexicographies of the world. For the purposes of the present work, the ideas of greatest interest are those set forth on this subject by two contemporary semantic schools: the Moscow School (Zholkovsky *et al.* 1961; Zholkovsky 1964*a*; *Mashinnyi perevod* 1964; Shcheglov 1964; Mel'čuk 1974*a*; J. Apresjan 1974; Mel'čuk and Zholkovsky 1984; Mel'čuk 1989; Apresjan 1995*b*) and the Polish School (Bogusławski 1966 and 1970; Wierzbicka 1969, 1972, 1980, 1985, 1987*b*, 1992).

## 1. The Approach of the Moscow Semantic School to the Language of Explications

### 1.1. THE COMPOSITION AND STRUCTURE OF A SEMANTIC METALANGUAGE

The basic ideas of the Moscow Semantic School were formulated in the 1960s in the following pioneering works: Zholkovsky *et al.* 1961; Zholkovsky 1964*a*; *Mashinnyi perevod* 1964; Shcheglov 1964. They were subsequently developed by Mel'čuk (1974*a*), J. Apresjan (1974), Mel'čuk and Zholkovsky (1984), Mel'čuk (1989), and Apresjan (1995*b*). They may be summarized as follows:

1. The meanings of words are described in a special formal metalanguage which has its own vocabulary and syntax.

Until the early 1980s it was presumed that the basis of its vocabulary (a list of semantic primitives) was formed of artificial words, or word-constructs. These were partly borrowed from the exact sciences (*mnozhestvo* [set (from mathematical set theory)], *sila* [power], *funktsiia* [function]), partly invented by researchers (*kauzirovat'* [to cause], *potok faktov* [current of events]), or taken from the vocabulary of natural language but shorn of some unnecessary semantic elements (*veshch'* [thing], *kolichestvo* [quantity], *chast'* [part], *norma* [norm], etc.). In addition to these relatively simple senses the vocabulary of the metalanguage also included many 'intermediate concepts', that is, semantically more complex words which in one or more steps could be reduced to primitives.

As for the syntax of the semantic language, it was an entirely artificial construct. Ideally it was the syntax of semantic graphs or dependency trees. A simplified and unified fragment of the syntax of natural language was used only as a palliative (Mel'čuk 1974*a*: 53, J. Apresjan 1974: 78–9 and Mel'čuk and Zholkovsky 1984).

It should be emphasized that in the period of the unchallenged dominance of componential analysis 'distinctive semantic features' were renounced on principle as being too feeble and inadequate a tool for the presentation of the meaning of linguistic units. Lexical or grammatical meaning is not merely the totality of 'values of distinctive semantic features', but a structure of senses with a complex organization and its own inner syntax.

2. Since the semantic language was constructed by the researcher as a kind of logical language using the inventory of the most basic human concepts, it was seen as universal in two respects. First, it was postulated that it could be used to describe any type of linguistic meaning, including that of morphological categories, syntactic constructions, and other meaningful linguistic units. Secondly, it was postulated that it could serve to describe the semantic material of any language. In this connection, in I. A. Mel'čuk's multi-level linguistic Meaning ⇔ Text model, semantics, unlike all other levels, was not divided into sublevels (surface and deep): what a surface-semantic level might correspond to was at the time unclear.

The research I have been engaged in for the past two decades, the first results of which were reported in J. Apresjan (1979; Chapter 1 in this volume; and 1980), and in J. Apresjan *et al.* (1979), has led me to the conclusion that the idea of an artificial metalanguage was in need of some clarification. In particular, in J. Apresjan (1980) I claimed that each natural language possesses large categories of lexical meanings, which, like grammatical meanings, *have* to be expressed, that is, they are expressed independently of the communicative intentions of the speaker. In Russian the verbs of locomotion *vyiti* [to go/come out], *vyletet'* [to fly out], *vypolzti* [to crawl out], and *vyplyt'* [to swim/sail out] signify a manner of locomotion in addition to everything else. A speaker is obliged to use one of these verbs even when it is utterly immaterial to him in what way a given being left a given place: *sobaka vyshla iz konury* [the dog came out of its kennel], *ptitsa vyletela iz gnezda* [the bird flew out of its nest], *zmeia vypolzla iz nory* [the snake crawled out of a burrow], *ryba vyplyla iz grota* [the fish swam out of a grotto]. We cannot say: *"sobaka pokinula konuru* [the dog left its kennel], *"ptitsa pokinula gnezdo* [the bird left its nest], *"zmeia pokinula noru* [the snake left the burrow], *"ryba pokinula grot* [the fish left the grotto]. In Russian these would sound comical, affected, unnatural, facetious, or would have a different sense ('to leave for good'). Yet in all these cases a Frenchman will use one and the same verb, *sortir*, which in its semantic composition more or less corresponds to the verb *pokidat'*. Only if it is important for some reason to indicate the nature of the movement will he inject the appropriate aspectual modification.

In any linguistic model which claims to provide a reasonably full description of the semantics of natural languages, provision must be made for a level at which such automatically expressed senses are described. For this reason, in the above-mentioned work (J. Apresjan 1980) it was proposed to divide the semantic level of representation of utterances into surface and deep sublevels. The former is handled by the surface-semantic component of the model. It deals with the national semantics of natural language.

To describe natural language semantics at the surface-semantic level it was proposed to use not an artificial language but a somewhat simplified and unified sub-language of the object language, that is, existing words and syntactic structures in their accepted senses, as is customary in traditional lexicography. It is assumed that such a metalanguage is best suited to the description of national semantics. We part company with traditional lexicography, however, in applying to this metalanguage the explicitly formulated and more strictly applicable requirements arising from the general ideas of the Moscow Semantic School. Here, for simplicity's sake, they will be exemplified only with lexical material, although in principle they are also fully applicable to the syntax of the metalanguage.

1. The lexical stock of the metalanguage, compared to that of Russian, is reduced by several orders of magnitude. In particular, all complex lexemes which cannot be used in the explication of other linguistic units are excluded (for example *shantazh* [blackmail], *insinuatsiia* [insinuation], *prisiaga* [oath], etc.). It retains words of two types: semantic primitives, that is, indefinable words which cannot undergo further semantic reduction, and semantically more complex words (the 'intermediate concepts' mentioned above), which can be reduced to primitives in a small number of steps.

2. The vocabulary of the metalanguage is unified to meet the requirement of a one-to-one correspondence between names and senses. This means that synonyms and homonyms are avoided. Usually the word which is most stylistically and semantically neutral is selected for the metalanguage from a given series of synonyms. *Glaza* and the bookish *ochi* [eyes] (as well as *burkaly, zenki*, and other colloquial and substandard synonyms for these) have one and the same referent, but only the stylistically unmarked *glaza* (or its syntactic derivative *glaznoi*) is used in the definition of words and expressions such as *zrachok* [pupil], *raduzhnaia obolochka* [iris], *belok* [white of eye], *brovi* [eyebrows], *veki* [eyelids], *resnitsy* [eyelashes], *trakhoma* [trachoma], *kon"iunktivit* [conjunctivitis], and *glaukoma* [glaucoma]. It would never occur to anyone to define, say, *zrachok* as 'chast' [part] oka', or *glaukoma* as 'bolezn' [disease] ochei'. Verbs such as *bresti* [to walk slowly or with difficulty], *plestis'* [to walk very slowly, as if tired], *shest-vovat'* [to walk triumphantly], *semenit'* [to walk with short mincing steps], and

*petliat'* [to dodge, double back while walking], and others are defined with the aid of the verb *idti* [to walk], and not its synonyms *stupat'* [to step] or *shagat'* [to stride], etc.

Consequently, as will be clear from the following, our metalanguage moves closer to the metalanguage of Anna Wierzbicka.

## 1.2. A THEORY OF EXPLICATION: CRITERIA FOR EXPLICATIONS AND THEIR FUNCTIONS

In recent years, in the course of work on the *New Explanatory Dictionary of Russian Synonyms*, the theory of explications has been somewhat amended.

In a dictionary of synonyms the process of explaining similarities and differences between synonyms is of primary importance. It is clear that, to explain how a given lexeme differs semantically from others, any means, in particular any periphrasis, may be used. In this connection periphrastic explications of lexemes (and other meaningful linguistic units) are divided into definitions (explications in the strict sense of the word) and freer forms of description.

Explication is only one of the periphrases of a linguistic unit, the most privileged, it is true. It performs the following four functions: (*a*) it explains the meaning of a given linguistic unit; (*b*) it serves as the basis in establishing its place in the semantic system of the language; (*c*) it is a semantic rule which may be applied in the transition from a syntactic representation of an utterance to a (surface-) semantic representation and vice versa; (*d*) it serves as the basis for the rules of semantic interaction between the given unit and other units within the utterance.

Only explications can perform functions (*b*), (*c*), and (*d*) and thus serve the needs of linguistic theory. Function (*a*), however—the metalinguistic function of explaining what a given unit means—may be performed by other periphrases, which we propose to call descriptions. If, for example, I am speaking to somebody who does not understand the verb *eliminirovat'* (*protivorechiia/prepiatstviia*) [to eliminate (differences/obstacles)] and I have reason to believe that he knows the word *ustraniat'* [to remove], I can say: 'It's the same as *ustraniat'* (*protivorechiia/prepiatstviia*).' Since the unknown word has been replaced by a known one we may regard the explanation as having taken place, although it did not take the form of an explication. The same purpose may be served by other means of communicating linguistic knowledge, among them pointing directly at the realia which are the referents in any given expression, or pointing out the practical conditions in which an expression is used. In their everyday speech native speakers of a language utilize appropriate methods when there is a need to communicate the meaning of an unfamiliar lexical unit. In this way they perform their metalinguistic activity.[1]

---

[1] A combination of definitions and descriptions is useful not only in a synonym dictionary. It should be an obligatory principle in any account of the semantics of natural languages which claims

As for explications in the strict sense, in connection with functions (*b–d*) the following four requirements were formulated: (1) they must be non-circular, (2) they must be necessary and sufficient, (3) they must be hierarchically structured, and (4) they must be explicit.

The first two criteria are purely logical and self-evident. The last two criteria are of a linguistic nature.

As will be clear from the foregoing, the presence in the metalanguage of intermediate words lays open the possibility of alternative, though synonymous explications. These may be constructed with the aid of a smaller number of large semantic blocks or a larger number of small semantic blocks. It is therefore possible to impose constraints from above on the semantic blocks (a minimum number) or from below (a maximum permissible number). The criteria regarding hierarchical structure and explicitness allow us to formulate these constraints.

### 1.2.1.  Hierarchical Structure

This means that the unit to be explicated should be presented in the form of the largest possible semantic blocks. However, there can never be fewer than two of these: if there is only one, it becomes impossible to avoid circularity. By substituting relatively large semantic blocks for the explicated meaning, a gradual breakdown is achieved of more complex senses into increasingly simple ones, down to semantic primitives.

We may take as an example an explication of the verb *obeshchat'* [to promise] by M. Ia. Glovinskaia and this writer but owing much to Wierzbicka (1987*b*: 205). '*X obeshchaet Y-u, chto sdelaet P*' [X promises Y that he will do P] = 'knowing or thinking that Y or some third person has an interest in P (presupposition), X tells Y that he will do P, in spite of possible difficulties (assertion); X says this because he wants to be believed and understands that if he does not do P people will stop believing him' (motivation).

In this explication the components 'to think', 'to know', 'to say/tell', and 'to do' constitute semantic primitives. We may note here that all these senses are used as primitives in Anna Wierzbicka's aforementioned semantic studies. The remaining components of the explication are not primitives and therefore need to be broken down further. They include the words *zainteresovan* [interested/having an interest], *nesmotria na* [in spite of], *trudno* [difficult] (see the component *trudnost'* [difficulty]), *verit'* [to believe] and *ponimat'* [to understand]. All of them can be reduced to semantic primitives in one or two steps. The respective explications follow: *A zainteresovan v B* [A has an interest in B] = 'A thinks

to be comprehensive. Only then will it be possible to conclude the protracted debate on whether circular descriptions are acceptable in accounts of meaning: they are impermissible in explications, but there is nothing to prevent their use in a freer explanation of meaning. Free paraphrase, like any other means of explaining meaning, models only the metalinguistic practice of speakers, while explications additionally model the scientific linguistic knowledge of a language.

that B is good for him and wants B to exist' (the level of primitives has been reached); *P nesmotria na R* [P in spite of R] = 'usually, if R exists, P cannot happen; in the given situation P has happened or will happen' (making an exception for the relatively simple and semantically transparent sense 'to happen', the level of primitives has been reached); *P trudno dlia A* [P is difficult for A] = 'when A does P he needs to [*neobkhodimo*] make much more effort than is normal'; *P neobkhodimo dlia R* [P is necessary for R] = 'R cannot happen if P does not exist' (the level of primitives has been reached); *X verit Y-u* [X believes Y] = 'X thinks Y is telling the truth; the only reason why X thinks this is his opinion that Y cannot tell him a lie' (the level of primitives has been reached); *X ponimaet, chto P* [X understands P] = 'X knows P; the source of this knowledge is the knowledge of the normal properties of situations of the type to which the given situation belongs' (the level of primitives has been reached).[2]

The proof that in the progress of semantic decomposition the level of primitives has been reached is the fact that it is impossible to explicate the semantic components obtained at the last stage of breakdown without circularity. *To see*, for example, can be explicated as 'to perceive with the eyes', *to hear* as 'to perceive with the ears', and so on. If we are to regard *perceive* as a semantic primitive, *eyes* and *ears* must also be accepted as semantic primitives: they cannot be explicated without mention of *sight* and *hearing* respectively, that is, without returning to the words *see* and *hear*. We may note in parenthesis that in such cases words whose referents can be demonstrated ostensively are selected as primitives.

Thus the principle of hierarchical structure, that is the gradual reduction of complex meaning to its semantic primitives, is an important feature of our general strategy of explication. As the semantic metalanguage does not permit synonyms, this strategy makes it possible to demonstrate directly all the systemic semantic links which the given unit has with a maximum number of other units within the entire lexicon. Indeed, the larger the semantic blocks from which meaning is constructed, the greater the number of intermediate steps to the level of semantic primitives, and hence the greater the number of words with which it will be explicitly linked. Let us consider some examples.

The usual dictionary explications of the words *ultimatum* and *blackmail* do not support the intuitive feeling that they have a large common semantic core. If, however, in explicating these two words we observe the simple conditions formulated above, we find quite a large area of overlap in their lexical meanings. In fact both *ultimatum* and *blackmail* include 'a demand that the addressee do something that the subject wants done, although very undesirable to the addressee, accompanied by a threat to do the addressee harm which in the subject's view greatly exceeds the undesirability of compliance, if he should fail to comply with the demand'. The difference in the semantics of *ultimatum* and *blackmail* can be reduced to the fact that *ultimatum* includes an indication of a

---

[2] The explication of *ponimat'* was subsequently modified, see Chapter 5 in this volume.

time limit (usually fairly short), in which the addressee must comply with the subject's demand, while *blackmail* involves an immoral threat to expose something shameful or illegal in the life or activity of the recipient, which he has concealed. As can be seen from these formulations, the shared area of the meanings of *ultimatum* and *blackmail*, both including such rich senses as 'demand' and 'threat', exceeds the sum of their differences.

All semantic links between various lexemes must be explicitly reflected in their explications not only when they belong to different words, as in the example examined above, but also when they belong to a single (polysemous) word. From this standpoint let us consider the lexemes *privyknut'* 1 (*rano vstavat'*, *delat' po utram zariadku*) [to become accustomed (to getting up early, to doing exercises in the morning)] and *privyknut'* 2 (*k postoiannomu shumu stankov, k novoi obstanovke*) [to become accustomed (to the constant noise of machine-tools, to a new situation)].

The difference between these two senses of the verb *privyknut'* (an action becomes a habit; a process of adaptation to some factor external to the subject takes place) is noted in all Russian explanatory dictionaries and dictionaries of synonyms. However, the usual explications do not make clear what exactly are the semantic similarities and differences between these two lexemes. See for example the following explications: *privyknut'* 1 = 'to acquire a habit (of doing something, acting in a certain way, etc.)'; *privyknut'* 2 = 'to become accustomed, get used to something' (*Shorter Academy Dictionary*); *privyknut'* 1 = 'to develop/ acquire a habit of doing something; to train oneself to do something/behave in a certain way'; *privyknut'* 2 = 'to become accustomed, get used to somebody/ something' (*Great Academy Dictionary*).

The use of metalanguage and the principles of explication described above permit us to resolve this difficulty in a natural way. *Privyknut'* 1 = 'after repeating a certain action or being in a certain state many times in the course of several periods of observation, to change as a result of this in such a way that doing this or being in this state becomes the subject's norm of behaviour or existence'. *Privyknut'* 2 = 'after spending some time in unusual conditions, to change as a result of this in such a way that these conditions become the norm or cease to be perceived as unusual'.

Two further problems are resolved at the same time.

First, explications built from relatively large blocks are psychologically most acceptable as they retain transparency. If a fairly complex lexical meaning is immediately reduced to primitives it may become virtually unrecognizable, however precise it may be. Consider the following explication, mostly (but not in every detail) reduced to primitives: *X obeshchaet Y-u, chto sdelaet P* [X promises Y that he will do P] = 'knowing or thinking that Y or some third person thinks that P is good for him and wants P to exist, X tells Y that he will do P; X knows or thinks that the situation may be such that P cannot normally happen and that X can do P only if he makes greater than normal efforts; X says this because he wants Y to think that X is telling the truth, thinking that X cannot tell him a lie; X knows that if he does not do P, Y or other people will stop thinking that X tells the truth; the source of X's knowledge is the knowledge of the normal properties of situations of the type to which the present situation belongs'.

Secondly, a basis is created not only for a qualitative appraisal of the systemic links between different linguistic units, but also for more precise quantitative appraisals. Such appraisals are desirable in at least two cases: in establishing polysemy (as distinct from homonymy) and synonymy (as distinct from freer thematic links between lexemes).[3]

At this point we may return to our explications of the words *ultimatum* and *blackmail*. A glance is all that is needed to see that the shared area of their meanings is almost double the sum of their differences. This might seem to be sufficient to pronounce them synonyms. Yet *ultimatum* and *blackmail*, like their equivalents in other languages, are not classed as synonyms in any dictionaries of synonyms. The reason for this is the semantic load and semantic value of the areas which do not coincide.

In order to provide a clearer idea of the semantic load and semantic value and at the same time introduce some measure of these properties, for simplicity's sake we shall present an explication free of inner syntax and represent each lexical sense via a list of its semantic components. In the present case this will mean components such as 'threat' (or 'to threaten'), 'aim' (cf. 'in order to'), 'demand' (or 'to demand'), 'immoral', 'exposure', 'shamefulness', 'illegality', 'short', 'time limit', etc. Each of these, as is clear from the foregoing, has a dual nature.

On the one hand they include some more basic semantic components, which in the final analysis can be reduced to the most basic (indefinable) senses— semantic primitives. *To demand*, for instance, can be reduced to semantic primitives such as 'to want' (somebody to do something), 'to say' (what the subject wants him to do), 'to think' (that he must do this), 'to do', and a number of others. In the same way we could present 'threat', 'aim', 'time limit', and all other components in the explication of *ultimatum* and *blackmail*.

On the other hand, each of these components forms part of the more complex units of the object language. The component 'demand', for example, forms part of the lexical meanings of words such as *blackmail*, *to extort*, *ultimatum*, *strike* (= a work stoppage by the workers of an enterprise, accompanied by a series of demands put to the management of the enterprise or state authority as a condition for resuming work) and many others.

It follows that each component may be quantitatively described by two figures: the number of semantic primitives which it contains, and the number of object-language units of which it is a component. We will term the former its

---

[3] This is not to assert that such appraisals can already be obtained, or that there is a need to obtain them. It is claimed only that explications formulated in the metalanguage proposed here, and observing all the conditions set forth above, provide a better basis for such appraisals than the traditional language of lexicography and traditional explications.

semantic load and the latter its semantic value. The semantic load of a given component is directly proportionate to the number of basic senses contained within it. Its semantic value, by contrast, is inversely proportionate to the number of lexical meanings which include it. The more often it occurs the more trivial it is. It is the very rarity of the component, like the scarcity of gold in rock or of pearls in oysters, which lends it heightened semantic value.[4]

Let us apply these considerations to our example. It is immediately obvious that 'immorality', 'exposure', 'shamefulness', and 'illegality' contained in the lexeme *blackmail* are extremely rich semantic components. Their aggregate weight, expressed by the number of basic semantic components contained in them, is very great.

The temporal component in the explication of *ultimatum* has much less load. In fact, *time limit* [srok] is naturally interpreted as 'a segment of time', and 'segment' and 'time' are clearly semantic primitives. The notion 'short' in the collocation *short time limit* comes down to three primitives: 'less than normal time'.

Therefore, if the component 'time limit' has any weight in the explication of *ultimatum*, this weight is defined not so much by its semantic load but rather by its semantic value. The semantic value of any component, as stated above, is inversely proportionate to the number of lexical meanings which contain it. The number of lexical meanings containing the idea of a time limit is extremely small. Three compact classes of such words come to mind: words meaning to acquire something for a while or for temporary use (*to rent, to hire, to let, to lend, to borrow, to recruit*, and their semantic derivatives); words meaning a pause during some activity (*interruption, stoppage, recess, cigarette break, armistice*, etc.); and prepositions such as *for* (*for two years*). By being so rare the 'time limit' component acquires high value, and therefore weight.

By comparing the weight of the components which coincide and those which differ in the structure of various lexical and grammatical meanings we are able to define more precisely the degree of their semantic closeness.

## 1.2.2. Explicitness

We move on to the next linguistic criterion to be applied to explications, that of explicitness. This stipulates that an explication should directly spell out all the semantic components with which the meanings of the other lexical or grammatical units of the given utterance interact. If, for example, a semantic rule establishes the interaction of lexeme A with semantic component X, that component must be explicitly included in the explication, even if this involves violating the criterion of hierarchical structure. This means that the criterion of explicitness takes precedence over that of hierarchical structure and fixes the lower limit of

---

[4] Here it should be borne in mind that it is not only the complex semantic components that vary in weight, but also the semantic primitives: compare, for example, the primitive *delat'* [to do/make] and the far more weighty (semantically more valuable) primitives *khotet'* [to want], *chuvstvovat'* [to feel], or *govorit'* [to speak/say].

semantic reduction: there must be as many semantic blocks in the structure of an explication as are required by the rules of semantic interaction.

Let us consider an example. A phrase of the type *khoroshaia retsenziia* [a good review] is ambiguous. It usually expresses a positive evaluation of the work under review: *on napisal khoroshuiu retsenziiu, no eta kniga zasluzhivaet luchshei* [he wrote a good review, but this book deserves better]. It is possible, however, to use the same phrase to express a positive evaluation of the literary and analytical properties of the review itself: *on napisal ochen' khoroshuiu retsenziiu: teper' vsem budet iasno, chto eta kniga nikuda ne goditsia* [he wrote a very good review: now it will be clear to everybody that this book is worthless]. Compare the unambiguous phrases *polozhitel'naia retsenziia* [a positive review] (praising only the book) and *interesnaia retsenziia* [an interesting review] (praising only the review itself).

The question arises: how much detail should go into the explication of the word *retsenziia* [review] in order to explain this ambiguity? The following explication seems to satisfy this condition: *retsenziia* (*Y-a na Z*) [review (by Y of Z)] = 'written analysis of a scholarly or artistic text Z by Y, in which Y gives an evaluation of Z'. The evaluative adjective 'good' may, by virtue of a special rule for words of the type *good, bad, positive, negative*, and certain others in the context of nouns of the type 'review', apply to the component of 'evaluation'. This gives us the first interpretation: 'a positive appraisal'. On the other hand, in accordance with the general rule for all qualitative adjectives, 'good' may apply to any component denoting an action or the result of an action. This gives the second interpretation: 'a good analysis'. In this way the ambiguity of the collocation 'a good review' acquires a formal explanation.

To sum up the foregoing, the metalanguage of lexicography is a sub-language of the object language, comprising a relatively small and unified vocabulary and syntax. The basis of this metalanguage is semantic primitives. With the aid of the metalanguage, complex semantic units of the object language (grammatical as well as lexical) are reduced to a fixed structure of semantic primitives by a process of hierarchical breakdown. The resulting explications (definitions) have a specific theoretical status: using them as a basis we may establish systematic paradigmatic links between various units of the language and formulate rules for the interaction of linguistic meanings.

## 2. The Approach of the Polish Semantic School to the Language of Explications

We now move on to the concept of a semantic metalanguage and semantic primitives developed by the Polish Semantic School. Among Polish linguists who have treated these problems, Anna Wierzbicka occupies the foremost position. She has carried out the immense and absolutely unique empirical task of establishing the set of primitives, given a profound theoretical analysis of this concept and applied the primitives she has discovered to the explication of a vast body of lexical and grammatical material in several dozen languages of different types. Her ideas in their present form (see Wierzbicka 1992: 6-18) may be summarized as follows:

1. Human languages display very extensive variety at the level of complex concepts (semantically complex lexemes), which are for the most part specific to a given language. However, at the level of the simplest concepts they display full unanimity: in one way or another (by lexemes, grammatical forms, or syntactic structures) these concepts are expressed in all human languages. Such simple concepts are very few in number. Wierzbicka's list of 1992 includes the following: *I, you, somebody, something, this, everything, two, to say, to want, not to want, to feel, to think, to know, to be able, to do, to happen, good, bad, similar, the same, where, when, after, because of, if.*

2. The words of the semantic metalanguage are not simply an inventory of concepts. They can be broken down into grammatical categories (nouns, determinatives, verbs, adjectives) from whose elements the simplest syntactic structures and sentences can be formed. Examples of such sentences are: *I think this; I want this; You are doing this; This happened; Somebody did something bad; Because of this something bad happened.* These most simple of syntactic structures in natural languages are also universal.

3. In the same way, in every natural language a universal mini-language, consisting of the simplest words and syntactic structures, may be identified. All the more complex units of that language, in terms of content (lexemes, grammemes, affixes, syntactic types), may be explicated in this mini-language. Moreover, they must be explicated in precisely this way, that is, directly via primitives. Only when this condition is met is it possible to compare all human languages and cultures on the same basis. It should be emphasized particularly that to describe any types of meaning (lexical, morphological, syntactic, etc.) the same semantic language, which Wierzbicka terms 'the language of thought', is applied.

4. Since mini-languages coincide it matters little which one is selected as a 'working' language: English, Russian, Polish, or others. In most of her writings Wierzbicka uses an English mini-language.

The fundamental similarity between the theories of the Moscow Semantic School and those of Anna Wierzbicka can be seen at a glance. It lies in the fact that a semantic metalanguage, understood as a language with its own vocabulary and syntax, is seen as the principal instrument of semantic description. This metalanguage is a sub-language of the object language and has nothing in common with the language of 'distinctive semantic features'. In both metalanguages a special role is allotted to semantic primitives. Both metalanguages are designed to describe both lexical and grammatical meanings.

However, there are also some differences.

The first concerns the status and function of explications in linguistic theory. In the Moscow School, explications are constructed hierarchically. This requirement has a theoretical status since compliance with it permits one to demonstrate a system in the organization of the lexicon. In Wierzbicka's scheme, hierarchical explications are permissible only as a technical device and only in exceptional cases. Furthermore, in the Moscow School, explications are the object of semantic rules by which the meaning of whole utterances is built from the meanings of the individual grammatical and lexical units. In the Polish School, the question of the interaction of meanings occupies a less prominent position.

The second difference, more substantial in the context of the present work, concerns the treatment of semantic primitives.

## 3. The Problem of Semantic Primitives

With regard to semantic primitives Wierzbicka's central thesis is that they represent the simplest and final atoms of sense and that they are therefore universal (cross-cultural, cross-linguistic). We shall endeavour to demonstrate that semantic primitives are not in fact necessarily so extremely simple in their meaning and that, generally speaking, they do not possess the property of universality.

In fact even the simplest words of natural language, in addition to a certain prototypical kernel, contain some particle of meaning which distinguishes a given word from its close synonyms. It is precisely this particle which is in many cases language-specific. We shall use the example of the semantic primitives *khotet'* [to want] and English *to want* to illustrate this point.

The English verb *to want*, used by Wierzbicka as a semantic primitive, undoubtedly shares a general semantic component with the verb *to wish*. The meanings of the two verbs intersect without matching: *want*, in addition to the wish proper, expresses the idea of need, deficiency, absence (*I want it badly*; *good advice is wanted*), while *wish* expresses the idea of abstract desire. It is no accident that *wish* is used in counter-factual constructions of the type *I wish he were here*. However, the unquestionably simpler semantic component which forms the point of intersection of the two meanings cannot be verbalized by a word or some other meaningful unit of the English language. It follows that *want* may be considered a primitive only in the sense that it is not amenable to further reduction within the framework of English.

The same applies to the Russian verbs *khotet'* [want] and *zhelat'* [wish]. Of the two, *khotet'* has the stronger claim to the role of primitive, being the more neutral and semantically less specific. However, its meaning does not exactly match that of the verb *zhelat'*. In addition to the basic idea of *wish* it expresses the idea of *need* (*Ia khochu est'* [I want to eat/I'm hungry]) and of active will and intention (compare *Ia khochu* [I want] and *Mne khochetsia* [I feel like]). In point of fact, Russian sentences such as *ia khotel rasskazat' ei, chto ia perezhil* [I wanted to tell her what I had been through] are ambiguous, meaning either 'I wanted to tell her . . .' (*ia tak khotel rasskazat' ei, chto ia perezhil* [I wanted so much to tell her what I had been through]), or 'I intended to tell her', (*Snachala ia khotel rasskazat' ei, chto ia perezhil, no potom razdumal* [At first I wanted to tell her what I'd been through, but then I changed my mind]). The notion of intention in the semantics of *khotet'* is so strong that it is included directly in the definition of this verb in Ozhegov's and Shvedova's dictionary ('to have a desire, intention (to do something)'), and the *Great* and *Shorter Academy Dictionaries* and some other explanatory dictionaries spell out a second meaning 'to intend'.

For its part the verb *zhelat'* may denote a 'spineless' wish: for example, 'Against these [Rudin *et al.*] he sets people with the ability not merely to wish [*zhelat'*] but to want [*khotet'*]' (A. Koni). In addition it may be used 'from the top down', to denote a wish which the subject regards as something to be performed by others: compare *Ia zhelaiu, chtoby tsygane peli vsiu noch'* [I wish to have the gypsies sing all night] and *Ia khochu poslushat' penie tsygan* [I want to hear the gypsies sing]; see also *Ne zhelaete li zakazat' obed v nomer* [Do you wish to order lunch in your room?] and *Chto zhelaete nadet'—khalatik ili pizhamu?* [What do you wish to put on—your dressing gown or your pyjamas?] (M. Bulgakov); '*Eti gospoda zhelaiut s toboi pobesedovat',' skazal Shuvalov* ['These gentlemen wish to speak to you,' said Shuvalov] (Iu. Daniel'). (For more detail see Chapter 6 in this volume.)

Thus both verbs are semantically complex: the meaning of each of them comprises a simpler general part (which for convenience we term 'the wish proper') and a number of specific accretions. However, since this general component cannot be verbalized by any single word or any other meaningful unit in Russian, one or other of these verbs should have the status of a primitive.[5] The verb *khotet'* has the stronger claim to this role, being the more neutral and semantically less specific.

---

[5] It may be thought that the collocation 'the wish proper' is the form required to express the corresponding semantic primitive. This hypothesis should be rejected. The word *chistoe* [pure, proper] in the collocation *chistoe zhelanie* [the wish/desire proper] may have either a limiting meaning 'only, exclusively' or a metalinguistic meaning 'strictly, in the strict sense'. Both these meanings are clearly much more complex than is permissible for semantic primitives. (See e.g. the explication of *tol'ko* [only] in I. Boguslavsky (1985: 88 ff.). Moreover, in both cases it is necessary to perform certain operations on the lexical meaning of the noun 'wish' in order to extract the meaning of the whole collocation. It is evident that such operations, particularly metalinguistic operations, are incompatible with the status of a semantic primitive, whose meaning must be immediately apparent. Nor can we accept the hypothesis that the noun *zhelanie* itself might serve as a semantic primitive. While it is simpler in certain respects than the verb *zhelat'*, it also has significant semantic accretions. Chief among them is the idea of the intensity of the state and the indication, linked with this, that it urgently requires resolution and realization: *nepreodolimoe zhelanie* [irrepressible desire], *ostroe zhelanie* [urgent wish], *goret' ⟨tomit'sia⟩ zhelaniem* [to burn with ⟨be in an agony of⟩ desire], *sderzhivat' svoi zhelaniia* [to curb one's desires]; *ia khochu videt' i ne mogu osvobodit'sia ot etogo zhelaniia* [I want to see and cannot free myself of this wish] (V. G. Korolenko); *ia pochuvstvoval nastoichivoe zhelanie rasskazat' komu-nibud' o babushke* [I felt an insistent desire to tell somebody about Granny] (M. Gor'kii). Furthermore, semantically speaking, *zhelanie* is closer to a stative verbal noun from *khotet'* than from *zhelat'*; *ia khochu spat'* [I want to sleep]—*moe zhelanie spat'* [my wish to sleep], but not [?]*ia zhelaiu spat'* [I wish to sleep].

Thus in Russian too the simpler semantic component forming the intersection of *khotet'* and *zhelat'* cannot be verbalized. Therefore, instead of a true primitive, i.e. the very simplest of senses, we are obliged to resort to the quasi-primitive *khotet'*.[6]

The position becomes even more complex if we consider other English and Russian verbs meaning 'wish', such as *desire, khotet'sia* [feel like], and others. *Desire* intensifies the notion of active will which is expressed by the verb *want* (*He received the position he desired*), while *khotet'sia*, by contrast, weakens it. This verb has the same semantic core as *khotet'*, but a different semantic accretion: the wish is seen as the result of the action of some ill-defined force which a person feels within himself. The shared part of the meaning of the two verbs in this case cannot be verbalized in Russian. As we move towards the periphery of corresponding series of synonyms in English and Russian the difference between them increases, as is usual in such cases. Compare the English verbs *to covet, to long, to yearn* and the Russian *mechtat'* (*sdelat' chto-to*) [to dream of doing something] and *zhazhdat'* (*sdelat' chto-to*) [to long to do something].

Thus we have established that neither *want* nor *khotet'*, which have a large common area of meaning, are semantically simple words. Furthermore the semantic accretions which complicate the sense of 'the wish proper' are specific to English and Russian respectively. It follows that neither of these lexemes has any advantage whatever as an element of a universal semantic language.

It is words of this kind, which are not amenable to further semantic decomposition within the limits of a given language, although not necessarily utterly simple in meaning, that we shall in future term 'semantic primitives'. Semantic primitiveness is determined, therefore, by the structure of the lexicon of the language being described: lexeme L is considered a primitive if the given language has no $L_1, L_2 \ldots L_n$ via which it might be explicated.

Similar considerations may be adduced for many other claimants to semantic primitiveness (*znat'* and *know; dumat'* and *think; govorit'* and *say*) but we shall not attempt this. It is more important to show why even such relatively simple words—semantically speaking—as *khotet'* and *want, znat'* and *know, govorit'* and *say*, and others do not fully coincide in meaning and why it cannot be otherwise.

The words of natural language which are selected for the role of primitives are always 'foreground' words, those most firmly established in a language and cul-

---

[6] From this it follows that the verb *khotet'* cannot be explicated without violating the minimal requirements of the theory of explication. Attempts to do so (see e.g. Trub (1993: 282) and Zalizniak (1992: 61)) give rise to objections. The most serious attempt is this: *X wants P* = 'X feels that P is good' (Zalizniak 1992: 61). It can easily be seen that this explication is deficient. It takes no account of such notions as need, active will, or intention (see above). I can feel that something is good without desiring it in the least, if my corresponding need is already satisfied, for example. On the other hand, *khorosho* [good] might equally well be explicated via *khotet'*: *P is good* = 'P is such that it is normal to want it'. This possibility in itself is evidence that we have reached the level of fundamental senses, i.e. those which cannot be further broken down. In fact the senses of *khotet'* and *khorosho* are not amenable to explication.

ture. They serve the greatest number of pragmatic situations, which lend them varying coloration. On the other hand, they are the most thoroughly exploited in a cultural tradition and therefore acquire the most varied associations. Take for example the contrast between *khotet'* and *khotet'sia* (see above), so typical of Russian culture, supported by other similarly contrasting pairs (*dumat'* [to think] —*dumat'sia*; *rabotat'* [to work]—*rabotat'sia*; *pisat'* [to write]—*pisat'sia*; *spat'* [to sleep]—*spat'sia*, and others). If semantically complex lexemes are specific to a language on account of the uniqueness of a combination of simpler senses, then semantically simple lexemes are specific to a language on account of the uniqueness of their denotational connections in the language and culture.

The foregoing argument, for all its lack of rigour, permits us to conclude that with the aid of a semantic metalanguage, conceived as a sub-language of the object language, the national semantics of that given language may be well described. A universal (cross-cultural) semantic metalanguage should evidently be based on an artificial logical language, the words of which are true primitives— the intersecting parts of words which partially translate one another in natural languages. We are dealing with a kind of semantic quark, with senses which actually exist but which are not materialized in the vocabulary of natural languages.

An example of such a quark is provided by stative verbs. As we know, stative verbs denoting homogeneous states, properties, and relations (*videt'* [to see], *slyshat'* [to hear], *khotet'* [to want], *zhelat'* [to wish], *znat'* [to know], *schitat'* [to consider], *dumat'* (*chto*) [to think (that)], *gordit'sia* [to be proud of], *stydit'sia* [to be ashamed], *zavidovat'* [to envy], *stoit'* [to cost/be worth], *vesit'* [to weigh], *izobrazhat'* [to depict] (*Kartina izobrazhaet zimnii les* [The painting depicts a forest in winter]), *otnosit'sia* [to belong to] (*Pumy otnosiatsia k semeistvu koshek* [Pumas belong to the cat family]), *vysit'sia* [to tower], *belet'* [to show white], etc.) behave almost identically in various natural languages.

(*a*) They are characterized by having a defective grammatical paradigm. They have no imperative, passive, or strictly aspectual perfective. (We cannot say, *\*Khoti uekhat'* [Want to go away!], *\*Vid' kartinu* [See a picture!]; *\*Kartina videlas' im* [A picture was seen by him], *\*Im schitalos', chto sem'e bez nego prishlos' trudno* [It was thought by him that it was hard for the family without him]; *\*Kartina izobrazila zimnii les* [The picture showed (pf) a forest in winter], *\*Pumy otneslis' k semeistvu koshek* [Pumas belonged (pf) to the cat family].) If a stative verb nominally possesses one of these forms it never has its prototypical sense. Thus, the imperative form of statives never conveys an urge to do something, but has instead one of a variety of modal meanings. Cf. *Gordis'! takov i ty, poet* [Be proud! You are his like, O poet.] (~ you should be proud), *Boisia danaitsev* [Fear the Greeks] (~ you ought to fear), *Schitai, chto tebe povezlo* [Consider yourself lucky] (~ you may consider, in spite of a rather slim basis), *Dumai, chto khochesh'* [Think what you like] (~ you may think whatever you like; what you think is a matter of indifference to me), *Znai, chto ona tebia liubit* [Know that she loves you] (shared knowledge). In none of these cases does the imperative have its usual imperative sense of a stimulus to action. For more details see J. Apresjan (1988: 30–2); see also the analysis of *znat'* in Bulygina (1982: 72).

(*b*) They are characterized by having a defective semantic paradigm. They are not used with progressive-durative meaning, future meaning, or certain other senses of the imperfective. (We cannot say, *\*On voshel, kogda ia videl pokhoron-nuiu protsessiiu na ulitse* ⟨*slyshal kakie-to strannye zvuki v uglu*⟩ [He entered while I was seeing a funeral procession in the street ⟨hearing some strange sounds in the corner⟩]; *\*Zavtra kilogramm kartoshki stoit piat'sot rublei* [Tomorrow a kilogram of potatoes costs a hundred roubles]; *\*Zavtra on znaet matematiku v ob"eme universitetskogo kursa* [Tomorrow he knows mathematics to the extent of a university course].)

(*c*) They cannot combine with inclusive temporal circumstances, purpose phrases, with most *Aktionsarten*, or with verbs such as *zanimat'sia* [to occupy oneself] or *delat'* [to do]. (The following are not possible: *\*On videl kartinu za odnu minutu* ⟨*znal matematiku za tri dnia*⟩ [He saw the picture in one minute ⟨knew mathematics in three days⟩]; *\*S tsel'iu postupit' v universitet on znaet matematiku* [With the aim of entering university he knows mathematics]; *\*S tsel'iu postavit' patsienta na nogi vrachi dumaiut, chto emu nuzhno prinimat' khvoinye vanny* [With the aim of getting the patient out of bed the doctors think he should take pine-needle baths]; *\*Lovko* ⟨*postepenno, tshchatel'no*⟩ *schital eti pretenzii nesostoiatel'nymi* [Adroitly ⟨gradually, meticulously⟩ I/you/he considered these complaints unfounded]; *\*Zanimalsia tem, chto gordilsia svoimi uspekhami* ⟨*stydilsia svoei bednosti*⟩ [He was engaged in priding himself on his successes ⟨being ashamed of his poverty⟩].)

It is clear that the shared reaction of stative verbs to other linguistic units of varying level (morphological, syntactic, semantic) is semantically motivated. We must posit the presence in their meanings of some common sense which is, however, so small that it cannot be materialized in the form of a word of natural language in the explication. A brief glance at the above short list of stative verbs is sufficient to show that no remotely sensible explication of them or of other similar words can contain any common denotational element.

It seems that there are other kinds of semantic quarks. T. V. Bulygina's hypothesis (conveyed orally to the author) is of interest in this connection. It concerns the categorial meaning of a part of speech as an element of the meaning of a word, always present in a word although it cannot be verbalized.

The sense which cannot be materialized in any individual word was termed in an earlier work (J. Apresjan 1980: 25 ff.) a non-trivial semantic feature. This is the true semantic primitive. It is precisely of such primitives (or 'constructs', or 'quarks') that the vocabulary of the universal semantic language will be built.

# 9

# Lexicographic Portraits (A Case Study of the Verb *byt'* [to be])

## 1. The Concept of the Lexicographic Portrait and the Lexicographic Type

### 1.1. THE LEXICOGRAPHIC PORTRAIT

The term 'portrait', applied to the description of words, was introduced by Zholkovsky (1964*b*). There, however, portrayal was understood only as the full semantic account of a lexeme, achieved by placing it in the broadest possible range of contexts and testing its applicability for the description of the broadest possible range of situations.

Views of the lexicographically relevant properties of lexemes have subsequently expanded considerably. In particular, a much fuller account of not only the semantic but also the co-occurrence properties of lexemes was undertaken in *The Explanatory and Combinatorial Dictionary of Modern Russian* (ECD) (Mel'čuk and Zholkovsky 1984). Another dictionary (Benson, Benson, Ilson 1986), based to a large extent on the ideas of ECD (but unfortunately not stating this explicitly), is also of interest.

Alongside the renewal of lexicography (for a fuller survey of lexicographical innovations see J. Apresjan 1990*a*), new tendencies in theoretical linguistics have been gathering momentum, and 'linguistic portrayal' has developed into an independent area. Suffice it to mention such works as Iordanskaja (1970 and 1972); Mel'čuk (1985); I. Boguslavsky (1985); Wierzbicka (1972, 1980, 1985, and 1987*b*).

Thus the prerequisites for a new synthesis of lexicography and linguistics have been established; see J. Apresjan (1986*b*) for an attempt at such a synthesis.

Developing further the ideas expounded in J. Apresjan (1986*b*: 57–70), by the term 'lexicographic portrait' we shall mean a description of *all the linguistically relevant properties of a lexeme* within the framework of an integrated description of a language.

An integrated description implies, in particular, that in the dictionary all properties to which linguistic rules may refer should be explicitly ascribed to each lexeme. In the present context these rules include not only strictly grammatical rules, but also semantic, pragmatic, communicative, and other rules.

Consideration of the lexeme against the background of a complete set of linguistic rules, with due account taken of all its connections in the lexicon and within an utterance, compels us to take an entirely new view of its lexicographically significant properties. It emerges that these are far more numerous and varied than has customarily been thought to date.

The metaphor of a lexicographic portrait is first of all meant to suggest that a dictionary entry should store new types of information hitherto not recorded in dictionaries, and should considerably expand the amount of traditional information.

Among the features never previously described or not described in any systematic fashion we may mention the prosodic, pragmatic, and communicative properties of lexemes (see the material on this subject in the entry for *byt'* given in § 3, and the discussion of factivity in this section).

As for the increased volume of traditional information, this bears above all on the co-occurrence properties of lexemes. In addition to lexical and semantic constraints, these now include prosodic, morphological, pragmatic, communicative, and syntactic co-occurrence constraints. Previously they had received less attention than was their due because they are clearly manifested only within a sentence or utterance.

Even the semantic information—the basis of any explanatory dictionary—has increased substantially in volume. A lexeme cannot, for example, become the object of effective rules of paraphrasing if its dictionary entry does not include different lexical functions—exact and inexact synonyms, conversives, antonyms, hyperonyms, syntactic and semantic derivatives and the semi-auxiliary words which serve them (see Mel'čuk 1974a on the lexical functions and rules of paraphrasing).

The second difference between a lexicographic portrait and a usual dictionary entry lies in the way in which the information is organized. In the past, dictionary-makers were content to register separately the various facets of a lexeme. The current principles of lexicographic portrayal require the dictionary entry to present the more complex picture of the *interaction between the different facets of the lexeme*. It is clear, for example, that the government and co-occurrence properties of a lexeme are to a large extent motivated by its meaning. The nature of its lexical meaning will in some cases also define its prosodic features, which in turn are linked with its communicative features.

This interdependence deserves further consideration and will be commented on at some length below, even at the cost of deviating slightly from our main topic. An instructive example is furnished by factive words.

The factive verbs *ponimat'* [to understand], *znat'* [to know], and *videt'* [to see, in the sense of 'understand'] in affirmative sentences may bear the main phrasal stress regardless of their position in the sentence: *On ↓znal, chto emu nichto ne ugrozhaet* [he knew that there was no threat to him]; *↓vizhu, kuda ty klonish'* [I can see what you're driving at, see your drift]. In general interrogative sentences, the main phrasal stress on the factive verb becomes almost a necessity: *vy ↑znaete ⟨vidite⟩, chto vam nichto ne ugrozhaet?* [do you know ⟨see⟩ that there's no threat to you?]. Thus the factives form part of the rhematic element of the utterance. This feature becomes especially noticeable against the background of the prototypical putative verbs *schitat'* [to consider], *polagat'* [to presume], *nakhodit'* [to find]. In comparable conditions (not at the end of a sentence), putatives cannot bear the main phrasal stress and belong to the theme of the utterance: *on schital ⟨polagal⟩, chto emu nichto ne ugrozhaet* [he believed ⟨assumed⟩ there was no threat to him]; *ia nakhozhu, chto vashi trevogi naprásny* [I find your concerns unnecessary]; *vy schitaete ⟨polagaete, nakhodite⟩, chto vam nichto ne ugrozháet?* [do you believe ⟨assume, find⟩ that there is no threat to you?]. The only possible type of prosodic emphasis for putatives is contrastive, not main phrasal stress: *vy ↑↑schitaete ⟨polagaete⟩, chto vam nichto ne ugrozhaet (ili vy eto ↓znaete)?* [do you believe ⟨assume⟩ that there is no threat to you (or do you know it)?].

Even verbs which are not prototypically factive acquire this property when they receive the main phrasal stress in certain syntactic conditions. Such is the verb *govorit'—skazat'* [to say], for example, in general interrogative sentences: *on ↑skazal, chto mat' bol'ná?* [did he say his mother was ill?] (factive; the speaker knows the mother is ill) vs. *on skazal, chto mat' ↑bol'na?* (putative; the speaker does not know whether the mother is ill and seeks information about this). The factive nature of the stressed *skazal* and the putative nature of the unstressed verb are further confirmed by the fact that stressed *skazat'* may freely co-occur with an indirect question, while the unstressed *skazat'* cannot: *on ↑skazal, kuda uekhal otets?* [did he say where his father had gone?] vs. *ᵎon skazal, kuda uekhal otets?* Compare also the following two uses of the English verb *to understand:* *I ↓understand your mother is ill* (factive: the mother is ill) vs. *I understand your mother is ↑ill* (putative; the speaker supposes that the mother is ill).

The link between factivity, main phrasal stress, and a certain type of communicative organization of the utterance may be traced in other classes of words. We may mention the factive adverb *deistvitel'no* [really] and the factive adjective *nastoiashchii* [real].

The adverb *deistvitel'no* has only factive meaning, expressed in two uses —circumstantial and parenthetic. In the former case it almost always bears the main phrasal stress: *ona stoiala spinoi, [. . .] no chuvstvovalas'—devushka ↓deistvitel'no grustit* [she was standing with her back to them, (. . .) but you could sense that the girl really was grief-stricken] (E. Katerli). In the latter, the main phrasal stress is possible, though not obligatory: *deistvitel'no, zagadochnye ptitsy okazalis' vinno-ognennymi list'iami klena* [the mysterious birds actually turned out to be fiery-purple maple leaves] (B. Pasternak); *govorili, chto Il'inu vezet. I ↓deistvitel'no, vse u nego poluchalos' udivitel'no vovremia i skladno* [It was said that Il'in was lucky. And indeed, everything he did turned out surprisingly timely and harmonious] (V. Kaverin). Unlike the factive *deistvitel'no*, putative adverbs and adverbial phrases such as *veroiatno* [probably], *vozmozhno* [possibly], and *dolzhno byt'* [it must be] never bear the main phrasal stress. The behaviour of *deistvitel'no* is the more interesting for the fact that parenthesis as a syntactic phenomenon is prosodically marked by precisely the impossibility (in the over-whelming majority of cases) of the main phrasal stress on the parenthetic word (see Zalizniak and Paducheva 1987).

The adjective *nastoiashchii* was first described from the prosodic point of view by A. V. Pavlova (1987). Comparing *borodach —↓nastoiashchii razboinik* [the one with the beard is a real gangster] (*nastoiashchii*—real, an outstanding specimen of smth.) and *borodach—nastoiashchii ↓razboinik* (*nastoiashchii*—real, undoubt-ed), Pavlova links the difference in the semantics and prosody of the two senses with the presence or absence of an evaluative component in the noun. 'The word *razboinik* in the first example has no evaluative connotation; in the second it expresses a negative evaluation' (Pavlova 1987: 8). In our view these observa-tions need to be amplified and qualified.

The adjective *nastoiashchii* is of particular interest, compared to the verbs and adverbs analysed above, in that it combines the factive and putative meanings in one word. The factive meaning is: *X nastoiashchii Y* = 'X possesses all the essential properties of objects belonging to class Y and none of the essential properties of objects of other classes'. (*Ia nikogda ne videl nastoiashchego nosoroga* [I have never seen a real rhinoceros]). The putative meaning is: *X nastoiashchii Y* = 'X has very many of the properties of objects belonging to class Y and is therefore perceived as something very like such an object, but X lacks the main essential property of objects of that class and therefore does not belong to it' (*Na kryshe khaty moei stoiala devushka . . . nastoiashchaia rusalka* [on the roof of my house stood a girl . . . a real mermaid] (M. Iu. Lermontov)).

As may be seen even in these two examples, the factive lexeme *nastoiashchii* does not always bear the main phrasal stress or fulfil the rhematic function. Its prosody and communicative function are determined by three factors.

First of all, the noun Y, with which the adjective *nastoiashchii* co-occurs, should be used in its basic meaning. If used in a comparative (metaphorical) meaning 'in some way similar to Y', it automatically reduces *nastoiashchii* to its putative meaning; for example, *eto—nastoiashchii stol* [this is a real table] (said of a large flat-topped tree-stump at which campers might eat a meal).

Secondly, the basic meaning of Y need not be purely evaluative. If it is, the adjective *nastoiashchii* displays its factive meaning regardless of prosody: *ona nastoiashchaia krasavitsa* [she's a real beauty].

The last condition applies to the syntactic structure of the sentence: noun Y should appear as a post-copula dependent and the adjective *nastoiashchii* as its qualifier. (If *nastoiashchii* itself occupies this position alone it can have only its factive meaning: *eti den'gi—nastoiashchie* [this money is real].) Constructions with factive, putative, descriptive, declarative, and other such copulas, in which Y occupies the position of direct object and the adjective *nastoiashchii* its second complement, are variants of the basic copula construction. Cf. *ego izobrazili nastoiashchim mafiozi* [he was shown as a real mafiosi]; *ia schitaiu ego nastoiash-chim mafiozi* [I regard him as a real mafiosi], etc.

If all these conditions are met, the adjective *nastoiashchii* in its factive meaning bears the main phrasal stress (*eto*—↓*nastoiashchee vino* [this is real wine]; *on*—↓*nastoiashchii artist* [he's a real artist]; *ia schitaiu ego* ↓*nastoiashchim artistom* [I consider him a real artist]) and forms the rheme of the utterance, with the noun Y in its basic meaning. In its putative sense *nastoiashchii* does not have the main phrasal stress (*Vash kvas*—*nastoiashchee vino* [your kvas is real wine], *vash rebenok*—*nastoiashchii artist* [your child as a real artist], *ia schitaiu vashego rebenka nastoiashchim artistom* [I regard your child as a real artist]) and is communicatively neutral, and the noun Y either has its comparative meaning (*artist* in the second example) or is used metaphorically (*vino* in the first example).

The fact that words with factive meaning attract the main phrasal stress and tend to a position in the rheme has profound pragmatic motivation. When aiming at co-operative dialogue it is natural to accentuate reliable information, i.e. knowledge. On the other hand, words with putative meaning repel the main phrasal stress and tend towards a position in the theme because their informational input into the utterance is insignificant: they simply make explicit the trivial modus 'ia schitaiu' which implicitly introduces every utterance.

The third difference between a lexicographic portrait and a standard dictionary description concerns the explication of the lexical meaning of the word. Standard dictionary explications are single-stratum semantic structures: all the elements used in them are treated as having equal status. Research over recent decades, however, has shown that within linguistic meanings there are several different layers: assertions, presuppositions, modal frames, observation frames, and motivations. Within assertions, strong and weak semantic components have been identified. The particular features of different layers of meaning and different components within one layer manifest themselves in the fact that they react in different ways to other meanings which are present in the utterance. All these facts should, of course, be fully reflected in the lexicographic portrait.

Finally, it should be noted that a lexicographic portrait should correspond to one or several lexicographic types. Only then is it possible to say that the lexicographic description meets the requirement that it be systematic. The concept of the lexicographic type is the subject of a separate work (Chapter 10 in this volume) so only a definition and one simple illustration are given here.

## 1.2. THE LEXICOGRAPHIC TYPE

'Lexicographic type' is the name we give to a more or less compact group of lexemes which have shared semantic, pragmatic, syntactic, combinatorial, prosodic, communicative, morphological, or other linguistically significant properties and therefore need homogeneous dictionary descriptions. The more interesting lexicographic types have a number of such shared properties and a number of linguistic rules which refer to them. They display motivated connections between the various facets of the member lexemes and reflect the nationally specific naïve picture of the world embodied in a given language. An empirically found set of lexicographic types is the most natural and reliable basis on which to compile any dictionary which purports to give a systematic description of the lexicon.

A good example of a lexicographic type is provided by the parametric nouns denoting the linear dimensions of a physical body: *dlina* [length], *vysota* [height], *shirina* [width, breadth], *tolshchina* [thickness], and *glubina* [depth]. These have a number of semantic, syntactic, and morphological properties in common.

Of primary semantic interest is the fact that these parametric nouns, like the corresponding adjectives, reflect the basic principles of a naïve conceptualization of spatial relations. The main principle is that of relativism: in the naïve picture of spatial relations, unlike scientific geometry (including non-Euclidean geometry), the linear dimensions of a physical body are not autonomous. They depend upon one another (except for depth, which is autonomous and absolute); on the features of external shape, inner structure, and the functions of the physical body to which they are ascribed; on whether it has support on the ground; on how many times its dimensions exceed those of the human body; on the position of the observer (who, incidentally, differs from the observer of the theory of relativity) in relation to the physical body; and on a number of other factors.

The linear dimensions of a body form a hierarchy, in which length and height come first, width second, and thickness third. Position in the hierarchy is determined by the nature of the object, by the dimensions it may have, and by the way its various linear dimensions relate to one another. Length and height may be ascribed to an object even when, from the standpoint of naïve geometry, it has no other linear dimensions; for example, the length of a railway line or the height of a mountain. Breadth requires a two-dimensional object, that is, an object with at least one other linear dimension; the length and breadth of a road, the height and width of a small, framed picture. Thickness is ascribed exclusively to three-dimensional objects, that is, to bodies. Moreover, thickness always has a lower rank than breadth and height, while breadth has a lower rank than length. Therefore each dimension has some end point, beyond which it turns into another dimension.

It follows from the above that the first two dimensions (length and height) have their transition points at the small pole, the last (thickness) at the large pole, and the second (breadth) at both poles. In other words, the length and height of a body may be increased infinitely and still be termed *length* and *height* respectively. They cannot, however, be reduced infinitely. If the other linear measurements are not reduced proportionately, at a certain point the length will become the breadth (e.g. a runway), and height becomes thickness (e.g. a flat board for chopping meat, obtained by cross-cutting a tall stump). On the other hand, thickness can be infinitely reduced and remain *thickness*. It follows, however, that it cannot be infinitely increased. If the other linear measurements of the body are not increased proportionately, thickness at some point becomes *height* (e.g. a solid metal cylinder) or *breadth* (e.g. a fortress wall seen from above). Lastly, breadth can neither increase nor diminish infinitely: when increased, at some point it becomes *length* (e.g. a field), and when reduced—*thickness* (e.g. a wooden board).

The dependency of linear dimensions on the shape of the body may be illustrated by the example of spheres and cubes, neither of which have length, breadth, height, or thickness, but only size in general.

Bodies of any internal structure whose vertical size exceeds the height of a normal human or are comparable with this, are said to have height; e.g. buildings and large rocks. If their dimensions are significantly less, all other conditions being equal, they may also be said to have thickness. The choice of one of these two dimensions is dictated by, among other factors, the internal structure of the body. Bodies with solid structure are said to have thickness (e.g. metal castings) while hollow bodies, such as boxes, have height.

Bodies with more or less the same external shape may be ascribed different linear dimensions depending on their function and the point at which they are supported. Compare a pole used for pole-vaulting, which has length, and one used as a flagstaff, which has height; a wooden or metal ladder placed against a wall to climb onto the roof (it may have height) and a rope ladder thrown out of a helicopter (it has length).

The same body may be said to have different dimensions according to the spatial position of the observer in relation to the body. The vertical size of a large container may be termed 'height' if observed from outside, and 'depth' if the observer is looking down into it.

We shall not set out the other features of naïve geometry (see J. Apresjan 1974: 58; Bierwisch 1967; J. Apresjan 1980: 102). It is clear they must all be considered in a lexicographic description of the corresponding parametric nouns and adjectives because they exemplify some of the most important aspects of the linguistic competence of speakers. It is also clear that this is no simple task.

We may mention another interesting though more superficial semantic feature of most (but not all) nouns denoting linear dimensions. They are characterized by the same type of regular polysemy, a combination of the meanings 'parameter' (*nebol'shaia* ⟨*sredniaia, bol'shaia*⟩ *vysota* ⟨*dlina, tolshchina*⟩ [small ⟨medium, great⟩ height ⟨length, thickness⟩]) and 'numerically large value of that parameter': *prygnut' s vysoty* [to jump from a height, i.e. from a great height]; *uiti v glubinu* [to dive to a depth, i.e. a great depth]. This combination of meanings forms a distinguishing feature of a larger lexicographic type which includes other parametric nouns; *idti na skorosti* [to move at speed, i.e. at high speed], *obrabatyvat' pod davleniem* [to process under pressure, i.e. under great pressure], etc. It should be noted that the words *dlina* and *shirina* lack this sense of 'numerically large value of a parameter'.

Nouns denoting linear dimensions have the following syntactic properties in common: (1) they have the same two-actant government patterns; compare *vysota* ⟨*dlina*⟩ *dereviannogo brusa* [the height ⟨length⟩ of a wooden beam] (a physical body to which the parameter is assigned) and *vysota* ⟨*dlina, shirina, tolshchina, glubina*⟩ *v piat' metrov* [five metres high ⟨long, wide, thick, deep⟩] (the numerical value of the parameter); (2) they may all be used in attributive constructions with the attribute having an obligatory dependent: *truby ogrom-noi vysoty* [chimneys of enormous height]; *truby dlinoi v sto metrov* [pipes a hundred metres in length], but not *\*truby vysoty* [chimneys of height]; *\*truby dlinoi* [pipes in length]; (3) they have the same type of syntactic homonymy, which is rooted in the partial coincidence of the outer form of the first and second actants: compare *vysota El'brusa* [the height of Mt El'brus], meaning (*a*) the height of El'brus itself and (*b*) the height of something else (another mountain, for example) equal in height to El'brus (*my podnimalis' na Everest i byli uzhe na vysote El'brusa* [we were climbing Everest and were already at the height of El'brus]); note a similar kind of homonymy in the collocations *skorost' sveta* [speed of light], *tsvet granata* [the colour of pomegranate], *ulybka rebenka* [the smile of a child], *muzhestvo soldata* [the courage of a soldier].

Finally, we should point out a common morphological property of all nouns denoting linear parameters: in their strictly parametric sense they either have no plural form (*shirina, tolshchina*), or their plural forms are marginal (*dlina, vysota, glubina*). In other words they tend towards the *singularia tantum* class.

It is clear that not all words or lexemes of a given lexicographic type must possess all properties of the type. It has been noted that the words *dlina* and *shirina* lack the meanings 'large numerical value of a parameter'. For this reason, when describing lexemes in the dictionary it is essential to attend both to their shared features (the problem of *unification*, or lexicographic types) and to their distinctive features (the problem of *individualization*, or lexicographic portraits). In a slightly paradoxical and over-stated form this principle may be reformulated as follows. Let us assume that a lexicographic portrait of lexeme $X_1$, which is considered to be a prototypical example of lexicographic type X, has already been obtained. If lexeme $X_2$ belongs to the same lexicographic type X, its lexicographic portrait should be copied from the lexicographic portrait of $X_1$ until the linguistic material begins to resist the procedure.

## 2. Preliminary Information Regarding the Dictionary Entry for the Verb *byt'*

### 2.1. REASONS FOR THE CHOICE OF *BYT'*

The verb *byt'* was selected deliberately to illustrate the idea of the lexicographic portrait. Being situated on the boundary of lexis and grammar it presents the lexicographer with a real challenge.

It possesses the fullest imaginable range of types of meanings, from the purely lexical to semi-auxiliary and modal on to the purely grammatical. Moreover the boundaries between the different meanings are so elusive that a pitfall awaits the lexicographer at every step.

The verb displays a full range of types of grammatical forms, including suppletives (*byt'*, *est'*, *sut'*) and the zero form Ø. These forms stand in extremely complex, sometimes confused or somewhat unstable relations with one another.

The range of its combinatory possibilities is vast. As a copula it has no equal in the freedom with which it may be used in constructions of different types and in collocations. Furthermore, even in its locative, possessive, and existential senses, which are prototypically expressed by the verbs *nakhodit'sia* [to be situated], *imet'* [to have], and *sushchestvovat'* [to exist] respectively, it far surpasses these verbs both in its general co-occurrence potential and the wealth of semantic, pragmatic, and communicative nuances which arise in specific combinatory conditions.

The verb *byt'* is capable of forming almost all possible types of verbal syntactic constructions and sentences, including most so-called impersonal sentences. At one pole of Russian syntax it functions as a meaningful verb; at the other it shades into the verbless nominative sentence (*krugom shum* [there is noise all around]).

The role of *byt'* in the lexis is also unique. Its semantic structure combines the meanings of four main groups: copula, locative, existential, and possessive. The first three groups of meanings are represented by many other classes of verbs which are semantically distant from *byt'*, such as the verbs of locomotion, for instance. This can be exemplified with the verb *vyiti*. Copula meanings: *vyiti zamuzh* ~ 'nachat' *byt'* zamuzhem' [to get married ~ to begin to be married (of a woman)]; *vyiti v generaly* ~ 'nachat' *byt'* generalom' [to become a general ~ to begin to be a general]; *vstrecha vyshla interesnoi* ~ 'vstrecha *byla* interesnoi' [the meeting turned out interesting ~ the meeting was interesting]. Localization meanings: *vyiti iz tiur'my* ~ 'perestat' *nakhodit'sia* v tiur'me' [to come out of prison ~ to cease *being* in prison]; *vyiti na rabotu* ~ 'nachat' *nakhodit'sia na rabote* [to go/come to work ~ to start *being* at work]. Existential meanings: *vyshla krupnaia nepriiatnost'* ~ 'stala *sushchestvuiushchei* krupnaia nepriiatnost'' [a large unpleasantness resulted ~ a large unpleasantness began *existing*]; *iz dvukh metrov materii vyshla odna iubka* ~ 'stala sushchestvovat' odna iubka' [two metres of material produced one skirt ~ . . . one skirt began to *exist*].

This combination of meanings characteristic of the copula is displayed by dozens if not hundreds of verbs. *Byt'* thus turns out to be one of the fundaments of the verbal lexis of Russian. One is justified in thinking that the copula in other languages has very much the same status. In the light of this it becomes clear which typical combinations of meaning the lexicographer should be prepared to seek in setting out to describe particular classes of verbs.

There is virtually no lexicographical problem that could not be illustrated with material from the verb *byt'*.

Lastly, the verb *byt'* has been fairly well studied (see for example the multi-volume series by Verhaar 1967–73, constructed on the typological material of several languages, and the monographs by Arutiunova and Shiriaev (1983) and Chvany (1975)), so it is convenient as a subject on which to test the technology for turning theoretical discoveries and findings into a lexicographic product. It has already been treated in J. Apresjan (1990*a*). But anything approaching a full picture is attainable only in the form of an extended dictionary entry, to which we now proceed. In order to ensure the autonomy of the present work it will be necessary to reproduce (with minor modifications) some of the general features from J. Apresjan (1990*a*).

## 2.2. GENERAL PATTERN OF THE DICTIONARY ENTRY

It is clear that the concept of the lexicographic portrait set forth above is an ideal which is difficult to attain but nevertheless useful to formulate. The ideal provides a landmark assisting us to draw that much closer to the fulfilment of the ultimate aims of linguistic description. From this point of view, the entry for *byt'*, given below, is no more than the first step along the way.

There is, however, another reason why this entry is not comprehensive. It was meant for an explanatory dictionary of the government and co-occurrence of the Russian verb and therefore preserves some of the limitations inherent in that particular lexicographical genre. Nevertheless, an attempt at an exhaustive description of the verb *byt'* within the framework of an integrated description of the language makes it possible to pin down certain of its unique features, so that the resulting dictionary entry may become an important part of a full lexicographic portrait of *byt'*. A comparison with the entry for *byt'* in the bilingual dictionary (J. Apresjan, Pall Erna 1982), from which much material was taken in compiling a monolingual Russian dictionary, will show how far the entry has moved from its prototype.

In the verb *byt'* six main groups of meanings may be separated: (1) copula, (2) locative, (3) possessive, (4) existential, (5) modal-existential, (6) auxiliary. Each of these may be represented by several meanings with their own numbering within the subgroup, so that a two-level hierarchy of meanings arises.

The general pattern (synopsis) of the entry for the verb *byt'*, with minimal explications of meanings and representative examples, takes the following form:

1.1. 'iavliat'sia' [to be]: *moi otets byl arkhitektorom* [my father was an architect];

1.2. 'byt' tozhdestvennym' [to be identical]; *eto byl Ivan* [it was Ivan];

2.1. 'nakhodit'sia' [to be situated]: *deti byli na ozere* [the children were by the lake];

2.2. 'pribyvat' kuda-libo' [to come]: *ego segodnia ne budet* [he won't be coming today];

3.1. 'imet'sia', 'imet'' [to be owned; to have]: *u nego byla prekrasnaia biblioteka* [he had a splendid library];

3.2. 'imet' vozrast' [to be of an age]: *emu bylo dvadtsat' let* [he was twenty];

4.1. 'sushchestvovat'' [to exist]: *est' eshche dobrye liudi na svete!* [there are still good people in the world];

4.2. 'imet' mesto', 'sluchat'sia' [to occur]: *byl ⟨budet⟩ dozhd'* [rain fell ⟨will fall⟩];

4.3. 'imet' mesto', 'nastupat'' [to take place, set in]: *bylo piat' chasov* [it was five o'clock];

4.4. 'sluchat'sia', 'postigat'' [to happen, occur]: *s drugom beda* [a misfortune has befallen my friend];

5.1. 'uverennost' v neizbezhnosti sobytiia' [certainty of an inevitable event]: *byt' groze* [there's a storm brewing];

5.2. 'uverennost' v neizbezhnosti plokhogo' [certainty of inevitable misfortune]: *nam teper' kryshka* [it's all up with us now];

5.3. 'nado prekratit' vozdeistvie' [an action must cease]: *budet s tebia* [that'll do];

6.1. part of the analytical future: *ne budu vam meshat'* [I won't get in your way];

6.2. part of the analytical passive: *proekt byl zakonchen* [the project was completed].

For comparative purposes an abridged form of the corresponding entry from the *Shorter Academy Dictionary* is included. (// stands for 'shades of meaning').

## I. The Independent Verb.

1. 'sushchestvovat'' [to exist]: *Est' pamiat' obo mne* [there is a memory of me]; // 'imet'sia' [to be available, on hand]: *cherez god budut u menia v stade dve gollandki* [in a year I shall have two Friesians in my herd];

2. 'nakhodit'sia' [to be situated], 'prisutstvovat'' [to be present]: *I tam ia byl* [I was there too]; // 'raspolagat'sia', 'razmeshchat'sia' [to be situated]: *Imenie bylo nedaleko ot derevni* [the estate was not far from the village]; // 'deistvie ili sostoianie', 'uchastie v chem-libo' [action or state, participation in smth.]: *On byl v iarosti* [He was in a rage];

3. 'proiskhodit'', 'sovershat'sia' [to happen]: *Ne ponimaiu, chto so mnoi bylo* [I don't understand what happened to me];

4. 'prikhodit'', 'poseshchat' kogo-libo' [to call on, visit smb.]: *Vy k nam budete zavtra?* [Will you come and see us tomorrow?];

## II. The Auxiliary Verb.

1. Copula between subject and substantival or adjectival predicate: *Bud' gotov* [Be prepared];

2. Formant of passive voice: *Ia byl gluboko oskorblen* [I was deeply offended];

3. Formant of future tense: *Budete vy streliat' ili net?* [Are you going to shoot or not?]

We leave it to the reader himself to establish the full measure of the divergence in the description and organization of the material between the *Shorter Academy Dictionary* and our dictionary; it is not possible to do this within the framework of the present chapter. Hereafter (see Notes) we shall mention only divergences of a fundamental nature or those which concern contentious matters of Russian grammar and lexicography.

2.3. TYPES OF INFORMATION ABOUT LEXEMES

Since we are dealing with types of information for the whole dictionary of government and co-occurrence, when necessary we shall cite verbs other than *byt'* as examples.

1. Morphological information. (1.1) Data on the paradigm. (1.2) Variant morphs of the same grammeme which express the same grammatical meaning; e.g. *est'* and Ø in all persons and numbers of the present tense. (1.3) Grammeme information: aspectual correlate, where one exists; constraints on aspectual forms, tense and mood forms, representation, person and number (see modal *byt'* 5.3, found only in the third-person singular future). (1.4) Information on participation in analytical grammatical forms (see § 6.1 and 6.2).

2. Stylistic information, conveyed with the aid of a traditional system of stylistic labels. The only innovation is that the object of stylistic classification is not only the lexeme, phraseme, and grammatical form but also more complex entities—constructions, free collocations, and certain types of sentences. For example, for *byt'* sense 1.1, the present-tense construction with post-copula instrumental (*On u nas povarom uzhe tri goda* [he's been our cook for three years]) is archaic, and for *byt'* sense 2.2 constructions of the type *vy budete k nam zavtra?* [will you be coming to see us tomorrow?] are obsolete.

3. Semantic information. (3.1) Analytical explication of the lexical meaning, not exhaustive, but sufficient for the requirements of a dictionary of government and co-occurrence; e.g. *byt'* 5.1 *X-u* = 'the speaker is sure that an event X, which in some way will affect him or another person about whom he is thinking at the moment of speech, will inevitably occur in the near future' (*Byt' bede* [there's trouble brewing]). (3.2) Information about possible semantic contrasts between outwardly differing manifestations of the same grammeme; compare the meaning of possession at a particular moment in *byt'* 3.1 = Ø (*U nego plastikovye lyzhi, i poetomu on tak bystro bezhit* [he has plastic skis on—that's why he's moving so fast]) and the meaning of ownership in *byt'* 3.1 = *est'* (*U nego est' plastikovye lyzhi* [he owns some plastic skis]). (3.3) Semantic modifications of the prototypical (dictionary) explication in different syntactic constructions and grammatical forms; compare the modification of the putative verb *dumat'* [to think] in the perfective form *podumat'* in the context of the modal *mozhno* [it is possible]: *Mozhno dumat'* ~ 'one should think' (*Mozhno dumat', chto peregovory poidut uspeshno* [we may suppose the negotiations will be successful]), and *Mozhno podumat'* ~ 'one should not think' (*Mozhno podumat', chto ty*

*nikogda ne opazdyvaesh'* [one might think you were never late], meaning that this is precisely what should not be thought as it is well known that this person is often late). (3.4) Constraints on the potential for realizing aspectual, tense, and other grammatical meanings in certain syntactic constructions or grammatical forms; compare the impossibility of progressive-durative meaning with the locative *byt'* 2.1 in negative sentences with the subject in the nominative, and the impossibility of general-factual resultative meaning in negative sentences with the subject in the genitive: *Otets ne byl na more* [my father has/had not been to the seaside] vs. *Ottsa ne bylo na more* [my father was not at the seaside (at a given moment)]. (3.5) Different syntactic uses within a single lexical meaning; e.g. the copula *byt'* 1.1 with a noun subject in the nominative (*Paren' byl slegka navesele* [the lad was a bit tipsy]), with an infinitive or proposition in the role of subject when there is a predicative (*Sidet' doma bylo skuchno* [staying at home was boring]), and with an infinitive as subject in a pronominal complex of the type *nekogo, negde* [nobody, nowhere] (*Spat' bylo negde* [there was nowhere to sleep]). (3.6) The paradigmatic semantic connections of a word—exact and inexact synonyms, analogues (~ co-hyponyms), conversives, and antonyms.

4. Pragmatic information; e.g. phrasemes *byt' po semu* [so be it], *tak i byt'* [so be it], which are used only performatively.

5. Prosodic and communicative information, that is, the accentuation of a lexeme with the aid of syntagmatic, main phrasal, contrastive (logical), and emphatic stress on the one hand, and its placement in the theme or rheme of an utterance on the other; compare *byt'* 3.2 in Ø form in the theme of the utterance and the stressed *byt'* 3.2 in the form *est'* in the rheme: *emu tri goda* [he's three years old (=exactly three)] vs. *emu est' tri goda* (=at least three).

6. Information on government. (6.1) The list of semantic valencies, identified by means of variables in the propositional form which provides the starting-point for the explication; see the explication of *byt'* 5.1 *X-u* in point 3.1 above. (6.2) Valency information. An indication is given of the part of speech of the governed word or its subclass (N—noun, A—adjective, V—verb, D—adverb or adverbial phrase, P—preposition, P$_3$—locative preposition, Conj—conjunction, Rel—interrogative word introducing a relative clause, Num—numeral), and of its grammatical form (case, number, person, representation). The description of syntactic constructions by symbols denoting parts of speech is geared towards prototypical situations. In real examples illustrating a given construction, a single part of speech symbol may be matched by a whole group of words with the same syntactic function. Where necessary the specific lexeme introducing the given valency is indicated (preposition, conjunction, etc.). Note is also made of the lexeme's ability to govern a whole clause (S) and the ability of a given valency to be expressed in different ways; e.g. *Paren' byl veselyi ⟨zol, navesele, zametno glupee svoei devushki, v unynii⟩* [the lad was merry ⟨angry, tipsy, noticeably more stupid than his girlfriend, dejected⟩]. Other ways of expressing the same valency are separated by a slash (/) and enclosed in pointed brackets.

(6.3) Information on whether a valency is syntactically optional or obligatory; e.g. *Inostrantsy arendovali sportkompleks 'Olimpiiskii'* [some foreigners rented the 'Olimpiiskii' sports complex], *Gorozhane neokhotno arendovali zemliu* (*u kolkhozov*) [the city-dwellers reluctantly rented some land (from the collective farms)], *Institut arendoval sportzal* (*za 1000 rublei*) [the institute rented the sports hall (for 1,000 roubles)], *My arendovali iakhtu* (*na dva mesiatsa*) [we rented a yacht (for two months)]. This is shown by appending the optional valencies (shown in round brackets in these examples) to the basic (first) construction, in which only the obligatory valencies are recorded. (6.4) Compatibility of valencies. This is shown explicitly in constructions which display optional valencies side by side with obligatory valencies, and implicitly in examples specially given for the purpose and preceded by the symbol +; e.g. + *Institut arendoval u zavoda stadion za 10,000 rublei na ves' letnii sezon* [the institute rented the stadium from the plant for 10,000 roubles for the whole summer season]. (6.5) Incompatibility of valencies, that is, the impossibility of their joint realization. This is shown by default—all valencies which are not shown explicitly as compatible are to be considered incompatible, cf. the incompatibility of the valencies of subject and measure of the parametric nouns like *vysota* 'height', *dlina* 'length', and the like: *\*vysota El'brusa v 5200 metrov* [the height of El'brus of 5,200 metres]. (6.6) Transformability of government patterns, that is, phenomena of the type *ia schitaiu, chto ona krasiva* [I consider that she is beautiful] ⇔ *ia schitaiu ee krasivoi* [I consider her beautiful].

7. Information on co-occurrence. (7.1) Morphological; e.g. verbs such as *privyknut'* [to become accustomed], *otvyknut'* [to become unaccustomed], etc., which normally govern an infinitive in the imperfective (except for the context of the coordinative construction, in which two or more perfective infinitives are used in the habitual meaning of the perfective). (7.2) Stylistic; e.g. constructions such as *moi brat byl ⟨budet⟩ professor* [my brother was ⟨will be⟩ a professor] with the copula *byt' 1.1* in the past and future tenses and the predicative in the nominative case are obsolete or bookish. (7.3) Semantic: (*a*) the governed nominal groups are constrained by the grammatical form of the verb or the ways in which its valencies are realized; e.g. *byt' 1.1* in the present tense zero form in the construction $N^1_{nom} VN^2_{inst}$ dictates that position $N^1$ be occupied by the name of a person and $N^2$ by an indication of his duties or trade: *Petr Fomich u nas dvornikom* [Petr Fomich is our caretaker], but not *\*on u nas veteranom truda* [he's our veteran of labour]; (*b*) a diametrically opposite type of constraint—the semantic class of the actant determines the choice of verb form or its variant; e.g. the choice of the zero variant of the present tense of *byt' 3.1* (possessive) in the context of normal anatomical nouns: *u nee kashtanovye volosy* [she has chestnut hair], but not *\*u nee est' kashtanovye volosy*, although it is possible to say *u nee est' rodinki* [she has birthmarks]. (7.4) Lexical; e.g. the list of seven *ne-K* units (*nekogo* [nobody], *nechego* [nothing], *negde* [nowhere, no place], *nekuda* [nowhere (to go)], *neotkuda* [from nowhere], *nekogda* [there is no time],

*nezachem* [there is no point]), which combine with the copula *byt' 1.1* in constructions of the type *nekomu bylo zhalovat'sia* [there was nobody to complain to], *negde bylo spat'* [there was nowhere to sleep], or the list of seven *K*-words (*kogo* [whom], *chego* [what], *gde* [where], *kuda* [whither], *otkuda* [whence], *kogda* [when], *zachem* [what for]), which combine with the existential *byt' 4.2* in constructions of the type *est' komu pozhalovat'sia* [there is somebody to complain to], *budet gde perenochevat'* [there will be a place to spend the night]. (7.5) Referential; e.g. the difference in denotative status (in E. V. Paducheva's sense) of the locative noun group with *byt' 2.1* in negative sentences. If the noun group signifies a spatially large area, in the general-factual resultative sense it is natural that it should be understood as having generic status: *za vsiu svoiu zhizn' ia ni razu ne byl na more* ⟨*v lesu, v gorode, v derevne*⟩ [in all my life I've never been to the seaside ⟨in a forest, in a city, in the country⟩]. In a general-factual two-directional or progressive-durative sense, the same noun group is naturally understood in the specific-referential status: *segodnia ia eshche ne byl na more* ⟨*v lesu, v gorode, v derevne*⟩ [I haven't been to the seaside ⟨in the forest, in the city, in the country⟩ yet today]; *ottsa ne bylo na more* ⟨*v lesu, v gorode, v derevne*⟩ [my father was not at the seaside ⟨in the forest, in the city, in the country⟩]. (7.6) Prosodic; e.g. the combination of the forms *byl, bylo, byli* with the negative particle *ne*, which attracts the main phrasal stress: *on tam né byl* [he has not been there], *ego tam né bylo* [he was not there], *oni tam né byli* [they have not been there]. (7.7) Communicative; e.g. the expulsion by the existential *byt' 4.1* of the subject into the rheme: *V Afrike est' l'vy* [in Africa there are lions]. (7.8) Syntactic: (*a*) the governed word must have a dependent, as in constructions of the type *u nee byli* kashtanovye *volosy* [she had *chestnut* hair]; (*b*) there must be a determinant or some stated adverbial modifier, as in constructions of the type *on* u nas *povarom* [he is *our* cook], *ia uzhe* tretii god *povarom* [I've been a cook *for two years*]; (*c*) a certain word order is fixed or preferable, as in the case of the existential *byt' 4.1* (see above); (*d*) a certain type of main clause is fixed, as in the case of the modal *byt' 5.3*, which may be used only in direct speech: *budet s tebia* [that'll do]; (*e*) a certain type of subordinate clause is fixed, as in the case of the existential *byt' 4.2*, which governs a subordinate subject introduced by a relative pronoun: *budet, chto vspomnit'* ⟨*s kem pogovorit'*⟩ [there will be something to remember ⟨someone to talk to⟩].

8. Phraseological information. See Δ.

We now proceed directly to the entry for *byt'*.

## 3. The Dictionary Entry for the Verb *byt'*

In order to read the dictionary entry below it is essential to be familiar with the lexicographic notation used therein. The majority of the conventional symbols have already been explained. Some of them, being transparent, are not explained.

Only the following observations are still required.

Within a particular meaning, several uses may be distinguished (each introduced by an Arabic numeral with a single bracket), which mainly reflect syntactic features of the construction expressing a given sense.

At any point the entry may be interrupted by commentary enclosed in square
brackets. If the commentary concerns the verb as a whole it is placed immediately after the headword, without brackets.

All constructions and types of collocation are illustrated by examples. The
sources of the illustrative material were the author's own card index and a number of linguistic and lexicographical works; in this respect M. Guiraud-Weber
(1984*b*) was particularly valuable. In the present chapter, for reasons of economy,
the illustrative material is reduced to a minimum.

BYT', future *búdu, búdesh'*; past *byl, bylá, býlo*; imperative *búd'(te)* ; past participle *bývshii*; verbal adverb *búduchi*; in the present only three forms are used—Ø
(for all personal forms), *est'* (for all personal forms)[1] and *sut'* (for the third person pl.),[2] which has only its copula functions 1.1 and 1.2,[3] while *est'* and Ø have
a complex distribution among the meanings (see below); the second person fu-

---

[1] In the *Shorter Academy Dictionary, est'* is considered a form of *byt'* only in the third person
present. The other uses are brought together in the independent verb *est'* with the following meanings (or 'shades of meaning'): (1) to be in reality: *ne dumaite obo mne luchshe, chem ia est'* [don't
think me better than I am]; (2) he/she/it/they exist(s): *est' strany, gde pasporta vovse ne trebuiut* [there
are countries where they don't ask for passports]; (3) he/she/it/they is (are) situated: *est' kto-nibud'
v komnate?* [is there anybody in the room?]; (4) is/are present (in smb.'s possession): *i noty est' u nas*
[we have music too].

It may easily be seen that the meanings identified in the *Shorter Academy Dictionary* exactly duplicate the four prototypical meanings of *byt'*: copula, existential, locational, and possessive. In the past
and future tenses, *est'* can be replaced by forms of *byt'* in all the instances given above. Thus no
serious semantic basis can be seen for treating *est'* as a separate verb. Nor are there sufficient formal
grounds. *Est'* and *byt'* stand in a strictly complementary distribution (with regard to the category of
tense). This corresponds to the formula of suppletion proposed in Mel'čuk 1972 and thus constitutes
a weighty argument in favour of a single lexeme. The sole argument against this treatment is that
the alternation of *est'* and Ø is not absolutely free (see meanings 1.1, 1.2, 3.2, and 4.3). However, an
attempt to divide this lexeme into two separate lexemes leads to *est'* being treated simultaneously as
a third person plural and third person singular form of the present tense (note the above formulations 'he/she/it/they exist(s)', etc.). But then the result is a grammatically proscribed intersection of
paradigms of two different verbs: *est'* as the third person singular present belongs simultaneously to
the verbs *byt'* and *est'*.

[2] Of *sut'*, the *Shorter Academy Dictionary* says the following: '3rd person pl present of *byt'* (see
*byt'*), also used as 3rd person sg.' From this description one might conclude technically that *sut'* is
a form of the verb *byt'* in all its senses. This interpretation is clearly false; we cannot say *\*deti sut'
vo dvore* [the children are in the yard] (locative meaning), *\*u moego ottsa sut' kitaiskie knigi* [my
father has some Chinese books] (possessive meaning), *\*sut' liudi, kotorye vsegda budut pomnit' obo
mne* [there are people who will always remember me] (existential meaning). In other words, the form
*sut'* has only one—copula—meaning, and this should be recorded in the dictionary. It is hazardous
to legitimize *sut'* as a form of the third person singular on the basis of uses such as *sie ne sut' ugroza,
no preduprezhdenie* [lit. these are no threat, but a warning] (M. Gor'kii), which are on the margins
of the literary norm, or on the basis of fossilized expressions such as *eto ne sut' vazhno* [that is
unimportant].    [3] See previous note.

ture may have present-tense meaning in questions: *Vy kakoi, izviniaius', budete natsii?—Ia budu evreiskoi natsii. A vy, prostite, kakoi natsii budete?* [Excuse me but what nationality might you be?—I might be of Jewish nationality. And excuse me but what nationality might you be?] (S. Dovlatov); no perfective; when combined with the negative particle *ne* in the past tense masc., neut., and pl., *ne* attracts phrasal stress while the verb becomes a clitic: ↓ *né byl*, ↓ *né bylo*, ↓ *né byli*.[4]

1.1. *A est' P* = 'Object or fact A has property P or is in state P'[5] [A classifying copula meaning; in the present represented by Ø (*zadacha trudnaia* [the task is difficult]) or the form *est'*; the latter is either archaic (*zhizn' eta* [. . .] *est' uzhe dostoianie literatury i poezii* [this life is already the stuff of literature and poetry]), or used in the genre of the pseudo-definition (*sotsrealizm est' umenie khvalit' nachal'stvo v dostupnoi dlia nego forme* [socialist realism is the art of flattering the management in a way it can understand];[6] SYN: *iavliat'sia* [to be]; ~ SYN: *stanovit'sia, delat'sia* [to become]; *okazyvat'sia* [to turn out]; *kazat'sia* [to seem]; *vosprinimat'sia* [to be perceived]; *risovat'sia* [to be seen as]; *videt'sia* [to be seen]; *byvat'* [to be (regularly)]].[7]

1) With a noun subject in the nominative.

N$^1_{nom}$ VD

*Paren' byl slegka navesele* [the lad was slightly tipsy]. *Vse bylo tak, kak on khotel* [everything was as he wanted].

N$^1_{nom}$ V {A$_{nom}$/A$_{short}$/A$_{comp}$} [when N$^1$ = polite *vy* the singular is the norm for A = nom: *Vy togda byli ochen' krasivaia* (you were very beautiful then); a plural form for A = nom is substandard: *Uzh bol'no vy obidchivye* (you're awfully

---

[4] The *Shorter Academy Dictionary* provides this prosodic information together with information on word stress. The fundamental difference between word stress and phrasal stress is consequently blurred.

[5] In the *Shorter Academy Dictionary* the copula meaning (*bud' gotov* [be prepared]) is separated from the meaning of a state (*on byl v iarosti* [he was in a rage]). In reality both constructions display the same meaning of the verb, which follows from the fact of their ability to be co-ordinated: *ia v nekotorom nedoumenii ot togo, chto mne o vas rasskazyvali, no gotov vas vyslushat'* [I'm somewhat perplexed by what I'm told about you, but I'm prepared to hear you out]. See also *ia v obide na vas* or *ia obizhen na vas* [I have a grudge against you].

[6] In the *Shorter Academy Dictionary* the present-tense forms *est'* and *sut'* are regarded as bookish. In our view their stylistic specifics (where they have any) are not a matter of register (bookish) but of genre, or, more precisely, they have illocutionary force: by using these forms we may wish to mark our utterances as definitions; *trud est' bor'ba cheloveka s prirodoi* [toil is the struggle of man against nature] (D. I. Pisarev). In fact they are not definitions. A definition logically requires the identifying meaning of *byt'*, that is, meaning 1.2, which allows the transposition of actants in relation to the copula: *priamaia est' kratchaishee rasstoianie mezhdu dvumia tochkami = kratchaishee rasstoianie mezhdu dvumia tochkami est' priamaia* [a straight line is the shortest distance between two points = the shortest distance between two points is a straight line] (for more detail on the identifying meaning see Arutiunova 1976).

[7] The synonyms, inexact synonyms, analogues, conversives, and antonyms are orientated towards prototypical cases of realization of a given lexical meaning, that is, its dictionary explication, its typical syntactic constructions and collocations.

quick to take offence); the plural is the norm for A = short: *Vy togda byli ochen'
krasivy* (you were very beautiful then); a singular form for A = short is unacceptable *\*Vy ochen' krasiva* (you are very beautiful)].[8]

*Noch' byla lunnaia* [the night was moonlit]. *Uchitel'* ⟨*byl*⟩ *bolen* [the teacher is
⟨was⟩ ill]. *Narod nash grub, on nekul'turen* [our people are coarse; they are un-
cultured] (M. Gor'kii).

$N^1_{nom}$ V {$A_{inst}$/$N^2_{inst}$} [if V is present tense, only $N^2$ can appear as the predicative; moreover (1) $N^1$ usually denotes a person while $N^2$ is his office, trade, etc.;
(2) the sentence contains a determinant meaning a place or referring to time;
(3) the construction as a whole is archaic; *on u nas povarom uzhe tri goda* (he's
been our cook for three years) but not *\*ssylka na nekhvatku vremeni u nas for-
muloi otkaza* (a reference to lack of time here is a way of refusing) or *\*on davno
narodnym artistom?* (has he been a people's artist for a long time?). In this construction the sense of *byt'* shifts towards 'to work'].[9]

*Noch' byla* ⟨*budet*⟩ *lunnoi* [the night was moonlit]. *Moi syn budet arkhitektorom*
[my son will be an architect].

$N^1_{nom}$ V $N^2_{nom}$ [obsolete or bookish in the past and especially the future, except
when $N^1$ = *eto* (this) or $N^2$ = nationality, citizenship, or a toponym derivative].

*Moi brat byl professor* [my brother was a professor]. *Eto byl* ⟨*budet*⟩ *zamechatel'nyi doklad* [it was ⟨will be⟩ a remarkable report]. *Ee muzh byl koreets* ⟨*mosk-
vich*⟩ [her husband was a Korean ⟨a Muscovite⟩]. *Muzyka—est'—bunt* [music is
rebellion] (M. Tsvetaeva).

$N^1_{nom}$ V P $N^2_x$

*Oleg byl s det'mi* [Oleg was with the children] [cf. *S kem byli deti?* (who were
the children with?)—see 2.1].[10] *Ivanov byl iz rabochei sem'i* [Ivanov came from

---

[8] Strictly speaking, these agreement rules with the long and short adjective (formulated in Chvany
1975: 70–1) really describe less the verb *byt'* than the 'polite' pronoun *vy*; note the agreement *Pochemu
vy, obychno takaia taktichnaia i chutkaia, sovsem ne poschitalis' s ego samoliubiem?* [why did you, who
are usually so tactful and sensitive, take no account of his self-esteem?]. They should therefore be
recorded in a comprehensive Russian dictionary in the entry for *vy*. However, in a dictionary of
government and co-occurrence it is reasonable to duplicate these rules in the entry for *byt'* since this
is the main verb governing the long and especially the short form of the adjective.

[9] At first glance it might seem plausible to suggest that in this construction it is not the zero variant of the copula which is displayed but the zero variant of the verb *rabotat'* [to work] in the present
tense. The counter argument is as follows: by recognizing a zero form for *rabotat'* we are postulating
a unique fact, whereas zero forms for *byt'* in the present are a well-established phenomenon.

[10] This commentary implicitly introduces the subject of 'oscillation' of meanings of polysemous
words (see Stern 1931: 190; J. Apresjan 1974: 179 ff.). In this case the copula and the locative meanings
are juxtaposed. The prototypical structures for them are *On byl studentom* [he was a student] and
*On byl v drugoi komnate* [he was in the other room], where they are clearly contrasted. In constructions removed from the prototype such as *Oleg Petrovich byl s det'mi* [Oleg Petrovich was with the
children] and *Deti byli s Olegom Petrovichem* [the children were with Oleg Petrovich] the clarity of
the contrast is blurred. The sentence *Oleg Petrovich byl s det'mi*, generally speaking, admits two interpretations: a copula meaning (*Oleg Petrovich byl s det'mi, no bez veshchei i slegka navesele* [Oleg

a working-class family]. *Otets byl v ot"ezde* [Father was away].

$N^1_{nom}$ V v $N^2_{prep}$ [$N^2$ = garment, item of uniform or harness, ornament, spectacles, etc.; $N^1$ = person or animal wearing this object].

*On byl v koroten'kom pal'to* [he was in a very short coat]. *Mal'chik byl v ochkakh* [the boy was wearing glasses] [cf. *byt'* 2.1—*Na nem bylo koroten'koe pal'to* [he had a very short coat on].[11]

$N^1_{nom}$ V $A_{gen}$ $N^2_{gen}$

*On byl vysokogo rosta* [he was of tall stature]. *Kolesa byli raznoi velichiny* [the wheels were of different sizes]. *Skatert' byla zheltogo tsveta* [the table-cloth was of a yellow colour].

2) With an infinitive or proposition as subject, and a predicative,[12] or in an impersonal construction with predicatives.[13]

---

Petrovich was with the children but without his things and slightly tipsy]), and locative (*Oleg Petrovich byl s det'mi, a Masha ushla na rynok* [Oleg Petrovich stayed with the children but Masha had gone to the market]). The same applies to *Deti byli s Olegom Petrovichem* [the children were with Oleg Petrovich]. Nevertheless, the first interpretation, given that Oleg Petrovich is independent, is more natural for the first sentence, and the second interpretation, since the children are dependent, is more natural for the second. It is our belief that these and similar cases of oscillation of meaning should be represented explicitly (via cross-references) in the dictionary.

[11] Constructions of the type *Oleg byl v novoi shapke* [Oleg was in his new hat] are synonymous with constructions such as *Na Oleg byla novaia shapka* [Oleg had his new hat on], but they display different senses of the verb *byt'*—the copula sense in the first and the possessive in the second. Here, as distinct from the example examined in n. 10, each sentence is perfectly unambiguous: there is no oscillation of meaning. How then are we to explain the synonymy of *Oleg byl v novoi shapke* ⇔ *Na Oleg byla novaia shapka*? The explanation seems to lie in the fact that in constructions of the type X *byl* 1.1 v Y-e and Y *byl* 2.1 na X-e where X = person (draught animal, etc.) and Y = garment (harness, etc.), a modification occurs of the dictionary senses of *byt'* v ~ 'to be dressed in smth.' and *byt' na* ~ 'to be worn by smb.'. This modification turns *byt'* 1.1 v chem-libo and *byt'* 2.1 na kom-libo into exact conversives (in terms of I. Mel'čuk's lexical functions—Real₁ and Fact₁).

[12] We do not consider this type of construction impersonal. The role of subject is filled by an infinitive or a subordinate clause. This is supported by the fact that the same syntactic position may be occupied by a propositional nominal pronoun such as *eto* [this], *chto* [what], *odno* [one thing], etc., providing what is indisputably the subject. Consider the following dialogue: – *Odno bylo zhal'* [one thing was a pity]—*Chto imenno?* [what precisely?]—*Chto on uekhal* [that he went away]. The traditional treatment of constructions with predicatives is inconsistent: constructions such as *odno bylo zhal'* are acknowledged to be subject-verb sentences while constructions of the type *bylo zhal', chto on uekhal* are treated as impersonal. In the latter case, incidentally, despite the obvious facts, the copula is presented as monovalent.

[13] From our point of view impersonal constructions differ from subject-verb constructions not in lacking a subject, but merely in the way it is expressed: in so-called impersonal clauses the subject is presented by a (superficial) syntactic zero (see Mel'čuk 1974b). From this it follows that the syntactic structure of clauses such as *Grustno* [it's sad]; *Rasstavat'sia grustno* [it's sad to part]; *Grustno, chto prikhoditsia rasstavat'sia* [it's sad that it's necessary to part] and *Eto grustno* [it's sad] is exactly the same, except for the differences in the type of subject (their semantic structures are, of course, different). In the light of this, the grammatical term 'impers' signifies specifically a type of agreement proper to a verb with a non-prototypical subject, including a zero subject: impers = (3rd p. sg pres/fut) or (neuter sg past). One should also bear in mind that there is a class of constructions in which

$V_{impers}$ {D/$A_{short}$/$A_{comp}$/$N^1_{nom}$}[D, A, $N^1$—predicatives].[14]

*Bylo veselo* ⟨*nelovko, stydno*⟩ [it was jolly ⟨awkward, shameful⟩]. *Khochetsia ei laiat', da len'* [she feels like barking, but is too lazy] (A. P. Chekhov).

{$D^1$/P $N^1_x$} $V_{impers}$ {$D^2$/$A_{short}$/$A_{comp}$} [$D^2$, A—predicatives].

*Zdes' budet melko* [it'll be shallow here]. *V komnate teplo i tikho* [in the room it is warm and quiet].

$N^1_{dat}$ $V_{impers}$ {D/$A_{short}$/$A_{comp}$/$N^2_{nom}$} [D, A, $N^2$—predicatives].

*Vsem bylo veselo* ⟨*nelovko, grustno, khorosho*⟩ [everybody felt happy ⟨awkward, sad, fine⟩]. *Mne pora* [time I was leaving]. *Vam otsiuda vidno?* [can you see from here?].

{$V_{inf}$/Conj S/Rel S/$N^1_{propos}$}[15] V {D/$A_{short}$/$A_{comp}$/$N^2_{nom}$} [D, A, $N^2$—predicatives].

*Nado bylo ukhodit'* [it was necessary to leave]. *I teper' emu skuchno, neinteresno byt' doma* [and now it's tedious for him and dull to be at home] (M. Zoshchenko). *Budet zhalko* ⟨*khorosho*⟩, *esli on uedet* [it'll be a shame ⟨it'll be good⟩ if he leaves]. *Odno bylo neiasno* [one thing was unclear].

s $N^1_{inst}$ $V_{impers}$ {D/$A_{short}$/$A_{comp}$/$N^2_{nom}$} [A, $N^2$—predicatives; D—predicative or *kak, tak, tak sebe* . . .].

*A kak u tebia s den'gami?* [how are you off for money?]. *S den'gami tugo* [the money's tight]. *S produktami bylo vse eshche trudno* [supplies were still hard to get] (V. Belov).

3) In modal constructions with an infinitive as subject and a pronominal complex of the type *nekogo* [nobody], *nechego* [nothing], *negde* [nowhere], *nezachem* [there is no point], *nekuda* [nowhere (to go)], *neotkuda* [from nowhere], *nekogda* [no time] (cf. 4.2.2).[16]

---

the verb agrees not with the subject but with a nominal predicative in the nominative: *s proektom byla polnaia neudacha* [the plan was a complete failure]. On these constructions see Zolotova 1966, Giro-Veber [Guiraud-Weber] 1984*a*: 336 ff.

[14] In our nomenclature of parts of speech there is no so-called 'category of state'. As we have attempted to show (J. Apresjan 1985: 301–8), the 'category of state' is not a part of speech but a syntactic feature of a number of adjectives, adverbs, and nouns. We may note, in particular, that the noun status of such categories of state as *vremia* [time], *len'* [laziness], *okhota* [wish], and some others is confirmed by their co-occurrence with attributive adjectives: *samoe vremia dumat' ob otpuske* [just the time to think about a holiday], *kakaia okhota idti zamuzh za cheloveka, kotoromu samomu est' nechego?* [who would want to marry a man who himself has nothing to eat?]. A similar point of view was expressed much earlier in an unjustly forgotten work (Anichkov 1964).

[15] 'Propos' is applied to pronominals such as *odno* [one], *chto* [what], *eto* [this], etc., which may replace a whole proposition; e.g. *odno mne neiasno—kak on tuda popal?* [one thing is not clear to me—how did he get there?], where *odno* stands for *kak on tuda popal*.

[16] Constructions of the type *Negde (bylo) spat'* [there is (was) nowhere to sleep] are closely connected with those of the type *Bylo gde spat'* [there was a place to sleep], but they display different senses of the verb *byt'*—copula in the first and existential in the second. The basis for this treatment of these constructions is given in J. Apresjan and L. Iomdin 1989, with a detailed argumentation for

$\{N^1_x/P \ N^1_y/D\} \ V \ V_{inf}$

*Nekomu bylo zhalovat'sia* [there was no one to complain to]. *Est' bylo nechego* [there was nothing to eat]. *Ne s kem pogovorit'* [there's nobody to talk to]. *Ne o chem bylo sporit'* [there was nothing to argue about]. *Spat' bylo negde* [there was nowhere to sleep]. *Nezachem tuda ekhat'* [there's no point going there].

$N^2_{dat} \ \{N^1_x/P \ N^1_y/D\} \ V \ V_{inf} \ [N^2$—agent of $V_{inf}]$.

*Vam nekomu budet zhalovat'sia* [you'll have nobody to complain to]. *Detiam nechego bylo est'* [the children had nothing to eat]. *Vam razvernut'sia negde* [you have no room to turn around] (V. Maiakovskii).

4) With the subject in the genitive in quantifying constructions [cf. 2.1.2), 3.1.2);[17] cf. also 4.1.2)].[18]

$N^1_{gen} \ V\{D/N^2_{nom}/Num_{nom}\} \ [D, N^2$—quantifier].

*Knig bylo mnogo* ⟨*po men'shei mere million*⟩ [there were lots of books ⟨at least a million⟩]. *Liudei bylo* ⟨*byla*⟩ *massa* [there were masses of people]. *Komnat bylo chetyre* [there were four rooms]. *Vintovok bylo nikak ne men'she* ⟨*bol'she, okolo*⟩

this non-traditional syntactic representation; see also Garde (1976) and Holthusen (1953). Here it will suffice to draw attention to the following obvious facts. In clauses such as *zhit' bylo negde* [there was nowhere to live] the verb *byt'* is a copula because it may be replaced by the copula verbs *stanovit'sia* and *delat'sia* [to become] which have no existential meaning: *zhit' stalo* ⟨*sdelalos'*⟩ *negde* [(suddenly) there was nowhere to live]. In clauses such as *bylo gde spat'*, *byt'* is existential, because it may be replaced by the existential verb *naitis'*, which has no copula meaning: *Naidetsia gde spat'* [a place to sleep will be found]; note also the typically existential *est'* in the present: *est' gde spat'* [there is a place to sleep]. Thus in these constructions there is an 'overflow', barely perceptible at first glance, of the copula sense of *byt'* into the existential and vice versa. This ambivalence is a feature of many other constructions with the verb *byt'*, as with its correlates in other languages; see Lyons 1967; Shvedova 1973; Chvani [Chvany] 1977.

[17] In n. 10 instances of oscillation of meanings were considered. They are similar to cases of homonymy of whole clauses due to lexical polysemy. The material of construction 1.1.4), contrasted with that of 2.1.2) and 3.1.2), provides an opportunity to discuss another type of ambivalence which is known in the literature as 'fuzziness', or in Russian 'diffuznost'' (D. Shmelev 1969: 8), or, more precisely, 'syncretism' (J. Apresjan 1974: 179 ff.). In the case of syncretism, the simultaneous realization occurs of two senses which are perceived as one. In sentences like *knig bylo mnogo* [there were a lot of books], the verb *byt'* displays its copula sense (see n. 18 below). In sentences like *knig v komnate bylo mnogo* [there were a lot of books in the room], *byt'* has locative meaning with elements of the copula. Finally, in sentences like *knig u nego bylo mnogo* [he had a lot of books], *byt'* has possessive meaning with elements of the copula. This syncretism of meanings is also reflected in the syntactic structure of the sentences, most particularly in the fact that *byt'* has three dependents at once: the subject (*knig*), the complement of place or possessor (*v komnate, u nego*) and the predicative (*mnogo*).

[18] Quantifying constructions of the type *plakatov bylo mnogo* and *bylo mnogo plakatov* [there were a lot of posters] are almost synonymous. However in the first the copula sense of the verb *byt'* is displayed, and in the second its existential meaning (4. 1.1)). This fact was noted in Zolotova (1973: 133–5), Ivanova (1973), Guiraud-Weber (1984b: 556). The principal argument for the copula nature of *byt'* in sentences of the first type is the preservation of the plural subject with small numbers: *plakatov bylo chetyre* ⟨*tri, dva*⟩ [there were four ⟨three, two⟩ posters]. If the noun were linked directly with the numeral, not via the verb, it would be in the singular: *bylo chetyre* ⟨*tri, dva*⟩ *plakata*. Thus in these quantifying constructions there is again an 'overflow' of the copula sense into the existential and vice versa.

*sta*[19] [there were no fewer than ⟨no more than, roughly⟩ a hundred rifles]. *Nas bylo tri devushki* [there were three of us girls].

1.2. *A est' X* = 'A est' 1.1 identichen X-u' [A is identical to X] [an identifying copula meaning; Ø in the present, except for the genre of definitions].

$N^1_{nom}$ V $N^2_{nom}$

*Eto byl stol ⟨Ivan⟩* [it was a table ⟨it was Ivan⟩]. *Pnompen'—stolitsa Kambodzhi* [Phnom Penh is the capital of Cambodia].

2.1. *A byl v ⟨na⟩ X-e* = 'A nakhoditsia v ⟨na⟩ X-e' [A is situated in ⟨on⟩ X] [locative meaning; in the present, expressed by Ø or *est'*; in negative sentences by the word *net*; in the past in a negative sentence with subject in the nominative usually has general-factual (resultative) meaning, but not progressive-durative; see *otets ne byl na more* = 'Father has/had never yet been to the seaside', in which the word *more* has the generic referential status and the meaning of the verb comes close to 2.2; in the same circumstances, but with the subject in the genitive, it usually has progressive-durative meaning: *Ottsa ne bylo na more* = 'Father was not at the seaside at the moment of observation';[20] SYN: *nakhodit'sia* (to be situated); ~ SYN: *prebyvat'* (to be, to stay), *prisutstvovat'* (to be present); substandard *torchat'* (to hang out); *byvat'* (to frequent, visit); coll. *vertet'sia*, coll. *krutit'sia*, substandard *okolachivat'sia* (to hang about), coll. *teret'sia*, coll. *toloch'sia*, coll. *toptat'sia* (to hang about, mark time, kill time, mix with)].

1) With a noun subject in the nominative.

$N^1_{nom}$ V{D/P$_3$ $N^2_x$}

*Andrei v shkole ⟨na rabote⟩* [Andrei is at school ⟨work⟩]. *Deti byli na ozere* [the children were at the lake]. *Gorod v shesti kilometrakh ot zheleznoi dorogi* [the town is six kilometres from the railway line].

$N^1_{nom}$ V P $N^2_x$

*Pri nem byli bol'shie den'gi* [he had lots of money on him]. *S nim byli deti* [the children were with him], [cf. 1.1—*on byl s det'mi* (he was with the children)]. *So mnoi byl chugunnyi chainik* [I had a cast-iron kettle with me] (M. Iu. Lermontov).

---

[19] In the government pattern no provision is made for the prepositions *ot, do,* and *okolo* or quantitative adverbs, although they appear in the examples. This is because such prepositions and adverbs introduce a so-called approximative-quantifier group which may replace a prepositionless noun group in the nominative, accusative, or genitive in any syntactic position. This is a general rule of Russian syntax, which does not need duplication in a government pattern. In the illustrative area, however, examples of approximative-quantifier groups are of value as they demonstrate paths of interaction between grammatical rules and lexical information within the framework of an integrated description of a language.

[20] For a more detailed discussion of this example see J. Apresjan 1980. A similar but less full description appeared earlier in Itskovich (1982).

$N^1_{nom}$ V na $N^2_{prep}$ [$N^1$—item of clothing, uniform, harness, ornament, etc.; $N^2$—person, creature or part of body clad in it; cf. 1.1.1)].

*Na nem byla seraia kurtka* [he had on a grey jacket] (A. Kuprin). *Na golovakh u nikh byli ryzhie metallicheskie tazy* [they had reddish metal basins on their heads] (M. Bulgakov).

2) With the subject in the genitive in a quantifying construction [cf. 1.1.4), 3.1.2)].[21]

$N^1_{gen}$ V{D/$N^2_{nom}$/Num$_{nom}$} {D/P$_3$ $N^3_x$}

*Komnat tam bylo chetyre* [there were four rooms there]. *Liudei na ploshchadi massa* [there are masses of people in the square]. *Sledovatelei v Peterburge bylo mnogo* [there were many investigators in St Petersburg] (A. F. Koni).

2.2. *A byl v ⟨na⟩ X-e* = 'person A went to X and was there to engage in some kind of activity' [usually in past or future form; in the past has general-factual two-directional meaning: 'came to X and then departed from it'; SYN: *poseshchat'* (to visit); ~ SYN: *naveshchat'* (to visit), *nanosit' vizit* (to pay a visit); *byvat'*, *pobyvat'* (to visit); *navedyvat'sia*; *provedyvat'* (to visit); *zakhodit'*, *zabegat'*, *zagliadyvat'* (to drop in, call in, look in); ANAL: *prikhodit'*, *priezzhat'*, *pribyvat'* (to come, arrive)].

$N^1_{nom}$ V

*Vrach segodnia uzhe byl* [the doctor has already called today]. *Glavnogo inzhenera zavtra ne budet* [the chief engineer won't be in tomorrow].

$N^1_{nom}$ V{D/P$_3$ $N^2_x$}

*Ty byl tam?* [have you been there?] [see also 2.1]. *Otets segodnia eshche ne byl na more* [Father hasn't been to the seaside yet today] [cf. § 2.1]. *Ia dazhe v magazine-to ne byl* [I haven't even been to the shop] (V. Shukshin).

$N^1_{nom}$ V k $N^2_{dat}$ [obs., future only; $N^2$—usually a person]—*Vy budete k nam zavtra?* [will you be coming to see us tomorrow?].

3.1. *U X-a est' A* = 'X owns A' [Possessive meaning; in the present, expressed by Ø or *est'*; in negative sentences by the word *net*; when combined with normal parts of the body—excluding pimples, tumours, birthmarks, and the like—and a descriptive adjective, usually as Ø: *U nee kashtanovye volosy* (she has chestnut hair), but not *\*U nee est' kashtanovye volosy*; a degree of contrast is possible between Ø and *est'* when these combine with the names of instruments and means: the former more often expresses current possession and the latter permanent ownership; compare *U nego plastikovye lyzhi (i poetomu on tak bystro*

---

[21] See n. 18.

*bezhit*) (he has plastic skis on [and that's why he's moving so fast]) and *U nego est' plastikovye lyzhi* (he owns some plastic skis); if the object possessed is some part of the subject's inner world (a thought, emotion, wish, etc.) the form *est'* is preferred and its meaning shifts towards 4.1: *U nego est' zhelanie* ⟨*namerenie, gotovnost'*⟩ *vystupit' s dokladom na seminare*[22] (he has a wish ⟨an intention, the readiness⟩ to deliver a paper at the seminar); with possessive meaning a preposed *u*-group is characteristic (before the verb), with the generic status of the subject; with a postposed *u*-group the meaning may shift towards the locative, while the subject has specific-referential status; compare *U menia est' den'gi* = 'I possess an object which belongs to the category of money' and *Den'gi u menia* = 'the money now being spoken of is with me'.[23] SYN: *imet'sia* (to be present); CONV: *imet'* (to have), *obladat'* (to possess)].

1) With a noun subject in the nominative.

$N^1_{nom}$ V u $N^2_{gen}$

*U nee mnogo knig* [she has a lot of books]. *U nego byla prekrasnaia laboratoriia* [he had a splendid laboratory].

2) With the subject in the genitive in a quantifying construction [cf. 1.1.4), 2.1.2)][24]

$N^1_{gen}$ V{D/$N^2_{nom}$/Num$_{nom}$} u $N^3_{gen}$

*Liudei u nas seichas men'she, chem do voiny* [we now have fewer people than before the war] (F. Abramov).

3.2. *X-u bylo A* = 'the age of X was equal to A' [in the present this is represented by Ø in the theme of the utterance or the form *est'* with the main phrasal stress or contrastive emphasis when *byt'* forms the rheme; in this case *est'* means 'has already completed no less than A';[25] in the present in a negated clause it is

---

[22] This occurs owing to the 'axiom of reality' which states that possession of some part of an inner world and the existence of that part in an inner world are one and the same thing; see J. Apresjan and L. Iomdin (1989).

[23] This is another instance of an 'overflow' of meanings.    [24] See n. 18.

[25] The curious fact that in rheme position parametric predicates of the type *vesit'* P [to weigh P], *dlit'sia* P [to last P], *stoit'* P [to be worth P], etc. mean not 'exactly P' but 'at least P' was noted by I. Boguslavsky (1985: 27 ff.). When negated they mean 'less than P'. I. Boguslavsky offered the following explanation for this shift of meaning: 'not at least P' = 'less than P'. It is clear that this explanation should be extended to cover similar uses of the parametric senses of *byt'* as well. I. Boguslavsky's description may be taken another step forward. The normal communicative position of verbs of the type *byt'* 3.2, *byt'* 4.3, *vesit'* [to weigh (intrans.)], *dlit'sia* [to last], *stoit'* [to cost, be worth] is in the theme of the sentence. This is due to the fact that they do not make any significant contribution to the content of the sentence. This function is performed fully by the corresponding quantifying groups. The relation between, for example, a sack of potatoes and 200 roubles or between a lecture and an hour and a half emerges clearly without the addition of a verb. This meaning is more or less contained in the meaning of the corresponding quantifying group, leaving the verb itself with only copula

represented by the word *net*; usually preposed to the subject; ~ SYN: *ispolniat'sia* (to be completed), *minut'* (to turn, pass); coll. *stuknut'*, substandard *sravniat'sia* (to reach, be equal to); ANAL: *idti* (to be in progress); CONV: *dostigat'* (to reach)].

$N^1_{nom} \; V \; N^2_{dat}$

*Emu tri goda* [his age is equal to three years]. *Emu ↓ est' tri goda* [he has already turned three; at least three]. *↓ Est' emu tri goda?* [has he already turned three?]. *V fevrale nashemu synu budet rovno god* [in February our son will be exactly one year old].

4.1. *Est' X* = 'X exists' [usually of objects and living beings; strictly existential meaning; in the present, expressed by the form *est'*; in negative sentences by the word *net*; usually precedes the subject; in simple sentences is usually marked by syntagmatic stress and, with the subject group, forms the rheme of the utterance; *↓ Est' eshche dobrye liudi na svete* (there are still good people in the world); in a complex sentence with a subordinate clause, it is phrasally stress-less and with the subject forms the theme of the utterance, while the subordinate clause forms the rheme; *Est' chelovek, kotoryi vsegda budet pomnit' obo mne* (there is a person who will always remember me); shifts towards 2.1 when determinants of place are present;[26] SYN: *sushchestvovat'* (to exist), *imet'sia* (to be present); ~ SYN: *vodit'sia* (to be found), *byvat'* (to happen from time to time)].

1) With a noun subject in the nominative.

$N^1_{nom} \; V$

*Est' liudi, kotorye nikogda ne zabyvaiut obid* [there are people who never forget insults]. *Est' mistika. Est' vera. Est' Gospod'. | Est' raznitsa mezh nikh. I est' edinstvo* [There is mysticism. There is faith. There is God. | There is a difference between them. And there is unity] (I. Brodskii).

$N^1_{nom} \; V \; \{D/P_3 \; N^2_x\}$

*V Afrike est' l'vy ⟨zhirafy, nosorogi⟩* [In Africa there are lions ⟨giraffes, rhinoceroses⟩]. *Est' eshche dobrye liudi na svete!* [there are still good people in the world!]. *Byli zdes' kogda-to smelye okhotniki* [once there were fearless hunters here].

---

function. In colloquial speech it may even be replaced by a copula: *Pochem (byla) kartoshka* [how much are (were) the potatoes?]. Thus a meaning of simple equivalence results. It remains to be explained why in rhematic position the meaning 'at least' arises. We should note that in order to transfer such a verb to the position of rheme in an affirmative sentence it is essential to use contrastive stress, not the usual phrasal stress. In other words, it is necessary to create a polemical context. But why does the speaker in his polemics with his addressee insist on the idea 'at least', in contrast to 'at most'? This is evidently explained by pragmatic considerations. If *Pal'to ↓ stoit tysiachu rublei* [the coat is worth a thousand roubles] is said by a shop assistant, he is pursuing an obvious material interest. If said by a customer, he is consoling himself with the thought that he has not wasted his money. Compare the behaviour of other classes of predicates in similar conditions (J. Apresjan 1980: 74–9).    [26] See n. 23.

2) With a quantifying group as the subject [cf. 1.1.4); usually preceding the subject].

V {D/N$^1_{nom}$}

*Vsego bylo okolo tysiachi demonstrantov* [there were about a thousand demonstrators altogether]. *Bylo mnogo plakatov* [there were a lot of placards]. *Est' mnogo otvetov na etot vopros* [there are many answers to that question].

4.2. *Bylo X* = 'Event, time period or state X occurred' [In the present, where N$^1$ = nom, represented by Ø, in which the construction approaches a nominating or predicateless status, especially when determinants are present:[27] *Noch'. Ponedel'nik. Krugom zavarukha, govor, krik* (Night. Monday. Commotion, hubbub and shouts all around); usually precedes the subject; ~ SYN: *idti* (to proceed), *stoiat'* (to prevail, reign); ANAL: *nastupat', nachinat'sia* (to set in, begin); *prokhodit'* (to be coming to an end)].

1) With a noun subject in the nominative.

N$^1_{nom}$ V

*Byla noch'* [it was night]. *Byl* ⟨*zavtra budet*⟩ *ponedel'nik* [it was ⟨tomorrow is⟩ Monday]. *Byla voina* [the war was on].

2) In modal constructions with an infinitive subject clause introduced by relative pronouns and the adverbs *kogo* [whom], *chto* [what], *gde* [where], *zachem* [what for], *kuda* [whither], *kogda* [when] [cf. 1.1.3)].

V Rel S

*Budet, chto vspomnit'* [there'll be something to remember]. *Bylo o chem zadumat'sia* [there was something to reflect on].

u N$^1_{gen}$ V Rel S [N$^1$—agent or u N$^1_{gen}$—the personal sphere of N$^1$].

*U nego est' chto vspomnit'* [he has something to remember]. *A u nego est' gde perenochevat'?* [but has he got anywhere for us/them etc. to spend the night?].

N$^1_{dat}$ V Rel S [N$^1$—agent].

*Mne est' chto chitat'* [I have something to read]. *Nam budet* ⟨*bylo*⟩ *o chem potolkovat'* [we shall have ⟨we had⟩ something to talk about]. + *U menia vam budet gde spat'* [at my place you'll have somewhere to sleep].

4.3. *Bylo X* = 'moment in time X occurred' [represented in the present by Ø or *est'*; if the latter, *est'* bears the main phrasal or contrastive stress and means 'not less than X';[28] with negation in the present, represented by the word *net*; usually precedes the subject; ANAL: *bit'* (to chime, strike)].

---

[27] See n. 23.    [28] See n. 25.

$N^1_{nom}$ V

*Bylo piat' chasov utra* [it was five o'clock in the morning]. *Seichas vosem' chasov vechera* [it's now eight in the evening]. *Seichas ↓ est' vosem' chasov* [at least eight]. *Seichas net vos'mi chasov* [not yet eight].

4.4. *A bylo s X-om* = 'An undesirable state or event A, or one difficult to define, occurred and its main protagonist was living being X, who was drawn into A regardless of his will' [in the present represented by Ø; usually precedes the subject, except for those cases where the subject is expressed by an interrogative; SYN: *proiskhodit'*, *sluchat'sia* (to happen); ~ SYN: *vykhodit'* (to turn out), *poluchat'sia* (to turn out); *delat'sia* (to become), coll. *prikliuchit'sia* (to happen), coll. *tvorit'sia* (to happen), substandard *deiat'sia* (to happen); *postigat'* (to befall)].

$N^1_{nom}$ V s $N^2_{inst}$ [$N^1$—pronoun or rarely *neschast'e* (misfortune), *nepriiatnosti* (unpleasantness), *beda* (disaster)].

*Ne ponimaiu, chto so mnoi bylo* [I don't understand what was wrong with me]. *S nim neschast'e* [a misfortune has befallen him].

5.1. *Byt' X-u* = 'The speaker is sure that an event X, which in some way will affect him or another person about whom he is thinking at the moment of speech, will inevitably occur in the near future'[29] [arch. or bookish: only in the infinitive; usually in affirmative sentences; in negative sentences the sense is usually expressed with the aid of the verb *byvat'*: *Ne byvat' etomu!* (this shall not be!); ~ SYN: *ne minovat'* (not to avoid, not to get around); *sluchat'sia*, *proiskhodit'* (to happen); ~ ANT: *izbezhat'* (to avoid)].[30]

---

[29] If the event does not personally affect the speaker or another person of whom he is thinking at the moment of speech, and if the speaker does not think the event is imminent, the form *budet groza* ⟨*svad'ba*⟩ [there will be a thunderstorm ⟨wedding⟩] should be used: *Kogda zakonchitsia sbor vinograda, budet mnogo svadeb* [when the grape harvest ends there will be a lot of weddings].

[30] Let us look at the alternative possibility of extracting the meaning of utterances such as *byt' groze* not from a single source—the existential-modal lexical meaning of the verb itself—but from two separate sources. The existential component of such utterances may follow from the purely existential sense of the verb *byt'*, for example, sense 4.2, while the modal sense (the speaker's certainty that an important event is inevitable) derives from the meaning of the syntactic construction type $N^1_{dat} V_{inf}$; e.g. *sadu tsvest'* [the garden will bloom] (V. Maiakovskii); *vam ne vidat' takikh srazhenii* [you will not see such battles] (M. Iu. Lermontov), etc. This solution may appear attractive as it makes it possible to reduce the number of entities: there is no need for sense 5.1. We shall adduce a number of arguments against this solution. Their central idea is the thesis that $N^1_{dat} V_{inf}$ is not the same syntactic construction as that on which sentences of the type *Byt' groze* are based. (1) In sentences of the *Byt' groze* type, in prototypical cases the event is denoted by an abstract noun in the dative, and the subject of the event is not directly named. On the other hand, in the *Sadu tsvest'* type, the event is denoted by the infinitive in prototypical cases, while the noun in the dative has concrete meaning and denotes the subject of the event. (2) In the *Byt' groze* type of sentence, the infinitive, following the general rule for existential verbs, normally precedes the noun in the dative, while in the *Sadu tsvest'* type it follows it. The only noticeable and easily explicable exceptions are sentences with copula verbs; e.g. *byt'* ⟨*ne byt'*⟩ *emu tvoim muzhem* [he is ⟨not⟩ to be your husband]. (3) In the

$V N^2_{dat}$

*Byt' groze* [there's a thunderstorm brewing]. *Byt' bede* [there's trouble brewing].
*Esli i dal'she tak delo poidet—byt' svad'be* [if things go on the way they are—
there'll be a wedding].

5.2. *A budet X-u* = 'The speaker is sure that an undesirable event A will inevitably befall object X' [represented in the present by Ø; usually precedes the subject; predominantly present and future; in the past and present the utterance
signifies a forthcoming event with regard to the point of reference: *Nam byl
konets* ~ 'we realized that it was all over with us'; ~ SYN: *postigat'* (to befall),
*nastigat'* (to overtake); *svalivat'sia, obrushivat'sia* (to crash down (upon))].[31]

$N^1_{dat} VN^2_{nom}$ [$N^2$—*chto* (what), *koe-chto* , *chto-to* (something) etc. or *gibel'*
(ruin, end), *konets* (end), substandard *kryshka, kaiuk, khana* ('curtains', end)].

*Nam teper' konets* ⟨*kryshka*⟩ [it's all up with us now]. *Srazu vse poimut, i tebe—
kaiuk, a s toboi—i drugim* [everyone will understand straight away: you've had
it and so have the others with you] (A. Fadeev) [see also 1.1.2)].

$N^1_{dat} VN^2_{nom}$ za $N^3_{acc}$

*Koe-chto tebe, konechno, za samovolku budet* [of course you'll get something for
absence without leave].

5.3. *Budet s X-a Y-a* = 'Deeming undesirable the continuation of situation Y
or a situation related to object Y, in which person X has been up to the moment
of speech, the speaker expresses the view that as from the moment of speech
that situation should be terminated' [usually in direct speech; SYN: *dovol'no,
dostatochno, khvatit* (enough)].

*Byt' groze* type, with existential *byt'*, there is only a rheme, while the *Sadu tsvest'* type has a theme
(a noun group in the dative) as well as a rheme (a verb or verb group with full meaning in the
infinitive). (4) Constructions of the *Byt' groze* type have lexical constraints: the position of the verb
can only be filled by *byt'* and that of the noun only by a noun signifying an event of importance in
the life of a person or many persons; *Byt' svad'be* [there's a wedding in the offing] is far more acceptable than '*Byt' svidaniiu* [there's a rendezvous in the offing]. In the *Sadu tsvest'* type, neither the
position of the verb nor that of the noun are lexically constrained.

[31] Strictly speaking, the meaning 'an undesirable event A will inevitably befall object X' is expressed
not only by *byt'* alone, but by the whole construction $N^1_{dat} V N^2_{nom}$, where the $N^2$ position is occupied
by words with the general meaning 'imminent death'—*gibel', kaiuk, konets, kryshka, khana*, etc. The
lexical meanings of precisely these words contain a temporal component indicating that the event
foreshadowed is undesirable and that it has been shifted into the future with reference to the moment of observation in the past or present. As for the idea of inevitability, it is most likely to be
conveyed by the combination of the dative and *byt'*, which appears here basically in its existential
sense. Thus, all in all, the identification of sense 5.2 is in some degree a lexicographic convenience.
It can be justified only by the fact that *byt'* holds a central position in the construction under consideration. Let us note one further difference between this construction and the outwardly similar type
*nam* ⟨*tam*⟩ *bylo razdol'e* [there we were at liberty], in which the usual copula sense of *byt'* is displayed. The construction as a whole does not have any sense of foretelling, but the meaning of a
simple statement of some situation at a fixed moment in the past, present, or future.

*Budet s* N$^1_{gen}$

*Budet s tebia* [that's enough for you; stop it!; you've had enough].

*Budet s* N$^1_{gen}$ N$^2_{gen}$ [rare].

*Budet s menia vashikh zhalob* [I've had enough of your complaints].
*Budet s tebia varen'ia* [you've had enough jam].

6.1. An auxiliary verb whose personal forms in the future combined with verb X in the imperfective infinitive give the forms of the analytical future indicative of that verb [any verb may be X except the verb *byt'* itself in all meanings and the verbs *byvat'* and *iavliat'sia* in the strictly copula sense;[32] note the impossibility of *\*on budet byt' zdes' zavtra* (he will be being here tomorrow); *?on budet byvat' veselym* (he will be being jolly); *\*vasha rabota budet iavliat'sia otkrytiem* (your work will be being a discovery); ~ SYN: *stat'* (to become)].

N$^1_{nom}$ V$^1_{fut}$ V$_{inf}$

*Ia budu ⟨ty budesh', on budet⟩ rabotat'* [I ⟨you, he⟩ will work]. *My budem nochevat' v khizhine* [we'll spend the night in the hut]. *Mne strashno podumat', chto vy ne budete bol'she byvat' u nas* [The thought that you won't be calling on us any more is dreadful for me].

6.2. An auxiliary verb which combines with a verb X in the past participle passive of the perfective to form the analytical passive voice of that verb; [as an auxiliary verb it has personal forms as well as the verbal adverb and infinitive; in the personal forms it combines mainly with short forms of the participle: *byl ⟨budet⟩ narisovan* (was ⟨will be⟩ sketched); in the gerundial form it combines with both short and long forms of the participle: *buduchi narisovan(nym)* (being drawn); in the infinitive it combines only with the long form: *byt' izobrazhennym takim masterom bol'shaia chest' dlia menia* (to be depicted by a professional painter of such stature is a great honour for me); ~ SYN: *byvat'; okazyvat'sia*].

N$^1_{nom}$ V$^1_{past\ part\ pass\ pf}$

*Portret byl ⟨budet⟩ zakonchen v sentiabre* [the portrait was ⟨will be⟩ finished in September].

Δ *mozhet byt'*, bookish *byt' mozhet* [perhaps] = 'govoriashchii predpolagaet ili dopuskaet, chto opredelennaia situatsiia imeet mesto' [the speaker assumes or acknowledges that a particular situation is taking place] [Parenthetic: *On, mozhet byt', ustal* (he may be tired)]; *dolzhno byt'* = 'govoriashchii dumaet, chto opredelennaia situatsiia imeet mesto, khotia i dopuskaet, chto mozhet oshibat'sia'

---

[32] Strange to say, this obvious constraint is not mentioned in any of the Russian explanatory dictionaries.

[the speaker believes that a particular situation is taking place, but allows that he may be mistaken] [Parenthetic: *On, dolzhno byt, ustal* (he must be tired)]; *byt' po semu* = 'Vlast'iu, kotoraia emu dana, govoriashchii ob"iavliaet obiazatel'nym k ispolneniiu sdelannoe tol'ko chto predlozhenie' [by the power vested in him, the speaker declares that a proposal only just made must be implemented] [arch.; performative; direct speech only];[33] *Byla ne byla!* = 'govoriashchii ob"iavliaet o svoei gotovnosti risknut'' [the speaker declares his readiness to take a risk] [direct speech only]; *stalo byt'* = 'sledovatel'no, znachit' [hence, therefore] [Parenthetic]; *Tak i byt'* = 'govoriashchii ob"iavliaet o svoem soglasii na sdelannoe emu predlozhenie, soobshchaia odnovremenno, chto ono ne vo vsem ego udovletvoriaet' [the speaker declares his acceptance of a proposal put to him, stating at the same time that he is not fully satisfied with it] [Performative; direct speech only]; *Kak byt'* = 'Govoriashchii sprashivaet, kak sleduet postupit' v slozhivsheisia situatsii' [the speaker asks how he should act in a given situation]; *I byl takov* = 'Tot, o kom idet rech', sdelav nechto, bystro pokinul mesto sobytii' [the person spoken of, having done something, quickly departed from the scene of the events]; *Bud' chto budet* = 'govoriashchii ob"iavliaet, chto on gotov k liubym posledstviiam priniatogo im resheniia, kak by plokhi oni ni byli' [the speaker declares that he is prepared for any consequences his decision may result in, however bad they may be] [direct speech only]; *Chto budet, to budet*[34] = 'govoriashchii ob"iavliaet, chto gotov priniat' liuboi iskhod sobytii' [the speaker declares that he is prepared to accept any outcome of events] [direct speech only]; *Chto bylo, to bylo*[35] = 'govoriashchii ob"iavliaet, chto gotov zabyt' o proshlom v interesakh budushchego' [the speaker declares that he is prepared to forget the past in the interests of the future] [direct speech only]; *Iz X-a budet tolk* = 'znaia svoistva sushchestva X ili ego predshestvuiushchuiu deiatel'nost', govoriashchii vyrazhaet uverennost', chto X budet umet' khorosho delat' chto-to' [knowing the qualities of person X or his previous activity, the speaker expresses his confidence that X will be capable of doing something well].[36]

---

[33] Being restricted to direct speech [not usable in indirect speech acts—the feature of unquotability] is an important pragmatic property of many lexical units. This property is lexicographically significant as it is lexicalized. We have already drawn attention to the fact that emphatic particles as close in meaning as *dazhe* [even] and *-to* also differ in this respect. *Dazhe* has the property of quotability (*on skazal, chto dazhe Serezha prishel* [he said that even Serezha had come]), whereas *-to* has not (*\*on skazal, chto Serezha-to prishel*). Those dictionaries with which we are familiar do not register this lexicographically significant feature.

[34] For an interesting discussion of phrasemes of the type *chto bylo, to bylo* and *chto budet, to budet,* etc. see Wierzbicka 1987*a*.

[35] See n. 34.

[36] The text of the present chapter was read by L. L. Iomdin, I. A. Mel'čuk, and E. V. Paducheva, to whom the author expresses his gratitude for valuable critical comments.

# 10

# A Lexicographic Portrait of the Verb *vyiti* [to emerge, come out]

## 1. The Concept of the Lexicographic Portrait

By a lexicographic portrait of a lexeme we mean a dictionary entry compiled within the framework of a unified or integrated description of a language. The general concept of this description is set out in J. Apresjan (1986*b*).

The integration principle requires that the dictionary and the grammar be co-ordinated in the types of information given in them and the ways in which they are recorded. Only then are the dictionary and the grammar able to interact with each other within the framework of an integrated linguistic model. In practical terms this means two things.

On the one hand, every lexeme in the dictionary should be assigned all the types of information that the rules of grammar may refer to (adjusting the lexis to grammar). By rules of grammar in this context we mean fairly general linguistic rules, including, for example, apart from grammatical rules proper, prosodic, semantic, pragmatic, communicative, and co-occurrence rules.

On the other hand, every grammatical rule should be formulated in such a way as to predict the behaviour of every lexeme falling within its scope, in all possible conditions and contexts except those which are described directly in its dictionary entry (adjusting the grammar to the lexis).

The lexicographic portrait as an element of a dictionary conceived as part of an integrated linguistic description differs considerably from the usual dictionary entry.

1. It includes certain fundamentally new types of information never previously included in a dictionary, such as information about the non-trivial prosodic, communicative, and pragmatic properties of a lexeme.

2. The traditional types of information are considerably expanded. Unified single-stratum explications are now divided into a number of layers (assertions, presuppositions, modal frames, frames of observation) differing by their reactions to different textual conditions. Within assertions the semantic components are divided into strong components (those which are preserved in all conditions of use of the lexeme) and weak components (those which may be cancelled out by stronger contextual elements). The volume of information on co-occurrence matters is also greatly expanded. Previously co-occurrence was considered mainly

from a lexical standpoint, although lexemes also have interesting prosodic, morphological, syntactic, semantic, pragmatic, and communicative co-occurrence properties and constraints.

3. All linguistic information in the dictionary is recorded in the same formal language as in a grammar.

The strictly linguistic differences between a lexicographic portrait and a usual dictionary entry come down to these three points. There are, however, metalinguistic differences as well. These derive from the fact that a dictionary of lexicographic portraits has an over-arching aim which is not shared by a standard explanatory dictionary. The over-arching aim of a dictionary of lexicographic portraits is to present the lexis of a language as a system. This results in two more points of difference.

4. An attempt is made to demonstrate the motivated links between the different properties of a lexeme, for example, its meaning, on the one hand, and its prosodic characteristics and government pattern, on the other.

5. The lexicographic portrait of a lexeme is compiled against the background of a particular lexicographic type. 'Lexicographic type' is the name for a more or less compact group of lexemes with shared properties (prosodic, syntactic, semantic, communicative, etc.) and therefore requiring a homogeneous dictionary account. The greater the number of such properties and linguistic rules requiring reference to them, the more interesting the lexicographic type.

All this means that each dictionary entry should reflect equally those properties of the lexeme which are shared with other lexemes (a problem of unification, or of lexicographic types), and those that distinguish it from other lexemes (a problem of individualization, or of lexicographic portraits).

At present the author is working on a dictionary of government and co-occurrence of the Russian verb, based on the Russian part of a bilingual dictionary (J. Apresjan and Pall Erna 1982). This new work was conceived as a dictionary of lexicographic portraits, with one important difference.

Certain restrictions on the treatment of lexemes are imposed by the mere fact that this is a dictionary of government and co-occurrence. For this reason certain important kinds of information, such as detail on syntactic and semantic derivatives of a verb (*lechit'* [to heal]—*lechenie* [treatment], *vrach* [doctor], *patsient* [patient], *bolezn'* [illness], *lekarstvo* [medicine], *bol'nitsa* [hospital], etc.), are not given. Nevertheless, within these limits we have tried to provide as full, integrated, and systematic a picture of verbs as possible, that is, to meet all the demands of the genre of the lexicographic portrait.

In addition to the features noted above, this genre also has the virtue of being able to draw together many signal achievements of contemporary theoretical linguistics.

By the 1960s it had become apparent that it was impossible to obtain any fundamentally new linguistic knowledge by working with such traditional material as word classes. Recognition of this fact led to a breakthrough into two completely new areas: in one direction, into the macrocosm of text linguistics; in another, into the microcosm of linguistic portraits.

Within the framework of the latter trend, individual words or even individual meanings of words became the subject of meticulous linguistic research and began to be described in unprecedented detail and fullness. For the first time in its long history, theoretical linguistics began to produce at least a semi-finished product for the lexicographer. To let slip this opportunity to make lexicographic use of the discoveries of the theoreticians would be to miss a chance to revitalize the whole business of dictionary-making.

In order to give a more complete picture of the proposed dictionary of lexicographic portraits, we shall consider the general format of a dictionary entry and the types of information included in it.

## 2. Format of a Dictionary Entry and Types of Lexicographic Information

In general terms the dictionary entry (the lexicographic portrait) of a verb comprises the following eight zones: (1) morphological, (2) stylistic, (3) semantic, (4) pragmatic, (5) prosodic and communicative, (6) syntactic (in the present form of the dictionary, this zone includes only government patterns, not syntactic (subcategorization) features, for example), (7) co-occurrence, (8) phraseological. Here the content of each of these zones, except the last, is considered in rather more detail and, where necessary, briefly illustrated by examples; any linguistic facts drawn from the Russian language, not only Russian verbs, may serve as illustrative material.

1. Morphological information: (1.1) type of paradigm (shown by a number of key forms); (1.2) aspectual correlate and constraints on aspect, tense, mood, person, number forms, etc. (e.g. in the senses 'to transpire, emerge' and 'to face a certain direction' the verb *vyiti* is used only in the imperfective: *vy, vykhodit, moi diadia* [it turns out you're my uncle], while *vy, vyshlo, moi diadia* is impossible, and *okna kukhni vykhodiat vo dvor* [the kitchen windows give onto the yard], while *okna kukhni vyshli vo dvor* is impossible); (1.3) variant morphs of the same grammeme (see the verbs *zavernut'* [to turn (intrans.)], *zagotovit'* [to stockpile], *osmyslit'* [to make sense of], *srézat'* [to cut off], *podseiat'* [to sow (more)], each of which has two imperfective forms: *zavorachivat'* and *zavertyvat'*, *zagotavlivat'* and *zagotovliat'*, *osmysliat'* and *osmyslivat'*, *srezát'* and *srezyvat'*, *podseivat'* and *podsevat'*); (1.4) capacity to form part of an analytical form (*byt'* in *budet chitat'* [he will work]).

2. In the version of the dictionary now being drafted, stylistic information is given by traditional stylistic tags. An important feature of the stylistic classification used in the dictionary is not so much the set of such tags themselves, but rather their application: the minimal objects of stylistic classification are not

words or word meanings but syntactic constructions or even free collocations manifesting the sense in question.

3. Semantic information: (3.1) an analytical explication of a given lexical meaning, specifying the assertive part (a finite verb form in what is syntactically the main clause of the explication), presuppositions (gerundial or participial phrases or subordinate clauses in the text of the explications) and modal frames; (3.2) various uses within the same lexical meaning (e.g. the copula sense of *byt'* [to be], used with a subject in the nominative, a subject in the genitive in quantitative constructions, and with an infinitive or propositional subject, etc.: *paren' byl slegka navesele* [the lad was slightly tipsy], *liudei bylo mnogo* [there were a lot of people there], *zhdat' bylo nekogda* [there was no time to wait]); (3.3) comments on the permissible combinations of lexical and grammatical meanings in various contextual conditions (e.g. constraints upon the aspectual meanings of *byt'* in its locative sense in negative sentences with the subject in the nominative or genitive: *otets ne byl na more* [father had never been to the seaside] (the general factual meaning of the imperfective, not the progressive-durative) vs. *ottsa ne bylo na more* (the progressive-durative meaning of the imperfective, not the general-factual)); (3.4) the possibility of semantic contrast between two different ways of expressing the same grammeme (e.g. the zero form vs. the form *est'* of the verb *byt'* in the [quasi-] possessive sense: *mal'chiku tri goda* [the boy is (exactly) three years old] vs. *mal'chiku ést' tri goda* [the boy is (at least) three years old]); (3.5) semantic links between the given lexeme and others on the paradigmatic axis of language, that is, in the lexis at large (exact and inexact synonyms, analogues, exact and inexact conversives, exact and inexact antonyms).

4. Pragmatic information: (4.1) pragmatic features, such as the capacity for performative use or inadmissibility in reported speech (cf. the phraseme *kak byt'* [what to do?], which may be used in indirect speech, vs. the phraseme *tak i byt'* [so be it], which is used only performatively in direct speech); (4.2) non-trivial illocutionary functions of a lexeme (e.g. statements with the verb *znat'* [to know] in the imperative in the context of subordinate clauses introduced by the conjunction *chto*, where the illocutionary function of urging is not present: *znai, chto ona tebia liubit* [know that she loves you]); (4.3) the relative status of speaker and addressee in social, age, educational or other hierarchy (e.g. use of the personal pronouns *ty* and *vy*); (4.4) lexical connotations or material associations as opposed to components of meaning in the strict sense (e.g. the connotation of monotony in the verb *pilit'* [to saw; to nag], of abruptness in *rubit'* [to chop], and of speed in *streliat'* [to shoot]).

5. Prosodic and communicative information: (5.1) the necessity, possibility, or impossibility of placing the main phrasal stress on the given lexeme; (5.2) the given lexeme's ability or inability to be the theme or rheme of a statement (note the inherently rhematic nature of factive verbs such as *ponimat'* [to understand], *znat'* [to know], *videt'* [to see], which stands out particularly sharply in comparison with the mainly thematic putative verbs such as *schitat'* [to consider],

*polagat'* [to suppose], *nakhodit'* [to find]: the former may and sometimes must bear the main phrasal stress, while the latter never do, although they may bear a contrasting (logical) stress: *vy ↑ponimaete, chto vam nichego ne ugrozhaet?* [you do realize that there is no threat to you?]; *vy schitaete, chto vam nichego ne ↑ugrozhaet?* [do you believe there is no threat to you?]).

6. Information about government patterns: (6.1) the semantic valencies of a lexeme, shown as variables in propositional form at the heading of the explication (*A verbuet B iz X-a dlia Y-a v/na C na T* [A recruits B from X for Y at C for T] where A—recruiter, B—the recruit, X—the body of people from which B is recruited, Y—the activity for which B is recruited, C—the place B must go to for his work and T—the period of time for which B is hired); (6.2) surface-syntactic ways of expressing semantic valencies (by case, preposition and case, and others); (6.3) the syntactic optionality or obligatoriness of valencies; (6.4) the syntactic compatibility or otherwise of valencies; (6.5) the transform-ability of government patterns with the same lexical meaning (cf. *ia shchitaiu, chto on chestnyi chelovek* [I consider that he is an honest person] – *ia shchitaiu ego chestnym chelovekom* [I consider him (to be) honest]).

7. Information about co-occurrence or co-occurrence constraints: (7.1) mor-phological (e.g. the combination of polite *vy* with long-form adjectives in the singular and short-form adjectives in the plural: *vy nedostatochno samostoia-tel'naia* (long-form singular) [you are not independent enough] and *vy nedosta-tochno samostoiatel'ny* (short-form plural) [you (polite form) are not indepen-dent enough], whereas *??vy nedostatochno samostoiatel'nye* and *\*vy nedostatochno samostoiatel'na* lie outside standard usage); (7.2) stylistic (the verb *byt'* in the sense 'to arrive' is used in stylistically neutral constructions of the type *Ivana segodnia ne budet* [Ivan won't be coming today] and in the obsolete construction *vy budete k nam zavtra?* [will you be coming to see us tomorrow?]); (7.3) seman-tic (the verb *vyiti* in the sense 'to run out, be expended' combines with the prepositional phrase 'za + $N_{acc}$', where N is any noun meaning a period of time: *za den'* ⟨*za nedeliu, za mesiats, za god . . .*⟩ *vykhodit okolo semidesiati rublei* [in a day ⟨week, month, year⟩ approximately seventy roubles are spent]); (7.4) lexical (the verb *vyiti* in the sense 'to cease to be in some state' combines with the prepositional phrase 'za + $N_{acc}$', in which N is a noun from a lexically closed list: *vasha stat'ia vyshla za ramki* ⟨*predely, granitsy*⟩ *ustanovlennogo ob"ema* [your article exceeded the agreed word-limit]); (7.5) pragmatic (in substandard usage polite *vy* may combine with a long-form adjective not only in the singular but also in the plural, but the speaker reveals his low level of education: *Uzh bol'no vy obidchivye* [you ain't half quick to take offence]); (7.6) prosodic (in the past tense of the verb *byt'* the main phrasal stress in negative clauses shifts onto the negative particle *ne* in all forms except fem: *né byl, né bylo, né byli* but *ne bylá*); (7.7) communicative (the verb *byt'* in the sense 'to exist' is usually preposed to the subject and forms the theme of the utterance: *est' liudi, kotorye ne liubiat muzyku* [there are those who don't like music]); (7.8) syntactic (e.g. an attribute

which is a parametric noun must have a dependent: *opukhol' velichinoi s iaitso* [a tumour the size of an egg]).

It may easily be seen that this list includes many (though not all) types of information foreseen in Mel'čuk and Zholkovsky (1984). On the other hand, the dictionary under discussion goes further in its design than the latter work as it aims to reflect all properties of the lexeme which are pertinent to the rules.

## 3. A Lexicographic Portrait of the Verb *vyiti*

### 3.1. LEXICOGRAPHIC TYPES FOR *VYITI*

The verb *vyiti* belongs to several lexicographic types at once.

First, it is a verb of locomotion. Like other verbs of locomotion, it has the valencies of point of departure, destination, and route (*vyiti iz lesa* [to come out of the forest], *vyiti na dorogu* [to emerge onto the road], *vyiti cherez chernyi khod* [to leave by the back door]), and combines easily with noun groups and infinitives denoting purpose (*vyiti za gazetami* [to go out to fetch the newspapers], *vyiti poguliat'* [to go out for a stroll]).

Secondly, it is a derivative of the verb *idti* [to walk]. It retains such features of *idti* as the ability to denote (*a*) the movement of a means of transport (*teplokhod vyshel iz Sevastopolia v Ialtu* [the vessel left Sebastopol for Yalta], *teplokhod idet iz Sevastopolia v Ialtu* [the vessel is sailing from Sebastopol to Yalta]); (*b*) activity (*vyiti na boi, idti v boi* [to go into battle, to take the field]); (*c*) a change of state (*vyiti v generaly* [to be promoted to general], *idti v soldaty* [to go for a soldier]; *vyiti zamuzh, idti zamuzh* [to get married (of a woman)]); (*d*) the existence of a situation (*vyshla nepriiatnost'* [some unpleasantness resulted], *idet eksperiment* [an experiment is in progress]).

Thirdly, it is derivative with the prefix *vy-*, which with verbs of locomotion has a particular sense not yet recorded in dictionaries. A *vyshel iz B v C* [A emerged from B into C] means that A moved from an enclosed space B into a more open space C. It is possible to *vyiti iz komnaty v koridor* [emerge from the room into the corridor] or *so dvora na ulitsu* [from the courtyard into the street], but impossible to *\*vyiti iz koridora v komnatu* [emerge from the corridor into the room] or *\*s ulitsy na dvor* [from the street into the courtyard]. Note that the differences between the more and less enclosed (more open) spaces are objective: in more enclosed spaces there are fewer possibilities for entry and exit and more obstacles to movement (*vyshel iz lesa na polianu* [he emerged from the forest into a clearing], but not *\*vyshel s poliany v les* [he emerged from a clearing into the forest]).

The prefix *vy-* in this sense is antonymous to the prefix *v-*: compare *voiti iz koridora v komnatu* ⟨*vo dvor s ulitsy, v les s poliany*⟩ [to enter the room from the corridor ⟨the courtyard from the street, the forest from the clearing⟩] = 'to move into an enclosed space from a more open space' and the impossible *\*voiti* *v koridor iz komnaty* ⟨*na ulitsu so dvora, na polianu iz lesu*⟩ [to enter the corridor from the room ⟨the street from the courtyard, the clearing from the forest⟩]. This difference is characteristic of all verbs of locomotion with the prefixes *vy-* and *v-*, including causatives: *vybezhat' iz komnaty v koridor* [to rush from the room into the corridor]—*vbezhat' v komnatu iz koridora* [to rush into the room from the corridor]; *vyletet' iz komnaty v sad* [to fly out of the room into the garden]—*vletet' v komnatu iz sada* [to fly into the room from the garden]; *vyvesti svidetelei iz zala zasedanii v koridor* [to lead the witnesses from the hearings room into the corridor]—*vvesti svidetelei v zal zasedanii iz koridora* [to lead the witnesses into the hearings room from the corridor].

This means, incidentally, that the lexicographic type 'vy- + verb of locomotion' should be described against the background of the lexicographic type 'v- + verb of locomotion', and vice versa. It is true that it would be rash to count on absolute mirror symmetry in the structures of polysemy of the verbs with *vy-* and *v-*. We may note, for example, that some verbs of locomotion with *vy-* may have a sense of motion away or dispatch, for which the opposition between enclosed and open spaces is irrelevant: *vsiu mebel' uzhe vyvezli* [all the furniture had already been carted away]; *kogda oni vyekhali* ⟨*vyleteli*⟩? [when did they leave?]. The corresponding verbs *vvezti, v"ekhat',* and *vletet'* do not possess direct analogues of these senses.

There are also less obvious links between *vyiti* and other lexicographic types.

It may be observed, for example, that at the basis of the meanings of all dynamic verbs denoting physical actions lie simple ideas of position (spatial location), property, state, or existence. These form the semantic framework, or perhaps the basis of the lexicon of verbs in many languages, because they depict the simplest situations in which objects from the material world are encountered and imagined. The dynamic verbs add to these the ideas of change (*idti* ~ 'to change location', *iz nego vyidet general* ~ 'he has the makings [the properties] of a general', *vyiti iz transa* ~ 'to cease to be in a state of trance'; *vyshla nepriiatnost'* ~ 'an unpleasantness began to exist') or cause of change (in causative verbs). We may also note that the combination of meanings 'to be situated', 'to have a property', 'to be in a state', and 'to exist' is characteristic of verbs of being in Russian and other languages, above all of the verb *to be* itself.

Lexicographically speaking, this means that in setting out to describe a dynamic verb denoting a physical action, the compiler should seek in it a combination of 'being' senses and, if present, set this out in the entry for that verb in the same way as in entries for 'being' verbs, allowing, of course, for complicating factors.

With the verb *vyiti* this becomes a problem of systematizing and arranging such meanings as *vyiti iz tiur'my* ~ 'to cease to be in prison', *vyiti na rabotu* ~ 'to begin to be at work', *vyiti iz sostava komissii* = 'to cease to be a committee member', *vyiti zamuzh* = 'to begin to be married' (of a woman), *za mesiats vyshlo okolo kubometra drov* [about a cubic metre of firewood was used up in a month] ~ 'ceased to exist', *vyshla nepriiatnost'* ~ 'began to exist', etc.

A complication is presented by the fact that in the underlying locative, copula, and existential senses of *vyiti*, as can be seen from our fragmentary examples, there are regular phasal accretions, in one case terminative, in another inchoative. The arrangement of lexical meanings must therefore follow not one but several lexicographical axes at once. As the primary basis for classification it is natural to select those axes which give the largest groupings of meanings. In accordance with this principle, the entry for *vyiti* begins with the group of terminative senses (subgroups 1 to 4 in 3.2), followed by the group of inchoative senses (subgroups 5 to 8 in 3.2). Within these groups the subgroups are ordered in the sequence 'locomotion'—'location'—'property or state'—'existence'. Lastly, the senses within a subgroup are ordered from literal to figurative and from less figurative to more figurative: *devochka vyshla iz komnaty* [the girl left the room] and *sudno vyshlo iz gavani* [the ship left harbour]; *vyiti na rabotu* [to go out to work] and *vyiti na ekrany* [to go to air (of television programmes), be released (of a film)]; *iz nego vyidet general* [he has the makings of a general] and *iz etoi zatei nichego ne vyidet* [nothing will come of this venture].

Another interesting problem of lexicographic portraits is linked with what might be termed minor lexicographic types. In order to explain what is meant, let us imagine a dictionary entry for a polysemous word in a standard explanatory dictionary. Broadly speaking, the senses are arranged as follows: first the literal or basic senses, then various derived or figurative senses and, finally, phraseologically bound senses. As is well known, the process of metaphorization and phraseological binding is often based on the removal of some semantic components of the literal or basic meanings, in which assertive components are prominent. At the same time, this process is accompanied by the appearance of evaluations, presuppositions, and other nuanced elements of meaning. As a result, at the end of the entry there is a concentration of senses which are not distinguished from the senses of some other polysemous words by their crude and obvious semantic components, but may differ from them in the finer evaluative, presuppositional, and other similar components. The (quasi-)synonymous series which arise in this way are a real stumbling block to the lexicographer: traditional explications fail to describe the semantic distinctions between such synonyms. These are the series we term 'minor lexicographic types'. It is particularly difficult to draw an exact lexicographic portrait for a minor lexicographic type.

In the entry for *vyiti* the lexicographer encounters several interesting minor types:

(1) *vyiti, uiti, izraskhodovat'sia, issiaknut', istoshchit'sia* (*Vse drova vyshli* [all the firewood's been used up]) [to run out, come to an end, be used up, be exhausted];

(2) *vyiti, poluchit'sia* (*Iz etikh studentov vyidut khoroshie inzhenery* [these students will make good engineers]) [to emerge, be produced];

(3) *vyiti, poluchit'sia, sluchit'sia, proizoiti* (*Vyshla krupnaia nepriiatnost'* [a very unpleasant incident occurred]) [to occur, arise, result];

(4) *vyiti, poluchit'sia, okazat'sia, vyiasnit'sia* (*Vykhodit, chto vy pravy* [it turns out that you are right]) [to emerge, turn out, transpire];

(5) *vyiti, poluchit'sia, vypast', vydat'sia* (*Roman vyshel* ⟨*poluchilsia*⟩ *neplokhoi* [the novel turned out quite good]; *Den' vypal trudnyi* [the day turned out to be difficult]; *Leto vydalos' zharkoe* [the summer turned out hot]) [to turn out to be].

In the last series, for example, the first two synonyms indicate human participation in the outcome, while the last two imply that the situation arose by chance thanks to the action of natural forces or higher powers.

In the dictionary entry for the verb *vyiti* given below we have done our best to take account of all the problems and difficulties described above. It begins with a synopsis or brief guide to the entry: the whole hierarchy of meanings is set out in simple terms and each meaning is illustrated by a brief example. This is followed by the text of the entry proper. For the most part the notation adopted by J. Apresjan and Pall Erna (1982) is used. Grammemes have been given new and more transparent labels which are fully self-evident and thus require no explanation. The text of the entry may be interrupted at any point by comments (given in square brackets), which are to be regarded as part of the dictionary.

## 3.2. DICTIONARY ENTRY FOR THE VERB *VYITI*

VYITI, *vyidu, vyidesh'*; past *vyshel, -shla, -shlo*; imperative *vyidi*; participle *vyshedshii*; verbal adverb *vyidia*; impf *vykhodít'*;

1.1. 'on foot, to move outside'; *vyiti iz komnaty* [to go out of a room];

1.2. 'to move outside'; *sudno vyshlo iz bukhty* [the ship sailed out of the bay];

1.3. 'to set out, depart'; *polk vykhodit zavtra* [the regiment moves out tomorrow];

2. 'to cease to be located somewhere'; *vyiti iz tiur'my* [to come out of prison];

3.1. 'to cease to be a part or member'; *vyiti iz sostava komissii* [to leave a committee, resign/step down from membership of a committee];

3.2. 'to cease to be in a given state'; *vyiti iz povinoveniia* [to cease to be obedient, get out of control];

3.3. 'to cease to do'; *vyiti iz boia* [to leave the field of battle, cease to fight];

4. 'to come to an end, run out, be used up'; *za mesiats vyshlo okolo kubometra drov* [about a cubic metre of firewood was used up in a month];

5.1. 'to come, appear'; *vyiti na rabotu* [to come to work, report for work];

5.2. 'to appear, become accessible'; *vyiti na ekrany* [to be released, go to air (of films, television programmes)];

5.3. 'to receive access': *vyiti na zamestitelia predsedatelia* [to obtain access to the deputy chairman];

6. 'to enter into matrimony'; *vyiti zamuzh* [to get married (of a woman)];

7.1. 'to turn into, become'; *vyiti v generaly* [to become a general];

7.2. 'to have the makings of'; *iz nego vyidet general* [he has the makings of a general];

7.3. 'to begin to exist'; *iz etoi zatei nichego ne vyidet* [nothing will come of this venture];

7.4. 'to turn out to be'; *vstrecha vyshla interesnoi* [the meeting turned out to be interesting];

8.1. 'to result, occur'; *vyshla nepriiatnost'* [some unpleasantness resulted];

8.2. 'to turn out, transpire'; *vykhodit, vy pravy* [it turns out that you are right];

9. 'to face a certain direction'; *okna vykhodiat v sad* [the windows look out over the garden].

1.1. *A vyshel iz B v C* = 'Living being A, on foot, moved out of enclosed space B into a more open space C' [The components 'enclosed space' and 'more open space' explain why it is impossible to say *\*on vyshel vo dvor s ulitsy* (he went out from the street into the courtyard); the correct form is *on voshel vo dvor s ulitsy* (he came into the courtyard from the street), although *on vyshel so dvora na ulitsu* (he went out from the courtyard into the street) is possible; ~ SYN: *uiti* (to go away); ANAL: *vysypat'* (to pour out (intrans.)); *vybezhat'* (to run out), *vyletet'* (to fly out), *vypolzti* (to crawl out), *vyplyt'* (to swim out); ANT: *voiti* (to come/go in)].

$N^1_{nom}$ V

*Mama vyshla* [Mummy's gone out].

$N^1_{nom}$ V {$A_{nom}/A_{inst}/P$ $N^1_x$ } [A, P, $N^2$—state of $N^1$].

*Deti vyshli razdetye* ⟨*razdetymi, bez pal'to i bez shapok*⟩ [the children went out in their indoor clothes ⟨without coats and hats⟩].

$N^1_{nom}$ V {$D/P_1$ $N^2_x$}

*Iz komnaty* ⟨*iz doma, iz lesa*⟩ *vyshel starik* [out of the room ⟨house, forest⟩ came an old man].

$N^1_{nom}$ V {$D/P_2$ $N^2_x$}

*Turisty vyshli na dorogu* [the hikers emerged onto the road].

$N^1_{nom}$ V {$D/P_3$ $N^2_x$} [Mostly for alighting from transport].

*Gde vy vykhodite* [where are you getting out?]; *Turisty vyshli u Bol'shogo teatra* [the tourists got off at the Bol'shoi Theatre].

$N^1_{nom}$ V {v $N^2_{acc}$/cherez $N^2_{acc}$} [$N^2$—an exit route or aperture].

*Grabiteli vyshli* (*iz doma*) *cherez balkon* [the burglars got out (of the house) over the balcony].

$N^1_{nom}$ V na $N^2_{acc}$ [$N^2$—aim of action].

*Deti vyshli na progulku* [the children went out for a walk].

$N^1_{nom}$ V za $N^2_{inst}$ [delivery or receipt of $N^2$—aim of action].

*Lena vyshla za khlebom ⟨pochtoi⟩* [Lena went out to get some bread ⟨the mail⟩].

$N^1_{nom}$ V pered $N^2_{inst}$ [$N^2$—a person or people].

*Novobrantsy vykhodili po odnomu pered stroem i proiznosili slova prisiagi* [the recruits stepped forward one by one in front of the ranks and swore the oath of allegiance].

$N^1_{nom}$ V $V_{inf}$ [$V_{inf}$—aim of action].

*Deti vyshli proguliat'sia ⟨podyshat' svezhim vozdukhom⟩* [the children went out for a walk ⟨to take the air⟩].

[figurative use]

*Zavod vyshel iz otstaiushchikh v peredovye* [the works advanced from being among the laggards to being a front-ranker].

1.2. *A vyshel iz B v C* = 'Vehicle A moved out of enclosed space B into a more open space C'. [See commentary to 1.1; also of people on boats, ships, etc.; ANAL: *uiti* (to go away); *vyletet'* (to fly out); *vyekhat'* (to drive away, depart), *vyplyt'* (to swim out, sail out); ANT: *voiti* (to go/come in).]

$N^1_{nom}$ V {D/P$_1$ $N^2_x$}

*Karavan vyshel iz oazisa* [the caravan left the oasis]; *Korabl' vyshel iz bukhty* [the ship sailed out of the bay].

$N^1_{nom}$ V {D/P$_2$ $N^2_x$}

*Avtomobil' vyshel na avtostradu* [the car drove onto the motorway]; *Kombainy vyshli v pole* [the combine harvesters drove out into the field].

1.3. *A vyshel iz X-a v Y* = 'People or vehicle A, located at point X and intending to reach point Y, began moving towards Y and are located on the route from X to Y' [~ SYN: *otpravit'sia*; *vystupit'*; ANAL: *vyekhat'*, *vyletet'*; ~ ANT: *ostat'sia* (to remain)].

$N^1_{nom}$ V {D/P $N^2_x$} [D, P $N^2$—time].

*Polk vykhodit zavtra ⟨na sleduiushchei nedele⟩* [the regiment moves out tomorrow ⟨next week⟩].

$N^1_{nom}$ V {D/P$_1$ $N^2_x$}

*Voiska eshche ne vyshli iz goroda* [the troops have not left the city yet].

$N^1_{nom}$ V {D/P$_2$ $N^2_x$}

*Pervyi avtobus vykhodit v Moskvu v shest' utra* [the first coach leaves for Moscow at six in the morning].

$N^1_{nom}$ V {v $N^2_{acc}$/na $N^2_{acc}$} [$N^2$—aim of action].

*Zavtra my vykhodim v pokhod* [we're setting out on an expedition tomorrow]; *Otriad vyshel na razvedku* [the detachment set out on a reconnaissance mission].

2. *A vyshel iz X-a* = 'Person A ceased to be situated in institution X, where he had been confined for treatment or punishment' [X—prison, camp, hospital, place of detention, but not, for example, exile; ~ SYN: *pokinut'* (to leave); *vypisat'sia* (to be discharged); *osvobodit'sia* (to be released); ANAL: *vernut'sia* (to return); ~ ANT: *popast'* (to go to/into); *lech'* (to go to/into (hospital)); *sest'* (to go to (prison))].

$N^1_{nom}$ V iz $N^2_{gen}$

*Moia zhena vyshla iz bol'nitsy* [my wife has come out of hospital].

$N^1_{nom}$ V na $N^2_{acc}$ [$N^2$—freedom, liberty].

*Chelovek vykhodit na svobodu* [the man is being released].

3.1. *A vyshel iz X-a* = 'Person A, not wishing to remain a member of organization or group X, took official steps to cease being a member and ceased being a member of X'. [~ SYN: *pokinut'* (to leave, abandon); *ostavit'* (to leave); ANAL: *otmezhevat'sia* (to distance oneself from); ~ CONV: *iskliuchit'* (to expel, exclude); ~ ANT: *voiti* (to join, enter)].

$N^1_{nom}$ V iz $N^2_{gen}$

*Chekhov i Korolenko vyshli iz Akademii v znak protesta* [Chekhov and Korolenko resigned from the Academy in protest].

3.2. *A vyshel iz X-a* = 'Object A ceased to be in state X' [~ ANT: *popast'* (to get into)].

$N^1_{nom}$ V iz $N^2_{gen}$

*Korotkie iubki vykhodiat iz mody* [short skirts are going out of fashion]; *Strana medlenno vykhodila iz krizisa* [the country was slowly emerging from the crisis].

$N^1_{nom}$ V iz-pod $N^2_{gen}$

*K chetyrnadtsati godam mal'chik sovsem vyshel iz-pod vliianiia roditelei* [by the age of 14 the boy had completely broken free of his parents' influence].

$N^1_{nom}$ V za $N^2_{acc}$ [$N^2$—framework, bounds, limits].

*Redaktsiia sledit za tem, chtoby kazhdyi iz pomeshchaemykh materialov ne vykhodil za ramki ustanovlennogo ob"ema* [the editorial board takes care that none of the published material exceeds the word-limit].

3.3. *A vyshel iz X-a* = 'Person or people A ceased to perform action X' [ ~ ANT: *vkliuchit'sia* (to enter, become involved in, start); coll. *vviazat'sia* (to become involved in, start)].

$N^1_{nom}$ V iz $N^2_{gen}$

*Rota vyshla iz boia, poteriav dvadtsat' chelovek* [the company withdrew from the battle after losing twenty men]; *S menia dovol'no: ia vykhozhu iz igry* [I've had enough: I'm not playing any more].

4. *A vyshel* = 'In the course of some human activity, a certain amount of resource A was used up' [Rare; in contemporary Russian, *vyiti* in this sense is being superseded by *uiti* ; SYN: *uiti* (to be used up, expended; to run out); ~ SYN: *istratit'sia* (to be spent), *izraskhodovat'sia* (to be spent, used up); *issiaknut'* (to dry up); *istoshchit'sia* (to be exhausted); ~ ANT: *pribavit'sia* (to increase), *pribyt'* (to increase)].

$N^1_{nom}$ V [often with the word *ves'* (*vsia, vse, vsë*) (all)—'to be fully used up, to come to an end'].

*Ves' tabak* ⟨*khleb*⟩ *vyshel* [the tobacco ⟨bread⟩ has run out]; *Kogda vyshli snariady, boitsy stali otstrelivat'sia iz vintovok* [when they ran out of shells the soldiers started returning fire with their rifles].

$N^1_{nom}$ V u $N^2_{gen}$

*U boitsov vyshli vse patrony* [the soldiers ran out of ammunition].

$N^1_{nom}$ V za $N^2_{acc}$ [$N^2$—time]

*Za nedeliu vykhodilo okolo semidesiati rublei* [about seventy roubles were spent per week]

$N^1_{nom}$ V na $N^2_{acc}$ [$N^2$—the object being acquired]

*Tol'ko na produkty vyshlo trista rublei* [three hundred roubles were spent on groceries alone].

5.1. *A vyshel na B* = 'Person A appeared at his place of usual activity B after a certain interval'. [B is usually *rabota, sluzhba* (work); ~ SYN: *iavit'sia, poiavit'sia* (to appear), *priiti* (to come, arrive); *pribyt'* (to arrive); ~ ANT: *uiti* (to leave, go away).]

$N^1_{nom}$ V iz otpuska

*Vash zavlab uzhe vyshel iz otpuska?* [has your lab chief come back from his holidays?]

$N^1_{nom}$ V na $N^2_{acc}$

*On vyidet na rabotu tol'ko cherez tri dnia* [he won't come to work for three days].

$N^1_{nom}$ V {iz otpuska / na $N^2_{acc}$} {D/P $N^3_x$} [D, $N^3$—time].

*Ia vyidu na rabotu v ponedel'nik* ⟨*posle prazdnikov*⟩ [I'll go back to work on Monday ⟨after the holidays⟩].

5.2. *A vyshel* = 'Object A was made public and became accessible to consumers' [~ CONV: *opublikovat'* (to publish), *napechatat'* (to print), *vypustit'* (to issue)].

$N^1_{nom}$ V [usually preceding subject].

*Vykhodili romany i fil'my* [novels and films were appearing].

$N^1_{nom}$ V iz pechati [$N^1$—work of literature].

*Vyshel iz pechati novyi roman Bulgakova* [A new novel by Bulgakov has appeared].

$N^1_{nom}$ V v svet [$N^1$—work of literature].

*Vyshli v svet stikhi Iuliia Kima* [Iulii Kim's poems have been published].

$N^1_{nom}$ V v efir [$N^1$—radio or television programme].

*Nasha peredacha vykhodit v efir vo vtornik na sleduiushchei nedele* [Our programme goes out on Tuesday of next week].

$N^1_{nom}$ V na ekran/na ekrany [$N^1$—film].

*Vyshel na ekrany zamechatel'nyi fil'm Abuladze* [Abuladze's remarkable film has been released].

$N^1_{nom}$ V v $N^2_{prep}$ [$N^2$—publishing house].

*Nasha monografiia vyshla v 'Nauke'* [our monograph has been published by 'Nauka'].

5.3. *A vyshel na X-a* = 'Person A, seeking to resolve a matter which can only be resolved by a person holding a high position in the hierarchy of power, gained access to person X; X either holds a sufficiently high position in the hierarchy of power to resolve the matter or can facilitate access to such a person' [low coll.; in the imperfective present used chiefly with potential meaning 'has ongoing opportunities to gain access to X': *Tvoi shef vykhodit na akademika* (your boss has the ear of an academician); ~ SYN: *probit'sia* (to reach, get through to, get at); *doiti* (to reach); *dobrat'sia* (to reach); ANAL: *popast'* (to get to)].

$N^1_{nom}$ V na $N^2_{acc}$

*Chtoby reshit' etot vopros, nado vyiti na prezidenta* [to resolve this matter it is necessary to gain access to the President].

$N^1_{nom}$ V na $N^2_{acc}$ cherez $N^3_{acc}$

*U Vadima est' znakomyi, cherez kotorogo mozhno vyiti na ministra* [Vadim has a friend through whom it is possible to reach the minister].

6. *A vyshla za X-a* = 'Woman A entered into matrimony with man X' [~ SYN: *zhenit'sia* (to get married); coll. *zaregistrirovat'sia* (to register one's marriage), substandard *raspisat'sia* (to register one's marriage); *venchat'sia*,

*obvenchat'sia, povenchat'sia* (to get married); CONV: *zhenit'sia* (to marry (of a man)); ~ CONV: *vydat' zamuzh* (to give in marriage); ANT: *razvestis'* (to get divorced), *razoitis'* (to separate)].

$N^1_{nom}$ V zamuzh

*Ol'ga nedavno vyshla zamuzh* [Ol'ga got married recently].

$N^1_{nom}$ V za $N^2_{acc}$

*Ol'ga vyshla za svoego byvshego odnoklassnika* [Ol'ga married her former class-mate].

7.1. *A vyshel iz X-ov v Y-i* = 'Person A, previously in the class of people X, by virtue of his success, has entered the class of people Y, whose social status is higher than that of class X' [The component 'whose social status is higher than that of class X' explains why it is impossible to say \**vyiti iz generalov v soldaty* (to be promoted from general to soldier) on the one hand, and \**vyiti v zheny* ⟨*v materi, v ottsy*⟩ (to be promoted to wife ⟨mother, father⟩), on the other: the first sentence is incorrect because the social status of generals (X) is higher than that of soldiers (Y), which conflicts with the explication (cf. the correct sentence *vyiti iz soldat v generaly* (to rise from the ranks to general)); the second is incorrect because the social status of wives ⟨mothers, fathers⟩ is not higher than the individual's previous status; cf. 7.2; ~ SYN: *vyrasti* (to grow up to be); *stat'* (to become); ANAL: *vyskochit'* (to become suddenly); ~ CONV: *vyiti* (to emerge); ~ ANT: *opustit'sia* (to descend)].

$N^1_{nom}$ V iz $N^2_{gen}$ [$N^2$—plural or collective].

*Ia sam iz krest'ian vyshel* [I come from a peasant background myself].

$N^1_{nom}$ V v $N^2_{prep}$ [$N^2$—plural].

*Kto-to iz ego detei vyshel v ofitsery* [one of his children has become an officer].

7.2. *A vyshel iz X-a* = 'Person X, whose qualities were such that with training and experience he might become a professional of class A, became such a professional' [A classifying and copula meaning; usually precedes the subject; the component 'professional of class A' explains why we cannot say [?]*Iz nego vyshel Geroi Sotsialisticheskogo Truda* (he made a Hero of Socialist Labour); the social status of X and A have no bearing: it is possible to say *Iz etogo soldata vyidet otlichnyi general* (this soldier will make a fine general) and *Iz etogo generala vyidet otlichnyi soldat* (this general will make a fine soldier); SYN: *poluchit'sia* (to result in); ~ SYN: *byt'* (to be); ~ CONV: *stat'* (to become); *vyiti* (to rise to); rare *vyrasti* (to grow into)].

$N^1_{nom}$ V iz $N^2_{gen}$

*Iz etikh studentov vyidut prevoskhodnye inzhenery* [these students will make superb engineeers]; *iz vashei docheri vyidet khoroshaia zhena* [your daughter will make a good wife] [see commentary to 7.1].

7.3. *A vyshel iz X-a* = 'From object X, whose properties and quantity were such that an object of class A could be made from it, an object of class A was made' [An existential meaning; usually precedes the subject; SYN: *poluchit'sia* (to result, turn out); ~ *byt'* (to be); ~ CONV: *prevratit'sia* (to turn into); *vylit'sia* (to turn out)].

$N^1_{nom}$ V

*Uberite dlinnoty, i vyidet neplokhoi roman* [cut out the longeurs and you'll have quite a good novel].

$N^1_{nom}$ V iz $N^2_{gen}$

*Iz etoi zatei nichego ne vyidet* [nothing will come of this venture]; *iz khoroshei povesti vyshla neplokhaia ekranizatsiia* [quite a good screen version came out of a good story].

$N^1_{nom}$ V u $N^2_{gen}$

*Roman u menia ne vyshel, a rasskaz poluchilsia* [my novel didn't turn out well, but my story did].

7.4. *A vyshel X-ym* = 'Object A could have had several properties different from property X; as a result of somebody's efforts, A acquired property X; the speaker presents this fact in such a way as to suggest that there is no causal connection between the intention of the agent and the acquisition of property X by object A' [A classifying and copula meaning; X is not a truth-functional property: it is not possible to say *\*Reshenie vyshlo nevernym ⟨oshibochnym, pravil'nym⟩* (the decision turned out incorrect ⟨correct⟩); SYN: *poluchit'sia* (to turn out); ~ SYN: *okazat'sia* (to turn out); *vydat'sia* (to turn out); *vypast'* (to turn out); ANAL: *byt'* (to be); ~ CONV: *vyiti* (to result)].

$N^1_{nom}$ V D [D—evaluative].

*Petr vyshel otlichno* [Petr turned out very well].

$N^1_{nom}$ V {$A_{nom}$/$A_{inst}$/$N^2_{inst}$} [$N^2$—victor, scapegoat . . .].

*Roman vyshel neplokhoi* [the novel turned out quite well]; *vecher vyshel neveselym* [the party was not very jolly]; *Kasparov vyshel pobeditelem* [Kasparov emerged the victor].

8.1. *Vyshel X* = 'Event or situation X need not have occurred; as a result of somebody's activity X did occur and the speaker presents this fact as if there is no causal connection between the intentions of the agent and X' [An existential meaning; usually precedes the subject; ~ SYN: *poluchit'sia* (to turn out, work out; to result), *sostoiat'sia* (to take place); *sluchit'sia* (to happen); *proizoiti* (to happen); *vydat'sia* (to turn out); *vypast'* (to turn out); *prikliuchit'sia* (to happen); *striastis'* (to befall); *byt'* (to be, occur); *byvat'* (to occur); ANAL: *sbyt'sia* (to come to pass, come true)].

V [often negated].

*Ne vyshlo, ne sbylos', ne sostoialos' snova* [it didn't turn out, it didn't come to pass, again it didn't happen].

{$A_{nom}$/$N^1_{nom}$} V

*Vyshla krupnaia nepriiatnost'* [a lot of unpleasantness resulted]; *vyshla zaderzhka v neskol'ko dnei* [a delay of several days resulted].

$N^1_{nom}$ V D

*Vse vyshlo inache* [it all turned out differently].

V tak, Conj S [Conj—chto, budto].

*Vyshlo tak, chto mne prishlos' uekhat'* [it turned out in such a way that I had to leave]; *I vykhodilo tak, budto u ego zhizni sovsem ne bylo nachala* [and it turned out as if his life had had no beginning at all] (L. Andreev).

8.2. *Vykhodit, chto P* = 'A chain of deductions exists, the concluding point of which is a judgement P' [Imperfective only; mainly parenthetic; ~ SYN: *okazyvat'sia* (to turn out, transpire), *poluchat'sia* (to turn out, emerge), *vyiasniat'sia* (to turn out, emerge)].

V

*Vy, vykhodit, moi diadia?* [it turns out you're my uncle].

V chto S

*Vot i vykhodit, chto mne nado uekhat'* [so it turns out I have to leave].

V S

*Vykhodit, ia vam ne nuzhen?* [it looks as if you don't need me?].

9. *A vykhodit na B* = 'Structure A, or part of it, or an aperture or exit from it, faces towards object B' [Imperfective only; ~ SYN: *byt' obrashchennym k* (to be turned towards)].

$N^1_{nom}$ V {D/$P^2$ $N^2_x$}

*Okna doma vykhodiat v sad* ⟨*na ulitsu*⟩ [the windows of the house give onto the garden ⟨the street⟩].

$N^1_{nom}$ V {D/$P^2$ $N^2_x$} $N^3_{inst}$ [$N^3$—exit or part of $N^1$].

*Dom vykhodil oknami vo dvor* [the windows of the house gave onto the courtyard]; *Zdanie fasadom vykhodit na naberezhnuiu* [the facade of the building looks out onto the embankment].

Δ *vyiti naruzhu* = 'obnaruzhit'sia', 'stat' iavnym' [to come out, emerge, become public]; *vyiti iz beregov* = 'razlit'sia v polovod'e' [to burst its banks]; *vyiti iz golovy* = 'zabyt'sia' (arch.) [to be forgotten]; *ne vykhodit' iz golovy ⟨iz uma⟩* = 'byt' postoianno v ch'em-libo soznanii' [to be constantly on smb.'s mind (imperfective only)]; *vyiti iz doveriia* = 'poteriat' ch'e-libo doverie' [to lose smb.'s trust]; *vyiti iz kolei* = 'perestat' vesti obychnuiu dlia sub"ekta zhizn'' [to cease to lead one's usual mode of life]; *vyiti iz polozheniia* = 'razreshit' sozdavsheesia zatrudnenie' [to resolve a difficulty] (cf. § 3.2); *vyiti iz roli* = 'sdelat' chto-libo, chto ne sootvetstvuet izbrannoi linii povedeniia' [to do smth. which does not correspond to one's chosen mode of behaviour] (cf. *vypast' iz obraza*); *vyiti iz sebia* = 'poteriat' samoobladanie' [to lose one's self-control]; *vyiti iz-pod kisti kogo-libo* = 'byt' napisannym kakim-libo khudozhnikom' [to be painted by an artist]; *vyiti iz-pod pera kogo-libo* = 'byt' napisannym kakim-libo pisatelem' [to be written by a writer]; *vyiti v liudi* = 'v rezul'tate dolgikh usilii poluchit' khoroshee polozhenie v obshchestve' [to obtain a good position in society as a result of persistent effort]; *vyiti v otstavku* = 'uvolit'sia so sluzhby do istecheniia sroka polnomochii po prichine nesoglasiia s rukovodstvom ili s tsel'iu zaniat'sia drugoi deiatel'nost'iu' [to resign from one's work before termination of duties because of disagreement with the management or in order to pursue other activities]; *vyiti v tirazh* = 'vyiti iz upotrebleniia v rezul'tate poteri interesnosti' [to go out of use by reason of becoming irrelevant]; *vyiti na pensiiu* = 'stat' pensionerom' [to retire, become a pensioner]; *vyiti na pervoe ⟨vtoroe⟩ mesto* = 'byt' pervym ⟨vtorym . . .⟩ v kakom-libo sorevnovanii po svoim rezul'tatam' [to take first ⟨second . . .⟩ place by results in a competition]; *ne vyiti X-om* (*litsom, rostom, umom . . .*) = 'imet' takoi X, kotoryi otkloniaetsia ot normy X-ov v khudshuiu storonu' [to have an X ⟨face, height, mind . . .⟩ which is inferior to the norm for X]; *vyiti sukhim iz vody* = 'buduchi vinovatym v chem-libo, sumet' ostat'sia beznakazannym' [being to blame for something, to succeed in remaining unpunished; to get off scot-free]; *vyiti bokom komu-libo* = 'konchit'sia plokho dlia kogo-libo', 'ne prinesti komu-libo nichego, krome nepriiatnostei' [to end badly for smb., to bring smb. nothing but unpleasantness].

# References

ANICHKOV, I. E. (1964). 'O tak nazyvaemykh novykh chastiakh rechi', in *Nekotorye voprosy teorii i metodiki prepodavaniia germanskikh iazykov*. Nizhnii Tagil.

APRESJAN, J. D. (1974). *Leksicheskaia semantika. Sinonimicheskie sredstva iazyka*. Moscow.

—— (1979). 'Angliiskie sinonimy i sinonimicheskii slovar'', in J. D. Apresjan, V. V. Botiakova *et al.*, *Anglo-russkii sinonimicheskii slovar'*. Moscow [Ch. 1 in this volume: 'English Synonyms and a Dictionary of Synonyms'].

—— (1980). 'Tipy informatsii dlia poverkhnostno-semanticheskogo komponenta modeli "Smysl ⇔ Tekst"'. *Wiener Slawistischer Almanach*, Sonderband 1. Also in J. D. Apresjan, (1995a, vol. ii).

—— (1985). 'Sintaksicheskie priznaki leksem'. *Russian Linguistics. International Journal for the Study of the Russian Language*, 9/2–3, 289–317.

—— (1986a). 'Deiksis v leksike i grammatike i naivnaia model' mira'. *Semiotika i informatika*, 28.

—— (1986b). 'Integral'noe opisanie iazyka i tolkovyi slovar''. *Voprosy iazykoznaniia*, 2: 57–70.

—— (1986c). 'Sintaksicheskaia informatsiia dlia tolkovogo slovaria'. *Linguistische Arbeitsberichte*, 54/5. Also in J. D. Apresjan (1995a, vol. ii).

—— (1988). 'Pragmaticheskaia informatsiia dlia tolkovogo slovaria', in *Pragmatika i problemy intensional'nosti*. Moscow. Also in J. D. Apresjan (1995a, vol. ii).

—— (1990a). 'Formal'naia model' iazyka i predstavlenie leksikograficheskikh znanii'. *Voprosy iazykoznaniia*, 6: 123–39.

—— (1990b). 'Leksikograficheskii portret glagola *vyiti*', in *Voprosy kibernetiki. Iazyk logiki i logika iazyka*. Moscow: 70–95 [Ch. 10 in this volume: 'A Lexicographic Portrait of the Verb *vyiti*'].

—— (1990c). 'Tipy leksikograficheskoi informatsii ob oznachaiushchem leksemy', in *Tipologiia i grammatika*. Moscow. Also in J. D. Apresjan (1995a, vol. ii).

—— (1992a). 'Leksikograficheskie portrety (na primere glagola *byt'*)'. *Nauchno-tekhnicheskaia informatsiia*. Series 2, No. 3. [Ch. 9 in this volume: 'Lexicographic Portraits: A Case Study of the Verb *byt'*'].

—— (1992b). 'O novom slovare sinonimov russkogo iazyka'. *Izvestiia RAN. Seriia literatury i iazyka*, 1.

—— (1992c). 'Systemic lexicography', in *Euralex '92. Proceedings I–II. Studia translatologica*. Tampere, ser. A, vol. ii, pt. 2.

—— (1993). 'Sinonimiia mental'nykh predikatov: gruppa *schitat'*', in *Logicheskii analiz iazyka. Mental'nye deistviia*. Moscow [Ch. 4 in this volume: 'The Synonymy of Mental Predicates: *schitat'* [to consider] and its Synonyms'].

—— (1994). 'O iazyke tolkovanii i semanticheskikh primitivakh'. *Izvestiia RAN. Seriia literatury i iazyka*, 4 [Ch. 8 in this volume: 'On the Language of Explications and Semantic Primitives'].

—— (1995a). *Izbrannye trudy*, 2 vols. Moscow.

APRESJAN, J. D. (1995*b*). 'Novyi slovar' sinonimov: kontseptsiia i tipy informatsii', in J. D. Apresjan, O. Iu. Boguslavskaia, I. B. Levontina, E. V. Uryson, *Novyi ob"iasnitel'nyi slovar' sinonimov russkogo iazyka. Prospekt.* Moscow.

—— (1995*c*). 'Theoretical Linguistics, Formal Models of Language and Systemic Lexicography', in *Linguistics in the Morning Calm 3: Selected papers from SICOL.* Seoul, 3–30.

—— BOGUSLAVSKAIA, O. Iu., LEVONTINA, I. B., URYSON, E. V. (1992). 'Obraztsy slovarnykh statei novogo slovaria sinonimov', *Izvestiia RAN. Seriia literatury i iazyka,* 2.

—— —— —— —— (1995). *Novyi ob"iasnitel'nyi slovar' sinonimov russkogo iazyka. Prospekt.* Moscow.

—— —— —— —— GLOVINSKAIA, M. Ia., KRYLOVA, T. V. (1997). *Novyi ob"iasnitel'nyi slovar' sinonimov russkogo iazyka. Pervyi vypusk.* Moscow.

—— BOTIAKOVA, V. V., LATYSHEVA, T. E., MOSIAGINA, M. A., POLIK, I. V., RAKITINA, V. I., ROZENMAN, A. I., SRETENSKAIA, E. E. (1979). *Anglo-russkii sinonimicheskii slovar'.* Moscow.

—— IOMDIN, L. L. (1989). 'Konstruktsii tipa *Negde spat'*: sintaksis, semantika, leksikografiia'. *Semiotika i informatika,* 29: 34–92.

—— PALL ERNA (1982). *Russkii glagol—vengerskii glagol. Upravlenie i sochetaemost'.* vols. i–ii. Budapest.

APRESJAN, V. (1995*a*). 'Emotsii: sovremennye amerikanskie issledovaniia'. *Semiotika i informatika,* 34.

—— (1995*b*). 'K opisaniiu glagolov so znacheniem prirodnogo protsessa (na primere glagolov *svetit'sia, merknut'* i *svetit'). Teoreticheskaia lingvistika i leksikografiia: k formal'nomu opisaniiu leksiki,* Moscow.

—— (1997*a*). '"Fear" and "Pity" in Russian and English from a lexicographic perspective'. *International Journal of Lexicography,* 10/2: 85–111.

—— (1997*b*). Synonym series for *boiat'sia,* in J. D. Apresjan, O. Iu. Boguslavskaia, I. B. Levontina, E. V. Uryson, M. Ia. Glovinskaia, T. V. Krylova, *Novyi ob"iasnitel'nyi slovar' sinonimov russkogo iazyka. Pervyi vypusk.* Moscow.

—— APRESJAN, J. (1993). 'Metafora v semanticheskom predstavlenii emotsii'. *Voprosy iazykoznaniia,* 3 [Ch. 7 in this volume: 'Metaphor in the Semantic Representation of Emotions'].

ARUTIUNOVA, N. D. (1976). *Predlozhenie i ego smysl.* Moscow.

—— (1988). *Tipy iazykovykh znachenii. Otsenka, sobytie, fakt.* Moscow.

—— (1989). '*Polagat'* i *videt'* (k probleme smeshannykh propozitsional'nykh ustanovok)', in *Logicheskii analiz iazyka. Problemy intensional'nykh i pragmaticheskikh kontekstov.* Moscow: 7–30.

—— SHIRIAEV, E. N. (1983). *Russkoe predlozhenie. Bytiinyi tip (struktura i znachenie).* Moscow.

BARANOV, A. N., PLUNGIAN, V. A., RAKHILINA, E. V. (1993). *Putevoditel' po diskursivnym slovam russkogo iazyka.* Moscow.

BARTMIŃSKI, J. (1980). 'Założenia teoretyczne słownika', in *Słownik ludowych stereotypów językowych. Zeszyt próbny.* Wrocław.

—— (1984). 'Definicja leksykograficzna a opis języka', *Słownictwo w opisie języka. Prace naukowe Uniwersytetu śląskiego.* Katowice.

BENSON, M., BENSON, E., ILSON R. (1986). *The BBI Combinatory Dictionary of English. A Guide to Word Combinations.* Amsterdam.

BIERWISCH, M. (1967). 'Some Semantic Universals of German Adjectivals'. *Foundations of Language. International Journal of Language and Philosophy*, 3/1.

BOGUSLAVSKY, I. M. (1984). Dictionary entry for *ponimat'*, in I. A. Mel'čuk, A. K. Zholkovsky, *Tolkovo-kombinatornyi slovar' sovremennogo russkogo iazyka. Opyt semantiko-sintaksicheskogo opisaniia russkoi leksiki*. Vienna.

—— (1985). *Issledovaniia po sintaksicheskoi semantike: sfery deistviia logicheskikh slov*. Moscow.

BOGUSŁAWSKI, A. (1966). *Semantyczne pojęcie liczebnika*, Wrocław.

—— (1970). 'On Semantic Primitives and Meaningfulness', in A. Greimas, R. Jakobson, M. Mayenowa. *Sign. Language. Culture*. The Hague: 143–52.

—— (1981). 'Wissen, Wahrheit, Glauben: Zur semantischen Beschaffenheit des kognitiven Vokabulars', in Th. Bungarten (ed.), *Wissenschaftssprache. Beiträge zur Methodologie, theoretischen Fundierung und Deskription*. Munich.

—— (1986). 'You can never know that you know'. *Semantikos*, 10: 1–2.

—— (1994a). '*Dlaczego wiemy, za co powinniśmy kochać Pana Profesora? dlaczego*?', in Andrzej Bogusławski, *Sprawy słowa*. Warsaw: 276–89.

—— (1994b). 'Ob ierarkhii epistemicheskikh poniatii i o prirode t. naz. propozitsional'nykh argumentov', in Andrzej Bogusławski, *Sprawy słowa*. Warsaw: 78-94.

—— (1994c). 'Savoir que *p* implique-t-il un autre état mental?', in Andrzej Bogusławski, *Sprawy słowa*. Warsaw: 257–75.

BORILLO, A. (1982). 'Deux aspects de la modalisation assertive: *croire* et *savoir*'. *Langages*, 67: 33–53

BULYGINA, T. V. (1982). 'K postroeniiu tipologii predikatov v russkom iazyke', in *Semanticheskie tipy predikatov*. Moscow.

—— SHMELEV, A. D. (1988), 'Vopros o kosvennykh voprosakh: iavliaetsia li ustanovlennym faktom ikh sviaz' s faktivnost'iu', in *Logicheskii analiz iazyka. Znanie i mnenie*. Moscow.

—— —— (1989). 'Mental'nye predikaty v aspekte aspektologii', in *Logicheskii analiz iazyka. Problemy intensional'nykh i pragmaticheskikh kontekstov*. Moscow.

CHISHOLM, Roderick M. (1966). *Theory of Knowledge*. Englewood Cliffs, NJ.

—— (1982). *The Foundations of Knowing*. Minneapolis.

CHVANI, K. V. [Chvany, Catherine V.] (1977). 'O sintaksicheskoi strukture predlozhenii s glagolom *byt'* v russkom iazyke', in *Grammatika russkogo iazyka v svete generativnoi lingvistiki. Referativnyi sbornik*. Moscow.

CHVANY, Catherine V. (1975). 'On the Syntax of BE-sentences in Russian'. Cambridge University, MA thesis.

COHEN, S. (1986). 'Knowledge and Context'. *The Journal of Philosophy*, 10.

DMITROVSKAIA, M. A. (1985). 'Glagoly znaniia i mneniia (znachenie i upotreblenie)'. Dissertation abstract, Moscow.

—— (1988a). 'Znanie i dostovernost'', in *Pragmatika i problemy intensional'nosti*. Moscow.

—— (1988b). 'Znanie i mnenie: obraz mira, obraz cheloveka', in *Logicheskii analiz iazyka. Znanie i mnenie*. Moscow.

EKMAN, P. (1984). 'Expression and the Nature of Emotion', in *Approaches to Emotion*, New York.

ESPERSEN, O. (1958) [JESPERSEN, O.]. *Filosofiia grammatiki*. Moscow. [*The Philosophy of Grammar*. London, 1958].

EVGEN'EVA, A. P. (1970–1). *Slovar' sinonimov russkogo iazyka*, 2 vols. Leningrad.

FILLMORE, C. (1968). 'Lexical Entries for Verbs'. *Foundations of Language. International journal of language and philosophy*, 4/4.

—— (1982). 'Frame Semantics', in *Linguistics in the Morning Calm 1: Selected papers from SICOL*. Seoul.

—— (1985). 'Frames and the Semantics of Understanding'. *Quaderni di semantica*, 6/2.

—— ATKINS, B. T. (1992). 'Towards a frame-based lexicon: the case of RISK', in A. Lehrer and E. Kittay (eds.), *Frames, Fields and Contrasts: new essays in semantic and lexical organization*. Hillsdale, NJ.

FRANK, S. L. (1991). 'Dukhovnye osnovy obshchestva. Vvedenie v sotsial'nuiu filosofiiu', *Russkoe zarubezh'e*. Leningrad.

FRIES, Norbert (1992). 'Emocje. Aspekty eksperimentalne i lingwistyczne', in *Wartościowanie w języku i tekście*. Warsaw.

GARDE, P. (1976). 'Analyse de la tournure russe *Mne nechego delat'*. *International Journal of Slavic Linguistics and Poetics*, 22.

GIRO-VEBER, M. [GUIRAUD-WEBER, M.] (1984*a*). 'Ustranenie podlezhashchego v russkom predlozhenii'. *Izvestiia AN SSSR. Seriia literatury i iazyka*, 6.

GLOVINSKAIA, M. Ia. (1982). *Semanticheskie tipy vidovogo protivopostavleniia russkogo glagola*, Moscow.

—— (1993). 'Semantika glagolov rechi s tochki zreniia teorii rechevykh aktov', in *Russkii iazyk i ego funktsionirovanie. Kommunikativno-pragmaticheskii aspekt*. Moscow.

GREENWOOD, T. G. (1993). 'International Cultural Differences in Software'. *Digital Technical Journal*, 5/3.

GRIFFITHS, A. P. (ed.) (1976). *Knowledge and Belief*. Oxford.

GUIRAUD-WEBER, M. (1984*b*). *Les propositions sans nominatifs en russe moderne*. Paris. (See also Giro-Veber, above.)

HOLTHUSEN, J. (1953). 'Russisch *nechego* und Verwandtes'. *Zeitschrift für Slawische Philologie*, 22/1.

HINTIKKA, K. J. (1962). *Knowledge and Belief: an Introduction to the Logic of two Notions*. Ithaca, NY.

IAKOVLEVA, E. S. (1993). 'O nekotorykh modeliakh prostranstva v russkoi iazykovoi kartine mira'. *Voprosy iazykoznaniia*, 4.

IOANESIAN, E. R. (1988*a*). 'Nekotorye osobennosti funktsionirovaniia predikata *ne znat'*, in *Logicheskii analiz iazyka. Znanie i mnenie*. Moscow.

—— (1988*b*). 'Znanie i vospriiatie', in *Pragmatika i problemy intensional'nosti*. Moscow.

IORDANSKAJA, L. N. (1970). 'Popytka leksikograficheskogo tolkovaniia gruppy russkikh slov so znacheniem chuvstva'. *Mashinnyi perevod i prikladnaia lingvistika*, 13: 3–26.

—— (1972). 'Leksikograficheskoe opisanie russkikh vyrazhenii, oboznachaiushchikh fizicheskie simptomy chuvstv'. *Mashinnyi perevod i prikladnaia lingvistika*, 16: 3–30.

—— (1984). Dictionary entries for *boiat'sia, vostorg, voskhishchat', gnev, strakh et al.*, in I. A. Mel'čuk, A. K. Zholkovsky, *Tolkovo-kombinatornyi slovar' sovremennogo russkogo iazyka. Opyty semantiko-sintaksicheskogo opisaniia russkoi leksiki*. Vienna.

—— MEL'ČUK, I. (1990). 'Semantics of Two Emotion Verbs in Russian: *bojat'sja* "to be afraid" and *nadejat'sja* "to hope"'. *Australian Journal of Linguistics*, 10/2: 307–57.

ITSKOVICH, V. A. (1982). *Ocherki sintaksicheskoi normy*. Moscow.

IVANOVA, V. F. (1973). 'Modeli kolichestvennykh predlozhenii'. *Russkii iazyk v shkole*, 3.

JESPERSEN, O. see ESPERSEN, O.

KENNY, A. (1963). *Action, Emotion and Will.* London.

KIBRIK, A. E. (1987). 'Semantika i sintaksis glagolov *khotet'* i *boiat'sia* (tipologicheskie nabliudeniia)', in *Propozitsional'nye predikaty v logicheskom i lingvisticheskom aspektakh: Tezisy rabochego soveshchaniia.* Moscow.

KÖVECSES, Zoltán. (1990). *Emotion Concepts.* New York.

LAKOFF, George and JOHNSON, Mark (1980). *Metaphors We Live By.* Chicago, London.

LEHRER, K. (1974). *Knowledge.* Oxford.

LIKHACHEV, D. S. (1993). 'Kontseptosfera russkogo iazyka', *Izvestiia RAN. Seriia literatury i iazyka,* 1.

*Logicheskii analiz iazyka. Istina i istinnost' v kul'ture i iazyke* (1995). Moscow.

LYONS, J. (1967). 'Note on Possessive, Existential, and Locative Sentences'. *Foundations of Language,* 3/4.

—— (1968). *An Introduction to Theoretical Linguistics.* Cambridge.

—— (1979). 'Knowledge and Truth: A Localistic Approach', in D. J. Allerton, E. Carney, and D. Holdcroft (eds.), *Function and Context in Linguistic Analysis.* London.

MALCOLM, N. (1963). *Knowledge and Certainty.* Englewood Cliffs, NJ.

MARTEM'IANOV, Iu. S. (1964). 'Zametki o stroenii situatsii i forme ee opisaniia'. *Mashinnyi perevod i prikladnaia lingvistika,* 8.

*Mashinnyi perevod i prikladnaia lingvistika* (1964), 8.

MEHLIG, H.-R. see MELIG.

MEL'ČUK, I. A. (1972). 'O suppletivizme', in *Problemy strukturnoi lingvistiki 1971.* Moscow.

—— (1974a). *Opyt teorii lingvisticheskikh modelei 'Smysl ⇔ Tekst'.* Moscow.

—— (1974b). 'O sintaksicheskom nule', in *Tipologiia passivnykh konstruktsii. Diatezy i zalogi.* Leningrad: 343–61.

—— (1985). 'Semanticheskie etiudy. 1. *Seichas* i *teper'* v russkom iazyke'. *Russian Linguistics,* 2/3: 257–79.

—— (1989). 'Semantic Primitives from the Viewpoint of the Meaning-Text Linguistic Theory'. *Quaderni di semantica,* 10/1.

—— ZHOLKOVSKY, A. K. (1984). 'Tolkovo-kombinatornyi slovar' sovremennogo russkogo iazyka'. *Opyty semantiko-sintaksicheskogo opisaniia russkoi leksiki.* Vienna.

MELIG, Kh. R. [Mehlig, Hans-Robert] (1985). 'Semantika predlozheniia i semantika vida v russkom iazyke', in *Novoe v zarubezhnoi lingvistike.* Moscow.

MOORE, G. E. (1959). *Philosophical Papers.* New York.

OATLEY, Keith (1992). *Best Laid Schemes: The Psychology of Emotions.* Cambridge.

ORTONY, Andrew, CLORE, Gerald L., COLLINS, Allan (1988). *The Cognitive Structure of Emotions.* Cambridge.

PADUCHEVA, E. V. (1988). 'Vyvodima li sposobnost' podchiniat' kosvennyi vopros iz semantiki slova?' in *Logicheskii analiz iazyka. Znanie i mnenie.* Moscow.

PAJDZIŃSKA, A. (1990a). 'Jak mówimy o uczuciach? Poprzez analizę frazeologizmów do językowego obrazu świata', in *Językowy obraz świata.* Lublin.

—— (1990b). *Językowy obraz świata.* Lublin.

PASTERNAK, B. (1982). 'Zamechaniia k perevodam iz Shekspira', in B. Pasternak, *Vozdushnye puti.* Moscow.

PAVLOVA, A. V. (1987). 'Aktsentnaia struktura vyskazyvaniia v ee sviaziakh s leksicheskoi semantikoi', dissertation for the degree of Candidate of Philological Sciences, Leningrad.

PERTSOVA, N. N. (1990). 'K poniatiiu "veshchnoi konnotatsiii"', *Voprosy kibernetiki. Iazyk logiki i logika iazyka*, Moscow.

ROBINSON, J. (1983). 'Emotion, Judgement and Desire'. *Journal of Philosophy*, 80/11.

RUWET, N. (1981). 'The "epistemic dative" Construction in French and its Relevance to some Current Problems in Generative Grammar', in *Festschrift Manfred Bierwisch*. Dordrecht.

SCHEFFLER, H. (1965). *Conditions of Knowledge*. Chicago.

SELEZNEV, M. G. (1988). 'Vera skvoz' prizmu iazyka', in *Pragmatika i problemy intensional'nosti*. Moscow.

SÉMON, J.-P. (1989). 'Le vouloir, la négation et l'aspect'. *La Licorne. Étude de linguistique*, Poitiers, 15.

SHATUNOVSKII, I. B. (1988*a*). 'Epistemicheskie glagoly: kommunikativnaia perspektiva, prezumptsii, pragmatika', in *Logicheskii analiz iazyka. Znanie i mnenie*. Moscow.

—— (1988*b*). 'Epistemicheskie predikaty v russkom iazyke (semantika, kommunikativnaia perspektiva, pragmatika)', in *Pragmatika i problemy intensional'nosti*. Moscow.

SHAVER, P. *et al.* (1987). 'Emotion Knowledge: Further Exploration of a Prototype Approach'. *Journal of Personality and Social Psychology*, 52/6.

SHCHEGLOV, Iu. K. (1964). 'Dve gruppy slov russkogo iazyka'. *Mashinnyi perevod i prikladnaia lingvistika*, 8.

SHMELEV, A. D. (1993). 'Khot' znaiu, da ne veriu', in *Logicheskii analiz iazyka. Mental'nye deistviia*, Moscow.

SHMELEV, D. N. (1969). 'Problemy semanticheskogo analiza leksiki', dissertation for the degree of Doctor of Philological Sciences. Moscow.

SHVEDOVA, N. Iu. (1973). 'Spornye voprosy opisaniia strukturnykh skhem prostogo predlozheniia i ego paradigm'. *Voprosy iazykoznaniia*, 4.

SPINOZA, B. (1957). *Izbrannye proizvedeniia*, vol. i. Moscow.

STELZNER, W. (1984). *Epistemische Logik. Zur logischen Analyse von Akzeptationsformen*. Berlin.

STERN, G. (1931). *Meaning and Change of Meaning*. Göteborg.

SUKALENKO, N. I. (1992). *Otrazhenie obydennogo soznaniia v obraznoi iazykovoi kartine mira*. Kiev.

SWANEPOEL, P. (1992). 'Getting a Grip on Emotions: Defining Lexical Items that Denote Emotions', in *Euralex '92. Proceedings I–II. Studia translatologica*. Tampere, Ser. A, vol. 2, pt. 2.

TOLSTOI, N. I. (1984). 'Ivan-aist', in *Slavianskoe i balkanskoe iazykoznanie. Iazyk v etnokul'turnom aspekte*. Moscow.

TRUB, V. M. (1993). 'K probleme semanticheskogo opisaniia zhelanii'. *Wiener Slawistischer Almanach*, 31.

ULLMANN, S. (1951). *The Principles of Semantics*. Glasgow.

URYSON, E. V. (1995*a*). 'Fundamental'nye sposobnosti cheloveka i naivnaia anatomiia'. *Voprosy iazykoznaniia*, 1995, 3.

—— (1995*b*). Synonym series for *strakh*, in J. D. Apresjan, O. Iu. Boguslavskaia, I. B. Levontina, E. V. Uryson, *Novyi ob"iasnitel'nyi slovar' sinonimov russkogo iazyka. Prospekt*. Moscow.

USPENSKY, V. A. (1979). 'O veshchnykh konnotatsiiakh abstraktnykh sushchestvitel'nykh'. *Semiotika i informatika*, 11.

VENDLER, Z. (1972). *Res Cogitans*. Ithaca, NY.

VERHAAR, John, (1967–73). 'The Verb BE and its Synonyms. Philosophical and Grammatical Studies', Parts 1–6, ed. John W. M. Verhaar, *Foundations of Language*. *Supplementary Series*, 1967, vol. 1; 1968, vol. 6; 1968, vol. 8; 1969, vol. 9; 1972, vol. 14; 1973, vol. 16.

VINOGRADOV, V. V. (1946). 'Iz istorii slova "lichnost'" v russkom iazyke do serediny XIX veka'. *Doklady i soobshcheniia filologicheskogo fakul'teta MGU*, 1.

—— (1974). *Russkii iazyk. Grammaticheskoe uchenie o slove*. Moscow.

—— (1994). 'Slovo i znachenie kak predmet istoriko-leksikologicheskogo issledovaniia', in V. V. Vinogradov, *Istoriia slov*. Moscow.

WEBSTER (1968). *Webster's New Dictionary of Synonyms, A Dictionary of Discriminated Synonyms with Antonyms and Contrasted Words*. Springfield, Mass.

WIERZBICKA, A. (1969). *Dociekania semantyczne*. Wrocław, Warsaw, Kraków.

—— (1972). *Semantic Primitives*. Frankfurt.

—— (1980). *Lingua Mentalis. The Semantics of Natural Language*. Sydney, New York.

—— (1985). *Lexicography and Conceptual Analysis*. Ann Arbor.

—— (1987a). 'Boys will be boys'. *Language*, 63/1.

—— (1987b). *English Speech Act Verbs. A Semantic Dictionary*. Sydney.

—— (1990a). '*Duša* ('soul'), *toska* ('yearning'), *sud'ba* ('fate'): three key concepts in Russian language and Russian culture', in Zygmunt Saloni (ed.), *Metody formalne w opisie języków słowiańskich*. Białystok.

—— (1990b). 'The Semantics of Emotions: Fear and its Relatives in English'. *Australian Journal of Linguistics*, 10/2: 359–75.

—— (1991). *Cross-Cultural Pragmatics: The Semantics of Human Interaction*. Berlin, New York.

—— (1992). *Semantics, Culture, and Cognition. Universal Human Concepts in Culture-Specific Configurations*. New York, Oxford.

WITTGENSTEIN, L. (1969). *On Certainty*. Oxford.

YOKOYAMA, O. T. (1986). *Discourse and Word Order*. Amsterdam, Philadelphia.

ZALIZNIAK, Anna A. (1983). 'Semantika glagola *boiat'sia* v russkom iazyke'. *Izvestiia AN SSSR. Seriia literatury i iazyka*, 42/1: 59–66.

—— (1984). 'Priznaki *kontrol'* i *zhelanie* v semantike predikatov vnutrennego sostoianiia', in *Semanticheskie problemy rechevoi deiatel'nosti*, Moscow: 86-95.

—— (1991a). '*Schitat'* i *dumat'*: dva vida mneniia', in *Logicheskii analiz iazyka. Kul'turnye kontsepty*. Moscow.

—— (1991b). 'Slovarnaia stat'ia glagola *govorit'*'. *Semiotika i informatika*, 32.

—— (1992). *Issledovaniia po semantike predikatov vnutrennego sostoianiia*, Munich.

—— PADUCHEVA, E. V. (1987). 'O semantike vvodnogo upotrebleniia glagolov', in *Voprosy kibernetiki. Prikladnye aspekty lingvisticheskoi teorii*. Moscow, 80-96.

ZHOLKOVSKY, A. K. (1964a). 'Leksika tselesoobraznoi deiatel'nosti'. *Mashinnyi perevod i prikladnaia lingvistika*, 8.

—— (1964b). 'Predislovie', *Mashinnyi perevod i prikladnaia lingvistika*, 8: 3–16.

—— LEONT'EVA, N. N., MARTEM'IANOV, Iu. S. (1961). 'O printsipial'nom ispol'zovanii smysla pri mashinnom perevode', *Mashinnyi perevod*, 2.

ZIFF, P. (1983). *Epistemic Analysis. A Coherence Theory of Knowledge*. Dordrecht.

ZOLOTOVA, G. A. (1966). 'K razvitiiu predlozhno-padezhnykh konstruktsii (sochetaniia s sushchestvitel'nymi v tvoritel'nom padezhe s predlogom s)', in *Razvitie sintaksisa sovremennogo russkogo iazyka*, Moscow, 147–73.

—— (1973). *Ocherk funktsional'nogo sintaksisa russkogo iazyka*, Moscow.

# Index of English Lexemes

# Index of Russian lexemes

# Subject Index

# Index of Names